WATER'S
EDGE

Contributions in Political Science
Series Editor: Bernard K. Johnpoll

WATER'S EDGE

Domestic Politics and the Making of American Foreign Policy

Paula Stern

Contributions in Political Science, Number 15

G P

GREENWOOD PRESS
WESTPORT, CONNECTICUT • LONDON, ENGLAND

Library of Congress Cataloging in Publication Data

Stern, Paula, 1945-
  Water's edge.

  (Contributions in political science ; no. 15 ISSN
0147-1066)
  Bibliography: p.
  1. Tariff—United States—Law. 2. Foreign trade
regulation—United   States.   3.   United
States—Foreign relations—Russia. 4. Russia-
Foreign relations—United States. Jews, Russia
Legal status, laws, etc. 6. Jackson, Henry Martin,
1912-   I. Title. II. Series.
KF6659.S74   343'.73'087   78-55331
ISBN 0-313-20520-5

Library of Congress Catalog Card Number: 78-55331
ISBN: 0-313-20520-5
ISSN: 0147-1066

First published in 1979

Greenwood Press, Inc.
51 Riverside Avenue, Westport, Connecticut 06880

Printed in the United States of America

10 9 8 7 6 5 4 3 2 1

To Paul, Gabriel, Lloyd, Margot, and Gerald

Contents

Preface

This is a study of the two- and one-half-year history of the Jackson amendment to the Trade Reform Act of 1974. This legislation, which today is law of the land, stipulates that the president not be authorized to extend trade concessions to the Soviet Union or any other so-called nonmarket country until he certifies to Congress that free emigration is permitted from these nations. The fight for the legislation led by Senator Henry Jackson (D.-Wash.), is a case study of policy-making in America. The immediate purpose of this book is to shed light on how foreign policy in America is created under conditions of high domestic political involvement. But many of the processes described are as applicable to domestic policy-making as to foreign policy-making.

Executive-congressional competition is examined in detail. The domestic debate over detente with the Soviet Union and the burning impact of Watergate are given major attention. The process by which a single, determined politician forms a congressional coalition reinforced by a broad, national interest-group alliance is also detailed. In this regard, the principal involvement of Jewish interest groups and the national leadership of the AFL-CIO, personified by President George Meany, is closely considered.

The theme of this book is that domestic politics neither stops at the water's edge nor does it necessarily begin at the water's edge of this nation. Interest groups and politicians in this country were stimulated by activities occurring overseas—Soviet interference in what was considered the right of Soviet Jews to emigrate. The domestic roots of the foreign policy issue of linking American trade concessions to freedom to emigrate from the Soviet Union were actually planted in foreign soil.

Once politicians involved themselves in the issue, it was transformed to fit both the needs of the original cause—Soviet Jewry—and to fit the requirements of the elected officials championing it. As other interest groups joined the cause, they also shaped it. To understand the events that occurred, it is necessary to bear in mind that elected officials involving themselves in foreign policy issues generally have dual requirements: domestic and diplomatic. These requirements may not always mesh neatly. Actions required to attain one objective in the American political context may contradict actions required to attain the other. Publicity, for example, may be helpful for an election campaign, but it may jeopardize low-profile diplomatic negotiations required to convince another sovereign nation, for example, the Soviet Union, to accommodate American demands.

That the Jackson amendment dealt with a human rights cause and a cause dear to the hearts of various ethnic, ideological, and economic interest groups in America reflected basic characteristics of American political life. That the Jackson amendment also attempted to use economic concessions to extract political concessions from another nation also illustrated a traditional theme in American foreign relations.

The study of the amendment's legislative history and related diplomatic negotiations illustrates both the strengths and weaknesses of politicizing foreign policy-making in this country. Ultimately, the limitations of policy-making in such highly politicized areas are determined by the ambitions of politicians who take it upon themselves to be foreign policy actors.

An earlier version of this book was prepared for The Fletcher School of Law and Diplomacy. At that time, The Brookings Institution graciously extended me guest scholar privileges. The generous help and guidance of Alan Henrikson and John Roche is gratefully acknowledged. So, too, are the informal chats with Capitol Hill acquaintances and friends. Senator Gaylord Nelson and his administrative assistants provided me employment security, and my dear friends in Nelson's office extended essential support, interest, and encouragement. The efforts of Jeff Angus, Edie Matricardi, Sue Miller, and Mary Thompson eased my work load. Linda Stern and typist Shirley Chipman willingly helped to pull together the earlier manuscript at a key moment in the project. Dalya Luttwack translated articles written in Hebrew. My brother Gerald Stern; Marvin Feuerwerger, Deputy Senior Adviser to President Carter; Charles Levy, formerly with Senator Adlai Stevenson III; Richard Gilmore, formerly with Senator Hubert Humphrey; Richard Perle, presently with Senator Henry Jackson; and Ira Silverman, presently with the American Jewish Committee, have read all or parts of this study. My husband, best friend, and critic, Paul A. London, gave me the emotional and intellectual support necessary to complete this work. While many have helped shoulder the burden of pulling together this book, I alone bear the responsibility for the shortcomings that may lie within.

Introduction: Domestic Politics and the Making of American Foreign Policy

> Once begin the dance of legislation, and you
> must struggle through its mazes as best you
> can to the breathless end—if any end there be.
> WOODROW WILSON

"Politics stops at the water's edge." This axiom is one of the more misleading ideas in American politics. Many of America's greatest architects, critics, and students of foreign policy either underestimate or misunderstand how American foreign policy is shaped by American political life. They tend to describe and/or prescribe policy to be the calculated product of a complex balancing of international power blocs or the expression of traditional policies and ideals.[1] Such analyses tend to explain foreign policy-making in terms of rational diplomatic goals that statesmen advance in the "national" interest of a given state. Such an approach, however, leaves little room for the possibility that domestic pressures also influence American foreign policy.

The "nation" can be dissected; competing economic, ideological, and ethnic groups can be identified. These groups and individual politicians often pursue goals that although rational from the point of view of a group or a politician, may not necessarily be rational for the nation as a whole. To understand fully the foreign policy of the United States, one needs to know the domestic politics shaping its development. The Jackson amendment to the Trade Reform Act of 1974 is a dramatic recent example of the interaction of United States domestic politics and American foreign policy-making. If one relied upon an approach to study the Jackson amendment struggle that presumed American statesmen were attempting to advance American interests vis-à-vis the Soviet Union and other nations, many of the events would be inexplicable. *Raison d'état* was not reason enough.

Of course domestic politics influences the foreign policy of any country. For example, some aspects of policy-making in Israel, another democracy, whose position on Soviet Jewry is relevant to this study, bears a remarkable resemblance to aspects of American policy-making. Even the foreign policy of dictatorships is shaped to some degree by the need to "satisfy" a domestic audience. The internal Soviet debate regarding detente with the West illustrated this phenomenon. However, several important characteristics of American political life give American foreign policy a distinct character.

The United States is a *democracy*. Individuals and interest groups have widely recognized legitimacy and relatively open access to the political process. They have a great deal of leverage over the foreign policy-makers in the government, since many policy-makers are politicians whose legitimacy and authority derive from being elected to serve in Congress or as president. (Career bureaucrats are relatively immune from the political process and thus tend to disregard it.) Politicians depend on organized, nonofficial groups to raise money and mobilize voters.

The United States is also a land of *immigrants*. Ethnic groups often try to influence American policy vis-à-vis other nations in ways that will aid their countrymen overseas. Two centuries of American diplomatic history yield numerous cases of politicians' (elected officials') concern for immigrants and their half-sisters—religious, racial, and ethnic groups—shaping what America did in the rest of the world.

As early as 1794, Irish-Americans actively opposed the Jay Treaty with Great Britian, their traditional enemy. The Irish were also instrumental in defeating an American fisheries treaty with British-controlled Canada in 1888 and the Anglo-American Arbitration Treaty of 1897. In 1888, German-Americans fought for the settlement of an American dispute over Pacific Samoa that was favorable to their ancestral homeland, Germany.

Religious groups have played a similar role. Catholic opinion played an important part in keeping the United States out of the Spanish Civil War, and Protestant protests forced President Harry S. Truman to change his plan to appoint an ambassador to the Vatican.

After World War II, the Poles in this country denounced the Yalta Agreement, which they claimed sanctioned Soviet hegemony over Poland; the Poles along with other immigrant groups from territory controlled by the Soviet Union after World War II were part of a broad national anticommunist consensus in this country during the Cold War.[2]

In 1912, Jewish pressure forced the abrogation of a commercial treaty with Russia as a means of protesting Russian treatment of Jews.[3] The 1912 episode bears a remarkably close resemblance to the subject of this study: the Jackson amendment. It is difficult to fit these examples of ethnic (or economic or ideological) group influence into a viewpoint that assumes politics in this country does or should not influence American foreign policy.

Furthermore, America has a historical sense of mission and a strong streak of *human rights* concern. It is commonly believed that the United States as a superpower possesses the capability—as well as some responsibility—to try to shape the world to meet America's moral and political standards. It is not uncommon to find attempts by the United States to exert *economic leverage*—to extract political concessions from other countries in exchange for American economic concessions.

Another major distinction between the United States and other nations is that under the United States' constitutional system of government,

Congress and the president, two separate but equal branches of government, share foreign policy-making power. Other nations may be democracies and therefore presumably reflect the will of the electorate. However, the United States' system is distinct from parliamentary democracies where the power resides in one branch of the government. Theoretically, this provides increased access for the people to affect governmental decisions. The Constitution also provides for congressional impeachment and removal of a president.

These traits of the American system affect the way the United States' domestic system influences American foreign policy. The question remains, however, under what circumstances these characteristics are most likely to be felt. When is domestic politics most influential on a final foreign policy product? The Jackson amendment case suggests some answers to this question.

The Jackson amendment debate lasted two and one-half years. Both Congress and the executive branch were actively involved. The issue attracted numerous interest groups, in particular Jews and organized labor, which are both politically active and knowledgeable. Formally, the debate centered on a tariff issue, an area where Congress had not abdicated its power to oversee foreign commerce in contrast to the erosion, for example, of Congress' war powers. It was not a life or death issue, again as in the case of many war power issues. The only time constraint operating seemed to have been the congressional timetable. Congress nearly exercised its impeachment prerogative during this period, and the intense domestic tension of Watergate accentuated the natural institutional competition between the president and Congress. This would suggest that maximum opportunity for open debate, discussion, and consideration and maximum interest in such debate are important prerequisites for the free play of domestic influences on foreign policy-making.

Another important dimension of full domestic political involvement in the foreign policy-making process is that there be a motivating force for these foreign policy decision-makers who are elected officials to involve themselves in the decision-making process. One may reasonably presume that the prospect of electoral impact drives politicians to take stands that a nonelected policy-maker would not take. Policy in the United States is the product of elected politicians, not simply the work of bureaucrats—even bureaucrats who are keenly aware of the American political scene. Elected politicians—in the Congress or White House—who act to shape foreign policy have other equally important objectives in mind. They must try to satisfy requirements at home, too.

This election imperative especially drives presidential hopefuls every four years and all 435 members of the House of Representatives and a third of the senators every other year. The normal tension between the two branches of government is increased by the fact that Congress—especially the Senate—has been the launching pad for five of the last seven elected presidents. In the time frame of this study, nearly one-third of the Senate during the Ninety-third Congress (1973-74) was running for the presidency or vice-presidency. Among the presidential candidates (announced and otherwise) discussed in this study are Henry Jackson, Edmund Muskie (D.-Maine), George McGovern (D.-S.D.), Hubert Humphrey (D.-Minn.), Walter Mondale (D.-Minn.), Birch Bayh (D.-Ind.), Edward Kennedy (D.-Mass.), Lloyd Bentsen (D.-Tex.), Richard Nixon (R.-Cal.), and Gerald Ford (R.-Mich.). Without understanding the election imperative of would-be president Henry Jackson and all the other politicians who had a role in the Jackson amendment struggle, one cannot fully understand the history of the Jackson amendment.

Jackson's stated foreign policy objective was to use trade as leverage on the Soviet Union to facilitate Soviet Jewish emigration. Relying on the stated objective of the amendment, however, to understand why decisions were made and certain thresholds crossed during the development of the legislation does not yield a complete picture. To understand better, one needs to bear in mind that Jackson and other major actors also had domestic political goals. This is not to say that Jackson or other politicians did not believe in his cause. But they certainly did not pursue this amendment willy-nilly without regard to possible political bonuses. The domestic politics of the amendment were very important.

JACKSON

Jackson—whom John F. Kennedy passed over as vice-president in 1960, whom the Democrats chose not to nominate for president in 1972, but who intended to run again for president in 1976—consciously linked domestic and foreign policy. For example, "The view of the American people on détente," Jackson explained, "is inseparable from its view on domestic issues."[4] He attacked detente by various means including the trade-emigration amendment. His amendment fulfilled both domestic and diplomatic objectives. His stated objective was to link trade and emigration, thereby using the extension of United States trade concessions as leverage on the Soviet Union to liberalize its emigration policies. Jackson also opposed the basic direction of Soviet-American trade negotiations being conducted at the time in the context of detente. The Jackson amendment appealed to American Jewry, an important group electorally and financially to Jackson and to other legislators who joined him in sponsoring the amendment. Jewry's primary interest in the amendment was Jewry. Haunted by the guilt of surviving the Nazi holocaust, it felt the need to act forcefully to aid its brethren under attack in the Soviet Union. Jackson also appealed to the AFL-CIO, whose president, George Meany, as much as anyone, spoke for organized labor in the United States. The view of Meany and Jackson on detente coincided. Meany, who wanted to slow down or block the expanding trade relationship with the Soviet Union and was also sympathetic to the plight of Soviet Jewry, also saw the amendment as a means to block the administration's bill liberalizing United States barriers to trade worldwide. The Jackson amendment, therefore, pleased the Jews, the AFL-CIO, and other groups spanning the political spectrum while advancing Jackson's strongly held foreign policy goals.

The coalescing of Jackson and other elected officials' views with the view of various important interest groups did not necessarily result from interest-group pressure per se. Politicians often anticipate the responses of target groups in the electorate and appeal to these groups by championing popular issues.[5] In addition, politicians may exert their own pressure on fellow politicians.

The system by which America selects its president has given Jews and the national leadership of the AFL-CIO a great deal of importance to Democratic presidential candidates like Jackson. A majority vote of the electoral college elects the president. Jews are grouped in the population centers in the states with the largest number of electoral votes: New York, New Jersey, Massachusetts, Florida, Pennsylvania, and California. Those six states cast 30 percent of the electoral votes in the college—161 from a total of 529. Jews have a great deal of leverage in those states. Since they tend to vote as a bloc and have a high turnout rate at the polls, the chances that Jews might "swing" an election are increased.[6] The Democratic party, where Jackson was running for nomination to be the party candidate for president in 1976, as he was in 1972, changed its rules for nomination, thereby spawning primaries in thirty states to determine how the delegates to the nominating convention in 1976 would vote on the first ballot. As it turned out, Jackson ran in the primaries in all of the above-mentioned six states where the Jewish vote was deemed significant. In New York State, for example, which was sending 274 of the 1,505 delegates necessary to nominate a candidate at the 1976 convention, Jews accounted for 36 percent of the statewide Democratic primary vote. Of Jackson's supporters, 61 percent were Jewish; Jackson gained 104 delegates in the April 6, 1976, primary balloting.[7]

Another important characteristic of presidential politics is that until January 1975 when campaign finance reforms took effect, campaigns were exclusively financed by private funds. A disproportionate amount of contributions to the Democratic party comes from Jews. Such contributions are especially important to Democratic hopefuls looking for seed money to start campaigns and to keep them going.[8] Until the campaign reforms took effect, individuals were free to give or loan just about as much as they

Q-why did you decide to write about this topic?

wanted to candidates. When the reforms took effect—almost two years before the election of 1976—Jackson had $1.2 million dollars in his campaign chest. Jewish contributions amounted to an estimated 40 to 70 percent of Jackson's funds.[9]

Labor, in particular the AFL-CIO, is another interest group that is especially important to presidential races in northern industrial cities. Union manpower in registration and election-day activities extending down to the precinct level is more important than labor money.[10] For example, Hubert Humphrey, labor's candidate in 1968, received extraordinary labor help financially and organizationally. Because of labor's efforts, 4.6 million voters were registered, 55 million pamphlets and leaflets were printed and distributed from Washington and another 60 million from local unions. Telephone banks in 638 localities using 8,055 telephones were manned. Also, 94,457 volunteers worked in car pools and as leaflet distributors, baby-sitters, poll-watchers, and telephone canvassers.[11] The promise of such assistance was, no doubt, enticing to a candidate.

APPROACH

what this book does

This book describes the two- and one-half-year history of the Jackson amendment as a case study of the domestic politics of American foreign policy-making. It shows that domestic politics is likely to have the greatest impact when popular feeling has been aroused, ethnic identities stimulated, economic interest affected, moral questions raised, and the two foreign policy-making branches of government are competing. The Jackson amendment case suggests that when these phenomena occur, it is almost impossible to depoliticize an issue and make it stop "at the water's edge."

One of the more striking aspects of this book is the process by which a coalition is forged by an individual using various forms of persuasion and coercion. The narrative history that follows is also a microcosm for demonstrating other characteristics of American political life that color the foreign policy-making process:

1. Congressional assertiveness in foreign policy-making against the will of the executive branch.

2. The role of interest groups—in particular Jews and organized labor—in policy formation in America. The internal politics of interest groups will be touched upon as will the role of so-called transnational interest groups in the international system.[12]

3. The attempted use of United States economic concessions to extract political concession from another country, i.e., the Soviet Union.

METHOD

The author worked as staff aide to a United States senator during the period of the study and followed the progress of the Jackson amendment closely. Extensive notes were kept of conversations with principals and their staff, who often were principal actors in their own right. Later, during a year that the author spent at the Brookings Institution, individuals in both the legislative and executive branches of the United States government were interviewed, as were diplomats and government officials from Israel and the Soviet Union. Discussions with leaders and professional staff members of the major Jewish organizations and with recent Soviet Jewish emigrés were conducted. Journalists, who followed the events on a daily basis, were also consulted.

Participant accounts bring out the fine detail and multiplicity of considerations of the many actors involved. However, it is important to analyze their accounts carefully. Some of them were contemporaneous with the events when participants stressed one point at one stage of the story and another point at a different stage in accordance with short-term tactical goals. Different individuals also have different allegiances even though they may be allies vis-à-vis a third party. Knowing what interest group, political ambition, government agency, branch of government, or government the individual represents is important and has to be considered in weighing the accounts of different sources. For that reason, brief statements about an individual's political, ethnic, and professional background have often been supplied in the narrative. Unless otherwise noted, quotations of individuals are taken from interviews or memoranda of conversations. Some of these individuals are nameless either by request or because I considered it unfair to identify individuals who discussed professional matters with me not knowing that I would later write this book.

Because of the author's legislative staff position and daily access to other staffers, the narrative may somewhat exaggerate the role of congressional staffers in the Jackson amendment process. However, the pressures felt by the staff are representative of pressures felt on the principal actors. While the staffers' employers had the formal responsibility and were the necessary condition for the staffers to operate, staff had a major role in drafting legislation and drawing together coalitions that were the foundation of the strength for many of the principal actors in the Jackson amendment.

Augmenting primary source material derived from interviews and conversations were public and private documents—legislative drafts, press releases, transcripts of press conferences, "dear colleague" letters circulated in Congress, memoranda, and testimony delivered at hearings held primarily in the Ways and Means Committee of the House of Representatives and the Senate Finance Committee.

Newspaper accounts from the *New York Times, Washington Post, Washington Star,* and *Wall Street Journal* as well as from the Israeli press were also helpful. To understand fully many of the newspaper accounts required reading between the lines, trying to identify the sources of the accounts, and speculating on reasons why the sources were publicly airing behind-the-scenes developments. Newsletters published by various interest groups involved in the debate—Jewish groups, business groups, and other ethnic groups, for example—also contributed to the research. Longer articles written by B'nai B'rith official William Korey, former Washington correspondent of Davar (Israel) Nahum Barnea, and *New York Times* contributor Joseph Albright were likewise useful.

ORGANIZATION

The book is divided into seven chapters. In between this introduction and a conclusion is a five-part narrative arranged chronologically and broken down to reflect the schedule of Congress and of the impeachment proceeding which influenced the timing and pace of the diplomatic drama. Chapter 1 discusses the Soviet Jewish emigration movement, which first raised the emigration issue and inspired political action in Israel and the United States. To discuss Soviet Jewish activism since 1967 is to trace the living roots of the Jackson amendment.

Chapter 2 tells how one politician—Henry Jackson—forged a link between the Soviet emigration issue and Soviet-American trade, an important element of the detente relationship that blossomed at the Nixon-Brezhnev summit in Moscow in May 1972. It discusses the original drafting and introduction of the Jackson amendment. It shows how Jackson assumed the leadership of the cause of Soviet Jewry, captured the support of three-quarters of the Senate, and neutralized the opposition of President Nixon on the eve of Nixon's reelection. All of this was necessary for Jackson to insure the development of his amendment while controlling it to fit his needs.

Chapter 3 covers the legislative struggle in the House of Representatives during 1973, the first session of the Ninety-third Congress. It contrasts the administration's handling of congressional relations with Jackson's mastery of the congressional process. It shows how the amendment advanced, passing first the House Ways and Means Committee and then the entire House of Representatives. Chapter 3 suggests that the standard image of the Washington lobby is at best a caricature. The popular image is a mechanistic one: the lobbyist pushes and the legislator reacts.[13] In reality, influence often flows the other way, with the legislator using interest groups for his own purposes. Another point to emerge from Chapter 3 is that appealing to one interest group is not sufficient to get a highly contested policy accepted by Congress. The Jackson amendment received broad press attention. It appealed to a broad constituency, not just to American Jews. America, a land of immigrants, was receptive to the notion that all people should be free to emigrate. Intellectuals in the liberal segments of the population who were appalled by Soviet repression of dissenters joined the cause. So did anticommunists who were consistently opposed to the Soviet Union. Other ethnic and religious groups with countrymen and coreligionists in Communist countries who stood to gain by the amendment also supported it. The AFL-CIO—for a combination of pragmatic and ideological reasons—also backed Jackson.

Chapter 4, covering January 1974 to August 1974, is the story of the launching of three-way negotiations among representatives of the legislative and executive branches of the United States government and a foreign government, the Soviet Union. These negotiations were conducted against the backdrop of Senate deliberations on the amendment in the second session of the Ninety-third Congress, 1974. The Watergate scandal of Richard Nixon clouded the progress of the talks.

Chapter 5 covers the tripartite talks from August 1974 to January 1975, which were spurred on by the appointment of a new president, Gerald Ford. In 1974, Jackson no longer possessed near exclusive control over the fate of the amendment, as he had during 1973. Actions taken by the administrations of Nixon and Ford and the Soviet Union in the negotiations, as well as the congressional timetable and the scheduling of the 1974 elections, were important constraints on Jackson. In Chapter 5, the close of the Ninety-third Congress approached as did the November elections, and Jackson wanted a settlement so he would have something to show for his efforts. This increased the leverage of Kissinger and the Soviet leadership as they sought to avoid passage of the amendment or to water it down by offering Jackson some rather unclear assurances.

Up to a point, Jackson managed to maintain support among his congressional cosponsors and from an alliance of disparate interest groups. His domestic and foreign policies had meshed neatly. When he finally agreed to a compromise within the framework of the three-way negotiations in the fall of 1974, however, Jackson angered some of his most important allies, who would have been happier to see no settlement at all. Chapter 5 demonstrates it can be more difficult for congressmen—especially publicity seeking ones—to negotiate than to legislate.

WATER'S
EDGE

The Soviet Emigration Movement: The U.S.S.R., Israel, and the United States

1

I have no use for those who come here from other countries and forget the countries of their origin. He who forgets the country of his birth and looks down upon his parents will never be a good American; he will change his loyalty as he forgets his ancestors.

CALVIN COOLIDGE[1]

Without too much exaggeration, it could be stated that the immigration process is the single most important determinant of American foreign policy. . . .immigration policy *is* foreign policy. . . .

NATHAN GLAZER
AND DANIEL MOYNIHAN[2]

Be he elected or appointed, the official is required to be sensitive to the possibility that casual chains forged abroad may acquire links at home.

JAMES ROSENAU[3]

INTRODUCTION

A small, disorganized band of activist Soviet Jews was the catalyst for the raging international debate in the 1970s concerning whether and how to link Soviet-American trade and Soviet Jewish emigration. Beginning in the late 1960s, Soviet activists focused the attention of political forces in the United States, the Soviet Union, and Israel. They and their allies in the West hardly qualified as an identifiable interest group in the political environments where they operated. They were amateur politicians, individual activists working on an *ad hoc* basis who lit fires and disappeared to let the regular political forces, including interest groups, bureaucrats, diplomats, politicians, or combinations of these, fan the flames or extinguish them.

Activist Soviet Jews wanting to emigrate goaded and/or inspired a few activists among American and Israeli Jewish populations, who themselves were often immigrants or sons of immigrant Soviet Jews, to join the cause of Soviet Jewry. They, in turn, appealed to the Golda Meir government of Israel and the Nixon administration in the United States to intervene with the Soviet authorities on behalf of Soviet Jewry. Eventually the alliance among Jews in the Soviet Union, Israel, and the United States was championed—and overshadowed—by Senator Henry Jackson, who piloted the cause through America's domestic political maze. Chapter 1 briefly traces this political chain reaction of the Soviet emigration movement from the Six-Day Arab-Israeli War in 1967 to the May 1972 Moscow Summit.

OVERVIEW OF SOVIET POLICY

As a result of a half century of Soviet policy to induce assimilation (as well as intimidation) among its national minorities, the majority of Jews in the Soviet Union were loyal citizens of the Soviet state.[4] In the words of prize-winning author Elie Wiesel, they were "the Jews of Silence." The Six-Day Arab-Israeli War in 1967, however, caused many Jews to find their voices. The war and Soviet attacks on the Jewish state dramatized the degree to which the Jews' fate was linked to the fate of Israel. In the past, some Jews had been prominent members of the Soviet dissent movement and had channeled their energies against suppression of the rights of artists, authors, and free thinkers in general. The June 1967 war uncovered Jewish self-identification buried under decades of compulsory assimilation. Activist Jews became increasingly interested in leaving the Soviet Union rather than staying and reforming it. As Jewish activist Yosef Kazakov explained, "Even if the democrats turned this into the country they dream of, there would be no place for us here."[5] In 1968, the Soviet invasion of Czechoslovakia further shattered hope of political liberalization in the Soviet Union.

From 1948 to the Six-Day War, Soviet authorities had allowed a total of six thousand mostly elderly pensioners to leave and be reunited with families in Israel. When hostilities broke out in the Middle East and the Soviet Union severed diplomatic relations with Israel, even that flow came to a standstill.

Strangely enough, Soviet authorities—apparently on their own initiative—resumed issuing exit visas in autumn 1968. Once it became known that the Moscow Office of Visas and Registration (OVIR) was accepting applications for exit visas in September 1968, thousands began to apply.[6] In all, 379 Jews actually left in 1968. This breakthrough may have encouraged dissidents to send the first petitions in 1968 appealing to Western Communist parties for help,[7] followed by the exit of the first group of Jewish activists[8] as part of a total group of 3,000 emigrants bound for Israel.[9]

There was a crackdown on Jewish activism in 1970. In all, only 1,044 Jews were permitted to leave. The Leningrad hijackers' trial held in December 1970 headlined a series of show trials. Soviet Jewish activists addressed appeals to the United States, and Western sympathizers responded with unprecedentedly vociferous protests against death sentences handed down for three of the alleged hijackers tried in Leningrad. Some argue that the protests were so effective that the Soviet leadership felt compelled to permit the number of emigrating Jews to rise in 1971.[10] Others interpret the events as more a product of Soviet desire to rid the country of undesirables. In any case, in the single month of March 1971, 636 were permitted to go—a dramatic upsurge almost equaling the number permitted for the entire year before.

Significantly, the March upsurge also preceded the Twenty-fourth Congress of the Communist Party of the Soviet Union held in April. Soviet and foreign delegates of close to one hundred foreign parties swarmed through Moscow, and newsmen's eyes were trained on the Congress, which officially reaffirmed a policy of peaceful coexistence and improved relations with the West. The jump in permissible emigration may have been an attempt (in vain) to pre-empt embarrassing and annoying criticism from Western Communist parties protesting Jewish persecution at the well-publicized Communist Party Congress. The presentation of the ninth Five-Year Plan, emphasizing modernization of the Soviet economy through technical inputs from the West and accelerated commercial relations with the United States, may have also had something to do with the spurt in permissible emigration.

One must be careful not to confuse coincidence with causality, especially when it comes to fathoming something so mysterious as fiats issued by the Kremlin. Nevertheless, it is perhaps not mere coincidence that all these phenomena—Western protests, Soviet concern about dealing with internal dissent, a new economic strategy based on Western imports, the Twenty-fourth Communist Party Congress, and the upsurge in permissible emigration—occurred in the same time frame.

By November-December 1971, a pattern was established of approximately twenty-five hundred Jews emigrating a month. It continued through

1972-73—up to and through the time that Senator Henry Jackson introduced his freedom of emigration amendment in October 1972 (see appendixes).

ISRAEL

If the Soviet authorities thought they were getting rid of their trouble-makers by permitting the activists to leave, they were only partially correct. They got the activists—some of them—out of the Soviet Union. But they could not stop the activist Jews once they were beyond Soviet borders.

Most came to Israel. The Israeli government's response to the rising Jewish consciousness in the Soviet Union is interesting because as a democracy, a land of immigrants, and a nation with a sense of responsibility for individuals (Jews) who are citizens of other sovereign countries, Israel's experience pre-saged the American response. The early Israeli government response to pleas for help from Soviet Jewish activists in the late 1960s was not what one would immediately expect. Nor was it what the Soviet activists would have wanted it to be. Rather than encouraging the indigenous Soviet Jewish activism, the Israeli government responded in silence, at least on the public level.[11] Although the Israeli government had encouraged Soviet Jews through radio broadcasts, contacts with Israeli diplomats in Moscow, and provision of Jewish materials, Israel's notion of pace and technique for changing Soviet policy toward emigration came to be considered inadequate by would-be emigrants. By 1969, official Israeli silence could no longer be effectively maintained. Larger numbers of Soviet activists reached Israel. They claim-ed, with some justification, to know the situation relating to Soviet Jewish emigration policies better than Israel's experts. They argued that the louder the protests, the better. Criticism from the growing number—roughly twen-ty thousand by the end of 1971—of emigrés who knew the Soviet scene first-hand aroused public opinion and captured the attention of the opposition party, Herut (now part of Likud and headed by Menachem Begin). Even-tually, the ruling Labor party government headed by Golda Meir reversed its traditional policy and spoke out publicly for Soviet emigration.

In November 1969, Meir made a dramatic statement to the Israeli Parlia-ment, the Knesset, which recognized and flatly supported the Jewish move-ment in the Soviet Union. Israel's ambassador to the United Nations also agreed to transmit some of the Soviet Jewish appeals to the United Nations.[12] Meir declared in a radio broadcast that the Soviet legal pro-ceedings of December 1970 against the Leningrad hijackers were a farce designed to frighten Soviet Jews. The Israeli government and various Jewish organizations even claimed the hijack attempt never occurred but was rather a fabrication of the KGB. In fact, for three years, the Israeli government reportedly suppressed the hijackers' testament, which revealed that the hijack attempt had been a desperate response to the "failure of Israel and Jews in the West to express vigorous commitment to Soviet Jewry."[13]

Another attack against the government's position raged from December 28, 1970, to May 1971, concerning a battle over Israel's citizenship law. Soviet activists and their allies in the opposition eventually forced a change in the Israeli law so that persons unable to settle in the country were still entitled to become Israeli citizens. Six months after the law was passed, the government, which was "markedly unenthusiastic" about the new law, had granted only fifty-eight certificates, although hundreds had applied.[14]

Israel was in a sensitive spot. On the one hand, the raison d'être of Israel was to gather in the Jews in the Diaspora, to be a homeland to homeless Jews. As the figures of immigrants from the Soviet Union mounted, the government also began to appreciate that the three million Jews in the Soviet Union were an important reservoir of new Jewish citizens. On the other hand, as a matter of *raison d'état,* Israel could not afford to alienate one of the world's two great superpowers, the Soviet Union. The Soviet Union was extremely wary of interference in its internal affairs from elements abroad. Despite all of Israel's cautious efforts, she was still accused of crass interference.

Israel played an important psychological role for Soviet activists under Soviet control. Radio broadcasts of Kol Yisrael gave the Jews in the Soviet Union confirmation that there was a haven, a national homeland for them outside their country. The mere existence of the state provided an address to which Soviet Jews could send appeals. The state and its highly symbolic capitol, Jerusalem, served as a goal toward which Soviet Jews could focus their hopes for the future and yearn for another kind of life.

Even so, Israel remained actively inactive, loudly silent. Its leaders may have been personally sympathetic, but officially, they refrained from activities that appeared to be overtly meddling in the domestic affairs of the Soviet Union. Israel's leaders tried to avoid exacerbating already tenuous relations with the Soviet Union on the theory that more Jews would be released if they avoided public criticism of the Soviet Union.

THE AMERICAN JEWISH COMMUNITY

The passiveness of Israeli policy was reflected in the early cautious response of Western Jewry to the new activism among Soviet Jews. American Jewry relies on Israel for basic data on the status of Jews in other lands and for interpretation of the data when choosing projects to devote the Jewish community's attention to. "Soviet Jewish activists inside and outside the Soviet Union have," in the words of one activist, "severely criticized Western Jewish organizations for unresponsiveness, inefficiency, inadequate commitment, and stupidity."[15] Until 1970, there was virtually no communication between Jews in Israel and the West and Jews in the Soviet Union. It was assumed that communication was impossible even though the Soviet Union was a member of the Universal Postal Union and a signatory of the International Postal Convention and the International

Telecommunications Convention. Western Jewish leadership discouraged trying to communicate, fearing that it might harm Soviet Jews.

In the early sixties, various American Jewish leaders including Jacob Javits (R.-N.Y.), Abraham Ribicoff (D.-Conn.), and Arthur Goldberg intervened on behalf of Soviet Jews. But their appeals generally dealt with religious, cultural, and spiritual freedom issues. The issue of freedom to emigrate was restricted to the reunification of families. In April 1964, the Jewish community in the United States established the American Conference on Soviet Jewry to deal specifically with the question of Soviet Jews. It was, however, a limited effort. It had no financing or staff of its own. Another organization, the National Jewish Community Relations Advisory Council, whose membership consisted of autonomous local Jewish community relations agencies in eighty-seven cities, contributed staff to handle the Soviet Jewish question. The American Conference on Soviet Jewry was, in effect, a name for a collection of delegates from the eighteen member groups that constituted the Jewish leadership in this country. While the leadership was organizing, a largely New York-based Student Struggle for Soviet Jewry was also created in 1964; it joined the American Jewish Conference on Soviet Jewry in 1971.

Meanwhile in Washington, the Jewish community's registered lobby, the American Israel Public Affairs Committee (AIPAC), focused on the State of Israel, almost to the exclusion of the Soviet Jewry issue. Safeguarding the 2.5 million Jews in Israel overshadowed concern in the American Jewish community and in this organization for the 3 million Soviet Jews. In the early 1970s for example, an AIPAC staff member told one frustrated independent activist for Soviet Jewry that "I just can't get too excited about Soviet Jewry."

The American Jewish Yearbook, a semiofficial publication of the Jewish community prepared by the American Jewish Committee, admitted to the timidity with which the Soviet Jewish issue was treated in the 1960s:

> With few exceptions, notably Jewish defense organizations in the United States, Jewish opinion had previously remained unconvinced of the special nature of anti-Jewish discrimination in the USSR. Most Jewish organizations in the United States had been content to employ 'quiet diplomacy' and to restrict their activities to meeting with low-echelon Soviet officials who had assured them that there was no Jewish problem in the USSR.[16]

Organizations following this restricted policy included the American Jewish Committee, American Jewish Congress, B'nai B'rith, and National Jewish Community Relations Advisory Council. In contrast, individual Jewish activists outside the mainstream of Jewish community leadership became active, and, as a result, they dominated the early Soviet emigration movement in the United States. The Leningrad Trial in December 1970 and the hijacking events that had led to the trial galvanized many of these people into the earliest organized efforts.

In late 1970 and early 1971, the Jewish Defense League (JDL) staged a number of violent, headline-grabbing, anti-Soviet incidents, which aroused the ire not only of the Soviet Union but also of United States and Israeli authorities, and of the American Jewish "establishment" leadership. The JDL's ten-point program included "an end to all Soviet-American talks including SALT, embargo on trade with the Soviet Union . . . political support of conservative politicians and political attacks on supporters of detente . . ."[17]

There may have been overlapping membership between the Jewish Defense League and another early organization, the Union of Councils for Soviet Jewry. The Union of Councils for Soviet Jewry was one of the earliest organized efforts on behalf of Soviet Jewry and considered itself more militant than the larger and better known Jewish organizations. In 1971, it grew from the first local group on Soviet Jewry, which was formed in Cleveland by Dr. Louis Rosenblum, into a federation of similar local groups in about a dozen communities, including the San Francisco Bay area and Los Angeles. Rosenblum recalled the hostile reception he also received from Israel: "The Israelis felt they could achieve a greater hold on the Soviet Jewry movement by working with established leadership circles in this country. But the problem was that these organizations weren't getting things done." Rosenblum has even stated that the chief of Israeli intelligence for Soviet Jewry matters threatened to "rub him out" for organizing the autonomous Union of Councils for Soviet Jewry.[18]

Soviet Jewish activists reaching Israel had managed to communicate successfully with friends and family remaining behind. They encouraged others in Israel and the United States to do the same. By 1971, an elaborate communications network existed featuring telephone networks and mail and tourist channels that reported and supported the would-be Jewish emigrants. Radio was an essential means of communication. Commented one scholar in testimony to Senator Jackson's inquiry on the subject in 1970, ". . . radio stations are heard universally . . . apparently the authorities can't prevent, or, anyway, can't prevent at the kind of cost they are prepared to pay . . . by restoring a complete police regime on Stalin's pattern. . . ."[19] Through broadcasts by the British Broadcasting Corporation, Kol Yisrael, Voice of America, and Radio Liberty, news flowed and dissidents derived a psychological lift.

Meanwhile an equally significant reverse flow of information emanated from the Soviet Union to the West. Senator Jackson, whose office apparently participated in the communication network, has commented, "there is an amazing flow of information out of the Soviet Union. It is incredible what these people have been able to do, policed as they are by the KGB, with all its intricate devices, to keep tabs on people." By radio, ". . .

we know that what happens in this body [the Senate] gets to them in a matter of hours, when it is publicly disseminated."[20]

Jewish activists outside the mainstream of American Jewish leadership had pushed the establishment organization to respond to the needs of the activists inside the Soviet Union. New life was breathed into the old organized coalition on Soviet Jewry, which was renamed the National Conference on Soviet Jewry.

Richard Maass, who had been chairman of the American Jewish Committee's Foreign Affairs Committee, vice-chairman of the old American Jewish Conference on Soviet Jewry, and second chairman of the National Conference on Soviet Jewry from 1972 to 1974, recalled an early confrontation between individual militant activists and the leadership. Maass was a delegate from the American Jewish Committee to the old American Conference on Soviet Jewry, which held a meeting at the Yeshiva University in New York in 1970 sometime between the June hijacking and the December Leningrad trial. Said Maass, a group of students who were not actually organized staged a confrontation and "made certain demands" for half a million dollars and the formation of a new group dedicated to Soviet Jewry. All the elected delegates but three walked out. Among the remaining three were Rabbi Herschel Schacter, who later became the first chairman of the new National Conference on Soviet Jewry and served from 1970 to 1972, and Maass, who was the second chairman succeeding Schacter.

This was a major step toward active involvement by the Jewish establishment. The Soviet emigration movement had developed rapidly. Soviet activists had gained Israeli government support after gaining more open support from sympathizers in the opposition parties in Israel and among organized groups for Soviet Jewry. Support was also gathering in the United States and elsewhere in the world. The fact that the Israeli government lent its support encouraged the establishment Jewish groups in America also to pay heed. Eventually, activists could boast that "of Soviet dissent movements, only the Jews have had a large, structured, well-financed, internationally distributed, strategically placed lobby in the West—world Jewry,"[21] the impact of which the government of the United States would come to feel. A pattern similar to that which had developed in Israel had recurred in the United States. The Soviet Jewry issue attracted politicians who found that attacking Soviet repression had an important constituency in the United States.

EARLY EFFORTS TO TIE TRADE TO EMIGRATION

Louis Rosenblum, chairman of the vanguard group Union of Councils for Soviet Jewry, is credited with first suggesting that freedom of emigration be linked to trade concessions that the United States government was considering granting to the Soviet Union. That was his position from 1969 on.[22] Rosenblum's Washington colleagues, Harvey Lieber of American University and Washington attorney Nathan Lewin, established the National Center for Jewish Policy Studies, which Lieber described as a "Jewish Nader's Raiders." In the summer of 1971, one of the earliest projects of the group was to assign a student to assess the Soviet need for trade from the West. It was the first attempt by a Jewish organization to consider what according to Lieber "appears to be so obvious now—dangle a carrot" before the Soviet Union to induce it to cooperate on the emigration question.

Lieber and Lewin drew up legislation tying Soviet concessions on emigration to the export control mechanism the United States had employed to regulate trade with countries in the Communist bloc. The proposed amendment to the Export Administration Act of 1969 gave the president discretionary authority to withhold exports as a means of pressuring the Soviet Union to liberalize its emigration policies.

Lieber became a self-appointed one-man lobby for the proposal. "Nobody [else] was lobbying [Soviet Jewry]—registered or unregistered. I was doing it on the side—on an *ad hoc* basis—pitching in when needed." Some might call Lieber a hobby-lobbyist.[23] He circulated several memoranda on Capitol Hill including a March 1972 memorandum prepared on his professional stationery of the School of Government and Public Administration of the American University, which combined data compiled from the Union of Councils for Soviet Jewry's press releases and selections from various congressional hearings.

Lieber had little support from the Israeli embassy, the American Jewish organizations, or anyone in Congress. Even though the Lieber legislation was a direct antecedent to the Jackson amendment, he was never in personal contact with Jackson or Jackson's staff. At this stage Jackson was satisfied with introducing a resolution cosponsored by Tennessee Republican Senator William Brock that expressed sympathy for the cause of Soviet Jewry and was supported by the Department of State.

Explained Lieber, "Jackson wasn't on the right committee . . . Richard [Perle, staffman for Jackson] wasn't in town; he was campaigning for Jackson. Secondly, Edmund Muskie (D.-Maine) and Jackson were fighting for a bill for refugee assistance for Soviet Jewry resettlement in Israel." Nor did Lieber contact the office of Senator Abraham Ribicoff (D.-Conn.). Ribicoff, who became a prominent sponsor of the Jackson Amendment, was not on the "right committee" either.

The "right" committee in the Senate, in Lieber's opinion, was the International Finance Subcommittee of the Senate Banking Committee. It was responsible for the Export Administration Act, to which Lieber aimed to attach his proposed legislation in early 1972. Senator Walter F. Mondale (D.-Minn.) was chairman of that subcommittee. Mondale's professional staff economist on the Banking Committee, Paul A. London, explained that Mondale tried to find a way to accommodate Lieber. Mondale wanted to do something for the Soviet Jews. But Mondale resisted linking emigration to Soviet-American trade, which he had worked hard and successfully to liberalize since 1969. After several efforts by London and Mondale's foreign policy assistant, Roger Morris, to redraft the Lieber proposal, Lieber was left disappointed.

On May 4, at the urging of Simon Frumkin of the Southern California Council for Soviet Jewry, Congressman Thomas M. Rees of California (D.-Calif.), introduced the legislation in the House of Representatives.[24] However, Lieber's experience with many of his co-religionists proved to be frustrating. He had no help from the Israeli embassy. Explained Lieber, "I want to stay clear of the Israeli Embassy. I don't know what their position was. It's always a difficult situation dealing with any foreign embassy."

Lieber tried to enlist the assistance of the National Conference on Soviet Jewry (NCSJ), which was the reembodiment of the American Conference on Soviet Jewry. In late December 1971, Lieber and Jerry Goodman, executive director of the National Conference on Soviet Jewry, had worked together to brief New York Congressman James Scheuer regarding the situation of Jews in the Soviet Union. Despite their prior experience of cooperation, Lieber's idea to link trade concessions to emigration received no support from Jerry Goodman, in particular, or his organization, in general.

Lieber called the National Conference on Soviet Jewry "very timid, very slow." "It was not backing it," Lieber said. "I had fights with the Director, Jerry Goodman. . . . Goodman was extremely ambivalent about the Export Administration Act. It [Lieber's project] was a personal thing but I was touching base with Jerry Goodman, who felt we should not tie trade with emigration."

In late June, when Goodman indicated to Congressman Rees that neither the NCSJ nor Goodman supported the bill, in spite of the fact that thirty cosponsors supported it, Congressman Rees' interest in the bill flagged. Congressman Bertram Podell, Karen Kravette, Washington representative of the Union of Councils, and Dr. Louis Rosenblum met with Rees, and reportedly revived Rees' efforts on behalf of the bill. However, in mid-July an effort to get the House Banking and Currency Committee to insert the emigration amendment into the Export Administration Act failed.[25]

THE NIXON ADMINISTRATION'S RESPONSE TO THE SOVIET EMIGRATION MOVEMENT

Richard Nixon was president of the United States during the period of rising Jewish agitation . . . and emigration. Even before he was sworn into office in January 1969, his political record reflected a concern for the question of Soviet Jewry and Communist repression in general. In 1959, when he was vice-president planning to run for president, Nixon was credited with establishing the practice of presenting Soviet authorities an official United States representation list or hardship list of individuals in the Soviet Union—many of whom were Jews—who had been denied permission to emigrate to reunite with family in the United States.

In 1964, still eyeing the presidency, Nixon criticized the Kennedy wheat deal and suggested instead that wheat be sold to the Communist-bloc countries only on condition that the regimes liberalize their domestic policies vis-à-vis their own population. Nixon construed East-West trade as a political tool—a bludgeon—to advance human rights objectives in Communist countries: "No United States trade should be approved if it strengthens a Communist government's stranglehold on the people."[26]

On September 30, 1968, in the heat of his successful run for the presidency, Nixon expressed his continuing concern for Soviet Jewry in a speech to the American Conference on Soviet Jewry: "I deplore the discriminatory measures imposed upon the Jews in the Soviet Union, and hope and trust that humanitarians throughout the world will continue vigorously to protest these restrictions and deprivations of human rights."[27]

If Nixon in office worried about repression in the Soviet Union as much as he did as a candidate, he did not reveal it publicly. Instead, the diplomats in his administration conducted "quiet diplomacy" by doing little more than presenting representation lists to Soviet officials. In October 1970, Secretary of State William Rogers handed over such a list to Soviet Foreign Minister Gromyko. Another list containing one hundred and fifty names was provided by United States Ambassador to Moscow Jacob Beam to Deputy Foreign Minister Kuznetsov on February 19, 1971. Again in September 1971, Secretary Rogers handed to Foreign Minister Gromyko a list when Gromyko was in New York for a session of the United Nations.[28]

When the Leningrad Trials death sentences were handed down, the Jewish national leaders called a conference December 30, 1970, and Schacter, Wexler, and Fisher met with Secretary Rogers and President Nixon to urge Nixon to intervene with the Soviet Union to ask for leniency for the two Leningrad Jews doomed to die. The Nixon administration petitioned Moscow, and the accused hijackers' lives were spared.[29]

Generally, however, the Jewish question paled before considerations dictated by the policy of detente with the Soviet Union, which Nixon and his national security adviser Henry Kissinger labored to establish. One of the major elements in that policy was that each superpower would refrain from intervening in the domestic affairs of the other.

The official administration position on Soviet Jewry was enunciated on November 1, 1971, by Deputy Assistant Secretary for European Affairs Richard Davies. The official told a congressional hearing that "a small number of outspoken Jewish activists has been dealt with arbitrarily and usually harshly. . . . Individual applications for emigration are sometimes harassed. We deplore this.'' But Davies was reluctant to do other than to deplore. He said that the United Nations was the best "regular forum for focusing world attention on the situation of Soviet Jews,'' and he referred to two such American protests lodged by United States Representative on the United Nations Human Rights Commission Rita Hauser. As for Jews wanting to go to Israel—in contrast with Jews wanting to reunite with American families—Davies flatly asserted, "We cannot be of direct assistance in cases of persons seeking emigration to other countries."[30]

As Nixon approached his reelection in 1972, however, it seemed he was compelled to pay greater attention to the emigration movement, which attracted greater attention in the Jewish community in the United States. In January 1971, the Democratic presidential front-runner Edmund Muskie took a trip to the Soviet Union accompanied by former United States Ambassador to the Soviet Union Averell Harriman. Muskie raised the question of Soviet Jews with Prime Minister Aleksei Kosygin.[31]

Muskie (who had run ahead of Nixon in the polls) and Jackson, both presidential hopefuls in 1972, cosponsored legislation to help Israel resettle Soviet emigrants. Soviet Jewry became a presidential political issue, which Nixon could not ignore. Appeals were sent to Nixon, Hubert Humphrey, George McGovern, and many other leading political figures in 1972 election campaigns. "In thirty-five different states, there was legislative action, gubernatorial proclamations, denunciations of Soviet persecution of Jews, and appeals asking the President to raise the question of Soviet Jews,'' reported the *American Jewish Yearbook.*[32]

Nixon's speechwriter William Safire recalled that Nixon personally sympathized with the cause. "He believed the Jews were right to stand up for their fellow Jews, and that the Soviets were making a mistake in allowing this to stand in the way of East-West détente.[33] In that case, the politics of the situation overlapped with the politician's personal point of view.

THE MOSCOW SUMMIT, 1972

The big test of Nixon's concern for the Soviet Jewry came at the May 1972 summit in Moscow. Safire recalled that Leonard Garment, a former Wall Street law partner of Nixon's and White House liaison with the Jewish community, "ran a delegation in to see Kissinger and the President before and after the Moscow summit; the Nixon men impressed on the Jewish leaders the need to let the Soviets back off without losing face. Kissinger kept pointing out that they were not telling us to solve our own race problems before dealing with them. . . . Kissinger did not want détente jeopardized by the admission of impediments like internal policy to the marriage of true minds."[34]

It is not clear how the president or Kissinger handled the question of Soviet Jews with Soviet officials at the summit. The administration told reporters in Moscow one thing and later told the Jewish leaders back in Washington the opposite. The issue was not included in the official agenda of issues to be discussed by Nixon and Brezhnev.[35] Kissinger counseled Safire and presidential aide Robert Haldeman to "say nothing while we're here. How would it be if Brezhnev comes to the United States with a petition about the Negroes in Mississippi?"[36] Reported Leonard Schroeter, who was very close to the Soviet activists in Moscow and in fact was in Moscow in 1972, there was "no indication that he [Nixon] ever raised any question with Soviet leaders."[37] An administration official who was involved in the Soviet-American trade negotiations also commented, "emigration never came into Administration interest in May and June 1972."

Apparent American inaction plus Soviet imprisonment of activists, disconnection of telephones, calling up of Jews to military service, and continuing jamming of Voice of America and Radio Liberty during the period of Nixon's stay in the Soviet Union caused "great bitterness" among Soviet Jews.

Soon after the summit, however, Governor Nelson Rockefeller—who was not in Moscow but who was a confidant of Kissinger's—reported that Nixon and the Soviet leadership had a "meeting of minds" and there was an understanding that the 1972 outflow of immigrants would reach thirty-five thousand. The *New York Times* correspondent reporting called the New York Republican's statement "a bit of political exaggeration" in reference to the upcoming Nixon reelection where the Jewish vote in New York was an important element. The correspondent reported that there was, nonetheless, an agreement. Soviet leaders told Nixon what their emigration figures were and probably made an annual projection.[38] It turned out that if Rockefeller had exaggerated, he did so only slightly; approximately thirty-two thousand Jews emigrated in 1972.

At a press conference after the president's return, Kissinger indicated that Soviet emigration was "mentioned" during summit talks. Months later the president personally told Jewish leaders the subject was discussed.[39] At the time, the administration in word—if not in deed—appeared to resist joining the mounting protests of Soviet emigration policies. Its "quiet diplomacy" was so quiet that it seemed imperceptible to the Jewish activists. Instead, Nixon appeared most concerned about not jeopardizing detente.

SUMMARY

By allowing some Soviet Jews to leave in the years after the 1967 June war in the Middle East, the Soviet authorities ironically whetted the appetites of others to try to emigrate. Eventually, pressure began to build as the Soviet authorities were unwilling to match the rising expectations in the Jewish community. The individuals who were frustrated in their attempts to leave became the core of the political activism that eventually was felt on

American shores. The Soviet emigration issue demonstrated that the source of United States political action can span the seas. In this case, the transnational links stretched back to the Soviet Union. United States politics not only does not stop at the water's edge; sometimes internal American politics even begins beyond the water's edge.

The Soviet activists as a group were clearly masters of the technologically sophisticated communications which were an important element of the transnational Soviet Jewish network. The core of the activists in the Soviet Union's major cities were members of a highly educated Soviet elite. This notable characteristic had important political consequences. Sociology students have generally observed that American immigrants today "are of quite different 'stock' from those of the past . . . the new immigrants are to an unprecedented degree professional, upper middle-class persons. What this means is that the process of gaining political influence as a small group, a process which took even the most successful of earlier groups two generations at least, is likely to be rapid for those most recent newcomers.''[40] The description of a special stock of immigrants fits the Soviet Jewish emigrants reaching Israel and America where they inspired political action on behalf of their brethren behind in the Soviet Union. Even though relatively few actually immigrated to the United States, advanced communications made it possible for them to influence America's foreign policy as had other ethnic groups in American history.

Success was due not only to the "stock" of the Soviet Jews and to technologically sophisticated communications. Another important factor was that these people were activating earlier Jewish immigrants to America who by then knew how to operate in the domestic political arena. Many of the American Jews who came to their coreligionists' assistance had made politics their vocation or at least avocation. The early idea for legislation linking trade and emigration toyed with by individual hobby-lobbyists illustrated the high level of political sophistication of some of the early activists in America who devoted their energies to helping Soviet Jews.

By the summer of 1972, the Soviet emigration issue was an important issue to nonestablishment and establishment Jews alike in the United States. The 1972 summit had offered hope that the way out of the Soviet Union would no longer be hampered by harassment and apparently arbitrary decisions about who among the applicants would actually be able to leave. However, the Jews were disappointed by an apparent reluctance of the Republican administration to broach the issue with Soviet officials forcefully. After the May summit, the time was ripe for a new actor to appear on the scene and take up the banner of Soviet Jewry. It would not be surprising, therefore, for a politically ambitious actor from the other branch of government with foreign policy-making powers—the Congress—and from the other party—the Democrats—to assume the role of champion of the Soviet Jewry cause.

Presidential Politics and Detente

2

The great rule of conduct for us in regard to foreign nations is, in extending our commercial relations to have with them as little political connection as possible.

GEORGE WASHINGTON

Be cautious of the ruling authorities, for they befriend a man only for their own interests; they appear as friends when it is to their own advantage, but do not stand by a man when he is in distress.

ETHICS OF THE FATHERS

If all the seas were ink, all the reeds were producing pens, the expanse of heaven were sheets of parchment, and all the children of men were scribes, yet it would not suffice to write down the devices of political government.

TRACTATE SABBATH,
THE BABYLONIAN TALMUD, 11b

INTRODUCTION

The presidential campaign summer of 1972 encouraged American politicians to focus on the disorganized protests of Jewish activists clamoring for free exit from the Soviet Union. In this way, Jewish activism emanating from the Soviet Union spread its political impact to the United States and shaped the course of American foreign policy.

The key actor in this period was Senator Henry Jackson, who took up the activists' cause both on its merits and no doubt for his own domestic political reasons. The amendment he drafted that summer brought the Norwegian-American senator from the state of Washington to the forefront. As Jackson orchestrated the movement to link trade and emigration in America's relations with the Soviet Union, the early Jewish activists were eclipsed by their new patron. They were reduced to issuing occasional choruses of protest and useful tidbits of information smuggled out of Soviet Russia to reinforce Jackson's legislative campaign.

To understand the events from late summer to early fall 1972, one must understand not only the transnational roots of the Soviet emigration movement. One must also explore the role Jews played in the 1972 presidential campaign, which set the domestic political context. Also, one must bear in mind the policy of detente, the quest for a ceasefire in Vietnam before election day, and related developments in the Soviet-American trade that formed diplomatic backdrops.

Senator Henry M. Jackson introduced his famous amendment on October 4, 1972, in the waning days of the Ninety-second Congress just as the legislature was recessing for the presidential election. In a letter written to his Senate colleagues dated September 27, 1972, he stated that the "principal and immediate cause of concern is the imposition by the Soviet Union of a head tax which was imposed on August 3, 1972."[1] However, one should not take this statement too literally. In fact, even before the August 3, 1972, Soviet edict levying an additional exit tax on educated emigrants (that in effect fell on Jews most heavily), Jackson was working on his own personal response to developments in the trade, emigration, and arms-control areas arising from the May summit between President Richard Nixon and Secretary Leonid Brezhnev.

The May summit represented the peak of detente, which President Nixon and Henry Kissinger had been shaping since 1969 from the earliest days of the Nixon administration. A SALT I treaty limiting antiballistic missile (ABM) sites and another agreement limiting offensive missile launchers were signed by the two leaders. Trade discussions—which had been carefully paced to progress in step with Soviet cooperation elsewhere, particularly Vietnam—had not advanced as far as some had expected. However, negotiations were scheduled to continue and future progress was promising.

Ostensibly the United States was unwilling to extend most-favored-nation (MFN) tariff treatment or government credit to finance Soviet purchases in the United States until the Soviet Union pledged to repay an agreed-upon amount of the Soviet lend-lease debt dating from World War II. The Soviet Union had been hopeful that a trade agreement would have been reached at the summit. As a compromise, Nixon and Brezhnev agreed to establish a commission to negotiate a settlement whereby the United States would grant most-favored-nation and Export-Import Bank credits in exchange for Soviet payment of its lend-lease debt. Presumably, more tangible evidence of Soviet cooperation in urging its North Vietnamese clients to negotiate a peace settlement with the United States was also a condition for Soviet-American agreement.

As for the issue of Jewish emigration, activists inside and outside the Soviet Union believed Nixon's promise to conduct quiet diplomacy was broken by, among other things, Kissinger's personal reluctance to bring up the subject at all. The Soviet decision to levy the August 1972 education tax on would-be emigrants, seemed to confirm Nixon's critics' worst suspicions about his administration's lack of interest or influence in the realm of human rights. It made a mockery of any professed advances the Nixon administration was making as far as Soviet emigration was concerned.

JACKSON SPOTS AN ISSUE

Jackson's chance to be the Democratic presidential nominee in 1972 was destroyed by his showing in the Florida, Ohio, and Wisconsin primaries. Even though he intended to run again in four years, his mind in midsummer of 1972 was probably as much on the summit postmortem as it was on his campaign postmortem.

Jackson looked at the results of the May summit and did not like what he saw. He was basically skeptical of detente with the Soviet Union. He thought the SALT agreement was a bad one. He thought that plans to trade with the Soviet Union were moving along at an unguardedly rapid pace. He was picking up advice at the same time from activists working on behalf of Soviet Jewish emigration about the oppressive domestic conditions inside the Soviet Union.

Soon after President Nixon and Secretary Brezhnev had initialed at the summit the SALT I treaty limiting ABMs and signed another agreement limiting offensive weapons, Jackson made known his objections to the SALT results. He said little publicly about the trade negotiations conducted during the summer of 1972, but his staff, in particular, Richard Perle, was at work on the topic of lend-lease at least by early June—even before the trade negotiations were completed.[2]

Perle's first approach to dealing with the developments in the trade field had nothing to do with emigration or with Jews: ". . . at first we explored an abortive idea which was to send it [the lend-lease agreement] back on the grounds that the lend-lease agreement was inadequate . . . by July we had disposed of the non-starter. . . . And then we thought of the Jackson Amendment" (linking trade to emigration).

Perle also explored linking the lend-lease agreement to the education tax levied by Soviet fiat in August 1972. He thought about taking the difference between what the Soviets owed, according to Perle's accounting, and what the Soviets would pay by agreement with the United States government, which amounted, said Perle, to billions of dollars, and "apply [ing] it as credit" toward payment of education taxes for Soviet emigrés.

Perle said he knew about both the tax and the developments in the trade negotiations on lend-lease and most-favored-nation treatment before either was officially announced. By August, "by the time the education tax was put on, we knew of a settlement on lend-lease," Perle recalled. If so, Perle had inside information. At the close of the round of negotiations on lend-lease, most-favored-nation, and credits, which was conducted in Moscow from July 20 to August 1, Secretary of Commerce Peter Peterson held a press conference where he revealed that the two sides were closer together on the matter of lend-lease, but that no final agreement had been reached. Reportedly the Soviets resisted paying lend-lease until after Congress granted most-favored-nation. In turn, absence of a lend-lease settlement barred the United States' granting Export-Import credits.[3] Perle indicated he knew more than Peterson was telling. Perle believed an agreement had been reached by then in which the "true lend-lease debt—the real debt of eleven billion dollars" had been reduced. "We knew that it [the agreement on the Soviet debt] was very small—a token." Perle referred to an $11 billion figure for the Soviet debts that the United States had officially dropped two decades before. (In 1952, the United States reduced its demand from $2.6 billion to $800 million.)

Jackson had trade-restricting language drafted at least by early June—months before the education tax was issued in early August. Thus, it is a mistake to view the Jackson amendment as a reaction to the August 3 tax announcement. Even less was it a reaction to the order of the Soviet Council of Ministers issued over Kosygin's signature on August 14 reaffirming the August 3 decree. Jackson had readied an initiative on trade—lend-lease—even before he drew a link to emigration. He drafted legislation linking emigration to trade even before the news of these two unpublished decisions leaked out to the world and before the United States and the Soviet Union had concluded their negotiations on most-favored-nation and lend-lease.

This point about timing is important for two reasons. First, it helps to put Jackson in the proper perspective vis-à-vis the Jewish community on this issue. Jackson was prepared to launch a tough legislative response on Soviet Jewry before the Jewish leadership was. Second, it demonstrates the mixture of motives behind Jackson's amendment. Jackson was concerned about Soviet Jewry, yes. But he also opposed the policy of accelerating detente and trade relations, an issue quite distinct from the Jewish question. The forces that impelled Jackson to advance his amendment linking trade and emigration, which launched a two-and one-half-year campaign for its passage, are important to explore. Jackson's amendment had a dual diplomatic aim: to liberalize Soviet emigration policy and to retard the development of trade and detente between the two superpowers. It should thus be viewed in the contexts of both Soviet-Jewry and Soviet-American trade.

Jackson was opposed to developing a trade relationship on the grounds that American national interest was not being served. He also objected to the "phoney" detente practiced by Henry Kissinger.[4] Both objectives are consistent with his personal belief that the Soviet Union should be dealt with in very strict terms. He did not shrink from the charge that he is a "hard-liner." He believed that "certainly the Cold War is still on."[5] These were important considerations underlying his critical response to the summitry of 1972. He also had a history of interest in Soviet Jewry and Jewish issues in general, although he had made statements in the past questioning the role that morality—and the human rights issue of emigration certainly came under that category—should play in world politics.[6]

JACKSON AND THE "JEWISH LOBBY"

Jackson's amendment was more an initiative than a response. On his own, Senator Jackson embraced the notion of linking trade and emigration even before the Jewish lobby did. This is an important distinction, as it contradicts strongly held myths about lobbyists in general and the "Jewish lobby" in particular.[7] If all of America's favorite stereotypes about the Jewish lobby were operating, the events would have been just the reverse. The popular image would have Senator Henry Jackson take a proposal from the Jewish lobby and then introduce it as his own.[8] It may be true that the sheer presence of a powerful Jewish community encouraged the Jackson initiative, and constituent considerations heavily influenced the attitude of a number of other legislators, as well as Nixon. However, there is an important distinction between a politician appealing to an interest group and a politician being pushed by a group to act, although a good politician admittedly anticipates constituents' desires.[9]

The idea of linking trade and emigration had been circulated to a few Senate offices, including those of Walter Mondale and Hubert Humphrey, by more militant activists in the Jewish community for at least six months before the Jackson amendment as such was actually discussed. Jackson's staff members might have heard about it, but they deny having borrowed the notion. Moreover, the established, organized, and well-known Jewish groups and Jewish leaders—in contrast to individual Jewish activists agitating on an *ad hoc,* "hobby-lobby" basis—actually objected to the notion of manipulating Soviet-American trade relations for the sake of Soviet Jews. Initially, they objected to what was regarded as the drastic measures embraced in the Jackson amendment. Israel's Ambassador Yitzhak Rabin at the time also agreed that "United States interference in Soviet internal affairs—no matter how warranted by the injustice of the exorbitant emigration tax—would be counter-productive."[10]

When the August tax was announced, Jackson—not the Jewish community—was prepared with legislation to launch a legislative counterattack. The Jewish groups in the Soviet Union and the United States could only issue mere verbal protests as they had done over the years. On August 15, a delegation of Jewish leaders met with Secretary of State William Rogers at the White House. Those attending included Max M. Fisher, a millionaire Jewish philanthropist and one of eight founders of the Committee to Reelect the President, the 1972 reelection campaign organization for Richard Nixon; Jacob Stein, head of the Conference of Presidents of Major American Jewish Organizations; and Richard Maass, the chairman of the National Conference on Soviet Jewry. "Ranking White House officials" also attended the meeting. The Jewish representatives were told that the United States government had expressed its concern over the fees to the Soviet government. Several prominent Jewish organizations also issued statements urging Nixon to explain to the Soviet Union that improved relations would be jeopardized by the new tax. On August eighteenth, the activist organization, The Greater New York Conference on Soviet Jewry, held a rally featuring recent Soviet emigrants and Democratic presidential nominee Senator George McGovern. On the twenty-ninth of August, McGovern also charged that Nixon "has never spoken out" on Soviet Jewry, a statement destined to have important ramifications in the Nixon White House in the months to come.

The following day Senator Jacob Javits (R.-N.Y.) appeared at another emergency rally for Soviet Jewry staged in New York's garment district on Seventh Avenue at Fortieth Street. Javits' aide, Roy Millenson, had helped prepare a short statement for Javits, expressing the notion of linking trade and emigration. While on the minority (Republican) staff of the Senate Labor and Public Welfare Committee, Millenson served as Javits' liaison with Jewish groups in New York. It was natural, therefore, for him to call up the executive director of the National Conference on Soviet Jewry, Jerry Goodman, to discuss the idea of linkage. Goodman recalled, "Millenson tried it out on me . . . as a speech, as an idea." Goodman approved. Javits' foreign policy aide Albert (Peter) Lakeland rewrote the Millenson statement, but the notion of linking trade and emigration stayed in the speech. Declared Javits, the first senator to do so, "We should properly demand justice for Soviet Jewry as a condition for close economic relations with the USSR in trade and finance."[11]

CONGRESSIONAL STAFF LINK TRADE AND EMIGRATION

The individuals most responsible for shaping legislation linking trade and emigration were congressional staff—in particular Richard Perle of Jackson's staff and Morris Amitay of the staff of Senator Abraham Ribicoff. A staff person cannot operate without permission—implicit or explicit—of his or her senator. Some senators supervise their staff more closely than others. When a senator feels he is not adequately controlling his staff, a senator can always fire his employee. In the cases of Perle and Amitay, staff was instrumental in drafting legislation and pulling together a coalition of supporters to reinforce their principals.[12] Said Jackson, "in all candor, it was the able staff of the three Senators who did the job. They were led largely by Mr. Richard Perle, of my staff, Morris Amitay of Senator Ribicoff's staff, and Mr. Lakeland, of Senator Javits' staff, and they all worked together as a team. They made our task a lot easier, let us face it, and they provided the professional expertise that resulted in what we were able to do."[13] Ribicoff has seconded Jackson's statement. "While Senators are out in front and take much of the credit, all of us know, realistically, that we have to rely on the hard work of many members of our staff. [They] worked hard in their research and in the legislative drafting. They were available twenty-four hours a day as assistants to the three of us in working out the Jackson Amendment."[14]

Richard Perle is a soft-spoken, chain-smoking Southern Californian in his midthirties. Trained as a military strategist, he has been described as a "SALT hawk with his own hot lines into the military and intelligence communities."[15] Perle received his political baptism and met his present boss, Jackson, when he served a short stint in Washington in 1969 with the pro-ABM lobby. Since then, he has been stashed away with at least eight other employees in the one-room office of the Senate Subcommittee on National Security and International Operations—now part of the Permanent Subcommittee on Investigations—chaired by Jackson.

Perle is not an observant, religious Jew. His Jewish affiliation is not so much religious as political. He works on Jewish political causes—Israel and Soviet Jewry—from a power base in the United States Senate. Thus his activity in things Jewish stems primarily from professional and intellectual sources. Until he went to work for Jackson, Perle was more interested in intercontinental missiles than Israeli affairs. "Scoop got me interested," he said, and "in fact, put me to work on the first Jackson Amendment, which provided five hundred million dollars for Phantoms and other equipment. My perspective is a little different from Morris' [Amitay] because I'm just very much convinced of the soundness of the foreign policy. I agree with John Roche, who says he'd be for defending Israel even if it were populated with South Vietnamese. There are sound strategic, political, economic reasons for supporting that piece of real estate *per se,* though obviously there's an emotional attachment beyond that" but it is "based largely on the profound respect for the competence and the dedication and toughness and the skill of the Israelis. They possess those values that Jackson admires and that, through him, at least initially, I've come increasingly to admire."[16] As one keen observer put it, Jackson "infected Richard with Jewish concern and then Richard reinfected Jackson"—at least on the Soviet Jewish idea.

Morris Amitay, a staffer for Abraham Ribicoff, worked closely with Perle on the Jackson amendment. Ribicoff claimed that Amitay spent 90 percent of his time on Jewish issues. Today, the former United States Foreign Service Officer is head of the American Israel Public Affairs Committee (AIPAC), the only registered lobby for Jewish issues, and spends 100 percent of his time on Jewish affairs. Compared to Perle, Amitay's attachment to Jewish issues arising in the United States Senate stemmed from a more personal, emotional source. Amitay traces his paternal ancestry back seven generations to Tiberius, Israel. Dark, moustachioed, speaking fluent Hebrew, and retaining a Hebrew family name, Amitay claims, for example, former Prime Minister of Israel Yitzhak Rabin as a good friend.

Amitay and Perle worked as a team on the Jackson amendment often calling upon other Jewish staff members to help push legislation that was in the interest of Jews. Amitay explained the importance of Jewish legislative staffers, which he contrasted to professional Jewish lobbyists:

> There are now a lot of guys at the working level up here who happen to be Jewish, who are willing to make a little bit of extra effort and to look at certain issues in terms of their Jewishness, and this is what has made this thing go very effectively in the last couple of years. These are all guys who are in a position to make the decisions in these areas for these senators. You don't need that many to get something done in the Senate. All you need is a certain commitment to get something done, if guys are willing to put time into that instead of a million other things they have to do, if they're willing to make a couple of calls, if they're willing to become involved, you can get an awful lot done just at the staff level. . . . The Senators have a million things to do [and] they'll take the recommendation [of their assistants] most times . . . a

few key senators with staff people who are willing to make this commitment in time and in energy, and who informally consult with each other on matters like this now [is the important element].[17]

STAFF MEETING I

Richard Perle and Morris Amitay—with the cooperation of I.L. Kenen, who represented AIPAC at the time—organized an early meeting of congressional staff and representatives of Jewish organizations. The group gathered in the Red Cross bandage room on the first floor of the Old Senate Office Building to discuss what action should be taken in response to the education tax announcement from the Soviet Union. The exact date of the meeting is in dispute, but everyone agrees the meeting came soon after the August tax announcement.

Perle and Amitay dominated the group as they would dominate policy made inside and out of Congress regarding Soviet Jewry for the next two and one-half years, the duration of the fight over the Jackson amendment. Other staffers at the first meeting included aides to Jacob Javits, Kenneth Gunther and Roy Millenson; Hubert Humphrey's foreign policy advisor, Richard Gilmore; Walter F. Mondale's foreign policy aide, Judith Davison; and Birch Bayh's administrative assistant, Jayson Berman.

Representing Jewish interest groups in addition to Kenen of AIPAC were Jerry Goodman, executive director of the National Conference on Soviet Jewry, and Yehuda Hellman, director of the Conference of Presidents of Major American Jewish Organizations. The distinction between professional workers for Jewish organizations and Jewish staffers whose power base was their desks in several congressional offices was not an unimportant distinction. The two groups of individuals were both Jewish and eventually became allied in the same cause, Soviet Jewry. But they represented different organizations with interests that did not always coincide.

At the early meeting, all did agree that Congress had to do something. Javits had already felt compelled to speak out. Humphrey's foreign policy aide had been contacted by Karen Kravette, the Washington representative of the more militant Union of Councils for Soviet Jewry; he had begun drafting a resolution that drew a connection between trade and emigration. Mondale, who had also been contacted by Jewish activists connected with the Union of Councils six months earlier, was still receiving constituent pleas that he intervene in special cases of Jews harassed in the Soviet Union. A Mondale aide recalled that Mondale was receiving "a lot of mail." It was an election year for Mondale, and he was willing to place calls to the Soviet Union to speak with some of the individual cases. Nonetheless Mondale was hesitant about linking emigration to East-West trade, which he had successfully worked to liberalize only a few years before. Mondale later stated, "It was with a heavy heart that I felt I had to join cosponsoring this proposal, because as the Senate well knows, I have been one of the consistent champions of expanding trade with the Soviet Union."[18] Even Jackson had constituents urging him to do more for the Jews in the Soviet Union. One of the most prominent was Washington State attorney Leonard Schroeter, who had worked on Soviet issues as the assistant to the attorney general of the State of Israel and later wrote the book *The Last Exodus,* criticizing Israel and American Jewry for acting too slowly and tentatively on behalf of Soviet Jewry.[19]

Several proposals were discussed at the September meeting in the Red Cross room. Perle tabled the notion of tieing freedom of emigration to the extension of most-favored-nation tariff treatment to the Soviet Union, which the president would have to ask Congress for authority to extend. Perle argued the case for binding legislation linking trade and emigration. He and Amitay, the only other participant at the meeting backing Perle, insisted that the education tax would be a permanent fixture of Soviet policy. Others argued that the tax might only be a temporary measure. Perle presented information from the Central Intelligence Agency to back up his argument. "They said that they [the Soviet authorities] were sending people out to villages to explain the tax which was [meant] to stir up anti-Semitism. . . ." Perle extrapolated from this intelligence that the Soviet leadership was committed to collecting the tax since it was mobilizing traditional anti-Semitism among the general population.

Perle and Amitay met resistance to the idea of linking trade and emigration both from representatives of the Jewish organizations at the meeting and from other Senate staffers. "The Jewish organizations were not for it [the Jackson Amendment]," Perle recalled, naming Yehuda Hellman, I.L. Kenen, and Jerry Goodman as personally not favoring the link.[20]

Javits' aide, Kenneth Gunther, was one of those opposing Perle's stringent measure. However, Gunther, an international trade expert, unwittingly toughened Perle's proposal. "My contribution was that I said it should logically include OPIC's [Overseas Private Investment Corporation] investment guarantees and credits" offered by the Export-Import Bank. Perle later thanked Gunther for his contribution, "even though you hated this proposal, we are indebted to you for your help." Henceforth, Jackson insisted that the Soviet Union liberalize emigration before Congress permitted the president to grant *MFN, credits,* or United States governmental *guarantees* for American private financing.

STAFF MEETING II

Perle, Amitay, and other Senate staffers held another meeting on September 11 to continue discussing linking trade to Soviet emigration. Amitay called together twelve staffers to meet in Ribicoff's office.[21] Representatives of Jewish interest groups who had attended earlier meetings and had proven recalcitrant were not included in the September 11 meeting. But Perle and Amitay still had a difficult time with the Senate staffers. Tempers were short at the meeting. Perle and Amitay were well known on Capitol Hill and downtown in offices of the White House and executive branch for eliciting hostility in others by threatening, accusing, and generally applying a power political philosophy to his workaday relationships.[22] That day, Perle's most vocal adversary was Richard Gilmore of Senator Hubert Humphrey's staff. Humphrey and Javits, said their staffmen, preferred gathering Senate signers on an open letter to the Soviet leadership or a nonbinding sense of the Senate resolution aimed at changing the Soviet leader's decision before the decree was to be promulgated formally on September 19. Gilmore had readied a draft resolution. Perle and Amitay had anticipated this argument and prepared a list of other nonbinding resolutions that had created more smoke than fire.[23]

Dispatching Humphrey and Javits to make a personal visit to Soviet Ambassador Anatoly Dobrynin was another proposal discussed. The purpose of the proposed secret mission was to have Humphrey, who felt he was on good personal terms with Dobrynin, warn the Soviet Union that action to withhold most-favored-nation treatment was afoot and that growing pressure in the Congress was serious. Javits was supposed to contact Humphrey, who was out of town, for the purpose of arranging a joint mission to ask Dobrynin to communicate to his superiors the need to head off the congressional move by reconsidering and ameliorating the tax policy. After several unsuccessful attempts to see Dobrynin, who at the time was returning to Moscow in conjunction with Kissinger's September Moscow visit, Javits and Humphrey gave up. Said Perle, the idea was "crazy and it didn't work."

Humphrey, meanwhile, was trying another approach. A week earlier, Humphrey had released a letter sent to President Nixon asking the president to have Kissinger raise the issue of Soviet Jewry with the Soviet leaders he was meeting in Moscow the very day that the Senate staffers were scrapping over Perle's proposal. No one could know whether or not Kissinger would take up the issue and, if so, how the Soviets would react. The Senate staffers agreed, however, to do several things simultaneously to reinforce publicly any quiet diplomatic effort that Kissinger might conduct in Moscow. It was agreed that several senators, whose staff had attended the meeting, would speak on the Senate floor and state that they would not support most-favored-nation treatment unless the Soviet Union reversed its education tax policy. Morris Amitay told the group that Ribicoff intended to denounce Soviet emigration policy and announce that he would not support the East-West Trade Relations Act (S.2060), which called for MFN tariff treatment for the Soviet Union. Gilmore was under the impression that the staffers had agreed that Senate speeches by Ribicoff or anyone else would not be immediately delivered. The Humphrey-Javits mission to Dobrynin and the circulation of a concurrent resolution accompanied by a "dear colleague" letter requesting Senate cosponsors, as proposed by Gilmore, were supposed to be given a chance to work first.

Amitay, however, did not wait to see the results of Humphrey and Javits' efforts or of the ongoing discussions between Kissinger and Brezhnev. The very next day, September 12, Ribicoff became the first senator to urge on the Senate floor that the "ransom question" be linked to improvement of Soviet-American trade relations. Ribicoff reversed his position articulated as early as June 1971 that the president be given the authority to grant MFN tariff treatment to Communist nations.[24] He had been an original sponsor of the East-West Trade Relations Act. Now he was opposing "any trade legislation granting the Soviet Union better trade terms as long as the ransom decree is in effect, and as long as similar draconian measures are applied to restrict emigration of *Soviet Jews.*"[25]

Javits issued a warning to the administration, to the Soviets, and to anyone else interested in reading his interview printed on the front page of the *New York Times* on September 15. He stated that "a determined group of legislators can block" trade if "justice" for the Jews wishing to emigrate from the Soviet Union was not assured. Javits listed a half dozen legislative steps that could be taken. White House spokesman Ronald Ziegler responded to this warning, saying "the Soviet Union is aware of the United States' position in this matter." Ziegler also elaborated on Kissinger's talks with Soviet leaders, which had just concluded in Moscow. "We are not hesitant to report that it [congressional sentiment against the education tax] was discussed" and "as I understand it, not just in passing."[26] Nevertheless, if Kissinger raised the issue of Jewish emigration, past statements on his part suggest he probably did so reluctantly. Moreover, it presumably carried little weight relative to the other topics under discussion—trade and Vietnam.[27]

KISSINGER LINKS TRADE AND VIETNAM

While Senate staff was discussing the idea of linking trade and emigration, Kissinger had been conducting discussions in Moscow where he was pursuing the Nixon administration's linkage of trade and Vietnam. The administration was holding out economic concessions to use as incentive for Soviet cooperation in resolving America's gravest foreign policy dilemma at that time: Vietnam. Kissinger had set the stage earlier when he met Brezhnev and other officials in Moscow in April to prepare for the May summit. The fourth draft of his speech prepared for delivery in April revealed how Kissinger connected peace in Vietnam, Nixon's reelection, and the question of opening up "billions of dollars of business activity."[28] In May at the summit, Nixon continued to hold out the possibility of normalizing trade relations. His trade negotiators, headed by Commerce Secretary Peter G. Peterson, held further talks with Soviet officials in July, but an agreement was not final at the time of Kissinger's trip to Moscow in September. Brezhnev was probably in a cooperative mood at the time. He was recuperating from the humiliation of having twenty-one thousand Soviet military advisers "invited" to leave Egypt that summer. He was also reeling from a short supply of grain in the Soviet Union brought on by a devastating harvest. His grain purchasers had managed to buy record volumes from private operators in the United States beginning in July, but a snag developed in shipments and the administration insisted upon renegotiating an agreement in September. The administration was also steadfastly withholding final agreement on MFN tariff treatment and credits. The announced reason for America's position was that it was waiting for Soviet agreement to pay back its lend-lease debt, an issue held over from post-World War II days. By September, it was clear that Soviet payment of its lend-lease debt at a rate acceptable to American negotiators was no longer an obstacle. Apparently, the remaining and most important issue was that Kissinger was waiting to see evidence that the Soviet Union's earlier offer made at the May summit to help American extricate itself from the Vietnam war was having a tangible effect on the Soviet client, North Vietnam.[29]

Two days before Kissinger embarked on his four-day trip (September 10-13) to Moscow, where his stay happened to overlap with a visit from Hanoi negotiator Le Duc Tho, the Vietcong issued a new proposal. The Soviets later informed Kissinger that that was the Vietnam peace breakthrough for which he had been waiting for three years. The Vietcong would accept a ceasefire without prior removal of South Vietnamese President Nguyen van Thieu.[30] All indications were that Kissinger was advancing by linking the Soviet's desire for MFN and credits and America's desire to end the Vietnam war, an objective that Kissinger was anxious to achieve before Nixon faced the voters in November. Accompanied by Under Secretary of Commerce James Lynn, Kissinger applied his economic tools to the Vietnam question.

After his talks with the Soviet leaders, Kissinger left Moscow for Paris where he conducted further secret talks with Le Duc Tho. In his wake came an article written by Victor Louis, a Soviet journalist with extraordinarily close connections to the Soviet intelligence community. Louis reported that the Soviets would be getting large credits and "probably" MFN since the lend-lease issue, which had been the ostensible barrier to credits and most-favored-nation, had been resolved.[31]

Ever since Nixon's first days in the White House, Kissinger's approach to the Soviet-American relations was to pace carefully progress on the economic front with progress on political objectives of the United States.

Getting the United States out of the Vietnam war was Kissinger's most pressing assignment, particularly as Nixon's reelection was fast approaching. Jewish emigration was of secondary importance. On his return from talks in Moscow and Paris, Kissinger told a press conference on September 16, that he had raised "in a number of ways" in Moscow the exit tax question. Kissinger postponed commenting on congressional threats to block trade legislation implementing any trade agreement that he negotiated with Moscow. "When and if we conclude an agreement, we will submit it to Congress for its approval" and "then there can be a full debate on this particular issue."[32]

One might interpret Kissinger's remarks as a coy suggestion that he was still using the prospects of trade concessions—promised though not yet formally agreed to in writing—as continuing leverage over the Soviet Union to guarantee continued cooperation on the Vietnam issue. In any event, Kissinger's remarks also indicated that he discounted the congressional threat that seriously jeopardized use of the available instruments of economic leverage.

Soviet officials also behaved as if the congressional challenge did not concern them. Reportedly they assumed President Nixon could push an MFN agreement through Congress in spite of protests from ninety congressmen who had signed a letter to Brezhnev in August, in spite of Ribicoff's threats, and in spite of Javits' warning of other challenges from "a determined group of legislators."[33] On September 22 further evidence of congressional intent came when Congressman Charles Vanik offered an amendment to the Foreign Assistance Bill (H.R. 16705), which the House of Representatives passed by a voice vote (in other words, there was no roll call with congressmen recording their personal "aye" or "nay"). Vanik's amendment denied Export-Import Bank credits and development loans to any country charging more than $50 in exit fees. The amendment, which technically would have also penalized Israel, whose exit fee then was $140, was dropped from the bill in a House-Senate conference that met September 28.[34] But the House action should have served as additional warning.

JACKSON SEIZES THE LEAD

In the White House, on Capitol Hill, and in the offices of the Jewish organizations themselves, pressure was building to respond to the education tax by means other than speech-making. This was a crucial period in the development of the Jackson amendment. With some careful guidance from both the administration, preoccupied with other aspects of Soviet-American affairs, and the Jewish interest groups, who had not decided on the best approach for responding to the education tax, Congress might never have started on the long march toward passage of the Jackson amendment. The

Jewish organizations did not send the administration or members of Congress a clear-cut signal on how to respond to events in the Soviet Union since they had no clear-cut policy. They embraced no remedy—legislative or otherwise—for dealing with the emigration issue. Meanwhile, the administration was mistakenly satisfied to meet with various Jewish leaders and to ignore the real threat to its position—the nascent congressional initiatives in the foreign policy field.

It was a time for decisiveness and determination, traits Jackson possessed. "I have a record of . . . what some people have fun poking at me, that I'm intransigent, that I'm difficult, that can become an asset."[35] Jackson was prepared for a tough legislative response—to withhold trade benefits from the Soviet Union pending liberalization of emigration. He had to convince others in Congress and in the Jewish community that this was the best approach, since, as he said, "unlike other such pleadings it has some teeth in it."[36] Javits had publicly embraced the idea, but coauthoring legislation was another matter. Javits and Humphrey felt that Soviet-American trade was a constructive development. At the time, they preferred having a non-binding resolution on emigration.

At this juncture, there were two separate proposals for congressional action, plus the alternative of the administration's quiet diplomacy conducted without interference from the Congress. The Jackson amendment insisted emigration be liberalized in the Soviet Union before trade concessions were granted. The Javits-Humphrey provision was a softer concurrent resolution deploring the tax, urging its removal, but also drawing a connection between the ongoing Soviet-American trade negotiations and liberalization of Soviet emigration policy. Even though a Humphrey aide contended that "it was not written to stop the Jackson Amendment," the two proposals competed for the attention of the rest of the Senate membership and for approval from the organized Jewish community. Humphrey's aide, Richard Gilmore, had taken a "dear colleague" letter and the resolution to a select group of Senate offices asking for cosponsors. He had gathered between sixteen and twenty-two actual signatures including what one staffer called "real stars": Edward M. Kennedy, Edmund Muskie, Walter F. Mondale, George McGovern. This formidable group, however, was no match for a determined Jackson.

The opportunity for Jackson to seize the leadership of the Soviet-Jewry issue presented itself on September 26, when the National Conference on Soviet Jewry (NCSJ), the umbrella organization representing thirty-two major Jewish organizations, sponsored an emergency rally in Washington to decide how to deal with the education tax.

The education tax announcement had galvanized the Jewish groups into action. It dramatized to them the limitations of all their candlelight vigils in front of Soviet diplomatic buildings and the futility of planting "Free

Soviet Jewry" signs in front of America's synagogues. The National Conference on Soviet Jewry had neither a Washington office nor a Washington representative. The rally—which was actually the regularly scheduled board meeting enlarged because of the emergency to a total of one hundred and fifty interested participants—met at the Mayflower Hotel in Washington. The National Conference on Soviet Jewry used the B'nai B'rith headquarters nearby at 1640 Rhode Island as temporary headquarters.

In contrast, Jackson was well-organized, prepared, and skillful. He was also forceful. "There was an agreement among staff that principals [i.e., senators or congressmen in contrast to their staff] would not come to the meeting," recalled a Javits staffman. "Jackson violated the agreement." He went out of his way to arrange an invitation to the meeting. Before the gathering at the Mayflower Hotel, Richard Maass, chairman of the National Conference on Soviet Jewry, and Jerry Goodman, the NCSJ's executive director, went to B'nai B'rith headquarters to use the telephones. While there, they received a call from Bostonian Moses Feuerstein who said his son Henry was working in Jackson's office. Young Feuerstein had been involved in presidential campaign fund-raising on a "high level" for Jackson to whom he had reported directly rather than through campaign finance officials or staff.[37] Elder Feuerstein, who was personally very influential in Boston's orthodox Jewish financial circles, informed Goodman and Maass that Jackson had a legislative proposal on Soviet Jewry and asked if it would be alright for Jackson to attend the rally. There was no one else around besides Maass and Goodman to decide yes or no. They said yes.

Jackson arrived early at the evening rally on his way home from the office before the two staffers for Javits and Humphrey even appeared. Jackson delivered a thumping twenty-minute speech. He spoke to the Jewish group like a general addressing his troops:

> The time has come to place our highest human values ahead of the trade dollar by firm and immediate action that the Russians can understand. You want to know what you can do? I'll give you some marching orders. Get behind my amendment. And let's stand firm.[38]

Jackson read the text of his legislation making trade with the Soviet Union conditional on reform of its emigration policy, cessation of harassment, and abolition of excessive emigration fees. Jackson claimed this approach was better than the weaker resolution of Javits and Humphrey. He argued that the time for compromise was not at the beginning of the battle but only after the enemy, the Soviet Union, had been weakened in the fight. His speech brought the applauding audience to their feet. He departed leaving behind Perle and Amitay to argue his case to the assemblage and urge the group to act. Amitay reminded the audience of the consequences of official Jewish silence during the Nazi holocaust, a theme that has generated Jewish political activism in recent decades.[39]

An unsuccessful effort was made to delete the section in the Jackson amendment requiring the president to report regularly to Congress on Soviet compliance with prior conditions established by Congress before it would approve trade concessions to nonmarket nations.[40]

Lawrence Goldberg, an attorney who ran the Jewish section of the Committee to Reelect the President (Nixon), tried unsuccessfully to get Chairman Maass to postpone the vote endorsing the Jackson approach. Goldberg asked for time to try and contact General Alexander Haig at the White House in hopes of getting a White House endorsement for a substitute to the Jackson amendment. Maass did not know who Haig was until Goldberg explained that he was Kissinger's top assistant. Maass agreed to wait forty minutes. Thirty-five minutes later, Goldberg called Maass on the telephone to report that he was unable to get in touch with Haig. He asked Maass to wait a couple of more hours but was refused.

Jackson's personal lobbying of the Jewish lobby paid off. The vote on the resolution was unanimous.[41] By the time Humphrey's aide arrived, as scheduled, to plead the case for the Humphrey-Javits resolution, the group had already voted. Said Gilmore, "I came. I spoke, I met opposition, and then I discovered they had already voted."

The actual resolution stated that the group "looked with favor" on the approach of Senator Jackson and other initiatives. They singled out Jackson without eliminating the Humphrey-Javits approach. The language was vaguer than what Jackson's militant aide had desired. Perle told a reporter, "I came out [of the meeting] wanting to vomit."[42]

Perle may have been disappointed with the cautiously worded resolution. But in effect it installed Jackson as the *de facto* leader of the Soviet Jewry campaign. The Jewish organizations entrusted their cause to Jackson. Some might say they abdicated their power to him. Clearly it was a reversal of the popular image of the Jewish lobby twisting a senator's arm.

"DEAR COLLEAGUE": ACT II OF JACKSON VS. JAVITS-HUMPHREY

One day after the National Conference on Soviet Jewry had endorsed the Jackson amendment more or less specifically, Perle and Amitay circulated a "dear colleague" letter with a copy of the legislation in the form of an amendment to the East-West Trade Act of 1971 attached.

Eleven influential senators signed that first letter inviting the rest of the senators to add their names to the legislation as cosponsors of the amendment. Their signatures helped to attract cosponsors and to demonstrate the power and seriousness of intention of the legislation.[43] It was important for the legislators to prove themselves not only to the Soviet Union, and to the Republican administration whose detente policy was challenged thereby, but also to Javits and Humphrey, who still had a competing resolution on

Soviet Jewry circulating in the Senate. More or less official Jewish activists joined Senate staffs in soliciting senators' signatures. Only in this marginal sense can one argue, as others have, that the Jackson amendment resulted from Jewish pressure. After the names of Jackson and Ribicoff, the letter bore the signature of Jackson's senior from the state of Washington, Warren G. Magnuson (D.-Wash.).[44] Other Democrats signing included Harrison A. Williams (D.-N.J.), Ernest Hollings (D.-S.C.), John Tunney (D.-Calif.), and Birch Bayh (D.-Ind.). Bayh and Tunney both had activist Jewish staffers in the mold Amitay had previously described. Bayh's administrative assistant, New York lawyer Jayson Berman, had worked hard on Bayh's abortive 1972 campaign for president, which, reported a former staffer, "attracted a great deal of Jewish money," and Bayh planned to try again for the presidency in 1976.

To make the appeal bipartisan, Jackson had succeeded in getting Republican signatures from Gordon S. Allott (R.-Colo.), the chairman of the Republican Policy Committee; Edward J. Gurney, who represented a large influential Jewish community concentrated in Dade County (Miami), Florida; and William V. Roth, Jr. (R.-Del.), who had been urged to sign by the offices of Jackson and Ribicoff and by Jewish activists in Washington, D.C. and Deleware. The inclusion of these Republicans may have constituted some degree of pressure on Republican Javits to sign. So perhaps did the inclusion of the other senator from the heavily Jewish state of New York, Conservative James Buckley.

At this stage of legislation—when a senator is asked to sign a letter asking the rest of the membership to cosponsor—it requires more conscious thinking on the part of a senator than simply cosponsoring. It requires the man's signature. Either the individual senator himself or someone specifically designated in his office must sign. In contrast to cosigning, cosponsoring merely takes the word of the senator who delegates a staffer to pass by word of mouth his decisions to cosponsor to staff in the office requesting cosponsorship. In some offices, staff takes the initiative of having its senator cosponsor legislation without even discussing the issue with the senator. In the week following circulation of a copy of the letter signed by the eleven senators, thirty-two names were gathered. Attesting to Jackson's success while also realistically pointing out the low level of political consciousness of some of the thirty-two cosponsors, one legislative aide has declared that Jackson is "the most effective [Senator] in rallying legislation. I'm convinced he gets people to be cosponsors [of his bills] before they know what they're cosponsoring."[45]

Nevertheless, cosponsoring a piece of legislation requires at least minimal conscious decision-making by the senator or by staff whom some senators authorize to deal with "dear colleague" letter requests arriving in the office.[46] There certainly is no rule that says one must cosponsor as there is presumably with voting. Cosponsoring a piece of legislation often is done for the purpose of attracting attention among targeted constituent groups. Indeed, it may attract more attention than a particular roll call vote, whose significance may be shrouded behind procedural veils sometimes thrown up deliberately by Congress to fuzz an issue.

Theoretically cosponsoring is easier than voting, because it is not as final as voting. The individual legislator can always cosponsor something and later—at a slight cost—decide it was not a good idea and vote otherwise. If he is lucky, he can cosponsor a piece of legislation for the sake of appealing to a particular constituency back home and the legislation never comes up for a vote.

The Jackson amendment was just such a case. The Ninety-second Congress was about to adjourn and the Jackson amendment could absolutely not come to a vote in either house of Congress before adjournment. One northern Senator posed this rhetorical question regarding Jackson's cosponsors: "Why did so many people sign the amendment?" He answered himself, "Because there is no political advantage in not signing. If you do sign, you don't offend anyone. If you don't sign, you might offend some Jews in your state."[47]

Just as important as who supported the Jackson amendment was who opposed it in the above-mentioned senator's calculation. In 1972, there was no organized opposition to the Jackson amendment, which helps to explain a great deal about the amendment's appeal. Business groups with business plans in the Soviet Union had not yet had an opportunity to begin trading on a large scale. They had not built up a strong interest in Soviet-American trade in the fall of 1972 when the two countries were still negotiating a trade agreement to clear the way to open trading although prospects for an agreement may have made some senators hesitant to sponsor.

William Saxbe (R.-Ohio), a cosponsor of the amendment, had second thoughts a year later and removed his name with a flourish as he attacked "Zionist" influence. Henry Jackson publicly debated Saxbe on his action, strongly suggesting that Saxbe had changed his mind after he received countervailing pressure from farm groups favoring trade and shipping grain to the Soviet Union.[48]

Although the Jackson amendment eventually picked up support from other important groups, Jewish interest and agitation was predominant in the early 1972 stages of the amendment. Jewish pressure, of course, meant different things to different politicians. The type of pressure was different on Jacob Javits, one of the two Jews then in the United States Senate and representative of the largest Jewish population in the country, than it was on James Buckley, the other senator from the same heavily Jewish state of New York. In 1970, "Buckley had campaigned hard for Jewish votes. Shortly before election day, for instance, his signature appeared on an advertisement in the *New York Times* condemning Russian treatment of Jews.''[49] In contrast Javits—who philosophically believed in free trade with all nations, a position that was also very appealing to his supporters on Wall Street—could afford to resist being one of the thirty-two original cosponsors of the Jackson amendment. He disappointed a group led by Rabbi Gilbert Klapperman, who urged him to cosponsor.[50] As a Jew, Javits was less vulnerable to charges of being anti-Jewish if he took a softer line on Soviet Jewry than a non-Jew.

Humphrey, who had a record as a friend of the Jewish community and who with Javits had his own resolution on Soviet Jewry, also stayed off the original list. Walter Mondale, who had also been represented at the earlier staff meetings on the Jackson amendment, may have felt comfortable following Humphrey's lead, as he often did. Both men also were philosophically liberal trade advocates—again an appealing position in Minnesota where the 1972 sale of grain and agriculturally related products was popular among large grain dealers, farmers, and farm implement manufacturers.

Until the National Conference on Soviet Jewry had endorsed—more or less equivocally—the Jackson amendment and not the Javits-Humphrey resolution, Javits and Humphrey were in good company in refusing to link trade and emigration. But once the Jewish leadership—with the notable exception of the American Jewish Congress[51]—had embraced the Jackson approach and the number of cosponsors grew to thirty-two, Humphrey and Javits found themselves increasingly isolated.

Javits and Humphrey, however, still resisted cosponsoring. Javits, a Republican, had not exhausted the possibility that his party's head, President Nixon, might aid him in finding a solution to the education tax crisis, which did not entail the Jackson amendment. Meanwhile, Javits assigned a new staffman to deal with Jackson's staff to negotiate altering parts of the Jackson amendment that Javits found offensive in the event Javits was left with no other choice but to cosponsor. Javits could bargain with Jackson as long as he refused to endorse the legislation. Albert (Peter) Lakeland, Javits' foreign policy aide, who had not been involved in the earlier staff meeting before the NCSJ September 26 emergency meeting, was given the task of dealing with Perle and Amitay.

Lakeland started by reinforcing Javits' bargaining position vis-à-vis Jackson. For three days he was able to hold off twenty-eight senators from signing the Jackson amendment, which reflected the fact that Gilmore, Humphrey's aide, had already gathered commitments from between sixteen and twenty-two senators to sign the Humphrey-Javits' concurrent resolution.

While Lakeland was working to hold Javits' position among his Senate colleagues, Kenneth Gunther, another Javits' staffman, tried to urge the administration to do something to avert the galloping growth of the Jackson amendment. "I personally called the office of Peter Flanigan [Council on International Economic Policy], the National Security Council [headed by Henry Kissinger] and Commerce Secretary Peter Peterson." Gunther said he spoke with Robert Hormats at the National Security Council; John Rose, with Flanigan; and Brandon Sweitzer with Peterson. "The message was that Jackson and Ribicoff had thirty-one sponsors on the Jackson Amendment. We [Humphrey and Javits] will go with a different approach—a concurrent resolution—if the Administration will go with us. The Administration came back to us" in a return telephone call from Sweitzer, with the following message: "The Administration position is that when we want to take a position on this, we will take a position."[52]

As his letter was circulating to all one hundred senators, who were also receiving telephone calls from their Jewish constituents, Jackson took to the Senate floor on September 27 to announce that he would be formally introducing his amendment in a matter of days.[53] The same day, Nixon's press secretary Ziegler told reporters that Nixon had informed several Jewish leaders that he would work through diplomatic channels and not by means of harsh confrontation tactics against the Soviet Union. This was a slap at the Jackson amendment but no comfort to Javits. The following day, State Department spokesman Charles Bray added that Nixon opposed linking trade to emigration and objected to any move to block the developing trade relationship with the Soviet Union. The administration opposed both the Jackson and Javits-Humphrey approaches since both linked trade and emigration.

Javits' mission to Dobrynin had failed. Jackson had stripped from Javits the backing of the Jewish groups at the National Conference on Soviet Jewry rally. The administration lent no support to Javits' search for a substitute. Javits had little choice but to try to soften Jackson's draft in exchange for his cosponsorship. Humphrey worked in concert with Javits.

"When [the Administration's response] came back, Lakeland and I opened negotiations with Perle and Amitay," Gunther recalled. "Rick Gilmore came later. The negotiations were a total flop in that Perle and Amitay took the deck. Only minor changes were made."[54] Admitted a Javits' staffer, "the changes were very cosmetic." After Lakeland agreed, Jackson's office quickly called the twenty-eight or so offices formerly committed to the Javits-Humphrey proposal to announce that Javits was going along with the thirty-two senators previously committed to the Jackson amendment.

It had been a slow but steady process by which Javits and Humphrey had relinquished their nonbinding resolution and their freedom to blunt Jackson's efforts. The final stage in this early period in the development of Jackson's strength came on September 30. The Senate was in session that Saturday as the legislature pushed to finish business in time to adjourn the

Ninety-second Congress before the November presidential elections. That gave Perle, Amitay, Gilmore, Lakeland, and Davison time to iron out the final details of the amendment in a series of last minute, hotly contested meetings. As one chagrined staffer put it, "Saturday, we capitulated."

A few minor changes were made in the originally drafted amendment, which was all Javits apparently believed he could get. For example, a requirement that the president discuss treatment of specific religious groups in his report to Congress on the emigration performances of Communist nations was deleted. In exchange for a few such concessions, Jackson's staffer Dorothy Fosdick, a hard-driving woman who had work dedicatedly for Jackson for several decades, insisted on a commitment from the others that no weaker substitues—like a resolution on Soviet Jewry—be introduced to compete with the stringent measures of the Jackson amendment.

The meeting bristled with hostility. Jackson's staff insisted on a commitment from Humphrey, but Richard Gilmore, his aide, was unable to commit his boss once and for all. Although staffs may negotiate among themselves, they may not always speak for their employers. That was the case with Gilmore. "I said I couldn't speak for Humphrey—there is no way I can commit him to an amendment he hadn't seen or to get off the resolution he had seen. . . . I called him on Saturday at Waverly [Minnesota]. He said he'd talk to Jackson on Monday. . . . It's possible that Javits [also] tried to get Humphrey. Javits probably succeeded [in reaching Humphrey] at Waverly. Javits was in Washington on Saturday and I remember having Peter [Lakeland] get [Javits] in touch with Humphrey." Some people have blamed Gilmore for Humphrey's wavering on initially sponsoring the Jackson amendment. Gilmore explained Humphrey's position and course of action. "It wasn't just me. But on this issue I played more of a role; in part it was because he was not in town. But Humphrey—like myself—was caught up in classical liberal notion of detente, and trade was part of liberalization of relations."

Javits' position was also still not completely clear. By the end of the legislative day on Saturday, recalled Gunther, "Javits flew to Texas for a speech with two statements—one going along and one blasting the Jackson Amendment. That's when Javits and Humphrey came on board. And that coalition has held since that time."

When Javits finally agreed to cosponsor the Jackson amendment, many other senators, who had waited to see which way the liberal Jewish Republican from New York would go, followed in his wake. In addition to Humphrey and Mondale, there were Edward M. Kennedy, Edmund Muskie, Charles Percy (R.-Ill.), Edward M. Brooke (R.-Mass.), and Richard Schweiker (R.-Pa.). A conspicuous number of those following Republican Javits' lead were liberal Democrats. Jackson's staff, who had attacked liberal Democrats for their consistent opposition to large defense budgets that Jackson defended, did not want the liberal Democrats to live down their waffling positions. One legislative assistant to a liberal Democratic senator recalled this attitude. When she heard that as a result of the Javits-Humphrey-Jackson agreement, changes had been made in the original Jackson amendment draft that had been circulated to all members of the Senate in the September 27 "dear colleague" letter, she wanted to see the changes. She walked over to Jackson's Subcommittee on International Security Operations, staffed by Perle, Fosdick, Tina Silber, and Charles Horner, a China specialist trained at the University of Chicago.

Fosdick overheard her ask for the draft of the revised Jackson amendment, jumped from her seat, and rushed to the front of the room exclaiming, "Oh, you liberal Democrats are all alike. You have to see where a Republican like Javits is going before you can follow." The staffer did not tell her that the particular liberal Democrat whom she worked for was a maverick. He was one of a handful not cosponsoring the Jackson amendment despite its increasing momentum.

NIXON'S AND JACKSON'S INTERESTS COINCIDE

While liberals in the Democratic and Republican parties joined Javits, there was still a group of Republican senators who marched not to Javits' beat, but to the political drum of President Richard M. Nixon. Jackson pursued his quest for sponsors of his amendment all the way to the White House where he asked Nixon not to oppose his effort to sign up cosponsors from the conservative wing of the Republican party. It was late September, virtually the eve of the president's reelection. Jackson's immediate search for cosponsors and Nixon's quest for four more years in office became intertwined.

Nixon's foreign policy advisers had resisted the notion of linking trade and MFN and reluctantly raised the question of Soviet Jewry in private diplomatic conversations with Soviet leaders. Kissinger had raised the topic of Soviet Jewry in his top-level talks in Moscow in September, but he had done so unenthusiastically. In the same period, he was privately advising members of the Foreign Relations Committee that the Jackson amendment might cause a serious political confrontation with the Soviet Union and, therefore, it should be opposed.

On the other hand, Nixon's political counselors were more receptive to the Jackson amendment. There were at least two major factors making Nixon feel disposed toward cooperating with Jackson on the Jewish emigration amendment by late September. First, it was the eve of Nixon's reelection and the president was anxious to avoid a wild-cat congressional action on Soviet Jewry that might reinforce his Democratic opponent George

McGovern's exploitation of the subject as an election issue. Second, Jackson possessed a great deal of personal influence during this period, which Nixon may have concluded was inadvisable to ignore.

THE JEWISH STRATEGY

Nixon's reelection strategy was based on the memory of his close 1968 race. Richard M. Nixon's most urgent objective after his narrow victory in 1968 was to broaden his political base.[55] Nixon beat Hubert Humphrey in 1968 by barely one percentage point, and he ran his 1972 race aware of the importance of certain swing votes. Nixon strategists appreciated the fact that even though Jews were 2.7 percent of the population, they carried much more political weight in terms of electoral votes and campaign contributions than that tiny number would indicate. Nixon's speech writer William Safire reported that in 1972 there was "an accent on Jewish money being collected by Detroit industrialist, Max Fisher, and New York financier, Bernard Lasker." Safire recalled that electorally Nixon at the time was also "openly trying to get Jews to switch." They ran a highly controlled reelection campaign, featuring among other things a "Jewish strategy."[56]

In 1968 only 17 percent of the Jewish vote went to Nixon.[57] Nixon strategists figured that every new vote for Nixon—a switch to the Republican party from habitually voting for the Democratic candidate—counted as two votes because it meant also a reduction in a vote against him. They figured they did not even need a majority of the Jewish vote to make a significant difference.[58]

Clearly it was not in Nixon's interest to have a highly volatile, moral issue like Republican apathy to Soviet repression of Jewry become an election issue. Nixon, the consummate politician, was therefore predisposed to Jackson when he requested that the president remain neutral rather than opposing the Jackson amendment, which his foreign policy adviser Henry Kissinger said would threaten a confrontation with the Soviet Union.

SALT

In late summer 1972, Jackson also appeared to be a formidable political force, inadvisable to ignore for other reasons.[59] Jackson was successfully challenging the achievements of Nixon's May summit. The first major assault on the agreements made at the May summit was Jackson's opposition to the Strategic Arms Limitation agreement covering offensive weapons and the treaty covering defensive weapon systems (ABMs) that was initiated by leaders of the two superpowers in Moscow. Jackson called the SALT achievements of Nixon a "bum deal." He drafted his own legislation—in the form of an amendment to the agreement that the president had submitted to Congress for approval as a concurrent resolution. The amendment reflected Jackson's personal thinking on the strategic military balance. It prescribed that any future agreements with the Soviet Union be based on what Jackson rather equivocally called "equality."

Jackson's SALT challenge must have appeared particularly menacing to Nixon in light of past events. Jackson was among a large number of prominent individuals to advise John F. Kennedy, the 1960 candidate for president against Vice-President Nixon, to charge that a missile gap had been allowed to develop during the Eisenhower-Nixon administration. That helped to set Nixon's scheduled entrance into the White House back eight years.[60] In election year 1972, Nixon was undoubtedly sensitive to the possibility that Jackson might have been raising another missile-gap scare.

Jackson introduced the SALT amendment on August 3. The White House opened negotiations with him immediately. During this period, Nixon's national security adviser Henry Kissinger spoke with Jackson on the telephone as frequently as three and four times daily.[61] The two men met over the weekend of August 5-6 at the White House. They worked out an agreement whereby the administration submitted the SALT agreement to congressional approval while Jackson introduced a softer version of his amendment, which the administration would not oppose. Each had the other's blessing.[62] Kissinger and Jackson's staffs exchanged drafts and counterdrafts until the wording was agreed upon by both sides. On September 14, the Senate passed the Jackson amendment, and both agreement and amendment were sent to the president to be signed on September 30.

Up through the White House ceremony on September 30, contacts between the White House and Jackson's office were close. These meetings touched on the emigration amendment as well as the SALT amendment, with Jackson's SALT amendment no doubt reinforcing the credibility of Jackson's threat to redirect trade with the Soviet Union.

Richard Perle's calendar revealed that he discussed trade developments with "State Department officials" on August 31. Perle also recalled lunching with Kissinger's Soviet expert Helmut Sonnenfeldt and other administration officials on September 20. The SALT issue was still pending, but Perle believed Jackson's trade amendment plans were also probably discussed at the meeting.

Perle also kept in close touch with John Lehman, who was doing legislative liaison work for the National Security Council. Perle recalled one particular discussion with "people in the White House" about the effect of one of Jackson's amendments on the other. "The Jackson Amendment to SALT was up at that time. I was weighing it [the amendment linking trade and emigration] with people at the White House. The people I was talking to were the hardliners down there, and they were fighting to support the

Jackson Amendment on SALT, and they said, 'for God's sake, don't [introduce the emigration amendment]. It would look prejudicial. Wait until after the SALT treaty is resolved. . . .' The Jackson Amendment on SALT was resolved in September."

In fact, Jackson's SALT amendment was resolved September 30 when the president signed the SALT agreement with the Jackson modification. Jackson attended the White House ceremony as part of a delegation of congressional leaders. His power and potential for wreaking havoc with detente must have appeared large at that moment.

Nixon had appeased Jackson by working out the softer version of the Jackson SALT amendment. By so doing, he also averted a possible missile-gap scare, averted criticism for what some interpreted to be asymmetries in the agreement, and silenced murmurings of discontent within the Pentagon concerning SALT. But even that day, Nixon could not breathe easily. Riding a wave of power thanks to his SALT victory, Jackson recognized an opportunity to raise the matter of his other amendment on Soviet-American trade and Soviet emigration restrictions.

Jackson and Nixon took a forty-five minute stroll in the White House Rose Garden after the SALT agreement ceremony. During the tête-à-tête, as one Jackson aide related it, Jackson urged Nixon to release the fifteen to eighteen Republican loyalists in the Senate who resisted becoming cosponsors without a presidential signal of assent. "In return, Jackson promised—I don't know if you call it a deal—Jackson in return said he would try to get Republicans and Democrats not to make the issue a political one—or simply let it stay as purely humanitarian." This deprived McGovern of an election issue against Nixon. Jackson also made it clear that he would not bring the amendment up for a vote in Congress. Since Congress was about to adjourn in two weeks anyway, Nixon could be sure that the amendment would become a dead letter in the Ninety-second Congress. Nixon—his attention focused on November 7, 1972—agreed. Jackson's amendment advanced one more step toward eventual legislative success.

Perle called Thomas ("Tom") Korologus, the White House liaison to the United States Senate, "to see if they had new orders" from the president reflecting the Nixon-Jackson arrangement. Korologus had not. After talking with Perle, Korologus checked with the White House and confirmed that Perle knew more about what was happening in the inner sanctum of the White House than even the official White House liaison.

Soon after, Jackson added eight more cosponsors from the ranks of the Republican Nixon loyalists to his list. When Jackson introduced his amendment on October 4, he had seventy-two Senate cosponsors—nearly three-quarters of the entire Senate. The legislation had no chance of becoming law, but it should have served the diplomatic purpose of adding to the pressure against Soviet emigration policies.

NIXON PUSHES THE SOVIETS ON ELECTION EVE

The September 30 Jackson-Nixon arrangement for Nixon to remain neutral on the Jackson trade amendment was not sufficient to fulfill the needs of Nixon's "Jewish strategy." Several forces were compelling the president to do more by personally raising the exit-tax issue with Soviet officials. The pressures on any elected politician on election eve were operating on Nixon. Taking up the issue was consistent with the behavior of any elected politician conducting foreign policy. It was aimed both at achieving domestic goals and a foreign political objective. As president, he was in charge of conducting foreign policy with foreign nations, regardless of what action Congress might have been taking. The enunciated policy of the administration was that dealing with the exit-fee issue should be left to quiet diplomacy at the highest levels. So it was incumbent upon him to raise the matter with the Soviet leadership. Second, Nixon's domestic political antennae were picking up a growing disaffection from those in the Jewish community who felt he was not doing enough for the cause. Since midsummer, his campaign strategists had felt confident that he could double the 17 percent of the national Jewish vote he had received in his 1968 race against Hubert Humphrey. But in early October, Nixon's political pulse takers detected the first signs of trouble for Nixon's Jewish strategy mostly over the issue of Soviet Jewry. The disaffection was felt in New York as well as in the Midwest declared the *New York Times* front page story entitled "GOP Intensified Drive to Attract Jews to Nixon."[63]

"At an October meeting between Jewish leaders and White House aide Leonard Garment, Garment was attacked for allegedly not pushing Mr. Nixon hard enough to get behind the amendment."[64] Rita Hauser, one of the seven cochairpersons of the Committee to Reelect the President, who is credited with sensing opportunities for Nixon among Jews, had also tried impressing on Kissinger the pressing nature of the Soviet Jewry issue.

Nixon's campaign director John N. Mitchell also warned Nixon that American Jewry was "totally worked up" over Soviet emigration restrictions and suggested that Nixon capitalize his gains among Jewish voters by publicly demanding a change in Moscow.[65]

The opportunity for Nixon to do something more than just remain neutral on the Jackson amendment presented itself on October 2 and 3, when Foreign Minister Andrei Gromyko visited Washington for the purpose, among other things, of signing the SALT treaty. The two leaders—joined by Kissinger and Dobrynin—met the evening of October 2 and again for breakfast October 3 before the actual White House signing ceremony of the treaty and the interim agreement. Although a well-placed administration source said there were no "burning issues" discussed between the two leaders, the trade negotiations were brought up and Nixon took the opportunity to explain that United States public opinion strongly opposed the education tax and that Congress might block the Soviet-American trade agreement that was in the final days of negotiations.

Also on October 2, Secretary of State William Rogers met with Jacob Stein, Max Fisher, and Richard Maass. A spokesman for the three Jewish community leaders said that "for the first time, we had a very positive feeling about the possibility of resolving the exit tax issue."[66] Maass maintained contact with the State Department and White House through presidential liaison Leonard Garment, and told a reporter during this period that "They have assured me that they are moving at every level and holding discussions on the subject. . . . I think the President got the signal."[67]

At a news conference on October 4, Jackson formally introduced his amendment to the Senate and to the national press. He portrayed his amendment as a complement to the quiet diplomacy conducted by the executive branch. He also indicated that Nixon was not opposing the amendment in spite of public statements from the White House and State Department to the contrary.

Meanwhile there were published reports that Gromyko had indicated to Nixon that Moscow might let the education tax "fade away." However, administration officials said it was only a "hope," since Moscow had not published the details of the tax, it might quietly lift the tax.[68]

A final round of Soviet-American trade talks began in late September and continued throughout the period that Jackson was organizing his cosponsors. On October 4, the White House announced that Foreign Trade Minister Nikolai Patolichev was expected soon to come to the United States to sign an agreement. He arrived October 11. A new maritime agreement readjusting the increasingly unpopular terms for shipping grain to the Soviet Union was signed October 14. Four days later, on October 18, the comprehensive trade agreement was initialed, in which the United States agreed to seek congressional approval to extend MFN treatment status to the Soviet Union, and the Soviets promised to pay $722 million of its World War II lend-lease debt. The same day, President Nixon also authorized the extension of Export-Import Bank credits to the Soviet Union by finding that such a move was in the country's national interest.

At a White House press conference where the new trade pact was hailed before the American public, a question was raised about the Jackson amendment, which would block all the trade advantages pledged in the October 18 trade pact until emigration from the Soviet Union was liberalized. Secretary of Commerce Peter Peterson answered by rejecting the Jackson amendment approach and advocating instead quiet diplomacy:

> We are going to handle that . . . through the channels we have been using. We think the channels of quiet diplomacy holds [sic] the greatest

promise of success, and after all that is what we are all interested in, so I have nothing further to say on that today.[69]

QUIET DIPLOMACY PLUS

In fact, the administration approach was really "quiet diplomacy plus." In other words, quiet discussions between officials of both nations were accompanied by American extension of trade advantages embodied in the October 18 trade agreement promises and in the mammoth Soviet grain purchases made in the American market and financed by credits from the United States Department of Agriculture's Commodity Credit Corporation, which began in the summer and continued throughout the fall of 1972. Selling $1.4 billion worth of grain to the Soviet Union, $750 million of which was financed by the United States Government Commodity Credit Corporation credits, likely helped to elicit Soviet cooperation regarding Vietnam. Trade advantages may have had a healthy effect on the position of Jews in the Soviet Union, too.

On the same day that the United States and the Soviet Union signed the trade agreement, October 18, exemptions from the emigration tax were granted to nineteen Jewish families leaving for Israel. Only forty-eight hours before, these people had been told they had to pay the tax.[70] The policy of granting full and partial exemptions continued and—significantly for Nixon's campaign—was reported in the *New York Times* several more times in the week after the agreement was signed. On October 26 the Soviet Council of Ministers approved waivers of fees for "justifiable" reasons, a policy enjoyed by as many as two hundred families in that one week who were among an unusually large group of Jews—four thousand five hundred a month—permitted to leave in the period preceding the presidential election.[71]

The *coup de grace* on behalf of Nixon came when the Soviet weekly *Za Rubezhom* denounced Nixon's Democratic opponent McGovern—not Jackson—for embracing the policy of linking trade and emigration.[72]

Remarks of highly placed Soviet journalists and officials portrayed the "noise on the emigration" question as a political campaign phenomenon that would disappear after the election—a view that indicated the exemptions that were granted at the same time that the Soviet government was publicly defending the tax might have been only a short-term accommodation.[73]

FOLLOWING UP THE OCTOBER 18 AGREEMENT IN CONGRESS

Exactly one day after United States and Soviet officials signed the trade pact in Washington on October 18, Henry Kissinger was in South Vietnam trying to persuade South Vietnam President Thieu to agree to the peace settlement that he had negotiated with the North Vietnamese in cooperation with the Soviet government. Kissinger was hoping to hop from Saigon to Hanoi on October 24, in time for an appearance right before the November 7 election. His plan was to initial the agreement in Hanoi, so the peace accord could be signed in Paris on October 31 by the four foreign ministers of the United States, Soviet Union, South Vietnam, and North Vietnam.[74]

The administration's preoccupation with Vietnam, which set the pace for the administration's timing of the Trade Agreement on October 18, had important implications for the future of the Jackson amendment. The Trade Pact of October 18 and the shipping of mammoth Soviet grain purchases coincided with progress on the Vietnam peace settlement, which the Soviet Union was helping to encourage. Had the Vietnam issue been settled earlier and thus had the trade negotiations been completed earlier, things might have been very different. The United States had resisted making trade commitments to the Soviet Union at the May summit, holding back to see a tangible demonstration that Soviet pressure was being exerted on the Vietnamese and that that pressure was working in America's favor. Had there been a trade agreement signed at the May Moscow Summit as some had anticipated, the administration might have requested and gotten MFN authority from Congress with little trouble in the summer of 1972 before the education tax was levied and before Jackson had prepared an effective counteroffensive.

Congress approved the SALT agreement and treaty after making some adjustments for the sake of Jackson, and it might have done the same for a trade agreement. After all, President Nixon and his summit talks and detente in general were at the peak of their popularity after the May summit. Opposing the results would have been much more difficult in midsummer[75] than in the fall when the grain deal was becoming a cropper as far as the American consumer was concerned and when the government felt compelled to insist upon a new shipping arrangement cutting the large shipping subsidies the Soviets were enjoying at America's expense.

By the time the Trade Agreement was initialed on October 18, 1972, time had run out for those in the administration who had wanted to rush the agreement to Congress for its approval before adjournment. Congress adjourned at 8:49 p.m. on October 18, 1972.

Some have argued that the trade agreement should never have been signed on October 18 since the warning signs from Jackson and three-quarters of the Senate were clearly indicating that what the administration was pledging to the Soviet Union in the agreement was not to be delivered so easily. In any case, attempting to get congressional approval for the trade pact had to wait until Congress reconvened in January, 1973.

MALIGN NEGLECT: THE POSTELECTION PERIOD

Richard M. Nixon achieved a landslide reelection victory over Democrat George McGovern by capturing every state in the Union except

Massachusetts. Nixon's Jewish strategy was also a success. Hundreds of thousands of Jews actually switched over to Nixon or at least did not vote for the Democratic candidate as they had habitually done before that time. Four out of every ten votes cast by Jews went to Nixon—double the total in 1960 and 1968.[76] Nixon attracted 37 percent of the Jewish vote in 1972 compared with 17 percent received in 1968.[77]

The intensity of domestic political considerations that motivated Nixon before the election to agree not to oppose the Jackson amendment and to apply quiet diplomatic pressure on the Soviet leadership diminished after the election. The reelection imperative that had driven him throughout his entire political career dissipated. Nixon interpreted the 1972 election results as an overwhelming stamp of approval for the past four years in office and an equally powerful mandate for the next four. Since the White House was presumably his for the next four years, after which he could not run for president again, the domestic constraints of getting reelected concerned him not at all. He was freer than he had ever been to conduct his foreign policy, regardless of domestic political ramifications. The only other constitutional check on him as president—impeachment—was unthinkable at this date in his presidential career.

The few months after Nixon's reelection and before his inauguration and the convening of the new Ninety-third Congress was a period of "malign neglect." The administration might have used the time after the election and in the lull of the congressional recess to try convincing the Soviet leadership that the harsh measures written into the Jackson amendment were avoidable if certain steps—including the permanent removal of the education tax—were taken. Soviet officials had already displayed flexibility in collecting the new tax in October before the election. Instead, the administration apparently thought it could ignore the amendment with impunity, and thus missed a crucial opportunity to derail the Jackson amendment.

Failure to explore an accommodation satisfactory to Jackson after the reelection has been characterized by officials within the Nixon administration as "arrogant." "Administration arrogance in general vis à vis the Congress from November, 1972, election day, when Nixon received a huge mandate, to April, 1973, when the Watergate tapes began to come out," was an administration mistake cited by a former well-placed East-West trade official.

An official serving on Henry Kissinger's National Security Council staff, who insisted on anonymity, suggested another reason why the administration may not have counseled the Soviet Union to liberalize its emigration policies to appease Jackson. Kissinger may have used the Jackson amendment as leverage for applying pressure on the Soviet Union to extract concessions on completely different issues:

The Jackson Amendment wasn't a big issue then. It had support. Everyone knew there were these pressures, and it would manifest itself

when the trade bill came up. But it was perceived as controllable. It
would be used to get the Soviet Union to acquiesce and get more. . . .
It could be used as a lever. The problem was to have it enough of a
lever to get results but not too much leverage. . . . No one ever thought
it would get to where it got to.

These remarks also suggest the administration was simply following its
own timetable. Congress was adjourned until January, so there was little
need to bother about the trade agreement and congressional protests until
Congress reconvened.

Another important reason why the administration "didn't treat" the
Jackson amendment as important, said one trade official, was that "Kiss-
inger was ninety-nine and nine-tenths involved with the rundown of the
Vietnam War and what he didn't give his attention to didn't get done."

Whatever the reasons, speeches delivered at this time by administration
officials attest to the remarkable disregard with which the congressional
protests were treated. For example, Assistant Secretary of State for
Economic and Business Affairs Willis C. Armstrong, speaking on
November 28, 1972, all but ignored the Soviet Jewry issue, which had
ralleyed seventy-two senators the previous month to sign the Jackson
amendment, in his observation that "the success of the Moscow summit,
the SALT negotiations, the quadripartite agreement over Berlin, the talks
between West and East Germany, progress in seeking peaceful solutions to
acute world problems—all have contributed to the fact that the trade
negotiations were able to proceed with remarkably *few intrusions of ex-
traneous pressures.*[78]

It is difficult to tell who was responsible for the policy of "malign
neglect"—for ignoring the Jackson amendment when it could have been
dealt with at a more controllable stage. The Nixon administration had a
well-known penchant for secrecy. One can, however, narrow down the
number of actors besides Nixon himself. Between November 1972, when
Secretary of Commerce Peter Peterson, who had led the United States
negotiating team for the October 1972 Soviet-American Trade Pact, left the
Department of Commerce, and February 1973, when George Schultz was
appointed secretary of treasury and official coordinator for economic affairs including East-West trade policy, there were few principal actors.
However, there were two prominent actors during this period: Peter M.
Flanigan, assistant to the president and executive director of the Council on
International Economic Policy, and Henry M. Kissinger, the president's
assistant for national security affairs and head of the National Security
Council staff. Charged a well-informed administration official: "Flanigan
and Kissinger didn't treat it seriously."

Steven Lazarus, then deputy assistant secretary of commerce and director
of the East-West Trade Bureau and executive secretary for the United States

negotiating team for the October 1972 trade agreement, believed that he (Lazarus) was just about the only official in the administration who could say, "I took the Jackson Amendment seriously." He assigned a researcher to work on the Jackson amendment in the fall of 1972. He spoke with congressional staffers Richard Perle of Jackson's office, Morris Amitay of Ribicoff's office, and Mark Talisman of the office of Charles Vanik. He also visited Israel and the Soviet Union in December 1972, where he unsuccessfully explored alternatives to the Jackson amendment.

SOVIET THINKING

Soviet officials, in particular Ambassador Dobrynin, accepted administration assurances that the Jackson amendment was of little concern when they should have been making their own independent assessments of Jackson's threat to block trade concessions until emigration policies were liberalized.[79] When Senator Hubert Humphrey visited the Soviet Union in December 1972, with a congressional delegation that included Senator H.L. Bellmon (R.- Okla.) and Congressman Henry Reuss (D.-Wisc.), he tried in vain to counter Soviet underestimation of the Jackson amendment. Premier Aleksei Kosygin reportedly rebuffed Humphrey when the Minnesotan tried to explain that the Jackson amendment was not an election ploy. The warning that Congress was serious about the subject of Soviet emigration and could set back progress on trade relations apparently fell on deaf ears.[80]

If the Soviet leadership was unwilling to heed the advice of visiting American legislators in early December, they were probably even less disposed to accommodating American concerns about the small Jewish minority in the Soviet Union after December 18 when President Nixon ordered "Operation Linebacker II," twelve ferocious days of American bombing of the Soviet ally North Vietnam.

For whatever combination of reasons, Soviet officials decided to get tougher, not softer, in their emigration policy in late December. The leadership took several significant steps toward reaffirming the original August 3 exit-tax decree. Clearly, the Soviet leadership was disregarding the danger signals that Jackson had thrown up over the months. At the end of December, Soviet Deputy Minister of Interior B. T. Shumilin stated publicly that although "as a rule" Soviet authorities might grant exit visas, "the Soviet Union does not intend to act as a philanthropist" toward people with higher educations, thereby defending the principle that the government had the right to impose an education tax.

On December 27, 1972, instead of lifting the tax, the Soviet authorities after months of delay formally published the decree of the Presidium of the Supreme Soviet of the USSR concerning the education tax in the Soviet equivalent of the *Federal Register*—the *Bulletin of the Supreme Soviet*. On the first of the new year, 1973, the actual text of the decree was published along with the implementing resolution of the Council of Ministers of the USSR containing the schedule of fees and conditions for waiving the fees.[81]

On December 29, there appeared to be some effort to make the emigration tax policy more palatable to the West when Shumilin announced that the education tax had been modified to exempt pensioners and to permit reductions in the tax according to the number of years that a would-be emigrant had worked for the state. The small concession over collecting the tax, however, was nullified in Jackson's eyes by the Soviet official and public embrace of the tax. Jackson attacked the published regulations—with the exemptions—as "totally unacceptable as a response . . ." and renewed his pledge that "so long as emigration is prevented by ransom taxes and other measures, we will use the votes we have to amend the appropriate trade bill."[82] November to January—the lost opportunity for quiet diplomacy—ended fittingly in acrimonious threats and counterthreats.

In January 1973, an administration spokesman predicted an uncertain future for Soviet-American trade. In a speech delivered at an International Business Workshop in Houston, Texas, Steven Lazarus forecast that in spite of Jackson's threatening response to the administrative hardening of the education tax policy in the Soviet Union, the Jackson amendment would not be reintroduced in the Ninety-third Congress when the administration would ask Congress for authorization to carry out its October 18, 1972 pledge to extend MFN to the Soviet Union:

> We have been following Soviet domestic policy very closely and I am somewhat encouraged that this policy is being moderated—at least to the degree that it will not elicit a reintroduction of legislative proposals akin to the Jackson Amendment—when we introduce the Most-Favored-Nation tariff legislation.[83]

Lazarus, however, added an important caveat: "Of course, this policy can turn momentarily and capriciously, and if it does, I think it could have unfortunate consequences." As events unfolded, Lazarus's second thought would prove to be prophetic.

SUMMARY

Doubtful of the benefits to the United States accruing from the policy of detente with the Soviet Union trade and sympathetic toward the Soviet emigration movement, Senator Henry Jackson linked both sentiments in the Jackson amendment, which made its debut in the fall of 1972. Jackson combined his staff's talents, his own determined personality and legislative skills, valuable information provided by the administration or smuggled out of the Soviet Union via the transnational channels of the Soviet emigration movement, and the support of the American Jewish community. Seizing the lead on the Soviet Jewry issue from the organized Jewish groups, he convinced three-quarters of the Senate to cosponsor his amendment and neutralized the opposition to it from President Richard Nixon who was on the eve of his reelection.

The administration had been carefully pacing the extension of trade concessions to gain diplomatic objectives; encouraging Soviet cooperation with America's efforts to extricate this nation from the Vietnam War was probably the most important objective. Jackson borrowed Kissinger's technique of linkage and applied it to his stated diplomatic objective of using trade concessions as leverage on the Soviet Union to liberalize its emigration policies.

Kissinger and Nixon had prepared the road toward detente with the Soviet Union, which would pay immediate dividends on the domestic scene in the United States as Nixon approached his reelection on November 7, 1972. A peace agreement with North Vietnam—with the Soviet Union cooperating—was welcomed, as were agreements on arms control, wheat sales, and trade. However, while pursuing these foreign policy objectives--and the immediate political benefits accruing therefrom—Nixon and Kissinger apparently failed to consider the longer term domestic political reaction to the ramifications of their major new policy of detente.

Looking beyond America's water's edge, Kremlinologists have advanced different theories to explain why the Soviet Union instituted the provocative education tax during the months after the May summit. The most likely theory is that the Soviet bureaucracies responsible for internal control like the K.G.B. and Ministry of Internal Affairs may have advanced the education tax, possibly arguing it was needed to maintain domestic control over Soviet society at a time when officials in the Foreign Ministry and Ministry of Foreign Trade were liberalizing foreign policy and advancing detente with the West and perhaps giving dissenters too many liberal notions for Soviet society. It may have been a case of two different bureaucracies inside the Soviet Union battling to carry out their separate policies. Under this hypothesis, the inconsistency of Soviet behavior may have reflected competing bureaucracies behaving consistently with their separate institution's mission. In other words, the education tax decision was like the emigration policy and the Jewish policy in general: subject to competing interests pulling from different directions.

Jackson's counterdetente policy drew strength from disparate elements on the American political scene. In turn, as a presidential has-been in 1972 and a presidential hopeful for 1976, Jackson reinforced his personal political position among the various groups to whom he appealed with initiatives on SALT, trade, and emigration.

Jackson's objection to Nixon's policy of trading with the Soviet Union, which he said was based on human rights considerations, echoed Nixon's campaign attacks on the Kennedy-Johnson wheat deal issued when Nixon was pursuing the presidency in 1963. Jackson pointed out, "I've been reading some statements that he [Nixon], made back in 1963. The United States, he said, should be willing to sell wheat to satellite countries as a business deal provided that the government involved gives some greater degree of freedom to the people in these countries, in particular the freedom to emigrate. Well, I couldn't agree more. I'm just trying to implement his 1963 promise.[84]

Ironically, for a brief interlude in October before his reelection, even Richard Nixon was willing to go along with Jackson's linkage of trade and emigration even though it jeopardized his policy of detente with the Soviet Union. Thus, both Jackson and Nixon demonstrated by their early involvement in the Jackson amendment that politics does not always stop at the water's edge.

Intialing the long-awaited trade pact on October 18, 1972, seemed to improve the atmosphere for Soviet emigration for the short term. The Soviets seemed to appreciate Richard Nixon's preoccupation with his reelection campaign and his desire to avoid a last-minute issue, Soviet Jewry, from exploding on the political scene. The Jackson amendment may have also reinforced administration efforts to achieve Soviet cooperation in the preelection period. Soviet authorities temporarily suspended collecting the tax right before the American presidential election, but by then the political damage had been done and Jackson was well on his way with his amendment linking Soviet-American trade to Soviet emigration policy. In the postelection period, the administration mostly ignored the long-term emigration issue.

Meanwhile, the Soviet Union appeared to harden its policy by reaffirming its education tax, although emigrants continued to leave at the rate of about thirty-two thousand in 1972. The policies of both the United States and Soviet governments embittered the supporters of the Jackson amendment. Indeed, Nixon later revealed in his memoirs that when he met with Ambassador Dobrynin on December 26, he expressed "my profound contempt for the alliance that had combined to defeat MFN."[85] The responsiveness in October on the part of both governments (when it was mistakenly believed by both governments that the Jackson amendment would not be a problem after the November election) had given the Jackson amendment credibility and visibility.

Jackson claimed that his "tough" tactics brought about an improvement in the lot of emigrating Jews.[86] On the other hand, the Nixon administration claimed success for "quiet diplomacy." The events in the preelection period of the fall 1972 indicate that quiet diplomacy, in addition to "tough" tactics and economic incentives were influential, at least for the short period before the November election.

Failure to remove some of the objects of protests after the election prepared the way for the reintroduction of the amendment when the Ninety-third Congress met in January 1973. The battle lines were formed for an all-out legislative-diplomatic battle to ensue.

The House of Representatives

3

A fusion of forces from opposite ends of the
political spectrum had resulted in a curious
coalition. My request in April 1973 for
Congressional authority to grant most-
favored-nation trade status to the Soviet
Union became the rallying point of both
groups: the liberals wanted M.F.N. legislation
to be conditioned on eased emigration
policies; the conservatives wanted M.F.N.
defeated on the principle that detente was
bad by definition.

I felt that we could accomplish a great deal
more on the Jewish emigration issue when we
were talking with the Soviets than when we
are not. RICHARD NIXON, 1978

It is said that I am stubborn and that's
true. . . . I make up my mind and I stay put
pretty well. HENRY JACKSON, 1978

INTRODUCTION

Jackson began the new year, 1973, with the new Congress, the Ninety-third, threatening to press ahead to pass the Jackson amendment if emigration was not liberalized in the Soviet Union. The votes Senator Jackson claimed to control were not Senate votes. Neither Jackson, nor his staffer Richard Perle, nor Ribicoff-aide Morris Amitay was collecting Senate votes during 1973. The emigration-trade fight of 1973 would occur not in the Senate but in the House of Representatives.

For President Nixon to implement the October 18, 1972, Soviet-American trade pact, he had to go to the House of Representatives for legislative authority. The Constitution of the United States assigns to Congress power to "lay and collect taxes, duties, imports, and excises" and "to regulate commerce with foreign nations." Over the year, the House of Representatives has retained a traditional prerogative of originating revenue-raising legislation. Tariffs are considered one means of raising revenue. Most-favored-nation (MFN) tariff treatment affects the tariff power and therefore falls within the jurisdiction of the House Ways and Means Committee. Thus, awarding MFN to the Soviet Union depended on how the House and particularly the Ways and Means Committee chose to exercise their prerogatives.

VANIK OF WAYS AND MEANS

Charles Vanik, an important member of the Ways and Means Committee, had taken an early interest in the Soviet emigration issue. Vanik, a third-generation Czech, who represented a district in Cleveland that was 11 percent Jewish, had intervened over the years for hundreds of his Slavic constituents who had tried to arrange reunification of families remaining behind Communist borders.

In September 1972, Vanik had introduced the first legislation aimed against the Soviet education tax. After his amendment failed, he became the sponsor of the House version of the Jackson amendment, which was introduced on October 10, 1972, a week before the Ninety-second Congress adjourned. In the new Ninety-third Congress, the Ohio Democrat took up the fight again, and the Jackson amendment was renamed the Jackson-Vanik amendment.

As in the Senate, staff was important to the outcome of Vanik's House effort. Vanik's administrative assistant Mark Talisman applied the legislative skills and knowledge of congressional folkways he had acquired from thirteen years in Vanik's service to block the administration's efforts to carry out its trade pledge to the Soviet Union. In ten days in January, he called the offices of all 435 members of the House of Representatives to ask them to cosponsor the Jackson amendment, which Vanik intended to reintroduce in the

Ninety-third Congress of the House of Representatives. By the time Talisman had finished telephoning, 235 members of Congress—a majority of the House membership—had decided to join the Jackson-Vanik crusade. His dynamic activity overshadowed the fact that another congressman, Representative Dominick V. Daniels (D.-N.J.), had actually preempted Vanik on the first day of the Ninety-third Congress by introducing the Jackson amendment as an "act for Freedom in Emigration of East-West Trade" (H.R. 151).[1]

Talisman recalled the activities of January 1973.

> . . . my plan: to call every member in Congress, every office. I didn't send out a "dear colleague" letter; this I did when I felt safe, to mop up. We were being pestered by the press and the State Department asking [how many sponsors we had lined up.] I didn't want any office to think it was a massive effort. I didn't want to stir up opposition. . . . No one knew how many cosponsors I had for the Vanik-Jackson Amendment. I had to call some offices fifteen times. [Representative Jonathan] Bingham [D.-N.Y.] and [Representative Sid] Yates [D.-Ill.] were trusted colleagues to help. . . . The first sixty members were easy to get because they were from large Jewish areas.[2] . . . Sixty would go on as cosponsors just because they were anti-Communist and anything like that was alright with them. Forty or fifty couldn't be categorized; they were key. They had to be convinced."

One of the first congressmen to cosponsor explained, "I just got on the bandwagon and it didn't hurt among my constituents. . . . You can do anything with one interest group if there is no one else lined up on the other side." This representative added that he also had substantive policy reasons for cosponsoring the amendment in addition to purely partisan reelection calculations. He "objected to the Export-Import Bank and credits to the Soviet Union anyway; I thought it [the Soviet-American Trade Pact] was a lousy deal."

To convince the various congressmen of varying political persuasions, Talisman used a variety of arguments. "The basic argument on the emigration side was unassailable . . . we have to draw the line . . . there was general guilt among a lot of members, guilt of the Nazi Holocaust." Talisman also capitalized on the fact that "there was pressure because of the wheat deal which was exploding." Moreover, he argued that there was "no prior consultation with Congress" before the Soviet-American trade pact was signed in October 1972. The administration, he said, "played it as if Congress did not exist; never did Kissinger speak or write. There was an open adversary arrangement, which was the keystone to their failure." In addition, he argued that there was no "effective *quid pro quo* for trade; Pepsico, for example. . . . They failed with regard to the public by not getting a *quid pro quo* on economic issues. . . ."

THE "JEWISH LOBBY"

Like Senate staffmen Perle and Amitay, Talisman was highly visible on Capitol Hill in battles for Jewish causes. Today, Talisman is the Washington representative of the Council of Jewish Federations and Welfare Funds. Talisman differed, however, from his Senate colleagues in his choice of political techniques he believed were best suited to activity in the House of Representatives. In contrast to the hard-pressure tactics of Perle and Amitay, Talisman said, "I refused to enlist pressure and use this method . . . . [the members of Congress] are here for two years [before they have to run for reelection]. They are either sensitive [to the desires of their constituents] or they are not."

Like Perle and Amitay, Talisman downplayed the role the organized Jewish lobby played in his efforts to collect House cosponsors for the Jackson-Vanik amendment:

> Either groups were doing their own thing [or] for the most part these groups hadn't got going. . . . They did their thing; it's a completely different mode of operation [on the House of Representatives side in contrast to the Senate]. It's a completely different place. I don't want to minimize the lobbying going on. I frankly don't remember. It wasn't anything compared to what it was later.

The National Conference on Soviet Jewry had not "got going," as Talisman put it. The organization had just hired a Washington representative, June Silver Rogul, who confirmed Talisman's assessment: "We had nothing to do with cosponsorship" in the House of Representatives.

While the National Conference on Soviet Jewry was just getting organized in Washington, another Jewish organization, well-established in Washington since the 1950s, initiated a massive letter-writing campaign that reinforced Talisman's efforts to gather cosponsors. By mid-January, Talisman had collected 144 sponsors.[3] I.L. Kenen of the American Israel Public Affairs Committee (AIPAC), which unlike the National Conference on Soviet Jewry is legally registered to lobby, sent a letter supporting the Jackson amendment dated January 18, 1973, to 1,000 key Jewish leaders throughout the nation. Kenen described the technique of generating pressure that is then felt in Washington—in Congress or the White House. "We will send out a notice to the leadership to the American Jewish Community letting them know what developments are occurring, they in turn will do what they can."[4] AIPAC played an important role, but said an AIPAC professional worker, Vanik's office did 80 to 90 percent of the work.

Through a combination of Jewish lobbying and Talisman's and other staffers' determination, a majority of the House membership was signed up as cosponsors by early February. However, one important member of

Congress—perhaps the most important at the time—was still not a cosponsor: Wilbur Mills (D.-Ark.), chairman of the House Ways and Means Committee. He became the target.

CHAIRMAN MILLS AND ADMINISTRATION STRATEGY

The Jackson-Vanik amendment came under Ways and Means legislative jurisdiction. With the behind-the-scenes aid of I.L. Kenen and his AIPAC staff, Vanik had rounded up a majority of the Ways and Means Committee members as cosponsors. But Chairman Mills was not a cosponsor and he was essential to insure the legislative future of the Jackson amendment. Over the years, Mills had demonstrated an impressive ability to steer the entire committee in whatever direction he desired. In fact, by virtue of his chairmanship of that committee where he presided over all legislation pertaining to tariffs as well as taxes, social security, medicare, and any other national means of raising revenue in the United States, Mills was the most powerful man in Congress. Some said he was the second most powerful man in the entire government, after the president of the United States.

"The Administration had to have a clear-cut signal that we were serious and so did the Soviet Union," Talisman explained. The two hundred and fifty congressional names were impressive. But the administration would know that together, they were hardly more impressive than the name of one man—Wilbur Mills. AIPAC director Kenen enlisted a Jewish friend of Mills's from Arkansas to convince Mills to cosponsor. Then on February 5, Vanik sent Mills a handwritten note asking him to take the leadership of the Jackson-Vanik amendment. On the sixth, Mills agreed to participate in a press conference on Soviet Jewry. Recalled Talisman, "The headlines were incredible." The newspapers reported the amendment, hitherto known as the Jackson amendment or the Jackson-Vanik amendment, as the Mills-Vanik amendment.

The administration response to the renewed congressional initiative was phlegmatic. State Department spokesman Charles M. Bray said the administration took the congressional threats "very seriously as we wish the Congress will take seriously the views of the Administration on this matter."[5] The administration view was that quiet diplomacy was more effective. Bray reminded the public that the issue had also been raised with the Soviet Union several times at several levels.

However, behind that calm statement, it appeared that the administration was beginning to stir into action to counter the threats it considered "very seriously." Peter M. Flanigan, presidential assistant and liaison with big business, had several private conversations with some of the key senators, in particular Abraham Ribicoff, but apparently did not get very far.[6] Soviet Ambassador Anatoly Dobrynin also met with Senator Jackson in early 1973, but it was apparently not a fruitful meeting for either party. It was the last time they met for the remainder of the battle over the Jackson amendment even though Third Secretary Grigoriy N. Rapota of the Soviet embassy continued to visit Perle on occasions.

The only route that seemed to hold some promise for the administration was to enlist Wilbur Mills to help work out a compromise substitute for the Jackson amendment in his committee. It seemed Mills's reason for cosponsoring the Jackson amendment was complex. Why had the most powerful man in Congress and perhaps the second most powerful man in the government decided to lend his name to the legislation? The day Mills agreed to do so, an unidentified Jackson aide took it upon himself to interpret Mills's behavior as "ideological" sympathy for oppressed Soviet citizens, not only Jews.[7]

There are indications, however, that Mills had other than an "ideological" affinity for the Jackson crusade. A number of well-informed observers have suggested that Mills, who reportedly foresaw a lucrative trade relationship between the United States and the Soviets, had hoped to work out a compromise in his committee with the administration.[8] Talisman posed the question, "Why did Mills go on the amendment?" and then answered his own question:

> My suspicion was to take control of the thing. He was absent because of illness. Knowing Mills, he would have been the first to cave [in]. He would have done something statesmanlike to cooperate with the Administration. That he could have succeeded? I don't know. It would have been a hell of a bloodbath. He went on and didn't have an opportunity to force a substitute later. It was a standard operating procedure [for Mills] to go on to something only after it was developed. He's a superb politician. To get a piece of legislation that was clean, ego-wise he was delighted with that kind of contact [with the Administration]. He was very flattered to be the expert, the consummate legislator, and he would have chosen the appropriate time [to compromise with the Administration over the Jackson Amendment].

Administration sources have confirmed that the administration tried to turn Jackson's signal of strength—the addition of Mills to the long list of cosponsors—against Jackson. According to one, "Peter Flanigan had gone up to see Mills. . . . He had worked out a strategy that Mills would offer an amendment that no country [should] discriminate in its emigration policy. They would argue that there was no discrimination since in the Soviet Union . . . their emigration policy treated all groups alike. Mills would offer it. The Administration would oppose it but encourage others to support it. . . . The Administration hung its whole case on beating the amendment with this. It was Mills's idea, I believe."[9]

THE "FIRST CRUCIAL DECISION": LINKING MFN TO THE TRADE BILL

The administration involved Mills in what one administration official called the "first crucial decision" in the administration strategy. The issue was how to handle legislatively the presidential request to Congress for authority to grant MFN to the Soviet Union.

A debate within the administration had been carried on by an interagency committee since summer 1972, even before the October 18, 1972, trade pact was signed. The committee organized by the Council on International Economic Policy (CIEP), whose executive director at the time was Peter M. Flanigan, debated what the best approach would be to achieve congressional authorization to fulfill the administration's trade objectives in the Soviet Union and elsewhere. The debate raged in the halls of the executive branch without regard to the Jackson amendment. Said one administration official, the "Jackson Amendment wasn't a big issue then . . . it was not an issue in the debate [about whether] to combine or not to combine" a request for authority to grant the Soviets MFN with a comprehensive Trade Bill or whether to leave the two separate.

The comprehensive bill was being prepared by the administration to request authority from Congress for the president's trade representatives to negotiate under the worldwide auspices of the General Agreement on Tariffs and Trade (GATT) the reduction of tariff and nontariff barriers with other nations of the world. The question was whether the administration would separate its request for congressional authority into one East-West Trade Bill and another comprehensive trade reform act or combine the two requests into a single bill.

The administration's major concern was the AFL-CIO, which opposed trade legislation in general on the grounds that it perpetuated American workers' vulnerability to unfair foreign trade competition. The legislative strategy for the Trade Bill was a crucial decision, because combining Soviet trade and the comprehensive Trade Bill would help forge a tight alliance between Jackson, his allies on Jewish emigration, and the formidable federation of unions.

Within the administration, there were those who argued to combine the request for both authorities; their principal congressional ally for that strategy was Chairman Wilbur Mills. Others, inside and outside of the administration, argued against that approach.

In February, the reelected Nixon administration reorganized the bureaucracy concerned with trade policy in general and East-West trade in particular. Secretary of Treasury George Shultz was entrusted as the "super" cabinet member for overall economic policy including international economic policy. On March 6 Shultz was also named chief representative on the United States-USSR Joint Commercial Commission and head of the East-West Trade Policy Committee.

Peter Flanigan, whose organization was under Shultz, was known to "grab" issues as one administration source put it. He did just that by "grabbing" the MFN section of the Trade Bill from William Eberle and William Pearce, the top officials in the office of the Special Trade Representative (STR) who were nominally in charge of the entire Trade Bill. Flanigan claimed to have the Jackson amendment under control in early 1973 because he thought he had close ties to the Jewish community. In addition, Kissinger had a say in the handling of the Soviet trade concessions.

The Special Trade Representative's Office wanted to handle the Soviet trade issue separately from the comprehensive Trade Bill. One of the chiefs of the office recalled, "We drafted the trade bill; it didn't have Title IV, the MFN authority. . . . I said if you put it on the trade bill they [Jackson and his allies] are getting the leverage that they want." Added another top STR official, the "Administration should not have linked MFN with trade. If they did, they should have had a strategy to get around Jackson. They failed at both."

A third official recalled that Secretary of Commerce Peter Peterson, who resigned in November 1972, had been on the fence. "Flanigan and [his Deputy] Deane R. Hinton made such a big fuss that they prevailed. . . . The Special Trade Representative's Office was against Flanigan. Peterson thought we [the] STR were right, but didn't make a big issue. Hinton dominated that decision if you want to put the finger on any one." Hinton made two arguments: The Soviets would be upset if the administration did not send the Soviet trade legislation to Congress and an MFN section, which was part of a generally popular detente, would actually strengthen the Trade Bill's chances of passage. In fairness, Hinton did predict that "the congressional battle will be extraordinarily difficult, whatever we do." The United States had run a trade deficit for two years after decades of trade surpluses. A deficit was forecast in 1973 also. Unemployment, which was then above 5 percent, made prospects of fierce union opposition even surer.[9]

After months of bureaucratic haggling, Flanigan's Council on International Economic Policy prevailed over the rest of the squabbling bureaucratic fiefdoms in the administration. Apparently Flanigan won because he had the strongest outside support against STR. Secretary of Treasury Shultz and Peterson's successor at Commerce, Secretary of Commerce Frederick Dent, backed him. Agriculture Secretary Earl Butz and the Commerce Department believed Soviet MFN would sail through Congress on its own.

Several individuals including members of Flanigan's staff, however, claimed that Kissinger had a larger say in the final decision and that Kissinger would not listen to Flanigan, who, as a result, was effectively frozen out of the final decision over how to deal with the Jackson amendment. Kissinger, it was said, had convinced the president that East-West trade was purely a foreign policy issue—not a domestic political or economic issue. However, even the insiders are not sure who made the ultimate decision to link MFN to the comprehensive Trade Bill. "To this day I have a hard time knowing who made the decision," said one official. Obviously, the final responsibility must be borne by the president.

In any case, the decision was taken only after Mills had been consulted. A meeting between Mills and Secretary of Treasury George Shultz is reported before January 8, 1973.[10] Another breakfast meeting occurred where Mills indicated he wanted an all-inclusive comprehensive Trade Bill sent to his committee, meaning that MFN for the Soviet Union would be included. Steven Lazarus, head of the East-West Trade Bureau, Department of Commerce, also got a similar message from Mills's staff economist Harold ("Harry") Lamar and from Robert Best, Lamar's counterpart on the Senate Finance Committee staff. Both men argued that MFN would be linked in congressional considerations, so the administration might as well link the two beforehand.

Others in Congress, however warned against the serious consequence of an administration decision to link MFN to the Trade Bill. Barber Conable (R.-N.Y.), a member of the Ways and Means Committee, wrote Kissinger warning of the trap. Even a relatively uninvolved member like Senator Gaylord Nelson (D.-Wisc.), wrote Flanigan in the early part of 1973, warning that if the MFN question was raised with the comprehensive Trade Bill, the Trade Bill's future would be jeopardized. Jackson had sworn to attach his amendment to any request for MFN. If the MFN was attached to the Trade Bill, surely the Jackson amendment would be hung on the Trade Bill.

Detaching the MFN request would have delayed congressional action on the Jackson amendment. It would have given the Soviet Union a longer and calmer time to review and respond to the concern Congress had expressed regarding the human rights question in the Soviet Union. It also might have eased the Soviets' decision to withdraw quietly from their untenable and unpopular position. But delaying the Jackson amendment, of course, meant delaying extending the trade concessions that had been promised. Rather than delay, the administration risked creating a direct confrontation with Congress, damaging to all parties concerned: the United States, the Soviet Union, and the Jewish community in the Soviet Union.

A Jackson staffer remembered being "delighted" that the administration had linked MFN to the Trade Bill. Amitay told Eberle that by tying the two issues together, "you guys are playing into our hands." Combining the MFN request and the comprehensive Trade Bill gave Jackson an even larger hostage to hold up to attain his emigration-and-trade objectives.

MORE ALLIES FOR JACKSON: THE AFL-CIO AND OTHERS

In addition to providing Jackson a bigger legislative hostage, the administration's decision to link its request for MFN to the comprehensive Trade Bill impelled the AFL-CIO, already backing the Jackson amendment in principle, into a tighter alliance for the Jackson amendment. Once it became clear that Soviet trade concessions would be attached to the administration's comprehensive Trade Bill, the Jackson amendment became for the AFL-CIO not only a sympathetic cause but also a means to fight and delay passage of the entire trade package, which it opposed on protectionist grounds.

Gaining the support of the AFL-CIO headed by outspoken anticommunist, octogenarian George Meany, reinforced Jackson's position vis-à-vis the administration. The Jackson-Meany alliance also promised to yield extremely important by-products for Jackson, the 1972 presidential has-been and 1976 would-be president.

Their alliance on the Soviet trade issue was consistent with their personal ideology as well as being mutually convenient politically. Meany and Jackson had both been conspicuously unenthusiastic about the nomination of George McGovern as the Democratic presidential candidate in 1972. After the 1972 campaign, the two kept in close touch directly and through staff. Their cold war suspicion of the Soviet Union, emotional attachment to Jewish issues, and rhetorical opposition to the major oil companies that surfaced during the oil boycott in winter 1973 all closely meshed. Meany's view of detente was harsher than that of Jackson's Jewish allies. However, during the House of Representatives fight, all parts of the Jackson amendment alliance were agreed on a legislative strategy that rejected compromising on the Jackson amendment. Meany was perfectly content with Jackson's position that any trade concessions to the Soviet Union should be linked to Soviet concessions on emigration. Jackson assured Meany that he would adhere strictly to that position.[11]

The Jackson amendment was also welcomed by various ethnic groups from the "Captive Nations," and other Eastern European territories controlled by the Soviet Union since World War II. These groups too had been strong anticommunists during the Cold War, and their views had changed little in the face of detente. Inclusion of these groups in the Jackson alliance also promised to pay fortuitous political dividends for Jackson even though his staff claimed the amendment's ethnic appeal came as a surprise. America's Slavic population of five million people live mostly in urban centers in the Northeast and Midwest states—swing vote areas in electorally significant states.[12]

ADMINISTRATION STRATEGY, PHASE II: QUIET DIPLOMACY

Backed by the Jews, unions, ethnics, and hard-liners inside and outside the military who traditionally support anti-Soviet measures, the Jackson amendment appeared to be a growing threat that the administration could no longer ignore. The administration, therefore, accelerated its efforts to deal with it.

On the eve of the administration's introduction of the comprehensive Trade Bill, which included provisions on East-West trade, it appeared that an agreement between the administration and Chairman Mills of the House Ways and Means Committee had been arranged whereby Mills would try to work out a compromise between the Jackson amendment—now know as the Jackson-Mills-Vanik amendment—and the administration position that trade concessions for the Soviet Union should be more or less unconditional. Mills's mission, however, could only have a chance if the Soviet Union showed some flexibility in its emigration policy. The administration sent a stream of officials to Moscow to discuss the emigration issue with Soviet officials.

The first trip to Moscow started out as "one last fling to Moscow" for White House Counsel Charles ("Chuck") Colson after "he had served his time" in Richard Nixon's White House, as one top East-West trade official described it. Colson's February trip to Moscow was officially billed as an opportunity to discuss office space for American companies in the Soviet capitol, but it was "probably decided at Kissinger's level" to be a mission to take up the emigration issue, speculated an administration insider.

During the discussions between Colson, who was accompanied by Steven Lazarus of the East-West Trade Bureau and Vasily V. Kuznetsov, Soviet deputy foreign minister, Colson explained that the Soviet education tax was endangering the fulfillment of the administration's promise to extend MFN status to the Soviet Union.[13] Kuznetsov twice replied, "We will do our part"—a response Lazarus interpreted as very significant.

Despite the Colson-Lazarus visit, the Soviet government publicly revealed little new appreciation of the seriousness of the congressional action on behalf of the Soviet Jewry. Several high-ranking Soviet officials visited Washington in late February and early March presumably to try to sway the American public in the Soviet's favor. Instead, their blunt and unyielding behavior provoked a hostile reaction in Congress and among the American public. V.S. Alkhimov, deputy minister of foreign trade; N.N. Inozemtsev, director of the Institute of World Economics and International Relations of the Soviet Academy of Sciences; and G.A. Arbatov, director of the Institute for United States Studies of the Soviet Academy, participated in a conference on Soviet-American trade conducted by the National Association of

Manufacturers in Washington, attended by eight hundred top American businessmen. Although reputed to be a principal adviser on American politics for the Soviet Politburo, Arbatov demonstrated a misunderstanding of the American scene in remarks delivered at a Washington press briefing on February 28, 1973. He threatened that "if normalization of trade relations" is disrupted by Congress, it would be a "harmful thing for Soviet-American relations as a whole" that could lead to "serious political repercussions." His prejudicial threats were hardly veiled as he explained that difficulties caused by a congressional action "would revive anti-Semitism in the Soviet Union" ostensibly because it would give "Soviet Jews a special status and treatment."[14]

Alkhimov's remarks also drew fire. He claimed the Soviet Union had liberalized its emigration policies to the extent that only 10 percent of all emigration Jews were paying the diploma tax. He also stated that "practically, 95.5 percent of all applications in 1972 have been settled and they have left" the country.[15] The National Conference on Soviet Jewry prepared a "fact sheet," which it distributed throughout Congress, indicating that the 95.5 percent figure represented the number of those granted permission to leave who had actually left. The real problem for the would-be emigrant, it claimed, came well before that stage.

After the National Association of Manufacturers Conference, the NAM arranged a luncheon at the request of the Soviet embassy for three Soviet officials—Deputy Minister Alkhimov and Soviet embassy economic officers K.G. Tretiakov and E.V. Bugrov—to meet with fifteen congressmen, including minority leader Gerald Ford and key Republican member of the Foreign Affairs Committee and chairman of the Republican party's Task Force on International Economic Policy Peter H.B. Frelinghuysen (R.-N.J.).[16] At the luncheon, Frelinghuysen explained that Congress drew a "close connection between the MFN treatment for the Soviet Union and the Soviet Government's emigration tax." Another participant, Democratic Representative James Symington of Missouri, came out of the meeting with the impression that the Soviet Union would not let the emigration dispute stand in the way of more trade.[17]

Underlining the administration's two-pronged strategy—quiet diplomatic discussions with the Soviets and heavy reliance on Wilbur Mills—Alkhimov and Chairman Mills met privately. Mills warned Alkhimov that two hundred and fifty members of the House would vote to stop the trade concessions if the exit tax continued in force. After the meeting, Alkhimov reportedly told Mills, "I can see we are not going to get MFN out of this Congress and my job is to tell Moscow that."[18] But Mills suggested to Alkhimov a possible way out for the Soviet Union: to remove the education tax. Mills promised that if the tax were dropped, he would personally make all efforts to have the admimistration Trade Bill passed without the Jackson-Vanik-Mills amendment.[19]

On the same day—March 11—that Alkhimov was meeting with Mills, Secretary of Treasury George P. Shultz was in Moscow meeting with Deputy Premier V.N. Novikov, Deputy Minister of Trade Mikhail R. Kuzmin, and Chairman of the Soviet State Bank M.N. Sveshnikov. He was there to discuss the Jackson amendment and to try to get private assurances from the Soviet Union that more Jews would be allowed to emigrate.[20] The following day, Shultz—accompanied by Kissinger's Soviet expert on the National Security Council staff Helmut Sonnenfeldt—met with party leader Leonid Brezhnev. In this meeting, Shultz tried to explain to the Soviet leadership the constitutional differences between the United States and the Soviet Union. Although President Nixon had pledged in the October 18, 1972, trade pact to get the Soviet Union MFN, congressional approval was also required. In Shultz's words, "I tried to explain the nature of the problem as we see it and to be sure that people were generally informed about that aspect. I also tried to explain the character of the American political process involving interaction between the President and the Congress."[21] Shultz reportedly pledged Nixon's assurances that he would try to overcome the congressional opposition to the trade pact. What Brezhnev pledged to Shultz in return was kept a closely guarded secret. Shultz did not indicate at the press conference after the meetings whether or not the Soviets would modify their education tax policy. He sent his report back to the president, using a supersecret reporting procedure arranged at Kissinger's behest. Instead of using the regular State Department channels, he reported via a channel using CIA codes, thus reducing circulation of the discussion results to a small group within the American bureaucracy. Even Harold Malmgren of the office of STR, who accompanied Shultz to Moscow but who did not attend the meeting with Brezhnev as did Sonnenfeldt, did not know the substance of discussions regarding emigration. Shultz did tell reporters, however, that the Soviet leaders had shown "willingness to tackle [the emigration problem] in very real terms."[22] A fortnight later, the well-informed columnist Marquis Childs wrote that Brezhnev had told Americans in Moscow that the tax was an error—a "bureaucratic bungle," in Brezhnev's words.[23]

ISRAEL: ANOTHER WAY AROUND JACKSON?

Thus far, the administration was exploring two ways to get around the Jackson amendment. Flanigan and Mills had agreed to try to get a compromise proposal at the appropriate moment. To help achieve a palatable compromise, Kissinger seemed to be orchestrating various discussions in pursuit of a "quiet diplomatic" solution to the education tax. Meanwhile, the administration also tried to get the Israeli government to help soften American Jewish support for Jackson's campaign. American Jewry had often deferred to Israeli judgment on world Jewry issues. Israel—its establishment and its assured security—has been top priority for Jewish groups petitioning the United States government on foreign policy matters. Jews in Russia had been an important issue at the turn of the century when the Czar was in power, and discrimination was legally imposed on the Jews there; however, for various historical reasons, the plight of Soviet Jewry had not dominated recent communal concerns of Jews in America. Like the Israeli government, Jews in the United States were anxious to avoid getting caught between Congress and the president. Like the government of Israel, American Jews did not want to jeopardize Israel's future by alienating the administration, which controlled vital military and economic aid and diplomatic support for Israel.

Nixon and the Israeli government had an excellent relationship. During 1972, the Nixon administration had provided Israel with arms at a rate satisfactory to the Israelis, and Israel's ambassador at the time, Yitzhak Rabin, supported Nixon's 1972 reelection efforts explaining in a public radio interview in Israel that Israelis "must see to it that we express our gratitude to those who have done something for Israel and not just spoken on behalf of Israel."[24] Rabin did little to stop the rumors in the American Jewish community that Israel wanted to see Nixon reelected.[25] In 1973, the administration found that Israel's need for continuing aid made it vulnerable to manipulation in the Jackson amendment dispute. Said one top presidential assistant at the time, "If the President's personal pledge to Brezhnev fails because of Israel and American Jews, we will take them on."[26]

Before Ambassador Rabin left his post in Washington, he tried in vain to convince Richard Perle that the Jackson amendment should not be reintroduced in the Ninety-third Congress. It was reintroduced. When Prime Minister Golda Meir visited Nixon at the White House on March 1, in search of aid commitments, Nixon tried to "enlist Israel's support for a compromise solution." According to one report, "Mrs. Meir made no commitment."[27] However, other reports indicated Meir did not disappoint Nixon completely. The Nixon administration had doubted that Israel would publicly disavow the amendment, but it received private assurances that Israel "will cool it" on the Jackson amendment, in the words of one administration official.[28]

A PREEMPTIVE STRIKE

In early March, the three channels explored by the administration looked promising. Chairman Mills, Soviet officials, and Prime Minister Meir all showed signs that they were accommodating the administration's strategy to compromise the Jackson amendment.

Senator Jackson was not waiting to learn the outcome of the administration's efforts. After the February 7 Mills-Vanik-Jackson press conference announcing Mills's nominal support, Jackson's office had circulated drafts for two "dear colleague" letters—one to senators who had not cosponsored the Jackson amendment in the Ninety-second Congress and one to the seventy-two senators who had been cosponsors. The actual "dear colleague" letters were sent February 21, emphasizing that the "principle and immediate cause of our concern is the imposition by the Soviet Union of a head tax ranging from five thousand dollars to thirty thousand dollars." Alongside the signature of Jackson and Ribicoff were the impressive names of Javits, Humphrey, and Kennedy.[29]

On March 15, Jackson formally introduced his amendment in the Senate for the second time. With seventy-three other Senators cosponsoring, the legislation took the form of an amendment to the East-West Trade Relations Bill. The March 15 floor statement delivered by Ribicoff, Jackson's cosponsor and primary ally in the battle for the Jackson amendment, sounded in the same breath conciliatory yet menacing: "There is still time to avoid confrontation over this issue. But the next move is up to the Soviet Union and I hope that our own leaders—at the highest levels—are conveying this message to Moscow."[30]

In his March 15 statement, Jackson apparently sensed that waiving the education tax was in the wind, but he made it very clear that that would not satisfy him.[31] His amendment called for semiannual reports on Soviet emigration policy in general and provided for retention of power in Congress to withdraw trade benefits if the Soviets were not satisfactorily maintaining a liberal exit policy.

Jackson was apparently in no mood to be conciliatory. Indeed, his action can even be interpreted as a preemptive strike against the Soviet Union and the United States administration.[32] In January and February, Jackson never hesitated to get cosponsors for the Jackson-Vanik amendment in the House or Senate. March 15, the day he formally reintroduced his amendment in the Senate, was one day after Shultz had completed his Moscow talks, but Jackson did not wait to see the results of that mission.

THE SOVIETS WAIVE EDUCATION TAX

In mid-March, Secretary of Treasury George Shultz had discussed the emigration issue with Brezhnev, and Mills had assured Alkimov that MFN would be granted if the tax were removed. Subsequently, there were indications that the Soviet officials had decided again to relax their education tax policy.[33] From March 19-20, forty-four Soviet Jews with higher educations were allowed to leave the Soviet Union without paying the diploma tax. The next day, a total of sixty families were permitted to leave without paying. Soviet officials were reporting that the tax was being "suspended indefinitely" although the law would remain on the books.[34]

The first news of a Soviet decision on the education tax policy was conveyed by Victor Louis, the Soviet journalist with ties to the KGB who had also been the first to announce in September 1972 an agreement in principle between America and the Soviet Union on lend-lease and MFN. On March 21, he wrote that the "diploma tax will not be enforced any more." "It seems," Louis acknowledged, "that the Soviet citizens who have decided to emigrate from the Soviet Union have won a victory in the six-months' war against the education tax."[35]

A Mills adviser claimed it was "Mills's assurance to them . . . [that] he would try to get MFN through the House if the tax were suspended . . . which got the Soviets to lift the education tax." Administration supporters insisted that quiet diplomacy exercised by Shultz and others should be credited for the waiver of the education tax. Meanwhile Jackson and his supporters claimed that Jackson deserved the credit for pushing the Soviet Union to so act.

There is also a fourth factor that may have been operating at the time: quiet diplomacy or, better yet, "quiet diplomacy plus." As in late 1972, extension of trade concessions to the Soviet Union in this same period may not have been entirely coincidental. On March 20, the Export-Import Bank signed its first loan agreement with the Soviet Union fulfilling in part the October 1972 Soviet-American trade pact. The Soviet Foreign Trade Bank was granted $101.2 million of direct loans and another $101.2 million in guaranteed American commercial bank loans for the purchase of industrial equipment in the United States.

Coupled with the word of new Soviet leniency in collecting the education tax was the airing by the White House of compromise proposals to replace the Jackson amendment, which principal sponsors of the Jackson amendment in both the House and Senate had reportedly rejected. Among the so-called unacceptable proposals was one giving the president a year to put in force a trade agreement including MFN with the Soviet Union and giving Congress the authority to veto the agreement after the year.[36]

Jackson's response to the news that the Soviets were waiving the education tax was swift and unyielding. On March 22, he addressed the National Press Club and repeated what he said on the Senate floor only days before at the time of the formal introduction of the Jackson Amendment: "Waiving the education tax was not enough . . . this week we have seen some encouraging signs that the Soviets are being more generous" and that "some tens of individuals have had the ramsom tax waived." Nevertheless, he emphasized, "We wrote the reporting requirement into the amendment after observing how capricious Soviet emigration policy has been." Terminating the tax he said was "a great first step." Jackson repeated that he intended to push for passage of his entire amendment despite the Soviet concessions on the tax: "Now, I have heard it said that the Soviets are going to keep the ransom tax on the statute books but they won't apply it in practice. I say that we are going to put the Jackson amendment on the statue books but in the hope that it won't apply to the Soviet Union because they will be in compliance with the free emigration provision."[37]

The National Conference on Soviet Jewry reaction was more guarded. It issued a statement saying it would take a cautious wait-and-see attitude to determine more definitely whether the tax was being waived in all cases.[38]

A week later, Deputy Secretary of State Kenneth Rush, standing in for Secretary of State William Rogers, spoke to six hundred members of the mass media at a State Department Foreign Policy Conference for Editors and Broadcasters. Rush referred to "commendable flexibility" on the part of the Kremlin and implied that quiet diplomacy had a great deal to do with the welcomed results. Echoing Arbatov, who had spoken in Washington in late February, Rush warned that conditions such as those embodied in the Jackson-Mills-Vanik amendment posed a "grave danger" by "bringing about a counter-productive reaction in Russia, producing anti-Semitism. . . ." He announced that the administration would soon formally "go forward with the proposed MFN treatment for Russia."[39]

Jackson, however, escalated his attack on what the administration official had called "commendable flexibility." Jackson called the reported Soviet leniency a "fraud" and vowed to push his amendment as drafted.

On April 10, President Nixon finally sent to the Congress the 124-page comprehensive Trade Reform Act authorizing the president to raise or lower tariffs and negotiate with the nations of the world mutually lowering trade barriers. The bill also included a provision to provide MFN to the Soviet Union. Nixon's formal statement included the following observation: "I do not believe a policy of denying MFN treatment to Soviet exports is a proper or even an effective way of dealing with this problem" of emigration.[40]

The same day that the president sent up his Trade Bill to Congress, Jackson and seventy-six other senators introduced the Jackson amendment in yet another form: as an amendment to the president's Trade Reform Act. Declaring himself one of the early supporters of expanded East-West Trade, Jackson said the issue was not really trade per se. "What is at issue here is whether to give the countries in question, in effect, economic assistance." By viewing this trade as "economic assistance," Jackson was echoing a favorite theme of the AFL-CIO, which was played by many senators and congressmen during the trade debate.[41]

EROSION OF JACKSON'S SUPPORT

By April 18, the administration could no longer be accused of ignoring the Jackson amendment. Following the introduction of the comprehensive Trade Reform Act, Nixon invited a group of six senators—Jackson, Ribicoff, Javits,

Majority Leader Mike Mansfield (D.-Mont.), Minority Leader Hugh Scott (R.-Pa.), and ranking Republican of the Senate Foreign Relations Committee George D. Aiken (R.-Vt.)—to the White House for an off-the-record discussion with him and Dr. Henry Kissinger. Nixon told the legislators that the Jackson amendment was endangering not only the Soviet-American trade agreement but also jeopardizing Brezhnev's planned visit to the United States in the summer and detente in general.[42]

Kissinger read to the senators two unsigned Soviet "communications" dated March 20 and April 10 indicating that the exit taxes had been waived for an unlimited period. The "communications" were apparently messages sent by the Soviet leadership to the Soviet embassy in Washington, which, in turn, were relayed to the president and his national security adviser.

Mansfield and Aiken, who were never cosponsors of the Jackson amendment, announced their full backing of the president's position opposing the Jackson amendment. Scott was a cosponsor of the amendment but sided with the leader of his Republican party in the White House. One of Jackson's aides described Scott's behavior at the time. "Scott . . . wasn't crazy about the Jackson Amendment and tried to get off of it in April when he and Jackson met with President Nixon. The understanding was that no one would tell the press about discussions at the meeting. Scott immediately did state that the tax had been abrogated, and Jackson hit back then with his own statement. That got Scott back on the Amendment."

On the opposite side of the spectrum from Mansfield and Aiken was Ribicoff, who blurted out to Nixon: "Mr. President, there's nothing new in this. We have known about the suspension for several weeks. But that in no way diminishes the need for passage of the Jackson Amendment."[43] According to a Jackson aide, Jackson's reply to Nixon was blunter, "Mr. President, if you believe that, you're being hoodwinked."[44] Jackson told the press afterwards that the President's reports of waivers were "old hat and not the heart of the emigration issue."[45] He issued a press release stating, "I am standing firm on my amendment, period."[46]

Underscoring Jackson's adamancy was George Meany who also issued a statement that "the Soviet Union has an unbroken record of breaking its word. . . ." Meany's Director of Legislation Andrew J. Biemiller circulated Meany's statement to most members of Congress so no one would underestimate the extent of Meany's commitment to the Jackson amendment.[47]

Jackson, Ribicoff, and Meany were obviously standing firmly behind the amendment as originally drafted. However, the Soviet notes announcing the tax waiver apparently convinced some very important sources of Jackson's support to change their minds—if only briefly before Jackson and his lieutenants got his forces back in marching formation. Reinforcements had to be rushed in to prevent Wilbur Mills and the Jewish leadership in America from succumbing in the face of Soviet concessions.

MILLS

While the president and Kissinger were meeting with the six senators, a presidential assistant was dispatched to show Chairman Mills a copy of the documents relaying the Soviets' announcement that they were waiving the tax. The documents convinced Mills that "any number will now be able to leave the Soviet Union except for national security reasons."[48] Mills recalled his March conversation with Alkhimov and concluded, "He's delivered on his end of the understanding and I intend to deliver on mine."[49] Mills had said he would try to get MFN through the House if the Soviets removed the education tax, the issue that had been the most publicized aspect of the debate and the one Jackson in his "dear colleague" letters, speeches, and releases had highlighted. When the Soviet leadership informed the administration in the communications Mills saw on April 18, Mills apparently figured there was no longer need for the harsh conditions of the Jackson amendment. He told the *Washington Post* that he was no longer in support of the amendment.

News of Mills's defection sent Jackson's office into action. Jackson enlisted both individual Jews personally close to Mills and the National Conference on Soviet Jewry. Mills had cosponsored after calculating—among other things—that as chairman of the committee he wanted to be in a better position during committee deliberations to manipulate the final outcome of the Jackson amendment, which the majority of his committee had cosponsored. A national reporter who closely followed the Ways and Means Committee and its chairman perceived the same pressure of the chairmanship pushing Mills back on the amendment in April. "When he tried to go off the amendment, he received pressure not from the Jews in Arkansas but from the House—from the fact that he didn't want to lose a vote on the floor [of the House of Representatives]. He's hardly lost any in fifteen years. . . ."

What this reporter did not know was that although there may or may not have been Jewish pressure from Arkansas, there was some from a personal friend of Mills in New York. When he announced he would no longer be a sponsor of the Jackson amendment, what followed was a near perfect example of lobbying. It has an extra twist that is also not atypical of the folkways of the Congress; the initiator of the pressure was not the interest-group lobby itself, but the office of another legislator.[50]

Ribicoff staffer Morris Amitay explained how so-called "grass-roots" support for the Jackson amendment got fertilized from Washington.

> . . . if we get a senator from an industrial state, a state with a sizable Jewish population, and he doesn't come out (for the Jackson Amendment), we don't let him get away with it. That's when we call for outside help. . . . What you have in this country is a fantastic, untapped reservoir of Jews who are in influential positions who were never asked to

help. And now it's just a matter of finding them and asking them to help. There are so many Jewish organizations, so many Jewish people sitting out in small towns in Iowa and in Oregon, and there are rabbis with congregations, who are just dying to get a call saying, "We need help with somebody. Can you help?" They understand the issue immediately—you're dealing with very sophisticated people.[51]

In Mills's case it seems that in 1971 Jackson did a small personal favor for Mills that Jackson managed to turn to his use in 1973. Mills had a friend in New York, an ex-shoe manufacturer named David Herman. Herman's wife, an activist on a committee for the American support of the Technion University in Haifa, Israel, was looking for a speaker for a gathering benefiting the Technion. Mills—on behalf of the Hermans—asked Jackson to deliver the speech, and Jackson consented. After the event, Jackson instructed his staff-man Richard Perle to maintain contact with Herman. When Perle learned that Mills had defected from the Jackson amendment, Perle enlisted Herman to intervene. Herman requested an immediate meeting with Mills and was told that Mills was in Arkansas and about to return on the weekend. So the next day, Herman flew to Washington accompanied by Richard Maass, chairman of the National Conference on Soviet Jewry.

Over a long lunch with Mills, Herman spoke with great emotion about the Nazi holocaust and said that Soviet Jewry was facing the danger of a new holocaust.[52] Maass made the NCSJ point that the Soviet official figures claiming over 95 percent of those applying for visas to emigrate have been allowed to go were false. Maass suggested that Mills speak with Jackson. Mills expressed skepticism about Jackson's motives saying Jackson was always against Soviet-American trade. Maass defended Jackson's record saying that Jackson had cosponsored the East-West Trade Bill of 1970 along with "only" twenty-seven other senators. Mills said, "Well, maybe I better speak with Jackson." Mills mentioned that he had also received a call from East-West trade businessman Armand Hammer, who opposed the Jackson amendment. Mills said he trusted Hammer less than the president. Said Mills, "I trust him as far as I can throw him, and I've got a bad back." At five that afternoon, Herman telephoned from Mills's office the news that Mills had been convinced. The same day, Mills issued a press release stating he was again on the Jackson amendment.[53]

Mills's decision to go back onto the Jackson amendment was probably the product of a combination of factors—the friendly persuasion of Herman, a desire of Mills not to lose control over the issue in his committee by dropping his cosponsorship status, and the fact that Mills had incorrectly assumed and told Alkhimov that if the Soviets removed the tax, then he could get MFN through the House. One of Mills's advisers summed up Mills's dilemma as he decided to rejoin the Jackson amendment after his brief defection, "Mills, after giving that commitment [to Alkhimov] within six weeks was overwhelmed by the momentum."

THE JEWISH LEADERSHIP

Mills was back in line. But then Jackson discovered an even larger and more dangerous hole in his line. The Jewish leadership's support of the Jackson amendment also began to weaken in face of Soviet concessions on the education tax. It was not entirely surprising to see Mills split with Senator Jackson, particularly since Mills seemed to be cooperating with the administration's search for a compromise. But it should be surprising, to those who have assumed that Jackson was doing the work of the Jewish lobby, to discover that the Jewish leadership was prepared to compromise on the Jackson amendment in the spring of 1973 until Jackson stopped them.

On April 19, a day after the president's meeting with the six Senate leaders, Nixon invited a group of fifteen Jewish leaders to the White House. This appeared to be part of an all out effort on the part of the administration to split off Jewish support from Jackson.[54] Nixon had not informed the senators of his plans to meet the Jewish leaders. When congressional aides discovered that the community leaders planned to see the president, they tried to arrange a hasty briefing before the White House meeting. Jackson said the offer to brief the leaders was not really intended to provide material for a "debate" with the president. However, the White House intervened and said that "correct procedure" deemed that the leaders should see no one on Capitol Hill until after their visit with the president. Max Fisher also insisted it was "inappropriate to see the Senator before the President."[55]

Nixon explained to them that in his view, the education tax was suspended. During the seventy-minute meeting, he had Kissinger show the leaders the two communications the six senators and Mills had seen the day before. The group included Charlotte J. Jacobson, vice-chairman of the National Conference on Soviet Jewry and head of the World Zionist Organization's American section; Max Fisher; and Jacob Stein, chairman of the Conference of Presidents of Major American Jewish Organizations. With a snap of his fingers Nixon told them he realized that if the vote on the Jackson Amendment was held that day, "I know the Amendment would go through like this."[56] Nixon argued that Jackson was a "hawk," that it was a mistake to think Brezhnev would ever capitulate before public pressure, and stated that as of then the tax was lifted and emigration would continue at a rate of between thirty-two and thirty-five thousand a year.[57]

Some of the Jewish leaders went away with the thought that as of April 1973, the Jews were back to where they were in August 1972, before the tax had been levied. Indeed, Kissinger told some of the participants, "You're now back to August 1972." Replied one participant who found the Soviet concessions on tax unimpressive, "We hope that the Soviets understand that, too." However, others left the meeting in a less skeptical mood. William Safire, the president's speechwriter, recalled that after the meeting one of the participants, "a life-long Democrat and an active McGovern supporter," confided in him, "This may be the only thing I trust him [Nixon] about."[58]

After the meeting, the Jewish leaders returned to Fisher's Washington office[59] where they issued a three-paragraph statement signed by Stein, Fisher, and Jacobson.[60] It referred to the documents on the waiver of the education tax, which they said "would be continued without any time limits." In the second paragraph, the three explained that they had specifically "asked the help of the President" for the one hundred thousand Jews who have been refused exit visas. The final paragraph expressed appreciation for the "historic meeting with President Nixon" and for his reaffirmation of "his concern for the plight of Soviet Jews."[61]

Although it appeared to be rather standard material, the third paragraph ignited a fierce fight inside the Jewish community. President Nixon had not asked them specifically to decide whether to continue endorsing the Jackson amendment.[62] The *New York Times,* reporting the results of the meeting with Nixon, said that the leaders "gave no indication they are slackening their support of the Jackson Amendment."[63] Nevertheless, the mere absence of a specific reaffirmation of support for the Jackson amendment, and the crediting of Nixon and not Jackson for helping Soviet Jewry, was interpreted by hard-line supporters of the Jackson amendment as a sign there was a move afoot among the Jewish leadership to back out of the Jackson amendment.

ISRAEL

Activities within Israel also seemed to signify that the leadership—with Israel's at least tacit consent—was removing its support for the amendment. The day that the Jewish leaders met with Nixon, Yehuda Hellman, executive director of the Conference of Presidents of Major American Jewish Organizations, flew to Israel for consultations with government officials there. Hellman may have been seeking allies for his chairman, Jacob Stein, who wanted to split off from Jackson. Stein himself arrived in Israel on May 3 to discuss the outcome of his meetings with Nixon and Kissinger and with Jackson.[64] Even if the Israeli government had decided to help Stein, it would have been difficult. One of Jackson's staff said that if Stein had come back to Jackson with word that the Israeli government was allied with Stein, it would have been clear to Jackson that Stein had actually initiated the Israeli government's decision. The Israeli government recognized the perils of taking sides and tried hard to avoid getting in between Jackson and Nixon over the Soviet emigration fray.

When Prime Minister Golda Meir returned from her visit with Nixon in early March, reports had circulated in Jerusalem that the "Israeli government was not supporting the Jackson Amendment or urging American Jews to support it."[65] On April 25, an official spokesman in Jerusalem still refused to deny or confirm that the United States had approached Israel to ask Israel to urge Jackson to drop his amendment. However, Israel's Absorption Minister Nathan Peled's first response to the news of Soviet concessions sounded a great deal like the statement of the Jewish leaders after they had met with President Nixon at the White House. Peled credited Nixon more than Jackson for the change in Soviet policy. Nixon and his administration, said Peled, "exerted their influence to the maximum." Almost as an afterthought, he added, that his words were not intended "to minimize in any way the important value of the pressures exemplified by the campaign of Senator Jackson."[66]

On April 30, the Israeli cabinet held an hour-long discussion on the Soviet Jewry question and the Jackson amendment in particular. The consensus appeared to be for the government to keep a low profile on the Jackson amendment dispute. The issue presented Israel with an embarassing dilemma because two of its staunchest friends, Nixon and Jackson, were at variance over an issue close to Israel's own heart.[67] Despite the cabinet consensus to assume a low profile, Mrs. Meir repeated to a Hebrew University audience on May 1 what her minister of absorption had said. Relaxation of Soviet emigration tax policy was mostly due to Nixon's involvement.[68]

This position was not an easy one for Mrs. Meir personally to maintain. She was facing a tough reelection fight of her own in October 1973. She experienced domestic political constraints on her conduct of foreign policy just as Nixon and other elected politicians in the United States did. Surely she had not forgotten the caustic criticism that had been levelled against her several years earlier by those in the Right Wing opposition parties and by newly arrived Soviet immigrants who charged that her government had been excessively cautious in withholding all-out support for Soviet Jewish dissidents.

On May 2, eight recent Soviet immigrants—part of a group calling itself the Movement for the Liberation of Soviet Jewry[69]—spent two and one-half hours with Meir trying "unsuccessfully to persuade her to openly support Senator Henry Jackson. . . ." The same day a "senior source" told the *Jerusalem Post* that "the Cabinet was united in its belief that Israel must encourage all efforts aimed at helping Soviet Jewry—but must not intervene in the dispute between President Nixon and Senator Jackson over the Jackson Amendment."[70]

Apparently, Mrs. Meir was convinced that the best position to take, considering her personal domestic political requirements and Israel's foreign policy requirements to avoid alienating the United States and the Soviet Union, was simply to straddle the issue. Earlier, the Israeli government had been reluctant to interfere overtly in the internal affairs of the Soviet Union in spite of demands from critics that Israel actively support the dissidents. In this affair, the government also took the public position that it should not interfere in the internal affairs of the United States by endorsing the Jackson amendment. This was as much as Meir presumably felt she could do and the administration could realistically expect. Meir repeated her position of official neutrality on several occasions. In a broadcast on the army radio station on April 28, she said as far as "the technical side of arrangements between the United States, Congress and the President . . . on behalf of Soviet Jewry, as a government, as a state, we must not interfere."[71] In another radio broadcast, Mrs. Meir stated that "the best way for the United States to act on this matter is the business of the Americans themselves, and through the differences of opinion among themselves, they will eventually find the way."[72]

Although Israel's public position was clearly neutral, many Israeli officials expressed personal approval of the Jackson amendment. The mixture of neutral official position and personal approval of the Jackson amendment created different impressions in the minds of different Jewish strategists in Washington. June Rogul, the Washington representative of the National Conference on Soviet Jewry, who before holding that position had lived and worked in Israel, considered the Israeli position entirely positive: "All the Israelis felt the Jackson Amendment was a great thing. They were very supportive of it. They were always very supportive of the Jackson Amendment all down the line. They couldn't speak about it since they were a foreign government. The conclusion was always the same—that Israel should never have a position publicly." A well-informed newspaper correspondent stationed in Jerusalem also said that "Israeli leadership—while they deep in their hearts liked the Jackson amendment—couldn't say anything." He believed, however, that "their lack of obvious support served to give excuse to some Jews in this country [America] for not supporting the amendment."

REINFORCEMENTS

Conflicting signals from Israel magnified the ambivalence and disunity within the American Jewish community. Until the meeting with President Nixon, the Jewish leaders had managed to avoid being squeezed between the White House and Congress. They were at least able to argue that their support for the Jackson amendment reinforced the leverage the president needed to conduct his quiet diplomacy. But when Nixon denounced it, Jewish leaders found themselves in a position where they had to choose between the amendment and quiet diplomacy as the best course for dealing with the Soviet Union. The American Jewish community needed friends in both Congress and the White House. The leaders wavered before the prospect of alienating the White House, particularly in light of contradictory signals from Israel.

At that moment, Jackson's dogged determination paid off again. Aided by activists within the National Conference on Soviet Jewry and the Union of

Councils for Soviet Jewry, Jackson mounted a campaign to put pressure on the Jewish leadership to issue a strong statement reaffirming support for the Jackson amendment.[73] This was a tense moment for Jackson. If Jewish official support in Israel and America vanished, he would have little reason to pursue his project. If members of Congress got wind of erosion of Jewish community support, it could put an end to the amendment.

For example, Senator Gaylord Nelson was exploring compromises between both Jackson's and the administration's positions. On Nelson's instructions, a substitute compromise was drafted together with an accompanying speech. It was a middle ground between the administration's proposal, which gave Congress only ninety days to veto extension of MFN for three years with an almost open-ended renewal provision, and Jackson's position, which required semiannual reports by the president indicating that the Soviet Union had free emigration as a precondition to granting MFN status. The Nelson amendment draft gave the Soviet Union MFN but retained power in Congress to withdraw it after one or two years if Soviet behavior was found to be unacceptable. (Coincidentally, this approach was similar to an administsration proposal raised in March but rejected by the principals sponsoring the Jackson amendment.)

The administration did not encourage Nelson or other congressmen to move in this direction although it did try to sow seeds of dissent within the Jewish community and to woo Mills into accepting a compromise. Perle and Amitay, however, were aware of the potential danger posed by Nelson. Earlier they had tried in vain to push Nelson to cosponsor the Jackson amendment. But with the help of various Jewish lobbyists, they contributed to Nelson's decision not to offer his compromise in the spring of 1973.

Since Nelson had never been a cosponsor of the amendment, his position was not so critical. It was, however, essential for Jackson to prevent defections of the Jewish leadership that might, in turn, stimulate dramatic defections by his cosponsors in Congress. Jackson moved swiftly to stiffen the original Jewish support for his amendment. The process illustrated the degree to which Jackson actually dominated the Jewish leadership during the campaign for the Jackson amendment. Jackson's response to the Jewish leaders' statement following up their meeting with President Nixon was reminiscent of his handling of the Jewish leadership in September 1972, when the National Conference on Soviet Jewry emergency rally endorsed Jackson's approach and in effect handed over the reins of power to the senator. The episode again demonstrated a reversal of the popular image of all-powerful "Jewish lobby."

After the Jewish leaders met with the president and issued their statement that did not include a reaffirmation of support of the Jackson amendment, Jackson's office went to work with the characteristic persistence that was demonstrated as recently as a month before when Mills temporarily dropped his name from the list of cosponsors. One high ranking officer of the National Conference on Soviet Jewry recalled:

> Jackson's office was no different from the Administration in that they were trying to manipulate the Jewish community. I didn't think it was right for Jackson to tell us what to do and what not to do. They [Jackson's office] became involved in the internal affairs of the Jewish community.

In turn, Jackson's staffer Perle has had even harsher words to say about the American Jewish community's political skills:

> You talk about Jews in politics. They're a pain in the neck. They're difficult to organize. . . . It's just a pity they're not better organized, because there are some crucial issues—whether Israel survives, whether we get the Russian Jews out—and if the American Jewish community were more sophisticated and better organized, if it had some political direction, if there were a commitment to these values, we'd be enormously more successful. . . . The Jewish organizations are incompetent and unrepresentative, indecisive, preoccupied with other areas. . . .[74]

Jackson used direct and indirect tactics to get the Jewish lobby in line on the Jackson Amendment. Directly, he demanded a strong statement of support.[75] Indirectly, his office got busy pumping up "grass-roots" pressure under the Jewish leaders. The most effective way for Jackson to keep the Jewish leadership in line was to remind them when necessary that they, too, had constituents and were subject to grass-roots pressure just like politicians. In the Mills case, Jackson used Jewish leaders to help him out. In this case, he used other more militant activists for Soviet Jewry to evoke cooperation from some of the Jewish leaders who seemed to be wavering.

After the White House meeting in April, one Jewish official recalled that "some people interpreted that meeting as a backsliding. . . . Jackson's office was hot and bothered and I knew people [at the grass-roots] were getting the word [but] I didn't draw the link [with Jackson's office]". Another participant in the White House meeting said he got calls from all over the country threatening him if he deserted the Jackson amendment; he believed that Perle was responsible for initiating these calls.

Perle telephoned Malcolm Honlein, director of the Greater New York Conference on Soviet Jewry.[76] Honlein was an orthodox, religious man with a healthy regard for power and a reputation as a skillful wielder of the same. As director of the Greater New York Conference of Soviet Jewry, he had much influence over the parent body of the National Conference on Soviet Jewry. Honlein exemplified how a constituent has the power to push the leadership of a lobby group to be tougher in defense of the group's interest than the leadership might prefer to think prudent.

direct & indirect influence on Jewish voters [handwritten marginal note]

Honlein was uncomfortable with the noncommittal statement of the Jewish leaders after the meeting with Nixon on April 10. His Greater New York Conference office, therefore, issued a statement April 26, 1973, reflecting a decision made by its leadership the previous week that clearly reaffirmed support for the amendment.[77] The Student Struggle for Soviet Jewry and the Long Island Council for Soviet Jewry also issued statements reaffirming the Jackson amendment.

An official of the parent NCSJ said that the Honlein organization "cannot take any policy different from us without clearing it" and that both Chairman Maass and Director Goodman said "yes." However, it is rather hard to see how the NCSJ could contradict the Greater New York group when Honlein's organization spoke for seventy-four organizations with an aggregate membership of two million people in New York, had organized rallies with a turnout of one hundred thousand people,[78] and paid approximately one quarter of the NCSJ's budget.[79] In any event, there seemed to be dissatisfaction with the Jewish leaders' statement among the professional workers for the NCSJ as well. June Rogul, the Washington representative for NCSJ, said that "There were times when I would have liked to have public statements to allay confusion . . . there was a certain sensitivity on the part of Jewish leaders not to offend the Administration."[80]

Another source of grass-roots pressure came from members of the Union of Councils for Soviet Jewry, which was generally regarded as more militant than the National Conference on Soviet Jewry. Harold B. Light, then chairman of the group, recalled the efforts made in April 1973 to change the minds of the leaders who had met with Nixon. "Happily, the Soviet Jewry activists went to work, and the fourteen Jews [half of whom were split about withdrawing support for the Jackson amendment] were 'convinced' that they should continue their backing."[81] Reported the *Jerusalem Post* at the time, "The grassroots support for the Amendment in Jewish communities across the United States reached the point where unless Jackson abandons it himself, the Jewish leadership—which in any event is neither monolithic or [sic] always effective—would do so only at its peril."[82]

Pressure on the Jewish leadership came from Jackson's office directly, from the Jewish grass-roots, and even from Soviet Jews themselves. Meanwhile, rumors about the wavering among American Jewish leaders reached Moscow quickly. It is not clear whether Jackson's office was also behind this, but his office has maintained contact by telephone and mail and is in close touch with American Jewish organizations communicating with Jews remaining inside the Soviet Union. On April 23, as recent Soviet emigrés demonstrated support for the Jackson amendment in the office of Golda Meir, more than one hundred Soviet Jewish activists sent an appeal from the Soviet Union to American Jewish leaders urging them to reject the Soviet notion that it should be able to refuse exit visas in cases affecting "national security" or for any other reasons, arguing that that "would have a tragic, irreparable effect and would mean a collapse of all hope of repatriation for many thousands of Soviet Jews."[83]

All of these pressures came to a head at an enlarged Executive Committee meeting of the NCSJ on April 26 where it was agreed that a public reaffirmation of support for the Jackson amendment was needed. Action was deferred, however, until a meeting April 30 of the Conference of Presidents of Major American Jewish Organizations. Both umbrella groups, the President's Conference and NCSJ, operated under the understanding that major policy questions required approval by both. Jacob Stein chaired the April 30 meeting where a bitter fight broke out. Stein tried to adjourn the meeting before a new public statement could be considered. According to the account in the *American Jewish Yearbook,* on one side of the "clash bordering almost on insurrection" was Stein and a "small minority, which, from the very beginning, had raised a principal objection to the working of the amendment," which was couched not in terms of Jews, but in general terms, "demanding that the USSR open its doors for any and all of its nationalities to leave," which tended to revive the "cold war." The challenge to Stein and the so-called minority was led by Balfour Brickner, a rabbi representing the Reform Jewish community, who threatened to keep the meeting in session until a new statement was accepted. Finally, the leadership agreed to issue another statement signed by Maass on behalf of the National Conference of Soviet Jewry; by Stein on behalf of the conference of Presidents of Major American Jewish Organizations; and by Max Fisher.[84]

Jackson's close involvement in the internal struggle of the Jewish community was dramatically demonstrated by the fact that Jackson's office reissued the entire joint statement reaffirming support for his amendment and signed by the three Jewish leaders. It was released on the press release form of Jackson's own office. The Jews felt, in the words of B'nai B'rith official Herman Edelsberg, that they were actually "beholden to Jackson" and could not let him down in his crusade on behalf of Soviet Jews.[85] The Synagogue Council of America, Anti-Defamation League of B'nai B'rith, and American Jewish Committee followed with reaffirming statements in the days following.[86]

After the wavering and discord, a new consensus was hammered out by April 30. The Jewish leaders, however, waited until May 2 to issue their new statement. In the interim, on May 1, Stein, Maass, and Fisher met with Kissinger who was about to embark for Moscow to prepare for the June summit visit of Brezhnev to the United States. The leaders apparently felt Kissinger should be informed of the new statement before it was actually released.[87] A spokesman for the National Conference on Soviet Jewry said that Kissinger had been "sympathetic and understanding" but that he repeated that Nixon felt it was necessary to carry out his "word" to the

Soviets said that they would receive trade concessions as part of a continuing process of improving Soviet-American relations.[88]

The three men also handed Kissinger a "hardship" list of one thousand cases of Soviet Jews, including forty-two who were imprisoned because of their efforts to emigrate. The leaders asked Kissinger to discuss the list with Soviet officials.[89]

At the meeting with the Jewish leaders in May, Kissinger set the stage for the coming months. "Look, you go your way and I'll take my road and we'll meet in the fall." (Kissinger added that he would pursue a quiet diplomacy approach in the coming months.)

BREZHNEV IN THE UNITED STATES

Kissinger was laying the groundwork for Brezhnev's visit to the United States scheduled for June. In May, he flew to Moscow for twenty-five hours of talks with Brezhnev, Foreign Minister Andrei Gromyko, and Soviet Ambassador Anatoly Dobrynin.[90]

Removing the tax had not removed the problem with the Jackson amendment. Jackson was determined and able not to yield. Chairman of the Ways and Means Committee Mills had deserted the Jackson amendment only to reenlist as a sponsor. For good measure, Senator Russell Long (D.-La.), the chairman of the Finance Committee, the Senate parallel to the Ways and Means Committee and the Committee that would be responsible for the Trade Bill when the House completed action on it, became a cosponsor of the Jackson amendment in the weeks before Brezhnev's arrival in Washington. Long, who was running for reelection the following year once confided that he decided to cosponsor after receiving several calls from Jewish supporters in his Louisiana constituency. Not unexpectedly, Jackson's office had a hand in this, too. Perle called a friend of his in Atlanta to ask for help getting the cosponsorship of Chairman Long. The Atlanta friend called department store owner Joe Lipsky of Alexandria, Louisiana. The next day, Lipsky called Perle to say "It will be okay. I am the treasurer of Long's election campaign." A few days later, Long joined the list of seventy-two senator cosponsors and 281 House cosponsors.[91]

It must have been an uncomfortable time for those in the administration and Soviet leadership who had overestimated the effect of Soviet concessions on the education tax. Kissinger, George Shultz, and Dobrynin, in particular, had been proven wrong.

Kissinger's talks in Moscow appeared to be a prelude to a new approach for convincing the American public and interested groups that the Soviet emigration issue should not impede Soviet-American trade. On his return from Moscow, Kissinger conveyed to the Jewish leaders that Brezhnev had told him Jews would continue to be permitted to emigrate at the current rate of thirty-six thousand to forty thousand a year and that the tax would remain suspended. Brezhnev also accepted the hardship list compiled by the American Jewish groups, which was construed as a sign of Soviet cooperation.[92]

It was rumored that Brezhnev's cooperation was gained on the condition that there would be no public demonstrations on Soviet Jewry marring Brezhnev's June trip to America.[93] Jacob Stein and Max Fisher heeded the administration's urging against demonstrations.[94] Denouncing Fisher as a "tool" of Nixon and dismissing Stein as "afraid" (presumably of the power of the Soviet and American governments), an official of the National Conference on Soviet Jewry explained that Stein and Fisher tried to keep the number of demonstrators down to ten thousand.

Indeed, the demonstrations were small when Brezhnev arrived in the United States. But the reason, said a NCSJ official, was not so much because Stein and Fisher had managed to keep an arrangement with Kissinger and the Soviet leadership, but because the date of Brezhnev's arrival in Washington was set only three and one-half weeks in advance, leaving little time to organize a larger demonstration. The reason the demonstration, which featured a rally where Jackson spoke and demanded free emigration in exchange for trade, was peaceful was because Jerry Goodman of the National Conference on Soviet Jewry and others managed to head off an attempt by the violent Jewish Defense League participants to march on the Soviet embassy in Washington. The Israeli government had already helped by confiscating the passport of JDL leader Rabbi Meir Kahane when he was in Israel, thus preventing him from returning to the United States to embarrass the Nixon administration during the summit.[95]

In Moscow, one the eve of Brezhnev's departure for the American summit, activists were rounded up, also apparently to prevent demonstrations in the Soviet Union marring the public relations campaign that Brezhnev intended to conduct in the United States. However, that move had an opposite effect from that intended. Reports of reduced emigration, denials of visa applications, harassment, and detention got back to the United States and poisoned the atmosphere.[96] That such activity could take place and contradict Brezhnev's diplomatic objectives may have been a sign that those who had objected to the March concessions on the education tax in the first place—concessions that had paid no diplomatic returns—were having their way for the time being.

Before Brezhnev left for the United States, he held his first meeting in the Kremlin with the American press. As part of his public relations campaign aimed at American audiences, he defended Soviet emigration policy. He claimed there were no laws restricting emigration except for those in "certain categories" who work in areas connected to national security. He maintained that Deputy Minister of Interior B.T. Shumilin had prepared "countless documentary materials" to be handed over to President Nixon demonstrating that Soviet Jews were leaving freely.[97]

Brezhnev also devoted significant time when he was in Washington trying to persuade selected congressmen and leaders in the American Jewish community that trade would be beneficial to the United States and that the Jackson amendment was not only damaging but that it was unnecessary since free emigration already existed in the Soviet Union. On June 19, Brezhnev presented his arguments to seventeen members of the Senate Foreign Relations Committee, of whom at least Fulbright, Mansfield, Aiken, and Scott were either opposed or shaky supporters of the amendment, and to eight other congressmen. Jackson and Javits were participants at the Blair House luncheon with Brezhnev. Javits and Robert P. Griffin (R.-Mich.) raised the issue of emigration. Brezhnev dug into his pocket, extracted a red book, and read statistics disputing the criticism of the U.S.S.R. emigration policy. Hubert H. Humphrey recalled Brezhnev's saying, "I have heard that the Soviets would change their minds and cheat. That is not true. Once we give our word we keep it." During the three-and-a-half-hour lunch, dominated by an hour-and-a-half informal, free-wheeling speech by Brezhnev, the party chairman told the congressman, "We came to consolidate good things, not to quarrel. We can stay at home and quarrel. Any of you who wants to spoil good relations can make up bad questions, spread the rumor that sometime in the future we will impose a new [emigration] tax. I can't understand why these things should impair good relations between us."[98]

Brezhnev and his foreign minister Andrei Gromyko also saw Jacob Stein and Max Fisher. Dobrynin introduced Stein to his superiors as "a reasonable Jewish leader."[99] However, both Stein and Fisher were becoming discredited in the eyes of others in the Soviet Jewry movement, particularly after the near insurrection in the Jewish community in April.

Stein and Fisher attended the June 18 White House dinner for Brezhnev without consulting the NCSJ or the Presidents' Conference. Students picketed Stein's home in New York, and some local Jewish groups condemned him.[100] Stein also attended a luncheon given by Gromyko and his wife. Even moderate leaders in the Soviet Jewry movement charge that Stein "mishandled" his opportunity to discuss the problems of the Jews with Gromyko. Said one leader, "He had no business there. He didn't know what to say and what to avoid. He had a four page single-spaced paper to give to Gromyko, but he didn't. [Instead] he mentioned human rights in the Soviet Union. Mrs. Gromyko blew up and said that the Soviet Union had human rights and a constitution and then Gromyko got into it." Stein's critic argued that Stein should have stuck to the narrower Jewish question because Jews in the Soviet Union wanted to leave, not to reform Soviet society. The net result was that the Jewish community remained disappointed by Soviet performance and "steadfast in their support" of the Jackson amendment.[101]

Predictably, Soviet officials had better luck with members of the American business community. At Secretary of Treasury Shultz's invitation, fifty-one business leaders—including Armand Hammer, oil millionaire with a lifetime of activity in joint ventures in the Soviet Union; Fred M. Seed, president of the grain-exporting company, Cargil Company; and Donald M. Kendall, who was involved in swapping Pepsi-Cola for Russian vodka—met with an expansive trade-promoting Brezhnev at Blair House Friday morning, June 22.

The National Association of Manufacturers followed up its February East-West Trade conference with another demonstration of business interest in East-West trade by hosting a luncheon for Foreign Minister Nikolai Patolichev where the business lobby pledged to wage a campaign to get congressional approval for MFN for the Soviet Union.[102]

SUMMER 1973: REPRESSION RENEWED; SO, TOO, IS JACKSON'S STRENGTH

Except for a pledge from business groups to help lobby against the Jackson amendment, Brezhnev returned with little hope that the Jackson amendment could be defeated. The Soviet leadership could have gone either way in deciding how to handle the issue of emigration and domestic dissent—more concessions or another crackdown. Brezhnev's spokesman L.M. Zamyatin upped the ante by suggesting another form of linkage—that trade be tied to further progress on arms limitations.[103] On June 26, the very day that Brezhnev was returning to Moscow from the United States, *Izvestia* reported that the Supreme Soviet, the Soviet Parliament, was considering—with the concurrence of its Presidium head Nikolai Podgorny, who was generally considered critical of the detente policy identified with Brezhnev—drafting new citizenship laws for the first time since 1938. This move was regarded as placing emigration restrictions on a more "authoritative" level.[104] The Presidium was also the first governmental organ to decree the education tax in 1972.

It seemed that a debate was taking place within the Kremlin in Brezhnev's absence regarding the policy of making concessions internally for the sake of Western public opinion. Moscow observers noticed the virtual disappearance of Brezhnev from public view after his return from the Washington summit. [105] After the disappointing American trip—with whatever serious consequences it might have had for Brezhnev's personal leadership position—Jackson's office perceived Kissinger taking the Jackson amendment so seriously that tension between Kissinger and Jackson, who had been on good terms, began to rise.

Kissinger saw Brezhnev again in Moscow in July. When he returned to the United States, he told Fisher, Stein, and Richard Maass that Brezhnev had conveyed to Nixon new assurances that some of the "refusniks"—Jewish applicants previously refused permission to leave—would be allowed to leave. Kissinger indicated that he personally believed the Soviet leadership was still trying to accommodate America concerning Soviet Jews. Kissinger showed the Jewish leaders their list of the 738 individuals that he had first discussed with the Jewish leaders in May. Kissinger had brought it up when he saw Brezhnev in June in Moscow, and Nixon had raised it again with Brezhnev in Washington in June. The Soviets had provided Kissinger a statement saying that 269 of the 738 had received permission to leave, 30 no longer were living in the Soviet Union, 177 no longer wanted to go, 80 were in the process of being cleared to leave, 149 were denied permission to leave, and 34 were unaccounted for. But like the concessions on the education tax, concessions on the several score of "refusniks" did not solve the basic problem of exiting from the Soviet Union. The three Jewish leaders told Kissinger they were still disappointed with the total record of the Soviet Union.[106] The number of emigrants perceptibly declined compared to the first half of 1973.[107]

There was additional evidence that hard-liners on emigration, who seemed to have a greater say after the Soviet concessions in March on the education tax had proven diplomatically unproductive, were prevailing. On July 17, 1973, dissident A.A. Amalrik was sentenced to a second two-year prison term.[108] In a heavy-handed display, well-recorded in the American press, a group of Soviets clashed with some twenty Soviet Jews in an ugly tussle after the Jews had cheered the visiting Israeli basketball team at the World University Games in Moscow in August.[109] In the same week, Soviet dissident physicist A.D. Sakharov was called in by Deputy Prosecutor General Mikhail Malyarov and warned against meeting with the foreign press. Sakharov, apparently believing his contacts with the West actually protected him from serious Soviet reprisals, contacted the Western press in Moscow and in an interview he stated that the United States should exact from the Soviet government unrestricted emigration as a very minimum for improved trade relations. The following week, Soviet authorities began the trial of V. A. Krasin and P. I. Yakir, dissenters who had recanted their former activities.[110] Moreover, an all-out press campaign was launched against Sakharov and Nobel Prize-winning author A. I. Solzhenitsyn, the first of its magnitude since the 1958 campaign against author Boris Pasternak.

The crackdown was possibly more a concession to Brezhnev's domestic critics who were criticizing him for allowing the Soviet Union to be pushed around, while reaping no diplomatic benefits and encouraging further dissident boldness, than it was a Soviet tactic in the battle with Jackson. The repression may have served some intragovernmental purpose in the Soviet Union, but it was a mistake as far as the Jackson amendment was concerned because it attracted even more allies to the Jackson campaign.[111]

Repression of Solzhenitsyn and Sakharov prodded other influential interest groups to join the Jackson amendment coalition. Joining Jackson's ranks were generally liberal groups including the Americans for Democratic Action, the Federation of American Scientists, the membership of National Academy of Sciences, and the American Psychiatric Association. The Association of American Publishers also expressed themselves in favor of the Jackson amendment, as did various church groups. Thanks to the clumsy clampdown on dissent in the Soviet Union, Jackson became the leader of a continually growing band of critics of the Soviet regime.

When Congress returned from summer recess, Andrei Sakharov penned an open letter to the United States Congress dated September 14, 1973, drawing a tight connection between the repression in the Soviet Union at that moment and the Jackson amendment, which he endorsed, pending in the Ways and Means Committee. This had the important effect of attracting even more American liberals to the cause. Arthur Schlesinger, Jr., a leading intellectual on the American Left, had opposed the Jackson amendment. After Sakharov wrote his letter urging congressional support for the Jackson amendment, Schlesinger wrote in the *Wall Street Journal*, "Always trust the man on the firing line." Writing in the *New York Review of Books*, I. F. Stone reached the same conclusion for basically the same reason. *New York Times* columnist Anthony Lewis also took a hard line vis-à-vis Moscow. Sixty-five intellectuals signed joint telegrams to Sakharov and Solzhenitsyn praising their "courageous efforts on behalf of peace and freedom" and dispatched a harshly phrased cable to Brezhnev denouncing the Soviet Union's violation of human rights.[112]

By the end of the summer of revived repression in the Soviet Union, news accounts and editorials indicated that American liberals in particular and public opinion in general were taking a tougher view of the Soviet Union. A Jackson aide believed that up until this point, "the Administration could have gotten its way. . . . We were vulnerable at times." Administration officials also have said that some sort of compromise to the Jackson amendment could have been worked out as late as August 1973 before the August recess. That possibility faded when the Ways and Means Committee took up the Jackson amendment from the docket.

WAYS AND MEANS DELIBERATIONS

Sakharov's September letter was a reiteration of a previous endorsement of the Jackson amendment, which he expressed to Western newsmen in August.[113] It came at a strategic moment in the House of Representatives' consideration of the Jackson amendment. On September 17, Congress returned from summer recess, and Jackson placed the letter in the *Congressional Record* that morning. "It is ironic," he commented, "that Sakharov's forceful argument should come to us at a moment when the trade bill is before the House Committee on Ways and Means—and when there is a move under way—which I am certain will not succeed—to kill the Mills-Vanik measure by a hastily drafted administration-backed Corman-Pettis alternative. . . ."[114]

The Ways and Means Committee was vulnerable to Jackson's pressure. Mills, still recuperating from back surgery, issued a harsh warning to the Soviet Union saying he would oppose trade concessions for the Soviet Union "if the price is to be paid in the martyrdom" of political dissidents.[115] But Mills was absent from Washington, and Acting Chairman Al Ullman's (D.-Ore.) control over the committee was weakened by the uncertainty of the timing of Mills's return. Without Mills, the administration had virtually no legislative strategy. A national reporter covering the committee at the time charged that officials in the administration "have a public policy and public relations positions but no legislative strategy. Timmons [William, the White House liaison to the House of Representatives] doesn't know a Title V from an MFN. Same for Korologus [Thomas, White House liaison to the Senate]. Pearce [William, the Deputy Special Trade Representative who was handling the day-to-day operations for the trade bill] has to check with Kissinger, Flanigan, and Eberle, every time he wants to do something. And they really haven't given the matter much thought."

Sakharov's letter was used as a Jackson-Vanik battering ram against half-hearted administration assistance for those committee members who devised compromise substitutes for the amendment.[116] The administration was disorganized and apparently lackadaisical at the time an effort to compromise the amendment in the Ways and Means Committee would have had to have absolute and full administration backing to succeed. In a twenty-six member committee, eighteen were cosponsors of the amendment. Vanik was "dead set against compromise," said Staffman Talisman. Jackson's staff supported him arguing that it was up to the Soviets—not Congress—to make compromises, and that the Soviets were learning that the president was not the only political force in America that had to be dealt with.

Sam Gibbons (D.-Fla.), a liberal trader on the Ways and Means Committee from the port city of Tampa, and in his words "not a fan of the Vanik amendment," was one of the key members who felt the pressure against compromise mounted by Jackson and Vanik's office. Gibbons related that "We tried to change it [the Jackson-Vanik amendment] but it was an emotional issue, a *cause célebrè*. You couldn't touch it with a ten foot pole. . . . I've spoken with most of the members of the Committee and they say, 'Sam, you may be right, but the Jewish community is thinking of the 1930's and is so emotionally tied in with that that they fear they will go along with genocide,' . . . [It is] the most emotional issue I've ever been involved in. I tried to make improvement in Vanik's Amendment and the word spread faster than the speed of light; I couldn't even touch a word. Corman had the same experience."

James C. Corman (D.-Calif.), another committee member, said he received a phone call at 2:00 a.m. Washington time (11:00 p.m. California time) saying, "Vote against the Gibbons proposal." Corman asked the caller, "What's the Gibbons proposal." The caller replied, "I don't know, but vote against it."

After the heavy lobbying dissuaded Gibbons from pursuing a compromise, Corman and another California member on the committee, Republican Jerry L. Pettis, suggested the compromise that was damned by Jackson on September 17 as the "hastily-drafted administration-backed" project.[117] Actually the proposal, of which there were two different versions, was drawn up by Wilbur Mills's special trade adviser Anthony Solomon. Basically, it would have granted the president authority to give MFN to a nonmarket country provided that he report "that such nation is evidencing reasonable progress in the observance of internationally agreed upon principles of human rights." Vanik objected to the absence of restrictions on credits and credit guarantees (in addition to MFN) in this approach and questioned how "reasonable progress" was to be measured.[118] But, the technicalities of the ill-fated compromise proposal made little difference because "Pettis, Corman, and Ullman ran like hell" and "chickened so fast," according to one staff insider.

What happened was Corman and Pettis—both original sponsors of the Jackson-Vanik amendment—ran into an all-out campaign against any compromise. When the proposal to break the deadlock between Jackson and the administration was discussed in committee, Vanik informed his staff aide, Talisman. Immediately, a call went out from Washington to the Southern California Soviet Jewry movement. Corman recalled what happened. "That very night, until 2:00, I was getting phone calls at home from good friends of mine who very irately wanted to know why I was selling out the Jewish cause."[119] This time the Jewish organizations obviously did not waver. They concurred with Jackson's view that the amendment should be passed "as is" in the House so if there were any compromising in the Senate, Jackson would be bargaining from an uneroded basis of strength.

Talisman personally denied initiating those phone calls. In any case, there were other staffers in the Senate and in the offices of Jewish groups involved in the fight for the amendment who could have made phone calls just as easily.

Neatly meshing with the constituent pressure accompanied by wide California press coverage on Corman was a well-orchestrated campaign in Washington to equate the Corman-Pettis compromise with a business effort to destroy the Jackson amendment for the sake of future profits in Soviet trade. Donald Kendall—a friend and former business associate of Nixon when he was a Wall Street lawyer representing Kendall's firm, Pepsico—directed the business community's lobbying. Kendall dispatched a telegram to rally sixty-five top executives of multinational banks and corporations.

However, his effort was "sandbagged" when Morris Amitay was tipped off about the businessmen's plans by a paid business lobbyist sympathetic to the Jackson amendment. Amitay leaked the business plans to the *Washington Post,* which printed the story on page one under the headline, "Big Firms to Press Hill on Soviet Trade Benefit."[120]

The article printed in the Kendall telegram in full:

> The President's request in the trade bill for authority to provide MFN treatment to the Soviet Union is in deep trouble in the House Ways and Means Committee. Soviet emigration policy and grain sales along with other considerations resulting in great hostility to granting MFN authority.
>
> President needs support from business community in order to win that authority from Congress. Ways and Means Committee likely to vote on MFN question on Wednesday, September 19. Vote will be exceedingly close. I urge you and other members of ECAT (Emergency Committee for American Trade) to contact by telephone or telegram each member of Ways and Means in support of MFN and its vital relationship to United States and Soviet detente. Suggest you note commercial and political importance of MFN and express hope that way can be found to grant President authority.[121]

The *Post* article also linked the businessmen's efforts to suggestions that Soviet Deputy Trade Minister Vladimir Alkhimov "might plan to do some lobbying of his own with Congress" when he was in Washington the week the committee planned to vote on the MFN proposals and counterproposals. Alkhimov rejected such suggestions when the *Post* reporter reached him by telephone at the tennis courts of Kendall's estate in Connecticut where he was a guest.[122]

Another attack against compromise came from AFL-CIO President George Meany. He sent his own telegram to each member of the committee dated September 17 arguing that to give the Soviets MFN was to abandon America's principles.[123]

The final blow to the Corman-Pettis proposal was delivered by the administration, which, Henry Jackson's claims notwithstanding, never gave the enterprise full support. Said one disgruntled administration official, "The Administration cut Corman-Pettis down at the knees." A worker for a Jewish organization considering compromise commented, "The Administration couldn't make up their cotton pickin' mind to say they would support Corman-Pettis and combine it with effective diplomacy." The worker dealt with White House official Leonard Garment and with State Department officials. "I got mixed signals. They were prepared to accept it but were making these extreme anti-linkage statements. They were waiting for Corman-Pettis to be shoved down their throat, but that was not enough."

Decisions like that were cleared through Kissinger, while Flanigan usually issued the orders. Although the Corman-Pettis compromise was preferable from the Soviets' point of view to the Jackson-Vanik amendment, it still added conditions to trade concessions and thus contradicted the administration's promises in the original trade pact of 1972. The administration's position made sense diplomatically, but it made little political sense given the existing situation within the Ways and Means Committee. It seemed as if assuaging the feelings of the Soviets in the short run had become more important than assuring their long-term interests via compromise.

Compounding the administration's inadequate handling of the committee was the fumbling of a scheduled appearance before the Ways and Means Committee of Henry Kissinger, who was then about to become the secretary of state. One of the committee members stated it simply, "We tried to get Kissinger, and he wouldn't or couldn't come up." The committee delayed voting on the MFN question until September 19 pending the appearance of Kissinger on September 18. However, Kissinger did not appear. He said he had several conflicts preventing him from appearing, but well-informed observers, including some in the administration itself, believed he might have avoided some of those "unavoidable" conflicts in his schedule.

It had been made clear to Kissinger that his appearance at the committee was crucial. Kissinger spoke to President Nixon, Melvin Laird, William Pearce, the administration's manager of the Trade Bill in the Ways and Means Committee, Chairman Ullman, and ranking Republican on the Committee Herman I. Schneebeli (R.-Pa.) about his appearing. Before the larger meeting, Pearce and Kissinger met with Nixon. Pearce said he could not resolve the issue unless Kissinger testified. Kissinger raised the question of his National Security Council status. Nixon said, "Well, you can limit your testimony." When the congressmen joined the administration officials, Schneebeli raised the subject of Kissinger's appearing, and it was agreed that Kissinger would testify. However, when it finally came time for him to go, Kissinger would not.

At the end of the week of September 17, Chairman Ullman—who apparently was unable to perceive a consensus in the committee—buffeted as it was by the Jewish groups, labor, Sakharov, big business, and lacking guidance from the administration—delayed action on the MFN question for one week "on the chance," he said, "that we can get more reason interjected into the discussion."[124]

Kissinger, who was sworn in as secretary of state on September 21, never made it to the Ways and Means Committee. His aide Helmut Sonnenfeldt also was unable to appear. Sonnenfeldt or someone on his staff allegedly felt it was important that Sonnenfeldt not appear because his appointment as under secretary of treasury was in jeopardy in the Senate Finance Committee. Thus Steven Lazarus, head of the East-West Trade Bureau, who could never talk with the authority of Kissinger, appeared. Lazarus had already gotten a bad name with the Soviet Jewish community when he was in Moscow with Charles Colson in February of 1973. He was thought there to have tried to trade Kissinger's influence with the Soviet authorities for a deal with Jewish dissidents to abandon their support for the Jackson amendment.[125] He ran into a great deal of trouble again at his committee appearance.

Mark Talisman called Lazarus's appearance a display of the "Administration's lack of understanding." He said that Steven Lazarus

> was sitting in executive session over in the Capitol saying things which simply weren't true. One [was] that Israel and the Soviet Union have MFN relationship. Israel doesn't have MFN. Two, [was] about economic trade data showing enormous trade [between Israel and the Soviet Union]. That was two things: trade in 1964 of Jaffa oranges in Israel for Russian Orthodox property [in Israel]—four hundred eighty-five thousand dollars in citrus—and the rest of what emigrés declared of value and shipments out of Israel of packages to relatives in the Soviet Union. [These were] red herrings raised by Lazarus. Vanik [sitting in the executive sessions of the committee which was restricted to members only and a few Executive Branch representatives] would call me up. And I'd get the call and check these [statements] out.

At least two days before the vote was finally taken in the Ways and Means Committee—on September 26—Kissinger recognized the unfavorable prospects for MFN for the Soviet Union and so warned Foreign Minister Gromyko.[126] In the few remaining days before the fateful vote, a new public hard line was detected in the Soviet Union. The United States was accused of "gross interference" in Soviet internal affairs and Soviet emigration policy was defended. (However, a continuing desire to trade with the United States was restated.) Brezhnev warned against "playing games" and "ambiguous maneuvers."[127] Gromyko, addressing the United Nations a day before the committee vote, also warned against interference in Soviet internal affairs.[128]

The vote on the controversial Jackson-Vanik amendment was taken in committee by voice vote—no head count, no names recorded. It was agreed that MFN would be denied to those nonmarket countries restricting emigration. That took care of the MFN half of the Jackson-Vanik amendment. Vanik proposed holding another committee session to deal with the credits and credit guarantee restrictions. At the follow-up session, the administration managed to weaken the credit restrictions by a parliamentary maneuver offered by Republican member Schneebeli. Schneebeli argued on a point of order that Jackson's provisions restricting credits and credit guarantees came under the jurisdiction of another committee, the House Banking and Currency Committee. Ullman upheld the point. Vanik moved to appeal the chairman's ruling. Vanik's motion lost in a twelve to twelve tie vote. The vote indicated that at least six of the eighteen cosponsors of the Jackson amendment defected on the procedural issue.[129] Mills, who was absent, could have broken the tie. He had cast a proxy on other votes, but on that one, he was nowhere to be found. Said one close observer of Mills's legislative life, "This demonstrates where Mills had stood on this issue all along. He has this burning desire never to lose—never to be on the losing side. This has determined his behavior all along. He'd just as soon dump the President and the Administration in this regard as anyone else."

Vanik and his allies in the committee were disappointed by the vote. To make things difficult for some of the members representing large Polish constituencies, Vanik raised the question why the committee should not include Poland as a nonmarket country subject to the Jackson-Vanik amendment just like the Soviet Union. By the wording of the amendment, Poland was a nonmarket country but not subject to the restrictions since it already had MFN treatment. But the answer an exasperated staffman gave to the Vanik group was "because Poland doesn't have a whole bunch of Jews."

The committee included in the bill part of the ill-fated Corman-Pettis provision requiring the president to determine annually whether nonmarket countries covered by the Ways and Means Committee definition had met some unspecific requirements for free emigration, which were then subject to congressional veto of trade concessions for these countries. The provision—originally intended to substitute for the Jackson-Vanik amendment—actually reinforced it.

On the final day of committee deliberation on the Trade Bill, Republican committee member Barber Conable (R.-N.Y.) wanted to offer an amendment striking the entire Title IV in the bill, which included both the Vanik restrictions and the administration's request for MFN authority for the Soviet Union. It would have permitted the administration at least to cut its losses incurred thus far in committee. Conable had actually advanced the idea earlier arguing that if anything on Soviet economic concessions was in the bill when it reached the House floor, the administration would get "clobbered on the floor." It took two weeks for William Pearce, the administration's representative in the closed-door committee mark-up sessions, to establish a line into the National Security Council so he could give the committee the administration's official position on Conable's suggestion. Until then, STR had been told not to concern itself with the MFN question. Eventually, said an STR official, "After a month of fighting, we won over Kissinger to the need to separate MFN out of the bill." But the green light did not come in time for Pearce to act forcefully on the Conable proposal. When Pearce was asked on the last day of mark-up for the administration's view of Conable's proposal, he could reach neither Kissinger nor any authoritative assistant to get clearance for the proposal. Pearce was reduced to repeating the administration line that the administration does not want the Jackson amendment and it wants MFN for the Soviet Union. Again, the White House let the committee down. It may not have been a conscious decision by Kissinger or others in authority, but they nevertheless must bear the responsibility for the legislative consequences.

Two days after the committee completed work on the Trade Bill, Soviet Foreign Minister Gromyko conferred with Nixon and Kissinger at the White House. A spokesman reported that the discussion between the leaders was concerned almost exclusively with MFN: "The current status of the Administration's [effort] to get most-favored-nation treatment . . . and . . . the Congressional situation." In addition to reiterating the administration's "commitment to seek MFN for the Russians," the president pledged to make a "diligent" attempt to overcome the committee passed restrictions.[130] Judging from Secretary of Treasury Shultz's impressions when he visited the Soviet Union from October 1 to 3 to discuss Soviet-American trade, the Soviet government was unwilling to make further concessions on the emigration question, which might have assisted a practically impossible effort to reverse the will of the Ways and Means Committee.[131] Shultz did reveal that the Soviets at least seemed to have "realistically accepted" that MFN would not be granted to the Soviet Union in 1973.[132]

That left the question of credits. By a tie vote the administration had managed to hold back the application of the Jackson amendment to credits or credit guarantees extended by the Export-Import Bank and other United States government agencies. But there still existed the possibility that Vanik and his allies could add these restrictions by amending the committee-reported bill when it reached the House floor.

A day after the committee vote, Jackson delivered a speech on the Senate floor calling the vote "a most welcome affirmation of the commitment of this country to the cause of human rights." As for the omission of the credit and credit guarantee restrictions, he predicted, "I am certain it [the full House] will move to include the full Jackson Amendment in the trade bill by adding the credit restrictions to those on MFN."[133]

Making Jackson's prediction a reality was Vanik's next task. It meant winding a narrow parliamentary path through the complex maze of rules of the House of Representatives. In most cases, Ways and Means legislation was handled in the House under a "closed rule," which barred amendments from the floor. When a congressman voted on Ways and Means Committee bills, he had to decide to vote for the entire bill or against the entire bill. He could not try to add or delete portions. To add the credit and credit guarantee restrictions, Vanik had to go to the Rules Committee and appeal for a rule "to open" the bill to an amendment to the bill from the floor.

To guarantee a favorable rule from the powerful Rules Committee, Vanik could go to the Democratic Caucus in the House with a petition of at least fifty House members. If the Democratic Caucus accepted the petition, it would recommend to the Democratic members of the Rules Committee—the majority of the committee—to vote for a rule giving Vanik an opportunity to offer one amendment to the bill. The Caucus recommendations were invariably binding. Vanik set out to gather more than fifty names to insure a dramatic success.

THE OCTOBER WAR

The committee votes had been cast; the bill, H.R. 10710, was officially reported out to the House floor on October 10, and a vote was scheduled for October 17 or 18. But on October 6—practically on the first anniversary of the original Soviet-American trade pact and of the original introduction of the Jackson amendment—the Yom Kippur War broke out drastically altering the legislative strategies of both Jackson-Vanik and the White House.

Soviet involvement in the war complicated the White House's task by hardening anti-Soviet feeling in the Congress. The Soviets became so unpopular in the war-spirited House of Representatives that when Congressman Richard H. Ichord (D.-Mo.), a conservative who had fifty names on his own petition to the Democratic Caucus to delete entirely all credits and all MFN to the Soviet Union under all circumstances, many were afraid it would pass. To avert Ichord, Chairman of the Ways and Means Committee Ullman agreed to let Vanik introduce his floor amendment to the bill without Vanik ever having to go to the Caucus or to the Rules Committee for a special rule. Ichord withdrew his amendment. Mark Talisman summed up the events to date. "Ullman was good about it in assisting rather than opposing it. It became clear that if this issue still festered without credits then the whole trade bill would sink. With the Schneebeli move to delete credit restrictions, [the administration] won their battle in the committee but lost the war in the full House."

The lines were drawn for the final battle on the House floor. The administration was faced with the task of deleting the portion of the Jackson-Vanik amendment dealing with MFN, which was already in the bill, while staving off a second attack by Vanik to add the credits restrictions. The Soviets were resigned to the defeat in 1973 on MFN, but how would they feel if the credits were lost, too? Complicating the entire matter was the fact that at the time Kissinger was trying to cajole the Soviets into putting pressure on its client state, Egypt, to bring about a cease-fire in the Middle East.

Kissinger tried snatching victory out of the jaws of defeat over the Jackson amendment and almost succeeded. Kissinger found an opportunity even in the dangers of superpower politics and client-state confrontation. The October War seemed to shatter any chance of averting the Jackson amendment, as a strong anti-Soviet feeling remaining below the surface in the American public became manifest. But paradoxically the war also shattered—at least temporarily—Jewish support in the country for Jackson's efforts.

The Jews had wavered in April; one of their reasons then was fear of incurring the wrath of the White House that might be directed against Israel. When the war broke out in October, Israel's position was much more vulnerable. After a week's fighting, Israel needed resupplies of Phantoms and M-60 tanks. Getting them became the top priority in every Jewish leader's mind. Kissinger was the key figure in the resupply decision.[134]

Kissinger wanted a cease-fire in the Middle East, and he tried influencing Israeli behavior by pacing shipments of American supplies. He also regarded cooperation of the Soviet Union to be essential since it was Egypt's major supplier. If avoiding alienation of the Soviet Union at this crucial juncture was necessary, delaying the vote scheduled for October 17 or 18 was essential.

Soon after the war broke out, White House liaison with the Jewish community Leonard Garment invited Jacob Stein and Max Fisher to the White House. He told them the time for consideration of the Jackson amendment was "not ripe." He asked them to convey to Ways and Means Committee Chairman Ullman the need to delay the House vote. A delegation including Stein, Maass, Mrs. Charlotte Jacobson, and Rabbi Arthur Hertzberg of the American Jewish Congress met with Chairman Ullman on October 12 to inform him that they supported a delay. Kissinger also requested and received from Speaker of the House of Representatives Carl Albert a delay until October 24 or 25 to give him more time to operate behind the scenes.[135] The Jewish leaders may have breathed a sigh of relief on October 19 when Nixon formally requested $2.2 billion for Israel's defense, even though complaints about actual shipment of arms continued.

As the scheduled day for the House vote approached and two ceasefires of October 22 and 24 tore apart, the need for another delay or a more definitive solution remained urgent. Leonard Garment called Stein and Fisher again on October 23 and invited them and Maass, Jacobson, and Jerry Goodman of the NCSJ to come to the White House on October 25 to discuss the ill-fated ceasefires with Kissinger's aide General Alexander Haig. At the last minute, Kissinger, who had just returned from a whirlwind trip to the Soviet Union in an effort to patch up the ceasefire, appeared instead of Haig. Kissinger sent his assistant away from the meeting, which he remarked resembled a *sanhedrin* (an ancient rabbinical court). The meeting was devoted almost entirely to the Middle East, but as the leaders were about to leave, Kissinger brought up the Jackson amendment. According to one participant, "He said that Israel's survival was at stake and that this was a very poor time to slap the Soviets in the face." The diary of another participant recorded Kissinger's words: "No matter how much the United States and Israel desire it, if the Russians were actively opposed, there would be no peace."[136]

Kissinger suggested dropping Title IV from the bill completely: the Conable approach. Kissinger had passed up or ignored the Conable approach in committee. But in the maelstrom of the war, he apparently was made cognizant of the issue and the greater danger of additional action to link credits to emigration. Kissinger improved on the by-then-outdated Conable proposal by adding a concession that came about when he and, later, Shultz asked a receptive Dobrynin to concede that the administration would extend no futher Export-Import Bank credits to the Soviet Union as long as the Trade Bill was in the House of Representatives (through December 1973). Kissinger pledged these two items if Jackson would give up the fight for his amendment in the House.[137]

One of the participants said the leaders were neither "buying it [Kissinger's proposal] or rejecting it. . . . They didn't give a yes or no." The group agreed to discuss the suggestion with the sponsors of the legislation.[138]

The administration made its new position official on October 29 when Peter Flanigan testified to a Senate Banking Subcommittee hearing:

> We believe that this issue is particularly sensitive in terms of the current situation in the Middle East, and the method that is underway to find not only a ceasefire to the shooting, but also an affirmative solution in that area. We think it would be inappropriate at this time to deal with that issue, either in the sense of removing any of the current, statutory limitations or in the sense of imposing additional statutory limitations. Therefore, it is the Administration's position that Title IV should be eliminated from the trade bill. Consonant with that position, it should not be attached to this legislation.[139]

The administration was initiating a policy that might have worked earlier but had little chance in October. To add insult to injury, it informed the House leadership and the Ways and Means Committee Chairman Ullman by using a platform in the Senate and in a Banking Committee. Ullman responded testily, "the Administration's new position has not been communicated to me. . . . The statement was made to the wrong forum. . . . This whole matter has been poorly handled by the White House." Ullman added that it is "totally unfair to have the entire trade bill endangered by the irresponsible delays and conflicting policies emanating from the Administration."[140] The next day, Speaker Albert echoed Ullman's exasperation, "I'm still waiting for the Administration to say what they want." Flanigan admitted to the press, "Our vaunted system down here at the White House is not functioning perfectly. We could have done a better job informing them that the statement was being made yesterday."[141]

Speaker Albert gave the White House an ultimatum: either take up the bill on the House floor soon or drop it for the year. The next evening, November 1, Kissinger requested scheduling debate on the bill to begin the week of November 12, the last week before Thanksgiving recess.[142]

From Kissinger's viewpoint, prospects were not completely bleak, perhaps helping to explain why he finally asked Albert to go ahead and schedule debate in the House. Kissinger was apparently hoping that the Jewish leaders with whom he had spoken would help him out. He also planned to ask Israeli Prime Minister Golda Meir to encourage the Jewish community to allow the compromise to pass in the House. Meir, who was in the United States at the time, was deeply involved in negotiating the disengagement of Israeli and Egyptian forces. According to an Israeli reporter with access to transcripts of top-level discussions,

> The price he eventually intended to extract from the Soviets for the trade agreement, Kissinger told the Israelis, was Soviet moderation at Geneva, and Israel should support him on this. . . . If Israel could persuade its friends in Congress and elsewhere to remove their support for Senator Jackson's amendment, Kissinger argued, the path would be cleared for a policy he considered beneficial for Israel in the long run.
> . . . When Ambassador Dinitz reminded him that Israel was not supporting Senator Jackson, Kissinger replied that it was not enough for Israel not to actively support the Jackson Amendment. He expected it to be active in opposition to Jackson. He could not understand what he saw as Israel's political blindness. "You only see what is under your nose," he kept saying over and over. "You don't see the global picture."[143]

Meir privately discussed the linkage of the Jackson amendment and Israel's predicament with top Jewish leaders who were in Washington on Friday, November 2, to hear her speak at a major public forum. It is not known what—if anything—Mrs. Meir advised. Based on past performances, she probably tried her best to avoid getting Israel or herself personally caught in the middle of the executive-legislative struggle. Different members of her government had been giving conflicting signals to the Jewish community so various parts of the Jewish community were reading what they wanted into them. Often the views of what Israel desired were contradictory. It was said that Ambassador Simcha Dinitz, former chief officer to Meir, conveyed to Jacob Stein and others the impression that nothing, including the Jackson amendment, should be allowed to interfere in the resupply of arms to Israel. But by November, that issue was subsiding.[144] On the other hand, a more militant American Jewish activist stated, "Israel made it clear that it didn't want us to sacrifice Soviet Jewry for Israel."

With apparently no more clear-cut guidance from Israel, the Jewish leaders tried to decide finally whether or not they should cooperate with the administration's plan to drop Title IV from the Trade Bill. Fisher wanted to go along with the administration. To a lesser extent, Maass and Jacobson seemed to agree.[145] The Jewish leaders agreed to meet with Vanik and Jackson and ask that Title IV be eliminated with the possibility that it could be renewed the next year when the Senate took up the bill.[146] Jackson resisted any arrangement that had the effect of dropping the Jackson-Vanik amendment in the House.

News leaked out about the leadership's decision, which represented a softer position than that taken by Jackson and the "rank and file" of the organizations.[147] On Monday, November 5, officials of the National Conference on Soviet Jewry held an emergency meeting to, in the words of one person closely identified with the organization, "help us clarify our position." According to one account of the meeting,

> a chorus of criticism among Jewish organizations arose. Denunciations of a policy of "capitulation" were accompanied, in some cases, by demands for the resignations of various Jewish Leaders. Insistence upon the maintenance of the basic Jewish position on the Jackson Amendment was the central theme which found expression in a decision reached at an emergency meeting of the National Conference on Soviet Jewry. The proposal that the Jewish leadership support removal of Title IV was rejected. Instead, the chairman of the National Conference, Richard Maass, was instructed to report to Senator Jackson what the White House position was and to seek his views.[148]

Some of the participants at the stormy New York session had to keep a previously scheduled meeting with Jackson the same day back in Washington. The group—Stein, Maass, Jacobson, Goodman—had survived the meeting and the shuttling from Washington on Friday to New York on Monday and back the same day to Washington. When they arrived a few minutes late at Jackson's office, the going was rough there, too. One member of the group remembered the aggressive greeting from Dorothy Fosdick, a loyal worker for over two decades for Jackson. She yelled down the Senate corridors to the delegation, "How dare you keep Jackson waiting?"

Apparently, they were keeping more than just Jackson waiting. Jackson was well aware that some of the group favored the administration proposal. Without their permission, Jackson had invited other known supporters to be on hand as a counterbalance. Ribicoff and his aide Morris Amitay were there, as were Jackson's aides Perle and Tina Silber, a former employee of the American-Israel Public Affairs Committee. Vanik was out of town, but Mark Talisman was included. David Blumberg and Herman Edelsberg, president and executive director of the B'nai B'rith, were also there. Elihu Bergman, a Harvard professor acting as a NCSJ consultant, was invited. Javits did not attend.[149]

The meeting began by Maass's relating what Kissinger had said on October 25. Stein added the editorial comment that "it is important to the Jewish leadership if Kissinger tells us his negotiating position would be strengthened by their going along with his latest proposal."[150] Charlotte

Jacobson said that even though Max Fisher, who avoided having any dealings with Jackson and Ribicoff, was not there, she thought the proposal Fisher supported should be raised. She added, "I know that this is a mistaken plea, but I feel we owe it to Max."[151] Later in the meeting, Stein remarked that American Jewish leaders had to concern themselves with the possibility that passing the Jackson amendment might hurt Jews in the Soviet Union. He added, "it is a gamble" whether Jackson's legislation might reduce Kissinger's leverage with the Soviet Union in the Middle East.[152]

Barely controlling his temper, Jackson answered, "If you believe détente will unravel, then you're foolish." Jackson said Kissinger was a "liar" for blaming the Department of Defense for Kissinger's own premeditated decision to delay resupplying Israel during the early days of the October War. In response to Stein's concerns, Jackson said he couldn't provide a written guarantee that his amendment held no risks. But, he said, it would be "naive" to think that dropping the proposal would assure Israel's security: "If we back down now, the Soviets will take advantage of it." He concluded: "The Administration is always using you. The only way to get Soviet Jews out of the Soviet Union is to stand firm on the Jackson-Vanik Amendment." He threatened that if the leaders did not heed him, "I'll go back to your people and tell them."

When Jackson left the room to take a telephone call, Ribicoff reiterated Jackson's view that Kissinger was a "liar."[153] He did not control his anger at those he regarded as spineless weaklings. The upshot of the meeting was that Jackson, Ribicoff, and Talisman said they would press to have the entire Jackson-Vanik amendment passed by both the House and the Senate.[154] Apparently objecting either to the way the meeting was going, to the lambasting of the Jewish officials for their so-called naiveté and foolishness, or to the threats to go over the heads of the Jewish leadership if they did not cooperate, Stein stomped out of the meeting. Maass joined Stein, and together they went to the White House where they spoke with Peter Flanigan, Helmut Sonnenfeldt, and William Pearce. Flanigan had apparently heard of the meeting from a news reporter's inquiry. According to one participant, Flanigan "didn't let up." Flanigan said it was not enough for the Jews just to say nothing more—to take a neutral position. He said they should call Ullman, House Democratic Majority Leader Thomas ("Tip") O'Neill, and other influential leaders and actively affirm that they didn't mind having Title IV removed from the bill. The Jews, visibly chastised by Jackson and Ribicoff, refused.

PUTTING OFF THE INEVITABLE

Kissinger was left with an equivocating Israel, a silenced American Jewish leadership, a sandbagged business lobby, an unyielding and threatening Soviet leadership, and an ailing Mills (who by then had returned to Wash-

ington but was unable to regain control over the Trade Bill). Basically all
Kissinger had was time, and he tried to use it. It was a sign of weakness, but
he had little choice.

On November 7 after the latest setback, Speaker Albert granted the administration another reprieve. President Nixon had personally requested the
third delay in a note slipped to Albert during a meeting.[155] The administration wanted a little more time to maneuver. All channels had been
explored and had failed. Kissinger was left with the harsh reality that if he
were to avoid a House vote incurring the Soviet Union's wrath, he had no
other choice but to go to Jackson directly. At the insistence of the administration's Trade Bill managers in the Special Trade Representative's Office, Kissinger took the initiative of setting up a meeting with Jackson for the
following week. A Jackson aide aptly described the effort to talk with Jackson
"as a last ditch effort." On November 21, Secretary of Treasury Shultz met
Jackson. The same evening at a dinner, Kissinger and Jackson had a general
airing of their differences. Kissinger got nowhere, as far as House action was
concerned. Jackson maintained his position. He was not ready to discuss
compromise or concessions until the House passed his amendment in its entirety. Only after that would he talk, and then he could talk with authority.

Suffering another setback, Kissinger aimed for another delay. The
president, however, was under strong pressure from his trade experts to delay
no longer. After months of arduous hearings and mark-up in the Ways and
Means Committee and years of internal administration preparation of the
Trade Bill before that, the trade officials feared for the bill's passage.
Kissinger, on the other hand, was known to prefer no bill at all to one offensive to the Soviet Union.[156]

Nixon finally agreed to reverse his earlier request for further delay and
asked Speaker Albert in a letter on December 3 to proceed with general
debate on the Trade Bill.[157] Pearce had drafted the letter to Albert. Secretary
of State Kissinger redrafted the letter so the president's opposition to the
Jackson-Vanik provision was prominently displayed at the beginning and a
presidential threat to veto the entire Trade Bill if the amendment stayed in
was conspicuous. But with Shultz's intervention on the side of the trade officials, at least the president sent the letter.

Kissinger was undaunted. In a fine bureaucratic application of guerrilla
tactics, he had breakfast with the House leadership. He told them that
although President Nixon had written Albert to commence floor action on
the Trade Bill, he still believed that passage of the anti-Soviet provisions
would be harmful and therefore debate should be postponed. A letter for
Kissinger's signature to Albert stating that view was drafted by Pearce and
again redrafted by Kissinger.[158]

The president finally overruled Kissinger, and the bill was sent to the
House floor for a vote on December 11. The day before, the full House ap-

proved by a vote of 230-147 the rule by which the bill would be considered. The rule—which had cleared the Rules Committee in October—was that three amendments would be permitted to the Trade Bill: Vanik's amendment to add the credit restrictions originally deemed inappropriate by the Ways and Means Committee; an amendment by Barber Conable to drop the entire Title IV, which by then contained the Jackson-Vanik amendment as amended plus a Corman-Pettis veto; and an amendment unrelated to the emigration debate.

As the final hour drew near for the vote, the State Department attempted to draw attention to the fact that Soviet authorities were letting a record number of Jews emigrate in spite of the October Yom Kippur War. Three thousand, six hundred and sixty Soviet Jews were allowed to leave in October, and the rate for November was estimated to approach that figure. According to the State Department, the number in 1973 had already reached thirty-two thousand—six hundred more than the 1972 total. State officials offered the press the opinion that the high numbers resulted from Brezhnev's promise to Nixon earlier in the year that thirty-five thousand were to be allowed to emigrate.[159]

The information impressed few. On the eleventh, the House voted by an overwhelming 319-80 to include the entire Jackson-Vanik amendment and defeated the Conable move to delete Title IV by an impressive 298 to 106. The entire Trade Bill passed as amended 272-140—the smaller margin indicating that organized labor was cutting into support for the bill as a whole. The bill was referred to the Senate for its consideration, and the Congress recessed until January 1974.

SUMMARY

Jackson seemed to begin and end 1973 with the same aim in mind: to achieve maximum bargaining leverage vis-à-vis the Soviet Union and the administration to advance his amendment. Legislatively, his tactic was to attach his amendment to legislation the administration badly wanted. He assiduously gathered backing in the crucial House Ways and Means Committee. In the House of Representatives at large, he and his House ally Charles Vanik lined up cosponsors and leading House personages as primary sponsors of the amendment. During 1973, Jackson also expanded his base of support principally among Jewish groups, but also added other ethnic, economic, and ideological groups as supporters. Labor, Eastern European ethnic groups, and liberal intellectuals were the most significant additions.

While building support, the Washington senator resisted compromises offered by the administration (in cooperation with the Soviet Union) by basically staying a step or two ahead of and generally outsmarting his adversaries.

Jackson's adept tactics were probably the most important factors in the executive-legislative contest that was played out in the Ways and Means Committee and the full House of Representatives in 1973. Once the administration woke up and began to appreciate the threat Jackson presented to the fulfillment of its trade pledge to the Soviet Union, a number of attempts were made to head off Jackson. Some were more skillful than others. But basically administration policy—heavily influenced by presidential assistant Peter M. Flanigan and National Security Assistant and Secretary of State Henry Kissinger—proved to be no match in Congress for Jackson and Representative Vanik. Each time it appeared that the administration was making headway in eroding Jackson's support—particularly in the Jewish community—Jackson managed to recoup and prevail. The most dramatic example of this came in April when the Soviets suspended the education tax and in October when the war in the Middle East broke out.

The administration was determined to fulfill its pledge to the Soviet Union embodied in the October 18, 1972, trade agreement. Before the Trade Bill was submitted to Congress, emphasis was placed on quiet diplomacy with the Soviets to encourage liberalization of its emigration policy. Once the Ways and Means Committee went into mark-up sessions, the administration tried to keep the amendment out of the committee version of the bill. When it became clear that that was impossible, delay was the administration's last resort, with the president threatening veto for some of that time.

Jackson, in contrast, adhered to a single no-compromise strategy. Among the possible explanations for Jackson's unyielding response was that Jackson resisted being maneuvered by a compromise that he was not party to. He may have also considered the concessions the administration received from the Soviets inadequate. His pledge to Meany that he would not compromise on his amendment until the Soviets had actually conceded to all the conditions laid down in the amendment probably reinforced this adamancy. In addition, Jackson may not have wanted to break a winning record that he had amassed since the Moscow summit in his challenge of the Kissinger-Nixon detente policy.

In May, as Kissinger left for Moscow to prepare for the Brezhnev Summit, he told the Jewish leaders that they should each go their separate ways and meet again in the fall. The fall, however, had proved to be disastrous as Ways and Means Committee action on September 26—with Mills absent—prevented the administration from giving MFN to the Soviet Union. What remained to be fought in October was the administration's desire for authority to give credits to the Soviet Union without the emigration conditions that had been linked to MFN. The October war in the Middle East presented some opportunities for Kissinger to maneuver, but eventually Jackson got his way completely in the House of Representatives.

Jackson, Vanik, and the Jewish organizations who for the most part had gone along with the strategy of no compromise were victorious. The margin of victory was nearly four to one. But labor, Jackson's other major ally acquired during the House fight, had, in the words of one observer, been "snookered." Ironically, the Jackson amendment helped insure passage of the labor-despised Trade Bill first by the Ways and Means Committee and then by the full House of Representatives. In the committee mark-up, members were voting for provisions in the Trade Bill that were counter to labor's view as they assumed that the AFL-CIO would be mollified so long as the Jackson amendment—championed by Meany—was included. Labor urged the members of the committee not to report the bill. After they did, the AFL-CIO issued a statement on October 19 that ironically concurred with Kissinger's assessment that the committee bill was "worse than no bill at all."[160] Labor worked hard for the two months before the final vote in the House, but again the attachment of the popular Jackson-Vanik amendment to the Trade Bill aided its passage, albeit by a lesser margin than had been recorded for the Jackson-Vanik amendment.

If Meany was chagrined, Dobrynin personally and the Soviet government generally were positively abashed by the results of the 1973 House battle. The Soviet embassy and Dobrynin personally were reprimanded by authorities in the Soviet Union for not having reported the threat of the Jackson amendment in Congress early enough and accurately enough. In April there had been published reports that Dobrynin would be posted in Moscow after Brezhnev's trip in June, but that never happened.[161] By early November, Anatoly Gromyko, son of Soviet Foreign Minister Andrei Gromyko and an expert on the United States by virtue of his former position as head of the Foreign Policy Section of the USA Institute, was stationed as a new minister counselor in the Soviet embassy possibly to establish another channel of communication to Moscow arguably to compensate for what was perceived to be a faulty channel in the person of Dobrynin.

As for the administration, so bungling were they in the House that one Ways and Means Committee member was heard to complain, "The Administration didn't fight until after the votes were taken though we warned them nine months ago. . . . The leadership in the White House has not been properly attuned to the problem and not able to lead and so poisoned the well." Representative Conable concluded, "The President and Mr. Kissinger may not have kept track of what was going on here. They did not realize that MFN was being opposed not just by the American Jewish community, but by a very impressive coalition."[162]

Little wonder then that a Jackson aide would boast in 1973: "Look at our record. When have we lost?"[163] Jackson, who had signed up three-quarters of the Senate, in 1972, was prepared for the 1974 fight in the upper house of Congress.

The Senate, Soviets, and
Nixon Negotiate

4

> The great mystery in this Administration is who's making the decisions. . . . Look at the impeachment schedule. How can Nixon focus? He prides himself on foreign policy, but he's distracted. . . .
>
> HENRY JACKSON[1]

> The acid test of a policy . . . is its ability to obtain domestic support.
>
> HENRY KISSINGER
> *A WORLD RESTORED*

INTRODUCTION

On January 21, 1974, the second session of the Ninety-third Congress convened, and the Jackson amendment battle was renewed in a new arena, the Senate. In 1973, the administration and the Soviet Union, which based its policy on advice from the administration, had tried first to ignore Jackson and his amendment. Later, the administration tried getting around Jackson with concessions on the education tax. Still later, it had tried to confront the amendment head-on in the House of Representatives. All failed. Having lost the legislative battle, the administration (and to a lesser degree, the Soviet government) had little alternative but to negotiate. After several months of preliminary jockeying for positions, trilateral talks began in spring 1974 involving two branches of the United States government and a foreign power.

The individuals involved were (1) Jackson, with Ribicoff generally reinforcing him and Javits sometimes challenging him; (2) Kissinger, whose presidential patron Richard Nixon was debilitated by the Watergate scandal; and (3) Dobrynin, who was reinforced by Foreign Minister Andrei Gromyko and General Secretary Leonid Brezhnev. The three Soviet officials apparently spoke on behalf of the dominant group in the Kremlin at the time. Although Jackson dominated his own forces, he could not control the action on his own terms as he had in Congress in 1973. Kissinger enjoyed a special status since he alone controlled the communications between Jackson and the Soviet Union. In effect, the secretary of state was the only one of the three parties involved who knew what all sides were saying in the secret, informal sessions.

Compared to these negotiations, the deliberations of the Senate Finance Committee, which was responsible for the Trade Reform Bill, was a sideshow. During this period, the Senate Banking Committee also considered the related Export-Import Bank Bill, which enormously complicated the legislative picture and clouded the trilateral negotiations.

LAUNCHING THE TRILATERAL NEGOTIATIONS

Like the Japanese legend of Rashomon, there are several versions of how the three-way negotiations actually began, each version differing depending on who tells it. Examining the various versions will help piece together why by early March 1974, Kissinger and Jackson were willing to begin negotiating a solution to the trade-emigration impasse.

VERSION ONE

According to an aide of Senator Javits, Javits was "the key." Javits had "contacts in Congress with the Republicans" and credibility as a Jew "to do what was best for Jewish interests." Thanks to him the negotiations got started. Operating "under general orders from Javits," Albert (Peter) Lakeland, a former foreign service officer in Javits' employ, conveyed a threat to Jackson's office. Lakeland found it personally difficult to conduct dealings with Jackson's aide Perle. So he conveyed the threat through Ribicoff's aide Morris Amitay. Lakeland told Amitay to tell Perle that Jackson had better meet with Kissinger. Lakeland also told Kissinger's executive assistant Lawrence Eagleberger that Kissinger should meet with Jackson.

Javits personally reinforced the message delivered by his aide when he saw White House aide Peter Flanigan at a Senate briefing on February 6, 1974. Javits also had a private meeting with Kissinger at the State Department where he warned Kissinger that he could never win in a head-on confrontation with Jackson. Javits guaranteed a favorable Senate response if Kissinger really worked on the emigration issue with the Soviets.[2]

VERSION TWO

Another version gives the impression that Jackson was the initiator of the negotiations. Accordingly, Perle met United States Special Trade Negotiator William Eberle on January 29, 1974, in a quiet spot in an Armed Services Committee room. Perle put out a feeler: If the Soviet Union would give specific assurance to the Nixon administration that it would grant about one hundred thousand visas a year and end harassment, Congress might be willing to allow the president to extend the trade benefits without insisting on prior Soviet performance.[3] According to a Jackson source, Eberle reportedly claimed he was authorized to negotiate with Dobrynin concerning the Jackson amendment. Jackson doubted Eberle's claim. To check it out, Jackson inquired with Kissinger. To check with Kissinger, he used the excuse of asking Kissinger to inquire about a fourteen-month delay in a Dobrynin response to a letter sent by Jackson. Using this convoluted excuse to contact Kissinger, Jackson got Kissinger to the negotiating table. According to a Jackson aide, Jackson never expected to insist on the "draconian measures" in the Jackson amendment. "All along, Jackson saw an outline for a compromise."[4]

VERSION THREE

A third version of how the negotiations began credits Ribicoff and is related by one of his aides. "For a year and a half," he said, "Kissinger never talked to Jackson about the trade-emigration issue. Then Ribicoff saw Kissinger at a party and said, 'Why don't you see Jackson; you've spoken to practically every Jew in the country' about this issue. And the next day, we had set up a meeting."

VERSION FOUR

The next version gives the administration entire credit for initiating discussions in the spring of 1974. Henry Jackson was the source for this version, which shows the administration giving in first. "Only after a change in Administration policy that resulted in the first reluctant approaches from the Administration early this year did negotiations aimed at the reconciliation . . . get underway."[5]

The administration's decision to have Kissinger open negotiations with Jackson was motivated by various factors. Javits and Ribicoff were urging such a move. So were various officials within the administration. Said one top Special Trade Representative official, "We got Henry stirred up." Secretary of Treasury George Shultz also had a hand in encouraging Kissinger to meet with Jackson.

VERSION FIVE

The administration's willingness to negotiate with Jackson was important. But Soviet willingness was also necessary. In the early months of 1974, several events occurred indicating the Soviet leadership was learning to appreciate the destructive potential of the Jackson amendment. The clearest sign of a changing Soviet attitude was that Soviet leader Leonid Brezhnev dispatched Foreign Minister Andrei Gromyko to Washington in early February. Gromyko "conveyed his government's decision to seek an agreement with Jackson." The meeting, which took place in the White House on February 4, was interpreted by some as a sign that the Soviets were now "ready to make concessions on Jewish emigration that will placate" Jackson.[6] It is not known whether this was an additional element impelling Kissinger to deal with Jackson or whether the administration had been a force impelling the Soviet Union to look for an accommodation with Jackson. What is known is that both the administration and the Soviet Union were indicating their willingness to deal with Jackson at approximately the same time.

For whatever combinations of reasons, Jackson and Kissinger finally sat down to talk at the State Department on the evening of March 6, 1974. Kissinger offered the idea—raised by the administration the year before—of granting trade concessions provided that after a time, Congress could review the situation and if it felt the situation merited it, Congress could withdraw the concessions. Jackson rejected the idea. Little else was accomplished. The negotiations were at least launched, albeit in a cloud of mutual suspicion. Quipped a Ribicoff aide, "Now at least [Kissinger] is talking out of both sides of his mouth; before [it was] only out of one side."

The two principals agreed to talk further. Jackson wanted to know just how far the Soviet Union was prepared to go to advance an agreement before Jackson would further commit himself. Jackson argued that "to make his case to the Senate, the Secretary of State must make our case to Moscow."[7] Kissinger had a meeting in Moscow scheduled for March, which provided an opportunity to get an answer for Jackson.

THE SENATE FINANCE COMMITTEE SIDESHOW

Before Kissinger embarked for Moscow to sound out the Soviet leaders, he had another obligation to fulfill. He was scheduled to appear at the Senate Finance Committee Hearings on the Trade Bill on March 7, 1974. In light of the private Jackson-Kissinger tête-à-tête the evening before and Kissinger's plans to go to Moscow, the hearings were, in effect, a sideshow to the trilateral negotiations that had been launched.

A Ribicoff aide had predicted that the hearings would be a "charade." It was, however, a very elaborate charade for the benefit at least of the press. The hearing room of the Finance Committee looked more like a reception hall for the benefit of all the individual actors and groups involved in the Jackson amendment debate. Heavily guarded by Capitol police and blinking in the lights of the national network television cameras, various senators waited for the privilege of shaking hands with Kissinger for photographs that would appear in the nation's newspapers the next day. On a lower echelon, the audience was packed with Israeli, Soviet and other nonmarket nation diplomats, American trade and State Department officials, congressional aides, and lobbyists for business, Jewish, and other interests. Finance Committee members sat at a U-shaped, raised dais. Behind them sat their staff who whispered advice to their superiors throughout the hearing.

Kissinger's statement on Soviet trade concessions was originally drafted by the Soviet desk in the State Department and reworked by Kissinger's personal assistants. Some of the remarks added by Kissinger's aides raised the ire of Jackson's supporters and the eyebrows of Soviet desk officers and trade specialists in the State Department. Kissinger warned that the number of emigrants might drop to zero. The Soviet desk said it had never heard Soviet authorities make such a claim. Kissinger also erroneously argued that the emigration issue had not been raised until after the October 18, 1972, trade agreement had been signed when in fact, Jackson's amendment was formally introduced in Congress on October 4. These remarks and the fact that he had been orally briefed beforehand, not by the economic bureaus or Soviet desk in the State Department, but by a few people around him like Executive Assistant Lawrence Eagleberger and Winston Lord, director of the State Department Policy Planning Staff, had yielded these *faux pas*.

However, at least one other person from outside Kissinger's inner circle did prepare Kissinger to testify. Thomas ("Tom") Korologus, the White House liaison to the Senate, sent Kissinger a memorandum reporting a compromise suggestion from the Congress. Korologus had heard the idea for a substitute to the Jackson amendment during an informal meeting with Senator Gaylord Nelson (D.-Wisc.). The Nelson idea, said William Eberle, had been "a source of inspiration for compromise" between the Senate and the administration.[8]

Kissinger had raised a similar idea the night before only to have Jackson flatly reject it. At the hearings, both Nelson and Senator Vance Hartke (D.-Ind.), who were unaware of the previous evening's meeting between Jackson and Kissinger, raised the idea again. It was the first public discussion of a compromise to the Jackson amendment. Until then, Jackson's staff had managed to squelch public airing of the private agonizing and searching for alternatives by Jewish groups and congressional offices. When Hartke and Nelson raised the subject at the public hearings, Kissinger was prepared, apparently thanks to Korologus. Kissinger reacted favorably making no reference to his meeting with Jackson or to Jackson's negative reaction to it.

NELSON: Would it not be more effective to accomplish the purpose of the Jackson Amendment and not destroy the trade reform legislation, by providing that the President could negotiate most-favored-nation status and credits with any country in the world not now enjoying this status and providing that at some subsequent date—every year or whatever—that those agreements would come back under the concept of the Reorganization Act. Either House may then veto any one of those agreements if it decided that the country receiving most-favored-nation status or credits, is conducting itself in a way that is offensive.

KISSINGER: Without committing myself to whether either House or both Houses should have the right; whether it should be one year or two years, I think that the concept by which the Congress can review an Executive determination, looking back for some reasonable period is one in which the direction of a compromise might well move. . . . it would have the advantage, at one and the same time, of achieving our objective of being able to grant most-favored-nations status and achieving the objective of the sponsors of the amendment by having their goals remain a live pressure on the process rather than be accomplished on the day that the amendment is signed.[9]

Kissinger testified that "I have not had a chance to study all the possible compromises that might be made. . . ."[10] However, Helmut Sonnenfeldt, Kissinger's aide, had discussed various formulas for compromise with Jackson aide Perle. Sonnenfeldt also consulted with the legal staff of the Special Trade Representative's office. "Sonnenfeldt would take them and talk with Henry and Perle," said a top STR official. Other times, Perle's formulas for compromise were passed to Kissinger over Eberle's signature. But Kissinger appeared not to follow up the staff suggestions, which rendered STR hamstrung and frustrated and the Finance Committee rudderless.

It can be argued that had Kissinger bothered to study the proposals for a compromise and to work with senators like Nelson, Hartke, and the others previously mentioned, he might have had a stronger position from which to bargain. This was the second time the administration had passed up the chance to encourage a compromise initiated by the committee in charge. The first time was during the Corman-Pettis fight in the Ways and Means Committee.

Kissinger explained, "I have hesitated putting forward a compromise proposal because I did not want to turn it into a contest between an administration proposal and that of the sponsors of these amendments because I am very hopeful that we can come up with something that everyone will agree to."[11] Kissinger apparently recognized the difficulty inherent in sidestepping Jackson and decided it was not worth the effort. The night before the hearings, Kissinger and Jackson had finally entered negotiations. Moreover, once in negotiations with Jackson, it was difficult to try the committee route. Kissinger agreed to negotiate only on the basis that Jackson would negotiate in good faith. It is not unlikely that Jackson extracted the same pledge from Kissinger.

Nevertheless, the possibility that a compromise might be worked out between Kissinger and the committee was a major concern in Jackson's office. Hours after Kissinger testified, Jackson's staffman Perle telephoned the office of Senator Nelson and accused Nelson of being part of a "prearranged dialogue" with Kissinger that was part of "an effort to do in the amendment." In 1973, Perle had taken pains to warn Nelson's office not to advance a compromise. On March 7, 1974, Nelson was theoretically in an even better position to push a compromise. He was a member of the Finance Committee where the legislation was under consideration. There were signs in the Senate of disaffection with the Jackson amendment. Perle said, "I'm going to spend my April recess apprising people of Nelson's idea; it would kill the amendment." Perle suggested he would focus his propaganda in Nelson's home state of Wisconsin, where Nelson was running for reelection.

Javits also continued to push Jackson to negotiate. When Javits' office learned that the Jackson-Kissinger meeting was occurring, it was demanded that henceforth Javits and Ribicoff must be at all subsequent meetings. Perle allegedly tried to resist the demand that Javits participate in future meetings. Javits' aide responded to Perle by threatening that even though it was twelve o'clock when the aides of Jackson and Javits were tussling, he could have fifty-one senators on a Javits-led compromise to the Jackson amendment by five o'clock in the evening. After that, Javits was at all subsequent meetings.

All three senators attended the next meeting with Kissinger on Friday, March 15. At Jackson's request, Richard Perle had prepared a memorandum, which, as Jackson explained, "set forth the general outlines along which a compromise aimed at breaking the deadlock between the two branches of government might be negotiated."[12] Ribicoff and Jackson said that Kissinger would have to get certain assurances from the Soviet Union on certain major points before the senators would consider compromising on the original terms of the Jackson amendment. They told the secretary of state, who was about to leave for Moscow, that harassment would have to end and the number of emigrants permitted to leave the Soviet Union would have to be "substantially increased." The figure they discussed was reported to be "well in excess of the current [sic] thirty-five thousand. . . . Aides of the two Senators would not divulge the specifics of the ideas presented, but other sources said that a guaranteed figure as high as one hundred thousand emigrants a year was mentioned to Mr. Kissinger as a possibility."[13] (Javits' views were not reported.)

OUTLINES OF AN AGREEMENT

Kissinger left for Moscow March 23. He called it "a more difficult period" than any of the past times he had visited Moscow. On the one hand, "Jackson and Ribicoff insisted he raise the question of Soviet emigration policy with Soviet officials."[14] On the other hand, the Soviet government was "impatient with the Nixon Administration for not having made good on promises to relax high American tariffs on Soviet goods" and had warned against injecting the emigration issue into the Moscow talks.[15] A March *Tass* commentary had just accused Jackson of following "a policy of extortion" and attacked him for not yielding to Kissinger on the trade issue.[16]

Aside from the Jackson amendment, it was a particularly touchy moment for Soviet-American trade discussions of any nature. On March 8, the United States General Accounting Office had announced that in its opinion, the president had not followed the law of the Export Expansion Finance Act under which the president was authorized to extend loans to the Soviet Union. From March 11 to 23, the Export-Import Bank ceased processing loans for the Soviet Union. On the eve of Kissinger's departure for Moscow, the attorney general issued an opinion disagreeing with the GAO, and $44.4 million of loans were released. The crisis had injected tension into the atmosphere. Discussing linkage of trade and emigration would only make matters worse. In Moscow the American party also got the impression that the Soviet leadership might be biding their time waiting to see the outcome of the domestic debate over Watergate.

Reporters were only able to glean news that the Soviet leadership had shown some slight flexibility on the Jewish emigration issue.[17] Kissinger told reporters that after twenty hours of talks with Brezhnev and Foreign Minister Andrei A. Gromyko, he believed he had some new "clarifications" to bring back to Congress that might encourage an eventual compromise.[18] The seriousness of the Jackson amendment had been driven home to the Soviet leadership. American diplomats had the "impression that the Kremlin now understands that trade concessions to Moscow have only a very slim chance of passing during the current session of Congress."[19]

When Kissinger returned to Washington, he happened to speak with Senator Alan Cranston on April 10. He described to him the Soviet position on the Jackson amendment as having given him "the surprise of his life." The Soviets were willing to make an "indirect deal" with Congress concerning their emigration practices.[20] One report said Kissinger stated that the Soviet leadership was agreeable to making assurances that the number of emigrants would be paced at the 1973 level—thirty-five thousand. This could not have been too much of a surprise; emigration figures had declined in early 1974, but the Soviet Union already had "guaranteed" (Kissinger's word) the Nixon administration that thirty-five thousand would leave in 1973.[21] What was surprising was that the Soviet leadership was willing to work on an arrangement in the face of Jackson's public demands. Kissinger had said Jackson's amendment constituted interference in Soviet domestic affairs in contrast with quiet diplomacy. But the Soviets seemed willing nonetheless to make concessions for Jackson's sake.

"American officials," however, were reported to believe that the Soviet offer was neither enough nor sufficiently concrete to sway Jackson.[22] Kissinger had an opportunity to see for himself when he took Senator Jackson aside at an Israeli embassy party the night before Kissinger left on his honeymoon. It is not known what Kissinger said; chances are he reported what he had told Cranston.

Two weeks later Kissinger saw Gromyko in Washington, and on April 26, 1974, Kissinger met with Senators Jackson, Ribicoff, and Javits. According to Javits' account of the breakfast meeting, Kissinger's report on his recent conversations in Moscow was a "very objective elucidation." Javits said, however, that there was no sign of Soviet "movement" on the trade-emigration issue. Javits said the "idea is that the Secretary go back and talk some more." Ribicoff reconfirmed what administration officials had feared would be the senator's reaction: "Nothing we got would satisfy the Senators," said Ribicoff. Jackson "suggested" a target figure of one hundred thousand Soviet Jewish emigrants annually. The figure was conceivably a tough bargaining position that Jackson was assuming. The day before the meeting, a Javits aide had said confidentially that "nobody is committed to one hundred thousand." Harassment was the other unresolved issue. "Figures don't mean much if people are being harassed every time they step near the American Embassy," Javits pointed out.[23]

According to Kissinger, "the three Senators agreed to an approach in which I would attempt to find clarifications of Soviet domestic practices from Soviet leaders. These explanations could then be transmitted to them in the form of a letter behind which our Government would stand. My point of departure was statements by General Secretary Brezhnev during his visit to the United States in 1973 to both our Executive and members of Congress to the effect that Soviet domestic law and practice placed no obstacles in the way of emigration."[24]

The substantive issues—numbers and harassment—had not been settled. However, the senators and Kissinger had agreed on the procedure for handling the Soviet assurances, which the senators demanded as preconditions to compromise. Apparently the letter device permitted communication of key points to the senators without embarrassing the Soviet government by making it appear as if it were capitulating to Jackson's demands. In this regard, Brezhnev had earlier indicated to Senator Edward Kennedy who was visiting Moscow in April that there was room for compromise provided Soviet cooperation was not whipped up in America for political gain. The letter device also permitted the institutionally jealous executive branch to maintain a monopoly over relations with foreign governments.

When the senators and the secretary of state met in late April, Kissinger had already planned another meeting with Foreign Minister Gromyko to take place in Geneva on Sunday and Monday, April 28 and 29.[25] The two foreign ministers discussed the trade-emigration issue in Geneva in April and in Cyprus in May.[26] Gromyko probably came to those meetings with an even fuller understanding of the constraints Congress was putting on the award of American trade concessions to the Soviet Union since he had just discussed the issue with Senator Edward Kennedy on April 21, 1974, when the visiting Democrat was in Moscow. The discussion with the well-informed and respected senator should have helped counteract the Soviets' initial underestimation of the broad American public appeal of the amendment.

During the month of May, while Kissinger was on his whirlwind shuttle (from April 28 to May 31), Kissinger and Gromyko met three or four more times to discuss the Middle East and other questions. Subsequently, it was reported that in a meeting with Kissinger in Cyprus, Gromyko was willing to talk about the figure of forty-five thousand Jewish emigrants per annum. Further, the Soviet authorities were willing to state that harassment was "inconsistent with Soviet laws."[27]

While Kissinger and Gromyko were making headway in their talks staged in the Middle East, several extraordinary events occurred in Washington that suggested the administration was rewarding Soviet cooperation in the emigration talks. Nixon personally intervened in a decision to expedite a major Export-Import Bank loan application for the Soviet Union. He wrote a letter to bank President William J. Casey, received Monday, May 20, requesting an end to the months of delay in the decision to grant the Soviet Union a low-interest loan for the unprecedented large sum of $180 million.

"There was no explanation for the timing of the Board's action," reported *The Washington Post*.[28] The timing of the loan might have been connected to the breakthrough on the trade-emigration issue. Rewarding the Soviet Union (or giving it an economic incentive for good behavior) was in keeping with Kissinger's use of the Export-Import Bank loans and other trade benefits as means for advancing diplomatic ends vis-à-vis the Soviet Union.

The president's personal intervention into the Export-Import Bank activity in the Soviet Union in late May coincided with a sudden meeting called by the chief executive with the chairman of the Finance Committee, Russell

Long, and its ranking minority member Wallace R. Bennett (R.-Utah). In the presence of Peter Flanigan and William Timmons, the president's liaison with Capitol Hill, Nixon requested Long to begin mark-up of the Trade Bill "as soon as possible." He told Long he was sure something could be devised on the emigration issue that he would not veto. After the meeting, Long issued a statement that he would hold a mark-up session, but his statement did not indicate how close the trade-emigration issue was to being resolved.[29]

The meeting with the Finance Committee leaders to clear the way for the Trade Bill and break the log jam on credits for the Soviet Union may have had an additional objective: to insure Soviet receptivity of Watergate-plagued Nixon in Moscow in late June. If it was intended to clear the path for Nixon in Moscow, Nixon should have been disappointed by how the Soviet press covered his reaffirmation of intentions to visit. The Soviet paper reporting a meeting between the president and the visiting parliamentary delegation headed by Ponomarev on May 23 ignored the president's strong statement of his plan to visit in June in spite of the threat of impeachment. This oversight was reported from Moscow as a signal of Soviet uncertainty of Nixon's ability to survive in office or to visit the Soviet capital the next month.[30]

JACKSON CONSOLIDATES HIS STRENGTH

Jackson seemed to be taking all precautionary measures possible to maintain maximum control during this period. The administration had not provided him direct information regarding the progress of the trade-emigration talks between Kissinger and Gromyko. On May 23, Ribicoff aide Morris Amitay stated his belief that "Kissinger hasn't even presented Jackson's position to the Soviets." Gromyko had suggested to Kissinger that forty-five thousand emigrants a year might be an agreeable number, and he had indicated that the Soviet authorities would state that harassment was inconsistent with Soviet law. But Jackson may not have known this, and if he did, Kissinger had not told him so formally. Kissinger did not return to the nation's capital until May 31. He did not convey the news of Soviet assurances to the Senate sponsors until June 5.

What Jackson did see quite clearly, however, was that Chairman Long had promised the president to begin mark-up of the Trade Bill and that Nixon had intervened at the Export-Import Bank to have millions of dollars of loans extended to the Soviet Union. It would be natural for Jackson not to want to lose control of the trade-emigration issue after having scored the successes he had to date. The anxious state of Nixon, who was besieged by scandal, also may have given Jackson cause for concern.

EXPORT-IMPORT BANK

An obvious target in any consolidation of Jackson's strength was the Export-Import Bank.

While the Nixon administration was using the Export-Import Bank to advance its relations with the Soviet government for various reasons, Jackson was simultaneously focusing on the institution to consolidate his leverage over administration trade policy with the Soviet Union and to insure his strong role in the trilateral negotiations. The Jackson amendment to the Trade Bill made both the granting of most-favored-nation treatment and the extension of credits (and credit guarantees) by the Export-Import Bank (and by other means such as the Commodity Credit Corporation) contingent upon the president's reporting semiannually to Congress that the Soviet Union was not restricting emigration. During the entire time that the Jackson amendment was debated in Congress, the president had no authority to give the Soviet Union MFN as he had promised to do in the October 18, 1972, trade agreement with the Soviet Union. He did, however, have the authority to extend credits. Credits had been arranged for the Soviet Union ever since the spring of 1973.

It so happened, however, that while the administration, Congress, and the Soviet Union were involved in the three-way negotiations over the Jackson amendment to the Trade Bill, the president's authority to use the Export-Import Bank was due to expire June 30, 1974. The administration requested congressional authorization to continue operations of the Bank. The legislative history of the authorizing bill, the Export-Import Bank Bill, became entangled in the fight over the Jackson amendment to the Trade Bill.

The close relationship between the two bills was perceived in Congress months earlier. When Congress convened after its recess in January 1974, conservative Congressman Richard Ichord and liberal Representative Les Aspin (D.-Wisc.) had introduced with eighty-nine cosponsors a resolution in the House of Representatives stating that the Export-Import Bank should not lend to the Soviet Union until the Senate had resolved the Jackson amendment controversy. The same resolution was introduced in the Senate on March 11 by Senators Dominick, Brock, Ribicoff, Williams, Buckley, and Helms. (By May, the measure had 225 House sponsors and was adopted by the House Committee on Banking and Currency.)

The Export-Import Bank had the potential for reinforcing Jackson's bargaining position vis-à-vis Kissinger by further restricting the administration's discretion to use trade as an instrument to advance its detente policy with the Soviet Union. At the same time, the bill also had the potential of becoming a substitute for the Jackson amendment. In that case, it had the potential for reinforcing the administration's search for a compromise.

From April through mid-June, a great debate took place behind the scenes in Congress, which ultimately determined which way the bill would actually go, and, by extension, whose position—Jackson's or Kissinger's—would benefit. Jackson and his staff kept close tabs on the Export-Import Bank Bill. The bill was being considered in the International Finance Subcommittee of the Senate Banking, Housing and Urban Affairs Committee. The Subcommittee Chairman Adlai Stevenson III solicited Jackson's views on the legislative future of the bill. Jackson and Stevenson met several times to discuss the subject during May and June. On the staff level, Perle held parallel sessions with Charles ("Chuck") Levy, legislative assistant to Senator Stevenson, and Stanley Marcuss, assistant staff counsel on Stevenson's subcommittee.

An early Jackson decision was to oppose adding the Jackson amendment to the Trade Bill to the Export-Import Bank Bill as well. In return for withholding support of any move to tack the amendment onto the Bank Bill, however, the principal sponsors of the Jackson amendment exacted a promise of favorable Banking Committee action on proposals for congressional review over Soviet credit transactions that would reinforce Jackson's emigration-related restrictions.

As one congressional aide active in those legislative strategy sessions said, "We're not going to let this [Export-Import Bank Bill] get away from us. We're not going to lose control of the amendment."[31] A Ribicoff aide explained, "We're not linking emigration to the Banking Committee Bill." However, he believed that Banking Committee limitations would reinforce the aims of the emigration movement. "If you have the Congress involved . . . you might get a lot more give on the Soviet side." For example, when large Export-Import Bank deals were pending and if Congress had some kind of veto over those transactions, Soviet behavior on emigration would likely be improved.

Insisting that the Banking Committee add congressional review procedures in exhange for not tacking on the Jackson amendment to the Bank Bill coincided with the desires of the AFL-CIO. As one Jackson ally explained, "For good economic and political reasons, Congress [ought] give Congress a veto" over major credit transactions with the Soviet Union. As in the Jackson amendment case, the economic and political concerns of Jackson and the AFL-CIO converged on the Export-Import Bank legislation. Both objected to the transfer of technology and productive capacity to the Soviet Union. Both objected to the use of Export-Import Bank loans to encourage such transfers. Andrew Biemiller, director of the Department of Legislation of the AFL-CIO, testified, "Why should the United States be using the American taxpayer's money to strengthen the war machine of the Soviet Union? . . . No matter how you slice it, such loans are free foreign aid to the Soviet Union."[32]

The Jewish leaders went along with Jackson's legislative strategy (as they had throughout the year) not to link the Jackson amendment on emigration directly and explicitly to the Bank Bill. Jewish representatives were invited to testify at the Senate Banking Committee hearings on the Bank Bill. An executive meeting of the National Conference on Soviet Jewry and the Conference of Presidents of Major American Jewish Organizations considered the invitation. NCSJ Washington representative June Rogul interpreted the proposed amendments to the Export-Import Bank Bill to be a backstop, a reinforcement to the Jackson amendment to the Trade Bill. The Jewish leaders decided, therefore, that they had nothing additional to request. So it was agreed that the chairman of the NCSJ would not appear personally before the Banking Committee.[33] Instead, Chairman Lowell sent a statement for the record reiterating support for the Jackson-Vanik amendment. He in no way recommended that the Jackson amendment be attached to the Export-Import Bank Bill.[34] For the remainder of the year, the Jewish groups failed to keep up with the development of the Bank Bill even though it was closely associated with the Jackson amendment.[35]

If others failed to recognize that the Export-Import Bank Bill, if amended, might potentially serve as a compromise substitute to the Jackson amendment, at least Adlai Stevenson III did. Stevenson also pushed his amendments because, he stated, there were strong economic and political reasons why Congress should exercise some oversight of the Export-Import Bank. The economic reasons echoed those laid down by the AFL-CIO. The political reasons were that Congress should have a say in major foreign policy issues.

The administration missed the opportunity Stevenson perceived and presented them with. Kissinger was in the Middle East during the month of May when the early discussions on the future shape of the Export-Import Bank Bill were taking place in Congress. Stevenson, however, tried to use one of his witnesses from the banking hearings, Marshall Shulman, then a professor at Columbia University, to establish a link between himself and Kissinger. At first, Kissinger cabled back not to discuss compromise with anyone except the principal sponsors of the Jackson amendment. In June when Kissinger returned from the Middle East, he spoke with Stevenson at least twice and possibly as many as six times. In one of their earlier conversations, Stevenson raised the idea of putting a $300 million credit ceiling on the Soviet Union. Stevenson told others that Kissinger "seemed receptive." Kissinger reportedly went further by suggesting that it might be used as a bargaining chip for dealing with the Soviet Union. Said Stevenson, "throughout consideration of the legislation, Administration spokesmen made it clear that the provision was one the Administration could live with and Secretary Kissinger, himself, raised no strenuous objections."[36] Kissinger's office paid so little attention to this potentially explosive legislation that one of his closest advisors actually gave "Jackson credit for not weighing down the Ex-Im bill."

The result of the months of behind-the-scene discussions manifested itself on June 17. Stevenson, Jackson, and eighteen other senators introduced a package of amendments to the Export-Import Bank Bill. Among the provisions of what was then known as the Stevenson-Jackson amendment was authority for Congress to review all bank transactions of more than $50 million and a ceiling of $300 million on new credits that could be extended to the Soviet Union alone. Speaking to the Senate when the amendments were formally introduced, Stevenson made clear the degree to which Jackson was author of the provisions. "This amendment reflects [Jackson's] concerns, as well as a prodigious commitment of his time and effort."[37]

The Senate Banking Committee considered the Stevenson-Jackson amendment the very next day. Stevenson may have thought he could accommodate himself to Jackson and the Export-Import Bank. However, administration officials at the bank opposed the restrictions of their lending discretion, and the committee cooperated with the administration by eliminating the ceiling. Nevertheless, the committee could not eliminate the possibility that the two senators would try again to add the ceiling in the form of an amendment offered from the floor of the Senate when it was debated by the full body.[38]

THE JEWS

Another target in consolidation of Jackson's strength would be those who had toyed with compromise in the past. In 1973, during the fight in the House of Representatives, the biggest threat came from within the Jewish community itself—from those who were close to Nixon and/or were fearful of having to choose between Israel's future and Soviet Jewry's future. To avoid that recurring in the Senate, the Jews tended to remove themselves from the fray completely.

Other considerations also placed the Jews in a more retiring position during 1974. The Yom Kippur War of October 1973 made both the state of Israel and its ruling Labor party preoccupied with regaining their strength. Israel was concerned about military security. The party was trying to recover from the debilitating December 1973 election from which Prime Minister Golda Meir never fully recovered. As late as March 1974, the Labor party was unable to form the necessary coalition to govern the country under its proportional representation parliamentary system. After the Labor party finally succeeded in forming a coalition in the spring, the government became immersed in an even tougher political exercise: negotiating a troop disengagement with Egypt that was acceptable to Israeli public opinion. In sum, the Israeli government was even less inclined to get involved in the American political debate over the Jackson amendment than it had been in 1973. This situation put the United States administration at a disadvantage since it could do little to influence Israel to side with the administration on the Jackson amendment.

The desire to avoid being wedged between two branches of the United States government applied equally to the state of Israel and the American Jewish community. In addition, lack of clear guidance from the Israeli government discouraged the taking of a sure and independent line adhered to by

American Jewry. In early 1974, changes in the top leadership of the two major organizations also made a difference. Jacob Stein, the chairman of the Conference of Presidents of Major American Jewish Organizations (Presidents' Conference), and an individual who had tended in the past to cooperate with the administration in calling for a compromise on the Jackson amendment more than his constituent membership might have wanted him to, tried unsuccessfully to retain his position at the end of his two-year term in office. Rabbi Israel Miller of the American Zionist Federation replaced him.

The Presidents' Conference and the National Conference on Soviet Jewry had earlier agreed that the two umbrella groups would represent American Jewry on the question of Soviet Jewry. The National Conference on Soviet Jewry also changed chairmen. Richard Maass, a supporter of George McGovern for president in 1972 and a man with a liberal political outlook, was replaced by Stanley Lowell, who has been described elsewhere as simply "tough."[39] A one-time aide to New York City Mayor Robert Wagner, attorney Lowell applied his political savvy acquired in New York politics to extracting maximum concessions from the Soviet authorities. The appointments of Miller and Lowell probably reinforced the tough stance of Henry Jackson.

Moreover, the few Jewish leaders who wanted to compromise on the Jackson amendment after having scored the dramatic victory in the House of Representatives were, for all practical purposes, silenced. In December 1973, several important Jewish leaders had broached the idea with Jackson, who reported shot back at them, "If we had listened to that kind of line, we wouldn't be where we are today." Jackson told his visitors that he would push ahead in the Senate fight regardless of their lack of support.[40]

The few Jews favoring compromise were virtually inconsequential. The prevailing viewpoint of the organized Jewish community was expressed in a confidential document circulated in early 1974 among Jewish activists involved in the struggle. The author prescribed the role the Jewish groups ultimately followed—with only one significant exception—throughout 1974:

> . . . public interest groups do not function independently of the Congressional sponsors, and certainly do not engage in activities that might affect the legislation without the sponsors' knowledge. . . .
>
> As a result of the community undertaking to back Jackson-Mills-Vanik, the leadership assumed two critical obligations: the first was to faithfully reflect and support the position of its constituency; and the second was to faithfully act in support of the legislative leadership. For the most part, the Jewish community leadership fulfilled these obligations. The exception to an almost universal pattern, and unfortunately the most damaging to the objective because it was the most visible, was reflected by the behavior of Max Fisher and Jacob Stein. . . .
>
> The behavior of Fisher and Stein reflected . . . a neglect of obligations

. . . to the congressional leadership with whom the constituency was allied for the enterprise at hand.[41]

Ironically, Henry Kissinger was slow to appreciate the degree to which organized Jewry was surrendering its independence to Jackson. He told a Senate gathering on March 7, 1974, that "I have been meeting regularly with the leaders of the Jewish community. . . . I think that in the contest that is now evolving, there is a possibility of getting a hearing for a compromise from the Jewish groups. . . ."[42] On April 10, National Conference on Soviet Jewry Chairman Lowell put a damper on Kissinger's talks with unauthorized Jewish leaders. Lowell testified to the Senate Finance Committee chaired for the occasion by Senator Abraham Ribicoff. Lowell was accompanied by NCSJ's Elihu Bergman and June Rogul and by Tina Silber of Jackson's staff. Lowell attacked Kissinger's efforts to court sympathetic members of the Jewish community and set the record straight as to who spoke officially for organized Jewry.

Lowell also took the occasion to "reject the efforts that have been made by some to tie Soviet Jewry and its problems to what happens in the Middle East and to Israel. We believe that this linkage is a scare tactic and should be rejected by the Senate." Lowell explicitly rejected the notion of compromising or finding alternatives to the Jackson amendment. Any form of substitute to the Jackson amendment was simply "wrong." In support of this uncompromising position, he quoted a Jackson statement as gospel: "Any serious effort to resolve the differences between Congress and the Administration on this issue must begin with the Soviet Union. That is where the problem and the potential for solution both lie."[43]

Lowell was attempting to counteract the airing of alternatives to the Jackson amendment that had occurred when Kissinger and Senators Gaylord Nelson and Vance Hartke had discussed substitutes at the Finance Committee hearings on March 7, 1974. Lowell's remarks were also intended to silence doubters within the Jewish community who might have wanted to work out a compromise sooner than Jackson's timing might have dictated. The so-called unauthorized Jewish leaders who met with Kissinger several times in April were well aware that Jacob Stein, who had dared to differ with Jackson, had become "persona non grata" in the Jewish community. They also knew that Jackson had threatened to go over the head of any other leader trying to follow Stein's example and search for a compromise without Jackson's say-so.

On April 23, a committee meeting of the Synagogue Council of America provided a rare opportunity to see behind the scenes into the Jewish community's internal debate regarding the best strategy to follow on emigration. At the Finance Committee hearings, Lowell had successfully papered over the differences with the community and muffled public debate. But there were still a few individuals who doubted that Jackson's approach was the best one. Elihu Bergman argued that the Jewish community should not deviate from Jackson's position because to deviate would be a dangerous signal to "the enemy." A few of the participants at the meeting mumbled that Bergman had become one of "Jackson's *apparatchiki*." Rabbi Arthur Hertzberg, president of the American Jewish Congress, whose membership is generally from professional, business, or academic backgrounds, openly debated Bergman. Hertzberg argued that while it was alright to pursue a bargaining game for a while, it was essential to back off eventually from confrontation with the Soviet government. He elaborated that in the long run confrontation would be of no benefit to those Soviet Jews who would eventually settle in Israel. Hertzberg also argued that the Jackson game, which Bergman was advocating adherence to, was proving to be very risky. He pointed to the decline in the number of Soviet Jews emigrating in the first quarter of 1974. It had dropped an estimated 25 to 30 percent from the previous year. Nothing was resolved at the meeting.

As for the Soviet Jews, on whose behalf the battle was being waged, said a National Conference on Soviet Jewry official, "The Soviet Jews kept telling us to support the Jackson Amendment . . . the most active spokesmen, at that time, were in unanimous agreement. They . . . sent out a lot of documents. . . . We solicited [them]. . . . We got documents. . . ." Even though "some of the language was naive," this contributed to the strong support in the American Jewish community for the single legislative approach of the Jackson amendment.

Jewish deviation would be no problem for Jackson. If Kissinger wanted to get a compromise, he had to deal with Jackson and Jackson alone. The Jewish community—either willingly or because it was cajoled into silence—more or less abdicated its power to Jackson who made all the decisions about legislative and negotiating strategies.

CONGRESS

Another potential source of discontent was from other legislators. Those who were cosponsors presented a greater threat than those who were not. In the Senate, Jackson had seventy-eight Senate cosponsors, an apparently formidable base of support. However, a closer examination of the collection revealed that Jackson did not completely control the group. Less than enthusiastic cosponsors of the original Jackson amendment included Edward M. Kennedy (D.-Mass.), Lloyd Bentsen (D.-Tex.), Hubert H. Humphrey (D.-Minn.), Edmund Muskie (D.-Maine), and Walter F. Mondale (D.-Minn.). There were others, too, but these men were particularly significant because, like Jackson, they were potential presidential candidates and would have a political stake in seeing Jackson's diplomatic campaign surpassed by a substitute amendment.[44]

Senator Ernest Hollings (D.-S.C.) was another senator in search of a compromise. He called Theodore Sorensen, formerly President Kennedy's speechwriter, who was working as an attorney in New York City. Hollings had read Sorensen's critique of the Jackson amendment in the winter 1973 issue of *Foreign Affairs* magazine. Hollings said Sorensen "asked for a way out of the Jackson Amendment." A staff member for Hollings met with staffers of Senator Alan Cranston (D.-Calif.) and Gaylord Nelson (D.-Wisc.) to discuss substitutes to the Jackson amendment in mid-April. Cranston, the self-appointed whip for the Senate liberals, had made a head count and discovered that forty-one members—twenty-four of whom were cosponsors of the amendment—would go for a Javits-sponsored compromise, if it were offered.[45] The erosion of cosponsorship support concerned the Jackson forces.

The toughest test of loyalty would come if Congress had the opportunity to vote for a Javits substitute compromise to the Jackson amendment since Javits was a Jewish senator and an original cosponsor of the Jackson amendment. Javits had all of these less-than-enthusiastic senators "in line," in the words of a Javits aide. They were "ready to follow Javits at any time." The aide recalled an exchange between himself and a Jackson aide about head counts in early 1974. The Jackson aide claimed Jackson would get a majority on an "up or down" vote. The other Senate aide retorted that there would be no "up or down" vote to test Jackson's strength. Rather the test could come on a Javits substitute and in that case Javits would win. But Javits was running for reelection in New York State—home of the world's largest Jewish community—he also had to be careful not to alienate his Jewish constituents who actively supported the Jackson amendment.

Alan Cranston also received a flood of telegrams from California regarding the Jackson amendment soon after one of his aides received a visit from June Rogul, the Washington representative of the NCSJ who worked closely with Jackson's office. Rogul came around to Cranston's office inquiring whether her information that Cranston was wavering in support of the Jackson amendment was true.

It was also deemed necessary to prevent Gaylord Nelson, who was not a cosponsor, from introducing a compromise at this unsure stage in the three-way negotiations. Ribicoff staff man Morris Amitay telephoned Nelson's office on May 23. He opened the conversation by remarking that the "Jewish community is pretty solid in support of us" (the Jackson amendment forces). "One of the things that has percolated back to me from Wisconsin," he said, "was a rumor that Nelson will introduce a substitute amendment to the Jackson amendment. . . . Since he is on the Finance Committee and a respected voice, to offer a substitute amendment" would be a threat to Jackson's monopoly. "It would seem to the Soviets that they can get" away without dealing with Jackson's demands. Another factor in Amitay's thinking was that "naturally we have erosion—lots of Republicans."

On the one hand, Amitay remarked, "We know he is sympathetic to the [Jackson] objective." But, he warned, if Nelson went through with his alleged plans, "we will fight it and it will get messy." The conversation closed as it had begun: "I would hope for the sake of the cause, [for] Nelson ['s sake], and your sake, if he has to do something, maybe he should talk to Jackson and Ribicoff" first.

Fearful that Nelson might still introduce a substitute compromise at what he argued was a strategic moment in the tripartite negotiation, Amitay placed a long-distance phone call to a leader in the Jewish community in Wisconsin who happened to be close to Nelson personally and politically. The man also happened to know the executive vice-president of the American-Israel Public Affairs Committee, I.L. Kenen. When Amitay called, he explained that he would soon succeed Kened as head of the Jewish lobby group.

Amitay explained in the hour-long call that he wanted the Wisconsinite's help in convincing Nelson not to offer a substitute to the Jackson amendment. Nelson was a "respected" member of the Finance Committee. He might pull support from liberal Democrats, from Republicans loyal to the administration, and from the twenty-two senators who had never cosponsored the amendment.[46] Instead of Nelson, the staffer suggested that a "President's man," a Republican who was willing at that late date in Nixon's political career to help out the Watergate-plagued president, introduce the amendment. Of course, legislation sponsored by any such "President's man"—if one indeed existed—would have only pulled the support of the declining number of Nixon loyalists. Apparently Ribicoff's aide wanted to make any compromise so weak it would be easily vulnerable to attack by Jackson and his forces.

Amitay argued that if Nelson, who was running for reelection that year in Wisconsin, introduced the compromise, it would hurt him among his Jewish constituents. The Jewish leader had been involved in discussions the year before between Nelson and the Jewish community on Nelson's stand on the Jackson amendment, so he knew how the Jewish community felt. He also was involved in Nelson's reelection campaign, so he had a good idea of Nelson's excellent chances for reelection. He disputed the staffer's thinly veiled concern about Nelson's political future. "It wouldn't hurt Nelson. The grassroot members of Hadassah [the Women's Zionist Organization] may grumble and mumble, but when it's all over" Nelson, who is well known as a maverick and reputed for his independence of thought, would not be hurt. The leader continued, "I won't ask the Senator not to introduce this amendment. He's very sincere and feels that détente must be assumed to have some merit and be best for the country, for the Jews, for Israel, etc."

After about an hour of conversation, the Wisconsin leader declared, "Why are you calling me? Why doesn't Javits, Jackson sit down with Nelson. . . . Don't call a constituent" to put pressure on his senator.

On May 28, a related phone call from the office of Senator Clifford Case (R.-N.J.) was placed to Nelson's office. Case's assistant said he had heard

Nelson was circulating a document to members of the Senate for cosponsorship. It was, he claimed to have heard, a substitute to the Jackson amendment. He asked if there was any truth to the rumor. Nelson's office indicated that Nelson was considering compromise solutions.

At 11:10, moments after Case's office had called, Richard Perle telephoned Nelson's office: "Do you want to tell us how you intend to introduce the amendment or shall we wait until it appears in the *Congressional Record?*" were his opening words. He quickly followed the first question with a second, "How many cosponsors do you have?"

Jackson's aide had the same objective in mind as had Amitay. It must have been an extraordinary coincidence that Case's aide telephoned only moments before Jackson's man. Jackson's staffer continued to argue as had Ribicoff's staffer, "We've got negotiations underway with Kissinger. He has taken our proposal to the Russians. We've asked for an increase in the number of visas and an end to harassment." He continued, "We would not write the number [of emigrants agreed upon] into the language of the bill but rather rely on private agreement, which remains to be worked out." Jackson's original position was the amendment itself. Jackson had made a major concession. Jackson was no longer insisting on the Jackson amendment as originally drafted. "That's come to an end. . . . It's a question now of getting something out of the Soviets. This will all come clear . . . we've done a memo which outlines the kind of harassment that is inconsistent with the Jackson Amendment and with the idea of free emigration. In addition to an agreed number of visas, there would be provision for applicants to take his place in [line]. . . . The flow is going to be limited but substantial compared to thirty-two thousand" and applicable to all Soviet citizens, not only to Jews.

He was asked how he could be asking for Soviet assurances in May 1974 when Jackson had charged (correctly) that the number of emigrants had declined, as Jackson's aide put it, "despite Russian assurances made in April, 1973 announced to Kissinger and to the President." Jackson's staffer replied, "We don't intend to take the Russian assurances. But we will take the assurance from the Administration and then also there is a way to keep legislation on the books as a last resort." He explained that to break the impasse on the Jackson amendment, "the amendment might provide a waiver [to Jackson's restriction]. The legislation would be changed." Allowing a waiver on these terms displayed a trust of the Soviets and Kissinger, which revealed how much Jackson would accept in order to get a final agreement.

Jackson's man was concerned that Nelson's involvement would create a contradictory signal to the Soviets that would bode ill for Jackson's bargaining position. He provided information to indicate Jackson's good faith in the negotiations. He argued that the time was key and that introducing an amendment would be damaging to the ongoing negotiations. He, too, talked about making a contribution to the Jewish cause. "It would be a real contribution to the cause" if Nelson did not introduce a compromise. Then his tone of voice became menacing. He warned Nelson not to "sell out" by implying that Nelson would be made a scapegoat if the dicussions broke down. He was warning Nelson "so no one can claim afterwards that he didn't know negotiations were underway. We know that your boss has an amendment. . . . I am cautioning you. It is wise not to get caught up into [this battle]. We will press it [the original Jackson Amendment] on the floor if we need [to]."

The tactical key to the telephone call was then revealed: "the only reason I care two hoots about Nelson's putting in the amendment" was that "if there is going to be an effort to kill the amendment—and it would kill the amendment and the Jewish community knows it—if there is going to be a gut, we'd rather fight the Republican Administration than fight" Nelson.

The day after the flurry of phone calls to Nelson, the Finance Committee returned from Memorial Day recess. Chairman Long held the first mark-up on the Trade Bill June 4 just as he had promised the president. Neither Nelson nor any other Finance Committee member introduced a substitute. But the possibility that a substitute would be introduced may have helped keep Jackson at the negotiating table.

Jackson, Ribicoff, and Javits saw Kissinger on June 5 and learned there was significant movement on the part of the Soviets. (The progress at the trilateral informal forum was reason enough for others who were not principal actors not to get involved with substitute language.)

On the same day that Kissinger saw the three senators, President Nixon delivered a hard-hitting speech at the United States Naval Academy in Annapolis, Maryland, which must have appealed to the Soviet leadership. He argued that "we cannot gear our foreign policy to transformation of other societies." The statement was aimed against the Jackson amendment. It may have also served the president's purpose of signaling the Soviet leadership that Nixon—in the weeks before the Moscow summit and in the maelstrom of Watergate—was still willing to stand up to the critics of detente, the shining achievement of his presidency.

After the speech, seven leaders of the Jewish community, including Max Fisher, Stanley Lowell, and Rabbi Israel Miller, arrived for a meeting with Nixon. Nixon's remarks had upset the Jewish leaders, who announced to Kissinger their intention to say something about it to Nixon. Kissinger's imprint on the speech was clear, so it was ironic that he suggested it would be better if they did not say anything to Nixon. Instead, he volunteered to speak with the president about it himself. After the meeting, the Jewish leaders reported that Nixon had "reaffirmed his concern for the fate of Soviet Jews."[47]

What the three senators and the Jewish leaders heard from Kissinger and the president on June 5 must have been encouraging. It was the first time that Jackson's Jewish forces saw fit to indicate publicly that they were no longer tied to the original language of the Jackson amendment. The June 5 NCSJ statement supported not so much the Jackson-Vanik bill per se, but rather the members who had voted for it in the House and who were cosponsors of the amendment in the Senate. The NCSJ—reflecting Jackson's lead—were no longer wedded to the original language of the Jackson amendment.[48] Over the weekend of June 8, Jackson was in Wisconsin where he sounded a note of reasonableness and moderation. Essentially he stated publicly for the first time what his staff and Ribicoff's staff had been saying privately to those who were anxious to see an accommodation in the protracted battle over the Jackson amendment: "We're not asking for everyone to be let out of Russia at once."[49]

Kissinger also seemed pleased with the progress in his talks and with Jackson's receptivity. He told the Senate Foreign Relations Committee on June 7 that it was time to start talking about changing the wording of the Jackson amendment. "It is my belief, that those concerned with Soviet emigration should now be working on a reformulation. . . ."[50]

The remarks of both men indicated the trilateral talks were running smoothly. However, the Jackson camp was nervous about not being in total control during the negotiations, perhaps from fear that Kissinger knew more about what both the Jackson forces and the Soviets were saying than Jackson himself did. They also recognized that Nixon was anxious to clear the way to a summit scheduled for late June, which might distract attention from Watergate.

Jackson had also experienced Soviet concessions before. The April 1973 suspension of the education tax was the most dramatic example. At that time, he had moved swiftly and effectively to reinforce his position lest the image of Soviet reasonableness erode support for his position as he bargained with the administration and the Soviet Union. In May of 1974 he had managed to forestall the Finance Committee from developing a compromise reminiscent of the Ways and Means struggle in the fall of 1973 during consideration of the Corman-Pettis compromise and during the Yom Kippur War. At this juncture, he reinforced his position by gaining control over the future disposition of the Export-Import Bank Bill, thus preventing it from becoming a jumping-off platform for impatient senators wishing to get off the Jackson amendment by adopting an amendment to the Ex-Im Bill embodying periodic congressional oversight of credit to the Soviet Union.

JACOB JAVITS AND INTERPRETING PROGRESS IN THE TRILATERAL TALKS

The big question was what Jackson was willing to settle for to justify forsaking his original amendment. There were signs of movement, but Jackson had not formally relinquished support of his original amendment. He may have discussed with Kissinger the possibility of moving away from that position, but that appeared to be the extent of his concessions. Without semblance of movement, however, it was difficult to keep some of his Jewish supporters and congressional colleagues from challenging his lead. "Javits and Ribicoff caved in several times in negotiations with Kissinger, but Jackson who is not Jewish had to spend the second half of at least one meeting propping them back up," said a Jackson aide. In negotiations, sometimes it seemed as if Jackson—the only non-Jew—had to lecture Kissinger, Sonnenfeldt, Javits, and Ribicoff—all Jews—about what was best for their coreligionists in the Soviet Union.

The issue over which the next challenge to Jackson arose concerned the interpretation of the report Kissinger delivered to the three senators at the June 5 meeting. It constituted the greatest challenge to Jackson's almost exclusive control of congressional will. The purpose of that meeting was for Kissinger to report on his latest talks with Gromyko. After the meeting, Ribicoff told reporters that he felt that "some progress has been made." Kissinger told the press the following day also that "while some progress is being made" on gaining Soviet assurances of emigration of Jews, he would not give details "until we have had some further discussions."[51] Jackson and Javits were noncommittal, except for the previously mentioned encouraging remarks Jackson had uttered in Wisconsin, far from the Washington or international press.[52]

By the third week of June, however, the participants were no longer noncommittal. They were in fact squabbling openly about what precisely Kissinger had said at the June 5 meeting. The *New York Times* reported that Kissinger had told the senators the Soviets were willing to guarantee in writing that forty-five thousand Jews a year would be permitted to emigrate; in addition, the Soviets were willing to deal with the problem of harassment of would-be emigrants by stating that such harassment was "inconsistent with Soviet laws." But the *Times* report went on to say significantly that "some [sources] said they understood that Mr. Gromyko actually put forward proposals. Others said that Mr. Kissinger merely undertook to state to the Senators what his understanding of the Soviet position was."[53]

The participants also disagreed in their interpretation of the significance of the June 5 meeting. Jackson seemed to perceive less progress than the others. Jackson's viewpoint was articulated by one of the *New York Times* "sources," which expressed continuing concern about "quality, extent and form" of the agreed figure.[54] Jackson's staff was concerned about what the so-called assurances assured: Would the agreed number of emigrants insure the departure of intellectuals and others from the Soviet cities of Moscow, Leningrad, Kiev? Many of the Soviet Union's most important Jewish activists fell into this category. Many had already been refused permission to leave. When Jackson reviewed the progress report on the latest Gromyko-

Kissinger meeting, he must have considered the reaction of the Jews who had been most vocal and who had shaped his emigration policies thus far. Activist Maria Slepak, the forty-seven-year old Moscow physician and wife of radio electronics engineer and Jewish activist Vladimir Slepak, expressed the sentiment of urbane intellectuals who had been refused permission to emigrate. "They can find forty-five thousand a year from Georgia, Dagestan, and Bukhara. They'll have enough for ten years without Jews from Moscow and Leningrad. The quota does not decide anything."[55]

Jackson also wanted to push for "well above" forty-five thousand.[56] An aide at the time believed the Soviet Jewish requests for invitations from abroad, the necessary first step to emigrate, were being solicited at a rate of sixty thousand a year. That may have been a clue to the number Jackson was seeking.

Personality and substantive differences over how to interpret progress in the trilateral talks formed the basis for a Jackson-Javits split, which led to the greatest crisis among primary Senate sponsors since Javits and Jackson had sparred over the original language of the amendment in September 1972. Until this point, Jackson and Javits had worked reasonably well together despite some underlying animosity at least on the staff level. So long as Jackson was negotiating and seemed receptive to the Kissinger-conveyed assurances from the Soviet Union, Javits had no reason to complain. That and the fact that he was in a close reelection race had been constraints on his offering a substitute to Jackson's amendment. By mid-June, however, it appeared there were disagreements over just how much more the Senate trio should demand from the Soviet Union.

Perle resorted to a by then familiar mode of operation. He telephoned his friend Malcolm Honlein, director of the Greater New York Conference of Soviet Jewry, and said he was worried about Javits' position. What followed, said a well-known New York Jewish organizer, was the second "showdown" with Javits—the first presumably being the September 1972 difficulties.

Honlein arranged an appointment for a delegation of New York Jewish leaders to see Javits in his New York office on June 24. Javits had expected a small group, but twenty-five or so pushed into the meeting. It was crowded and confusing. Honlein was there. So was Eugene Gold, the Brooklyn district attorney and chairman of the Greater New York Conference on Soviet Jewry. One of the Jewish leaders, who was in touch with Javits "fairly regularly," said that Javits "was under tremendous pressure" because he had "strong reservations" about the Jackson position. Javits was "intellectually honest," and made some "unfortunate statements about the amendment and compromise. He refused to say" what the group wanted to hear—that there were no difficulties or differences of opinion about the approach that the senators should take. Instead Javits told the group, "I'm not your Moses." He simply did not say all the "key phrases" in support of Jackson's demands.

After the meeting, the *Jewish Press* in New York ran an editorial criticizing Javits.[57] The kind of opposition generated by the editorial was extremely dangerous to Javits, whose Senate seat was being seriously challenged by former Attorney General Ramsey Clark. A knowledgeable Jewish leader in New York said, "Javits was a dead man. He didn't understand how vulnerable" he was. Later in the fall, for example, a New York rally for Soviet Jewry was held where the crowd booed Javits. But Javits—or at least his campaign and legislative staffs—did appreciate how vulnerable Javits was. One of his campaign executives said the Jewish vote was "absolutely key"; the traditional 45 percent of the Jewish vote that Javits drew in the past was "crucial" in the year 1974.

Javits had had close calls in previous reelections and had turned to Jewish appeals at the last minute with success. In 1962 he lost the Jewish vote to Catholic Democrat James Donavan. Six years earlier, he also lost the Jewish vote although he pledged at the last moment to visit Israel if elected. In 1968 he gained 60 percent of the Jewish vote.[58] In the summer of 1974, when the Jewish groups approached him, and the *Jewish Press* reproached him, Javits "responded to pressure. . . . ," to quote a Jewish activist closely involved at the time. Jackson continued to press for more detailed assurances from the Soviets and an agreement on a number over forty-five thousand, and Javits probably decided not to resist Jackson for the time being.

THE MOSCOW SUMMIT AND STAGNATION

Nixon, no doubt, had hoped that the concessions Kissinger had brought back at the end of May would be sufficient for him to announce a breakthrough either at the summit scheduled in June or as he embarked for Moscow. That became an impossible goal. Instead, the Moscow Summit became yet another opportunity to refine the kinds of concessions the Soviet leaders were willing to make in the face of Jackson's demands.

Days before the summit, Jackson had admitted in a speech to the Women's National Democratic Club that there had been some Soviet movement on Jewish emigration. But he militantly insisted that more concessions were possible "if we remain steadfast. . . . Why give them concessions and ask for nothing back?" he argued. "In the case of emigration we do not ask anything for ourselves nor are we asking the Russians to change their image. We are seeking freedom for others." Jackson did little to improve Nixon's chances of making any progress on the emigration issue once he finally arrived in Moscow. Jackson criticized Nixon for going in the first place. He charged that the trip was intended merely to divert the American public from Nixon's Watergate woes.[59]

In a presummit press conference, Kissinger said he would be looking for a result "in which there is no disagreement between the Senators and ourselves."[60] But there was a third party to accommodate: the Soviets. Even before Nixon arrived in Moscow, the Soviets were signaling that they were not prepared to make any major new concessions on the emigration question. Soviet Jewish dissidents began noting a crack-down on their activities by Soviet authorities.[61] On June 17, Lev Tolgunov, editor of *Izvestia*, wrote a major article construed as a warning to Washington that Moscow was not prepared to make further concessions on the Jewish emigration issue. In the most outspoken report on Soviet-American trade relations appearing to date in the Soviet press, Tolgunov referred to Henry Jackson and his "notorious amendment." He said the legislation provided that expanded Soviet-American trade be accompanied by "American supervision over freedom of emigration of Soviet citizens from the USSR. That is how détente, Jackson-style looks: the Soviet Union under American pressure unimaginable in former times."[62]

In his first public toast to President Nixon upon his arrival, Brezhnev clearly indicated his discomfort with developments in the trade field as a result of activities of certain unnamed individuals—an allusion, of course, to Senator Jackson:

> We all know that much remains to be done here, both in the sense of making economic ties more balanced and stable, and in the sense of clearly establishing the principles of equality and respect for each other's interests in this area of relations. . . . There is no need to dwell on this subject since our American guests know better and in more detail than we about those who oppose international détente, who favor whipping up the arms race and returning to the methods and mores of the cold war. I just want to express my firm conviction that the policy of such individuals . . . has nothing in common with the interests of the peoples.[63]

The emigration question was undoubtedly discussed. Newsmen, however, were treated to the same public response they had heard at the 1972 Moscow Summit. Soviet spokesman Leonid M. Zamyatin announced that emigration "has no relation whatsoever to Soviet-American trade." As Kissinger argued in 1972, Zamyatin said, "I could put the following question to you: Would you agree to making United States trade with the USSR dependent on the solution of the racial problems in the United States?"[64]

Kissinger was in little hurry to report the meager results of the summit to the senators. He arrived in Washington after a trip to Europe on July 10, and met with the three senators on July 18. Soviet leaders had taken exception to reports emanating from the previous meeting between Kissinger and the senators. The reports had said the Soviets might agree to a forty-five thousand emigration figure, a figure that incidentally Jackson had thought too low. The Soviets objected to reports stating that they could not agree to any publicly announced quota for emigration.

Kissinger, however, was able to state that the Soviets had told Nixon they were willing to settle a number of the issues so long as it would not embarrass them publicly. Jackson indicated he understood the Soviets' desire to avoid public embarrassment. It has been an issue previously discussed in the spring when Kissinger proposed and the senators accepted a letter arrangement. It was a point that would become key as the negotiations unfolded in the remaining months of 1974. After the meeting, Jackson said, "I think it's fair to say we made some progress, there is some indication that the Russians want to do something in this area." He emphasized that "The biggest problem we face; we have to find a way to improve the situation on emigration without the Russians' losing face and this is the biggest part of the problem. . . . The Secretary feels encouraged that there can be worked out a formula which will be acceptable which will not embarrass the Russians or cause any problem of face."

The participants at the breakfast, therefore, agreed to work not so much for a publishable quota, but rather to work out procedures that the Soviet Union could agree to that would insure a satisfactory rate of emigration. They agreed to try to develop a detailed proposal to present to the Soviet Union that would contain certain guidelines that would permit a high emigration rate and guard against harassment.

Parts of this plan suited Jackson fine. He, too, wanted to avoid the pitfalls of a quota. As stated earlier, he suspected the Soviets might fill any quota with Jews who were not the most pressing concern to him or to the organized Jewish groups in America. The Jews they were most in touch with were the intelligentsia of Moscow and the Soviet Union's other major cities. To assure their exit, Jackson insisted on an agreement on guidelines he had originally offered to Kissinger in March regarding "quality, form and content" of the Jews emigrating. After the meeting, he explained, "The heart of our problem in working out an agreement is the issue of harassment. It isn't just the numbers of people that will come out, but are there means by which we can be assured that those who apply will be able to get out?"

It was also reported that in return for Soviet concessions, the senators would permit the originally worded Jackson amendment to be replaced with other language that would permit the extension of trade concessions to the Soviet Union that the president had promised two years before. The authority would be granted in such a way that should the Congress be disappointed with Soviet behavior in permitting a given number to leave or in harassing those choosing to go, Congress could rescind the tariff and credit concessions.[65] (This notion was more or less embodied in the Corman-Pettis and Nelson approaches mentioned earlier.)

The summit was an anticlimax. It seemed as if the Soviets were wary of dealing with Nixon who was in his last days in office. It seemed as if Jackson, too, was holding back. Perhaps he, like the Soviets, resisted making a deal with Nixon who was not destined to remain in office for long. The delay, however, made some doubters of the purity of Jackson's motives question whether Jackson was actually negotiating in good faith, just as the Jackson forces had doubted Kissinger's good faith efforts. Was his an effort to find a way out of the emigration impasse? Or was Jackson using the negotiations—much to George Meany's liking—as a tactic for delaying and possibly killing the Trade Bill? The AFL-CIO, chaired by Meany, actively supported the Jackson amendment. The amendment was attached to the Trade Bill, which was opposed by organized labor intent on protecting its workers from foreign competition. Meany objected to liberalizing trade policy if it failed to stop job losses for workers in America. In his view, the bill permitted—even encouraged—export of American technology and factories and, with that, jobs from the United States.

Moreover, Meany claimed that even if the Jackson amendment restrictions on Soviet trade had not been attached to the Trade Reform Act, he still would have been against granting trade concessions to the Soviets. Meany had said, "I trace my anticommunism back to the 1920's, when the Communists made a determined effort to take over our labor movement." Meany thought detente was "an absolute fraud." "Détente," he said, "is appeasement. Nothing else pure and simple, but appeasement. It's a give away in search of profits for our corporations through a combination of American capital and Soviet slave labor."[66]

Nixon was threatening to veto the Trade Bill if the Jackson amendment stayed attached as it had been in the House Bill in 1973. That was precisely what Meany wanted. As long as Jackson held out for his maximum demands on the Soviet Union—as long as Jackson did not weaken the original tough restrictions in the Jackson amendment—Meany was satisfied.

Some keen observers on the scene privately suspected that "Jackson [wa]s without a doubt aiding, abetting, and supporting the unions." According to this view, Jackson's argument that he still had to hammer out the harassment issue was actually an excuse. It was a "vehicle," not a "substantive issue" to drag out the Trade Bill to see it die.

If that were the case, time was on Jackson's side. Chairman of the Finance Committee Russell Long had already announced that nothing would be resolved on the Trade Bill before the November election. Before the November election recess, the committee hardly met. After the recess, there would be a mere month or so until Congress would adjourn the Ninety-third Congress and go into winter recess. In that short time, the Finance Committee would have to mark up the entire, minutely detailed, 124-page bill; the entire Senate would have to vote on it; then there would have to be a conference between the House and Senate to iron out the differences between the Trade Bill as passed in the House of Representatives and as passed by the Senate. If the Congress did not complete all of these necessary steps before adjournment, the Trade Bill would be dead. All the work that had gone into it since early 1973 and all the bargains that had been struck since then would be null and void. Action would have to begin all over again in the Ninety-fourth Congress. That prospect delighted the AFL-CIO, which opposed the Trade Bill in general and the Soviet trade concessions in particular. The longer things dragged out, the more likely the bill would be killed. That is why some people thought that Jackson's strict demands were a way of doing Meany's dirty work to kill the bill.

THE SOVIET JEWS

Others believed that Jackson was sincerely and exclusively concerned about using trade as a lever to extract concessions from the Soviet Union for the sake of Soviet Jewry. If that were the case, time was not necessarily on Jackson's side. It did not make sense to try to drag out the negotiations indefinitely. In the first place, the rate of Jewish emigration in 1974 was down 45 percent from 1973 levels. That should have suggested to Jackson that holding out any longer was becoming a losing proposition, as far as Soviet Jewry was concerned.

Second, if the Trade Bill was dragged out to its death in the Ninety-third Congress, Jackson and the Jews would lose all the leverage on the Soviet Union that Jackson thought he had maneuvered to gain. Jackson thought his leverage derived from withholding trade concessions until the Soviets capitulated. However, if Congress adjourned without passing the Trade Bill, that would be the end of that exercise under optimum conditions in which the amendment had passed one house and was close to passage in the second house.

Finally, while Jackson was using trade as a lever by withholding concessions, the Nixon administration was trying to use trade as a lever by extending concessions. Nixon had offered incentives for future good behavior and had given rewards for past Soviet cooperation. He had tried to smooth the way to the summit, by extending Export-Import Bank loans. That approach had not been entirely successful. The Soviets had seemed to cooperate just so far, but the summit was a disappointment. After that disappointment, there was little chance that extending such large concessions would be tried again. It would seem that if the Soviets had not come around further at the summit, it was unlikely they would do so in the future. Moreover, after Nixon, the next president would not be so desperate to extend such huge amounts of credits.

APPEARING TOUGH FOR THE SOVIETS

One of Jackson's chief aides considered these arguments. But he believed it was not quite time to make a deal. He insisted that time was still on Jackson's side. He argued this from the point of view of what was best for Soviet Jewry. He rejected the suggestions of others that the AFL-CIO's desire to kill the bill was a cross-cutting factor in Jackson's calculations on timing. The most important difference between Meany and Jackson was, "When push comes to shove we'd rather have the trade bill with Title IV [The Jackson amendment] than no trade bill at all. . . ."

His argument was premised on diplomatic calculations, not domestic political calculations, although the two meshed nicely. "We're not going to back down in response to tightening pressure. . . when they [Soviet leaders] see the trade bill going down the tubes, that's the time the Russians will come around. If they [the trade concessions for the Soviet Union] get disassociated from the trade bill, they will never get MFN." He was convinced that Jackson's taking the toughest line was the only way of dealing with the Soviet Union. He did not worry that if the bill passed with Title IV, it might be vetoed at Kissinger's urging. If it were not vetoed, he was not worried that the Soviets might still reject Jackson's conditions. He apparently believed the Soviets would come around before Jackson would ever have to.

A day after the July 18 meeting between Kissinger and the three senators, this same aide commented that contrary to press reports there had been "no discussion about revising the amendment . . . no discussion on changing the language . . . the test is performance on the Soviet side. It would be very bad given the fact that Russia [is] cut[ting] back to permit our position to weaken." Jackson was willing to concede very little. Only, "We've indicated to the Russians—if you solve this deal—that's it. Jackson won't anymore link trade and human rights. This is the one human rights linkage. We won't next demand freedom of press in the Soviet Union," for example.

Another reason for resisting accommodation at this juncture may have been Jackson's desire not to make a deal that the discredited Nixon would have to guarantee.

APPEARING CONCILIATORY FOR HIS ALLIES

While Jackson had to appear tough vis-à-vis the Soviets and Kissinger—his adversaries—he had to appear conciliatory before his allies in Congress and the Jewish community who were anxious to resolve the two-year struggle. This required delicate balancing. While one of Jackson's aides was talking tough in the conversation noted above, another Jackson aide, Tina Silber, spoke of progress toward compromise before an assemblage of congressional aides and Jewish activists.

On the same day as the July 18 Kissinger-Jackson-et al. breakfast meeting, about twenty people gathered in one of the hearing rooms on the second floor of the Old Senate Office Building that was assigned to the Armed Services Committee, one of Jackson's committees. A Jewish activist who had his doubts about Jackson's approach construed the purpose of the meeting conducted by Silber to be "to keep those people with cold feet from actually quitting the Jackson Amendment. . . . There had to be some idea that the game is being played—both in terms of moving toward passage [of the Trade Bill] and of moving toward compromise [of the Jackson amendment]." The meeting therefore was "namby-pamby—'we're making progress and will continue to meet [with Kissinger] again.'" Such reassurance was needed to maintain the silent cooperation of some of the Jewish leaders who were beginning to doubt Jackson's approach in light of the declining number of emigrants.

Some of the Senate staffers who attended the meeting also interpreted the purpose of the meeting as an effort to keep Jackson's forces reined in. While the Jewish activists thought the target of the meeting was the Jewish supporters with "cold feet," the Senate staffers perceived the target of the operation to be Senate cosponsors. "It was an effort to keep everyone together [in a] united front [so as to] speak with one voice." Presumably the one voice was that of Henry Jackson.

Silber took some jabs from skeptical staffers. One asked whether the Jackson amendment would apply to Chinese emigrants since the People's Republic of China was a nonmarket country. Jackson had returned in July from a successful visit there where he met Mao Tse-tung.

Silber preempted other jabs by raising and laying to rest other items that had been used to challenge Jackson. She mentioned that two of the cosponsors of the Jackson amendment were talking about a compromise. One of them was a Republican. This was presumably another attempt to have any challenger to the Jackson amendment painted with the same brush as Richard Nixon who was in his last scandal-filled days in office.

"Tina raised the union argument as a straw man," reported another Senate participant at the meeting. This was an effort to lay to rest the doubts in a growing number of minds in the Senate that Jackson was more interested in killing the Trade Bill for the sake of the AFL-CIO than in finding a resolution to the Soviet Jewry issue in negotiations with Kissinger and the Soviet Union.

Silber also had Charles Levy and Stanley Marcuss, both representing Senator Stevenson, stand up and as one eye-witness said, "give the pitch" that Jackson and Stevenson saw eye-to-eye on legislative strategy for both the Trade Bill and the Export-Import Bank Bill.

A number of Senate sponsors required close attention to assure their loyalty to Jackson's tough stance. Mondale and Kennedy were both represented at the meeting. One Senate staff member was convinced that Jackson put columnists Robert Novak and Rowland Evans up to writing a column suggesting that Mondale and Edward M. Kennedy were wavering in support of the Jackson amendment. Leaking such a notion to the press was apparently intended to push the two men back in line. The column reported that the two Democrat senators were approached to go along with a "ploy by businessmen, hungry for profits from United States-Soviet trade, to use pro-détente liberals as a battering ram against the Jackson Amendment."[67] The column had the happy coincidence for Jackson of enforcing discipline among cosponsors while in the words of one staff member, "it also helps to screw Mondale" and Kennedy—both potential Democratic presidential rivals of Jackson.

Jacob Javits remained the main threat to Jackson from his cosponsors. Javits kept pressure on Jackson to cooperate with Kissinger in the discussions. Lakeland of Javits's staff told an Israeli reporter during this period, "Many Senators were putting pressure on Javits to put forward his own proposal that would have put an end to the Jackson Amendment. This pressure can come up even now if Jackson and his supporters will not be flexible."[68] Publicly, however, Javits had been effectively silenced in late June by a critical editorial in the *Jewish Press* in New York. On July 23 Javits was visited again by a smaller group of New York Jewish activists. In a letter to the editor of the *Jewish Press* one of the participants, Marvin Schick, reported two separate discussions the group held with Javits and with Jackson. Apparently the Jewish leaders who saw Javits in his private office in the Capitol were satisfied that time with what they heard. They concluded that what Javits had said that day and what Jackson had said when he met with Schick and Eugene Gold later in the day were close enough together. Wrote Schick

> We continued to show [the Soviets] and the world that there is a united front on the Jackson Amendment as there is on the issue of freedom for Soviet Jews. Splits and infighting among the supporters of the Amendment, in the Jewish community or in the Senate, is something we cannot afford or tolerate. But had we not found a willingness on the part of the Senator to clarify his earlier remarks or if we had found his answer unsatisfactory, it would certainly not have been kept quiet.[69]

Schick went on to decry "harmful speculation and misrepresentation" carried in headlines stating "Jackson Softens" and "Is Jackson Compromising on Soviet Jewry?" Schick said that "While in Washington, Mr. Gold and I also met with Senator Henry Jackson. . . . the answer [as far as both Jackson and Javits are concerned] is an unqualified 'no.' "

Another complaint voiced by the cosponsors at the time was that Jackson was taking too much time making a counterproposal after the July 18 meeting. A Ribicoff aide defended the senators. He said the administration "puts up a proposal and takes a long time formulating it but then it expects us to offer a counterproposal immediately." The two sides, he said, "need to agree on two more items and get a signature on something."

On August 6, Kissinger proposed to Jackson five ways to express what the Soviets had conveyed to Kissinger: "We have been advised that. . ."; "We are informed that. . ."; "We are satisfied that. . ."; "We are confident that . . ." or "I have reason to believe that . . . ." Neither Jackson nor Lowell of the National Conference on Soviet Jewry was satisfied with the choice presented them. All of them were too "vague." They believed the phrase that Kissinger's letter should contain should read "We have received assurances that. . . ."[70]

This issue was settled soon after Gerald Ford became president at twelve noon on August 9, 1974.

SUMMARY

After an initial period of jockeying for position in early 1974, Jackson and Kissinger (with the Soviet Union in the wings) began negotiating in March. Jackson presented a memorandum discussing the necessary commitments that Kissinger would have to obtain from the Soviets before Jackson would permit any tampering with his originally drafted amendment. Kissinger and the senators agreed on a letter approach by which Kissinger would try to obtain and convey certain clarifications from the Soviets to accommodate the points contained in Jackson's memorandum.

Kissinger returned from Moscow in March with news that the Soviets were willing to cooperate with the senators who were making public demands as they had cooperated in the past with the administration whose demands were couched in quiet diplomatic language. To encourage the Soviets to agree to these demands without public embarassment, Kissinger suggested and the senators agreed to an exchange of correspondence between the two branches of government stating what the Soviets would assure. Evidence suggests that in exchange for Soviet cooperation during this phase of the negotiations, the United States extended the Soviet Union large amounts of low-interest Export-Import Bank loans. Nixon personally interceded with the bank on this question. At the same time, Nixon convinced Chairman of the Finance Committee Russell Long that there was sufficient progress on the trade-emigration question to merit holding the first committee mark-up meeting on the Trade Reform Bill.

By spring a suitable substitute or variations thereof were aired publicly by others: Congress would authorize the president to extend trade concessions for a given period—a year or two. During that time, Congress would monitor Soviet behavior. At the end of the period, Congress had the power to decide whether or not to renew trade concessions. The outline of an agreement was perceivable, but by summer the talks seemed to bog down as Watergate sapped America's political energy.

Behind the sequences of events is the more interesting issue of the political forces driving the tripartite negotiations.

THE ADMINISTRATION

The administration had exhausted three other alternatives: ignoring the amendment, trying to get around it, and confronting it. The 1973 House of Representatives' vote was adequate indication of failure. It was a clear warning of what might be in store for the administration in the Senate if it did not come to terms with Jackson.

Kissinger's career was closely identified with the policy of detente. Kissinger, no doubt, wanted the removal of the Jackson amendment barrier so the administration could make good on its original October 1972 pledge to extend trade concessions to the Soviet Union, which was an important element of detente with the Soviets. Failure to fulfill promises raised questions about America's steadfastness in the diplomatic arena. It even raised questions about Kissinger's personal reliability.

Nixon also needed a breakthrough on the Jackson amendment for both personal and diplomatic reasons. The amendment barred increasing trade with the Soviet Union, which, in turn, was the keystone to the one accomplishment—detente—that Nixon could cling to as an asset amidst all his liabilities related to the Watergate scandal. In January 1974, polls showed only 29 percent of those polled approving Nixon's handling of his job.[71] Eventually, however, Nixon's participation retarded progress in the talks. He was reluctant to alienate the Soviet Union, his partner in detente, which he clung to as a diplomatic achievement that might mask his deteriorating domestic position. His discredited position probably discouraged Jackson and the Soviets from making an accommodation that his administration would have to guarantee.

THE SOVIET UNION

The Soviet Union was learning that dealing exclusively with Nixon and Kissinger was insufficient and that Congress was a force that also had to be dealt with. Senator Edward M. Kennedy (D.-Mass.) was invited to visit Moscow with the understanding that Brezhnev would see him. In the spring, the Kremlin also "took the unprecedented step . . . of dispatching a high-level parliamentary delegation to open relations with Congress, which the Soviet leadership had not previously deigned to recognize officially. Simultaneously, the Soviet press began noticing the bipartisan nature of support for detente among American politicians."[72] The slow process of understanding by spring 1974 of the Watergate scandal probably sharpened appreciation of congressional will vis-à-vis the president.[73]

JACKSON

Jackson was, of course, the third party who had to be willing to negotiate. Like the administration and the Soviet regime, he, no doubt, had a multiplicity of reasons for coming to the negotiating table in March. Primarily, he had—for the first time—someone to negotiate with. Kissinger and the Soviet Union were both indicating a willingness to come to grips with his amendment. Jackson had also achieved a strong bargaining position. He had insisted he needed that before he would consider compromising. The overwhelming four-to-one margin on the House vote and the fact that the Jackson amendment had not been watered down during the legislative process in the House must have given Jackson the confident feeling that he was negotiating from maximum strength.

A number of other domestic and foreign political considerations may have pushed Jackson toward negotiation in early 1974. Jackson's diverse foreign and domestic political targets boiled down to either using trade as a lever to encourage freer emigration, which appealed to American Jewry, or retarding trade with the Soviet Union, which appealed to the AFL-CIO, which also wanted to block the entire Trade Bill.

SCENARIO ONE

Assuming that Jackson was primarily interested in using trade as a lever to force open the gates for more Soviet emigrants, negotiations would have to lead eventually to a compromise on Jackson's original legislation which prevented extending MFN and credits to the Soviet Union until the president certified that exit from the Soviet Union (and other nonmarket nations) was free. Refusing to compromise by blocking trade concessions permanently would mean losing whatever leverage his amendment had given him thus far. If his primary objective was free emigration, Jackson would not want this to happen and would negotiate a compromise before that.

A number of developments in early 1974 indicated that the leverage over the emigration policy derived from the Jackson amendment was beginning to slip. That leverage depended upon a number of factors. One was Soviet economic vulnerability. Speaking in the fall of 1974, Jackson said, "I made a judgment over two years ago that the Russians were in deep economic trouble. . . . I was convinced that we had something that they wanted badly, and that if we stayed firm, we could get concessions out of them. . . . I can just tell you that it is paying off."

Economic Leverage: Throughout the history of the Jackson amendment, Jackson never changed his assessment of Soviet economic vulnerability.

Nevertheless, Soviet economic health improved dramatically between the fall of 1972 when Jackson first introduced his amendment and the early months of 1974 when there had been a recovery thanks to, among other things, a quadrupling in the price of Soviet oil as well as increased earnings for other Soviet exports, which helped gain for them hard currency and a better balance of payments and as a corollary, less need for American trade concessions and less vulnerability to leverage applied by Jackson.[74]

Jackson preferred to read the economic tea leaves in such a way that he was not losing the leverage over the Soviet Union that he supposedly possessed by means of controlling the trade concessions. He persisted in presuming that the Soviet government wanted credits and was willing to make concessions to get them. Soviet economic fortunes may have been shifting during this period, but it did not affect Jackson's calculations. It was not a factor impelling him to negotiate.

Emigration Figures: However, another factor in Jackson's diplomatic calculations had to be the glaring fact that the Soviet Union was responding to Jackson's challenges regarding Jewish emigration in exceedingly harsh terms. The number of emigrants from the Soviet Union began to decline in the months following the House vote. At first the rate was down by 25 to 30 percent. By midyear, the numbers had dropped by 40 percent. The drop was attributable to a new official Soviet restrictive policy and to a decline in the number of applications since the Yom Kippur War in Israel. If Jackson's aim was to help the Soviet Jews, he had to consider that his tough approach might not work for long. If he persisted and refused to negotiate, he might lose all the gains he believed he had made vis-à-vis the Soviet Union. Domestically, he also stood to alienate the Jews in this country and American public opinion in general if his approach turned out to be a dismal failure with serious consequences for the Jews whom he claimed to be helping.

If Jackson interpreted this trend as a sign that the Soviet Union was no longer responsive to leverage applied by his amendment, it was time to change tactics and negotiate a compromise. One clue to Jackson's thinking may have been the National Conference on Soviet Jewry's view, which almost coincided with the thinking of the Jackson office about the facts and interpretations of facts on issues relating to the Jackson amendment. According to the interpretation of an important NCSJ worker, "the drop in emigration was clearly intended to show they [the Soviet leadership] couldn't be pushed around—that the United States legislation was not going to make a difference." Although it may have appeared to observers that Jackson was concerned about this decline, he has subsequently revealed that he was unaware that emigration was declining at this time.[75]

The Soviet response was a tough response to Jackson's hard-line ap-approach. It may very well have been an important incentive to negotiate for

Jackson, the would-be diplomat in pursuit of liberalized emigration for Soviet Jews. This factor also had implications for Jackson, the politician, whose career stood to suffer in the event he was charged with misjudging and miscalculating his campaign to help the Jews. He did not want to have the blood of the Jews stain his career should his hard-line approach fail and the Soviet leaders retaliate against their Jewish population. It was said at the time that Kissinger actually threatened Jackson that if the administration turned out to be right and the number of emigrants actually went down to zero, the administration would wait to blame Jackson when Jackson was in the thick of his presidential campaign.

Controlling the Coalition: A factor leading to Jackson's decision to negotiate was the desire to appear reasonable. Negotiating gave him control over any members of his coalition who might try entering into negotiations without him. A few Jewish leaders and some senators privately voiced their misgivings with the Jackson amendment. A comment of a Jackson aide revealed Jackson's sensitivity to certain elements in the domestic audience that kept him at the negotiating table and eventually pushed him to compromise. "If the negotiations break down, then we have to defend the proposition that we've been reasonable." Jacob Javits was an important part of any assessment Jackson made of the cohesiveness of his original seventy-eight cosponsors and his ability to control his Senate coalition. Jackson could not afford to disregard Javits's and other senators' desire for a compromise. As an aide to Javits puts it, Javits at least could "keep the pot boiling" under Jackson to make him negotiate.

Administration's Interest in the Trade Bill: Another more subtle element developed in 1974 that may have undermined Jackson's strength and thus impelled him to negotiate in the spring and then compromise in June. This was the weight of importance the Nixon administration placed on passage of the Trade Bill relative to the importance it vested in avoiding passage of the Jackson-Vanik restrictions on Soviet-American trade.

Originally, Jackson's amendment to the Trade Bill had been designed to give him maximum leverage in bargaining with the administration. This was achieved by attaching the amendment to the Trade Bill, which the Nixon administration in 1973 had made a priority legislative item. Jackson assumed that if he could hold the passage of the Trade Bill hostage to his amendment, he could eventually force the administration to deal with his emigration demands on his own terms. Up until final passage of the Jackson-Vanik amendment in the House of Representatives, the strategy worked. But in the end of 1973, Kissinger entered the picture in sharp focus. An internal administration debate between Kissinger and the Special Trade Representative's office ensued over whether the president should threaten to veto the Trade Bill with the Jackson amendment. At Kissinger's urging, the Nixon administration took the position that the bill should be vetoed because it considered that the adverse consequences relating to Soviet-American detente of having the Jackson amendment in the Trade Bill outweighed the advantages of the Trade Bill itself.[76]

When Kissinger appeared before the Finance Committee on March 7, Chairman Long asked him "if the bill reached the President's desk in its present form, would you recommend that he sign it or veto it?" Kissinger replied, "It would give us a very, very serious dilemma because we require the provisions of the agreement for the conduct of our negotiations. At the same time, I believe that the bill as it has emerged from the House would do serious and perhaps irreparable damage to our relations with the Soviet Union. I would think very seriously about recommending a veto."[77] He told Senator Hartke at the same hearings that "I would suspect that if the President asked my opinion today I would be inclined to recommend a veto."[78]

At the time, President Nixon was relying heavily on Kissinger as the Nixon administration came under increasing attack because of the Watergate scandal. Kissinger was overheard to say that "In the last year and a half in office . . . in the last nine months, he barely governed."[79] Clearly Kissinger's influence grew as he, personally, and his achievements in foreign policy, professionally, became the single shining asset in the Nixon administration and as the president's attention was diverted to withstanding the domestic attacks on him stemming from Watergate. Kissinger's views dominated the administration's position in those areas that Kissinger really cared about. Kissinger cared a great deal about avoiding a rupture in the detente relationship that he had been constructing since 1969. Kissinger was most concerned about the ramifications of the Jackson amendment on the policy of detente with the Soviet Union. His interest in having a Trade Bill pass to begin international tariff and nontariff barrier negotiations was minimal.[80] Given the choice of having the Trade Bill with the Jackson amendment or doing away with both the Trade Bill and the Jackson amendment together, Kissinger was apparently willing to let the two die. He was not going to let anything, including the Special Trade Representative's office or business lobbies, stand in the way of detente.

Jackson may have taken that into consideration. If Kissinger's view that the Trade Bill was disposable prevailed upon Nixon and if Noxon actually made good on the threat to veto the entire bill including the Jackson amendment, Jackson would be left with nothing at all to show for all his efforts. The possibility of losing all leverage over the administration that had been gained by attaching the amendment to the Trade Bill in the first place may have been another factor impelling Jackson to negotiate by March 1974.

SCENARIO TWO

The above discussion assumed that Jackson was primarily concerned about using economic leverage to liberalize Soviet emigration. If, however,

Jackson's primary diplomatic concern was to retard Soviet-American trade or if it was a domestic political concern to please the AFL-CIO by blocking passage of the Trade Reform Bill, or both (since they coincide), Jackson's calculations about when, if ever, was the time to negotiate and later to compromise would have been different. If he was not primarily concerned about Soviet emigration, the only reason he might have negotiated was at least to appear concerned. As long as he was only negotiating, he did not have to choose between his objectives. He did not have to disappoint Meany who wanted no compromise. From the beginning of the fight for the amendment, Jackson was in the position of achieving all his objectives simultaneously. Choosing between objectives would come only if he decided to compromise to attain one of the objectives that would contradict other aims. By May, the Soviets recognized the seriousness of Nixon's domestic position. Because the talks bogged down in the final discredited days of the Nixon administration, a test of Jackson's commitment to finding a negotiated settlement on emigration was postponed until a new president took office.

President Ford

5

I know the cynicism which surrounds politicians, and I know the cynicism which sur-
rounded the fact that this cause would be
taken up because it was a popular political
cause. But, . . . the deep proof of whether it
is politics or hardened principle . . . is how
the matter was resolved.[1]

JACOB JAVITS

INTRODUCTION

The talks hardly progressed during the summer of Richard Nixon's political demise. Both Jackson and the Soviet government seemed to be treading water until the uncertain element in the three-corner arrangement—Richard Nixon—removed himself. From March, the negotiations had been trilateral. The Soviets had moved slightly toward agreement. Jackson also had edged a little closer to an accommodation. The Nixon administration had been more or less a mediator, undertaking no commitments on its part. To break the stalemate, the new Ford administration found that it, too, had to make some accommodations as had Jackson and the Soviets.

Gerald Ford could break the diplomatic logjam created during the Nixon administration since Ford had the authority to make commitments on behalf of the United States that Nixon came to lack. Ford also viewed the controversy from a different personal and political perspective. As a congressman, he had signed a number of resolutions sympathizing with Soviet Jewry. Yet as minority leader in the House of Representatives, his outstanding quality was loyalty to the position of the administration of Richard Nixon, and he never cosponsored the Jackson-Vanik amendment.[2] As the unelected president appointed by Nixon, Ford could demonstrate his mettle by arranging an accommodation to the Soviet emigration controversy. Finding a way out of the impasse would also be a feather in his cap from the points of view of the various domestic and foreign audiences who were interested. Individuals and interest groups—inside and out of the bureaucracy—who had had little contact with Nixon had access to Ford. The views of business and free traders who wanted a resolution to the Jackson amendment to clear the way for final passage of the Trade Reform Bill competed with the views of Kissinger who saw the bill as an instrument of diplomatic relations toward the Soviet Union.

The advent of November elections and December congressional adjournment concentrated decisions by the major actors to resolve their conflicting views. As the tripartite negotiations reached the end, events accelerated and political calculations of the particpants were compressed. For example, the best time for Jackson to get an agreement on emigration was before the November election and before Congress adjourned in December. One-third of the Senate and an even greater percentage of the Finance Committee were standing for reelection. After the fateful first Tuesday in November, senators were less vulnerable to pressure generated by Jackson's office to keep cosponsors steadfast and to prevent challenges by substitutes or alternatives to the Jackson amendment. Moreover, if Jackson waited too long to agree, Congress would adjourn and the Trade Bill and the Jackson amendment would become dead letters.

RELAUNCHING THE NEGOTIATIONS

Ambassador William Eberle, the president's Special Trade Representative, had tried to convince the Nixon administration to adopt in some form Jackson's compromise suggestions. Eberle found Ford to a better audience than was Nixon, who was insulated by Kissinger from contrary advice. Eberle saw Perle in August right after Ford assumed office. Perle complained, "You know, we have delivered letters to Kissinger but nothing has come of them." Eberle was anxious to push final passage of the Trade Bill. He was looking for a way, in his words, to "get the thing started again." Eberle discussed the problem with William Timmons, the liaison between the White House and Congress. Said another trade official, "Timmons agreed it was festering. He went to Ford on this. Then, the effort was made to get outsiders to nudge Ford along. Someone talked to Melvin Laird [a former colleague of Ford in the House of Representatives and a political adviser to the White House] to bring him in, to tickle him. Timmons got Ford focused on it."

Then, said Eberle, "I wrote a memo to the President explaining it to him. . . . I found out then what was acceptable from Perle: numbers—forty-five to fifty thousand and a procedure [for congressional review of a presidential discretionary authority to grant trade concessions]. . . . The President said, 'This sounds okay to me. I'll have to check with Henry.' . . . [Ford] did pick up."

Another trade official added this to the narrative. "The President told Kissinger, 'you can't sit on this.' . . . Kissinger got the message that he was to find a solution. Kissinger called Jackson and suggested they get together again. When the President heard about the meeting, he said, 'if you are going to meet, meet in my office.' "

In his first speech to Congress on August 12, Ford pledged to make a "good marriage" with Congress. The very next day, congressional aides were telling reporters that a meeting with Kissinger and the three senators had been tentatively scheduled for the fifteenth of August and that the president might personally join the discussions.[3]

The following day, August 14, President Ford met with Ambassador Dobrynin, who had just returned from Moscow. The major topic of the Ford-Dobrynin discussion was trade. J.F. ter Horst, Ford's press secretary, said that:

> Ford successfully persuaded Dobrynin that there never could be a trade bill unless the Soviets accepted some version of the Jackson Amendment. Additionally, Ford impressed the Russians that he personally was sympathetic to the emigration argument and that it should apply not only to Soviet Jews, but also to other Soviet nations from

such countries as Latvia and Estonia that were swallowed up by the Soviets during and after World War II.[4]

The following day, Ford invited the three senators, Kissinger, his deputy Major General Brent Scowcroft, and William F. Timmons for breakfast. During the meeting, which lasted from 8:00 a.m. to 9:10 a.m., ter Horst said his boss displayed "his acknowledged talents as a Congressional arbiter. . . . He convinced his old colleagues on Capitol Hill, specifically Jackson, that he fully understood their legislative objectives in the Jackson Amendment, but would need several weeks to sell the Russians on its merits. He convinced Kissinger that Congressional leaders could be trusted not to surface the details of confidential exchanges between Moscow and Washington which provided a basis for the Soviet-American agreement on the trade pact."[5]

After the meeting with Kissinger and the senators, ter Horst escorted the three senators to the White House briefing room where an official White House press conference was called. Jackson credited "the President's direct participation" for progress in the negotiations. "The President's direct intervention in this matter, which is the new development—this had not taken place before—has given it new momentum, new movement. . . ."[6] Jackson told the press conference that "the issues that we are struggling with, of course, are basically harassment, for those who try to apply, and numbers. . . ."[7] Responding to the suggestion that he was backing away from his original position of "completely free movement," Jackson denied that "the three of us have . . . ever insisted that the amendment would contemplate that those who want to leave all leave at once." Jackson indicated that the decline in the number of emigrants affected his thinking at the time. ". . . what we want is progress, and we want more than what is happening now. They have cut back to one thousand a month, and that is going in the wrong direction."

Jackson tried—successfully—to convey the impression that there had been some "significant Russian movement," which precipitated progress in the talks. He excused himself from providing further details because of Soviet sensitivity to publicity: "Obviously, when you are in the area of negotiations, we cannot discuss the substance of those talks, otherwise we defeat the whole objective here of reaching an accord."

Jackson had often warned of Soviet duplicity. However, at this juncture he did not insist that the Soviets clearly state what they were willing to do. He seemed anxious to trust them. He revealed no desire for something in writing from them. "That is up to the President, he is the one who will have to guarantee, and what arrangements he makes with the Russians, that will be a matter for him. But he has assured us that whatever is worked out that he will see that the guarantees are there, period. And we will rely on his integrity for those assurances, and we have faith in that integrity." He was putting the onus on Gerald Ford. If the agreement broke down, Ford had volunteered to be the scapegoat. Jackson willingly accepted Ford's offer.

Whatever Jackson's term *significant Russian movement* meant, it did not mean new Soviet commitments. Henry Brandon, a reporter who in the past had had very close relations with Kissinger, said he had "a very good source" for the following statement: "The President had no new concessions to offer from the Kremlin, but he took the risk of proposing to hold the Soviet Union personally accountable for more humane immigration [sic] and of assuming responsibility for monitoring the Kremlin's compliance."[7] A Soviet embassy official who visited Capitol Hill offices frequently also said there had only been "clarifications from Dobrynin." That was a far cry from the impression Jackson gave that the Soviets were giving any assurances or commitments. Explained a diplomatic reporter close to the story, "The Russians always said 'no' to any formal concessions. They were not even willing privately to commit themselves." They may have "implied they would have an open mind," the reporter explained. "And perhaps they said their emigration policy would be applied 'in accordance with our law, but we will interpret it in a flexible way.' "

What complicated the interpretation of Soviet behavior was that after the August 15 breakfast meeting in the White House, NCSJ Chairman Lowell was told that Kissinger had conceded to write in the proposed letter to Jackson that "we have received assurances . . ."—the last issue over which the talks had bogged down under the Nixon administration.[8] Naturally the various Jewish groups in the battle believed the Soviets had made some new commitments. Lowell's group was so pleased with what they perceived as "the cooperative attitude adopted by the Soviet leadership through Ambassador Dobrynin, that they actually sang his praise in a press statement.[9] Said another representative of an influential Jewish organization, "Dobrynin did come back to Washington with something new on the Jackson Amendment for Ford and they all decided why not give Ford credit for breaking the logjam."

All three senators told the press that they believed a Trade Bill could be passed. But some skeptics believed that Jackson had not given up thinking about killing the Trade Bill for the sake of the AFL-CIO rather than finding a solution on Soviet Jewry in time to save the bill. They read doubt into Jackson's statement: "We are hopeful that we will be able to resolve this matter *in time* for appropriate action by this Congress."[10] Only time would tell how much effort Jackson would make to resolve the issue *in time*. Until all the details of an agreement on Soviet Jewry were laid down to his satisfaction, the delays involved in negotiating served the AFL-CIO's purpose.

As for the details of the agreement made public to date, there would be an exchange of letters between the president and Congress and some kind of assurance on harassment. A benchmark number of anywhere between forty-five and fifty thousand would be conveyed. Ford would personally guarantee the assurances. The senators were not insisting upon anything in writing from the Soviet Union. In addition, a new clause would be added to the Trade Bill granting presidential discretion to waive the Jackson amendment and extend MFN for at least a year. To renew the waiver of Jackson's requirement that the president file semiannual reports on Soviet adherence to Jackson's criteria for free emigration spelled out, the president would have to make an affirmative move, over which the Congress would still have final authority to veto. A Jackson aide said that while "the report language would be nullified . . . it will be kept in and if there is a breakdown, then the waiver would not count and the criteria would remain."

Several items remained to be resolved relating to the letters to be exchanged between Jackson and the new Ford administration and relating to the waiver authority that would be grafted onto the Jackson amendment. While staff were working on that, the Finance Committee was holding sporadic mark-up sessions on the rest of the Trade Bill. On August 22, the eve of Labor Day recess, which extended from August 23 to September 3, Ribicoff, who was both part of the trilateral negotiations and a member of the Finance Committee, briefed his committee colleagues on the progress of the negotiations. He predicted the agreement would be worked out by early September.[11]

Behind closed doors, some of the committee members expressed discomfort with the situation. One participant at the meeting complained, "The Congress has delegated its authority to a man and his two lieutenants."[12] The power of Chairman Russell Long—who by tradition should have controlled the entire Trade Bill—paled before Jackson, Ribicoff, and Javits, the three self-appointed leaders for the Senate on behalf of Soviet Jewry. Chairman Long said, chuckling, "It's your game, Abe." Long is not known for giving away his innermost thoughts or his considerable power. His cryptic remark at least revealed that the committee was not happy about handing over its oversight authority and policy-making powers to the three senators or to Kissinger. Added to the jealous guarding of prerogatives that prevails as members of Congress jockey for optimum power positions was the skepticism stemming from the Watergate affair. One hesitated to take anyone's word, particularly the word of an extraordinary letter exchange between self-appointed representatives of two branches of the government.

The Finance Committee decided, therefore, that even if it was not involved in drafting legislative language embodying the trilateral agreement, which was due to conclude in early September, it still insisted on hearing from the secretary of state in person before it would report the bill to the Senate floor for full Senate action.

SIXTY THOUSAND JEWS

A "diplomatic finale" was planned to coincide with Foreign Minister Gromyko's visit to Washington on September 20. Ford had arranged successive meetings on that day with Jackson and Gromyko.[13] Forty-five to fifty thousand had been discussed as target figures for annual emigration from the Soviet Union in the wake of the White House meeting with Ford. In June after Kissinger's Middle East discussions with Gromyko, the forty-five thousand figure was originally publicly aired. During the Javits-Jackson strain in July, there were signs that Jackson was pushing for more. Then during the congressional recess that followed the White House meeting, the figure sixty thousand began circulating. A Jackson staffer told a colleague on August 25 that that would be the number in the compromise soon to be revealed. In August, Perle reportedly had increased Jackson's demand to seventy-five thousand. Javits and Ribicoff had rejected that figure outright. The aides of the three senators agreed, however, to Jackson's attempting to get sixty thousand. If that proved impossible, they would all drop back to the earlier demand of forty-five thousand.

Some skeptics, suspicious of Jackson's motives, read the effort to raise the annual agreed-upon emigration is upping the ante to kick the negotiations back to square one. Several observers of the Senate and labor scene believed that Jackson did not want a compromise with the administration and the Soviet Union, but rather Jackson was really doing labor's business. They construed Jackson's behavior as motivated less by concern to reach an agreement with the Soviet Union on Soviet emigration and more by a desire to kill the entire Trade Bill by forcing a breakdown of the negotiations by raising his demands. A breakdown would delay the negotiations and ultimate passage of the Trade Bill before the end of the Ninety-third Congress, which was scheduled to adjourn—at the latest—in time for Christmas.

A related scenario of the skeptics portrayed Jackson making demands that were so tough as to justify Soviet withdrawal from the trilateral negotiations. In that event, the bill would remain with the Jackson amendment's original restrictions as passed by the House of Representatives. Kissinger would then make good on his threat to recommend to the president to veto the entire Trade Bill to kill the Jackson amendment. Since the Trade Bill would be dead too, labor would be happy. In either scenario, labor would gets its way.

Another interpretation of Jackson's increased demand for sixty thousand is that he was squeezing out one last concession before the diplomatic finale. At least Javits was convinced that Jackson's demand was a fair one and added his voice to it. ". . . we expressed it as our view that the *sixty thousand* per annual initial figure given for persons who have applied to emigrate and wish to leave Russia each year remains a solid one, because it is the benchmark which we would apply in the event that the President sought to extend the waiver beyond the first eighteen-month period."[14]

The impression—publicly and privately—was that the Soviet leaders and Kissinger agreed to the larger figure. Sixty thousand "did not raise an eyebrow" at the State Department, recalled an aide to Javits. He did not know why. He said that "surprisingly" the Soviets Kissinger consulted apparently accepted the figures, too. A top administration official in charge of the Trade Bill also recalled, "Henry, I learned, had agreed to sixty thousand; that surprised me." However, there was one contemporaneous report that some congressional sources indicated that a specific number was not completely sure.[15] Since then, Javits has stated "that the Soviets had never provided a figure or a quota of persons who would be permitted to leave."[16] A close associate of Kissinger's has stated that the Soviets never came closer to negotiating a specific figure on numbers than in Cyprus in May when Gromyko talked about forty-five thousand.

By the evening of September 6, Kissinger, Jackson, and Dobrynin had agreed that letters would be exchanged within two weeks—a time when Gromyko was scheduled to be in Washington. Most news accounts perpetuated the impression that sixty thousand was acceptable and foretold an agreement including the following elements:

1. An end to persons being fired from their jobs after applying for permission to emigrate.
2. An end to arbitrary arrests and imprisonment of applicants because they have applied.
3. Stripping such impediments as requiring parental consent for adult applicants to leave.
4. Considering and acting on visa requests in the order in which they are filed. The last specifically applies to a list of Soviet Jews that Kissinger carried to the Soviet Union on a recent visit. Most of the persons on the list have not been allowed to leave.

These points and others would be laid down in an exchange of three letters:

The first letter, signed either by President Ford, or Mr. Kissinger, would go to Mr. Jackson. It would assert that the Administration understood the objectives of his amendment to increase emigration and to end harassment and would report that the Administration has assurances that Moscow would be responsive. In return, Mr. Jackson would send a letter accepting with pleasure the Administration's assurances and asserting his understanding of what they meant by an end to harassment. . . . Mr. Jackson would then assert that if the harassments actually ended, he would have confidence that at least sixty thousand people would be permitted to leave annually. Mr. Ford or Mr. Kissinger would then send a third letter asserting that he concurred with Mr. Jackson's understandings.[17]

LOSING LABOR

Jackson had successfully followed a game plan pleasing not only to the Jewish cause but also to labor's cause. By September, however, Jackson had to choose between the two. If Jackson were to salvage anything from his two-year fight for the Jackson amendment, he had to decide to compromise with Ford in time for Gromyko's visit to the United States on September 20.

The November election was also fast approaching. The most vulnerable moment for Jackson's amendment would be after November. Senators cosponsoring the amendment would be beyond their reelection campaign and feel less anxious about bucking any vocal anticompromise Jewish organizations existing in their constituency. Approximately one-third of the Senate was running for reelection. A majority of the Finance Committee were either running for Senate reelection or running for president and were, as a group, particularly sensitive to pressures emanating from the well-organized Jewish organizations. But in postelection session, if Jackson resisted compromise, many keen observers thought his amendment would probably lose in a Senate vote. Jackson's office conceded that in an "up-or-down" vote on the Jackson amendment, it would be harder for Jackson to succeed after November. Refusing to compromise therefore would risk losing the entire battle. It would also upset his Jewish allies, who saw the fight as a means of exercising leverage on the Soviet Union. It would confirm the suspicions of many of his critics that Jackson had merely been using the Jewish issue to advance his true views as an unreconstructed cold warrior or to mask his efforts to kill the labor-despised Trade Bill.

Compromising to get an agreement on Soviet Jewish emigration meant disappointing Jackson's most powerful potential ally in his bid for the presidency—George Meany. Tension had been building in their personal relationship ever since Jackson's trip to the People's Republic of China during the fourth of July recess. "While Jackson is Meany's favored horse," observed a follower of labor activities, "at this point, he must feel a little miffed that Scoop took off on a trip to China to play the game of détente there. Mao Tse-tung doesn't stand any higher in Meany's estimation than Brezhnev."[18] Victor Riesel, another close observer of labor, wrote after Jackson's China trip that "it's beginning to be said for the first time in their labor circles that they're not wedded to Scoop Jackson."[19]

On Thursday, September 12, the relationship suffered a critical reversal. Meany—accompanied by I.W. Abel, president of the United Steelworkers, Paul Hall of the Seafarers Union, and Lane Kirkland who with Hall was rumored to be a successor to Meany—paid Jackson a visit. Jackson told Meany that he was on the verge of reaching a compromise agreement on the emigration issue that he could not pass up. Meany, Jackson, and everyone involved in the battle knew that if Jackson compromised, it would remove the last block to final passage of the Trade Bill. In fact, it would probably assure the bill's passage as it had in the House of Representatives the year before.

Meany was willing to trust the Soviets less than the traditionally hard-line Jackson was. The labor leader was simply and unalterably opposed to trading with the Soviet Union regardless of whether the Soviet Union had MFN and credits.[20] Meany asked Jackson what would happen if the Soviets cheated. Jackson argued that the agreement would work and if it did not, Congress retained a safeguard—the power to withdraw the Soviet's trade benefits. Meany was unconvinced.[21] "We couldn't buy it," Meany told a questioner after his talk with Jackson.[22] He told Jackson and others that Jackson is "being had."

Reported others, "Meany felt betrayed. He turned on Jackson as if he had been caught in some heinous offense. Almost overnight Jackson was banished. Knowing that Meany might change his mind in a one hundred and eighty degree turn, a reporter asked him under what conditions would he change his mind about Jackson. Meany replied, 'That's something I'll have to sleep on.' Reporter: 'What would you expect to find under your pillow in the morning?' Meany: 'A switch hitter.' "[23] Another reporter said, "I spoke with George Meany, and he physically hated Jackson."

Jackson probably hoped that Meany would not react so harshly. After all, compared to other presidential candidates, Jackson had gone to the well often enough for Meany. His views and those of organized labor tended to overlap on many issues. In the field of East-West trade alone, Jackson had sponsored amendments not only to the Trade Bill but also to the Export-Import Bank Bill setting a ceiling of $300 million on loans to the Soviet Union, and placing a member of organized labor on the Board of Directors of the Export-Import Bank. The latter amendment was called by some legislators the "Andy Biemiller Amendment" in honor of the AFL-CIO's legislative director. Jackson also fought for legislation amending the Export Administration Act to tighten restrictions on export to the Soviet Union of manufacturing capabilities that simultaneously endangered American national security and encouraged foreign competition with goods manufactured by American labor.

Meany stayed on Jackson's right. He remained there, unalterably opposed to compromising with the Soviets or to clearing the way for final passage of the Trade Bill, which he said would adversely affect American workers. Disappointing the AFL-CIO was a price Jackson had to pay to get a final agreement on the two-year-long emigration battle.

The AFL-CIO was not the only dissatisfied group. Jackson's original success in the House fight was the product of a broad-based coalition built of Jews, labor, conservative critics of the Soviet Union, liberals concerned about human rights within the Soviet Union, and other ethnic groups who thought their relatives should be getting out of the Soviet Union along with the Jews. As news of Jackson's decision to compromise with Kissinger and the Soviets became known, labor, some of the conservative groups, some of the other non-Jewish ethnic groups, and even militant Jewish groups like the Jewish Defense League, complained.

LAST-MINUTE DETAILS

On September 19, the day before Gromyko was scheduled to see the president, Kissinger called another meeting with the senators. Aside from the Jackson-induced demand for an annual emigration of sixty thousand, which seemed at the time to have been resolved, several other issues remained outstanding.

SECRET LETTERS

A major question was whether the letters to be exchanged by the administration and Jackson would be kept secret. As early as June, it had been reported that at least some participants in the June 6 meeting had expected assurances from the Soviet Union regarding the earlier number of forty-five thousand. But it was also revealed that the Soviets had objected to publication of any concessions. Most of the details of the talks had thus far been leaked.[24] Stanley Lowell believed Kissinger had inspired the idea of having the contents of letters handled by means of a "definitive leak" to the *New York Times.* Ford passed on the idea to a Jewish leader at a White House State dinner honoring Israeli Prime Minister, Yitzhak Rabin.[25] Said an administration insider, "The Russians don't mind if they [the letters] are leaked, but they insisted Kissinger couldn't release them."

Jackson, however, refused to have the letters handled that way, as did Lowell. The senators wanted as much as possible made public. Probably they perceived the rising concern in Congress that it was not proper to legislate merely on the basis of undocumented word of a triumvirate of senators and of Kissinger. Watergate had made many in Congress skeptical of anyone's words. Constitutionalists also objected to an unpublished exchange of letters trilaterally negotiated between two branches of the United States government and a foreign government that substituted for a public agreement or treaty. In effect, the Kremlin was a "silent partner" to an administration-Senate understanding, and that was no way to conduct United States foreign policy. Members of the Finance Committee, including Chairman Long, resented Jackson's becoming the self-declared spokesman for Congress on an issue of trade that was under his committee's jurisdiction. The committee insisted on having at least a look at whatever understanding came out of the three-way discussion.

DRAFTING LEGISLATION

The second issue still outstanding was what the actual legislative arrangement would be permitting the president to renew the mutually acceptable waiver of the Jackson amendment. The senators argued that both houses of Congress should not have to act affirmatively to stop continuation of trade benefits once the initial waiver had been invoked. The senators wanted trade concessions to lapse unless both houses took affirmative action to renew them. Kissinger wanted the authority to remain in effect unless Congress acted to end it.

Jackson and Ford discussed the question of the renewal of the waiver on September 20. Kissinger and National Security Deputy Assistant Scowcroft sat in on the meeting. Jackson had the impression that Ford seemed less accommodating than he had in previous meetings. Ford expressed concern about weakening the power of the presidency. After the meeting Jackson and Ford were "still hung up on one issue—mainly how to handle it legislatively." Jackson, nevertheless, took the opportunity to announce to the press that "The Russians have come one hundred and eighty degrees."[26] As he left the president's office he encountered Foreign Minister Andrei A. Gromyko entering to see the president as scheduled at 11:00 a.m. According to one version of the chance meeting in the antechamber, "Trying to make a joke, Jackson put his index fingers up above his ears and remarked he guessed he was the devil in this negotiation. But Gromyko didn't get it, and for a long nervous moment the interpreter couldn't explain to the Foreign Minister what Jackson was doing with his fingers on his head."

Gromyko and Ford spoke for two and a half hours on subjects ranging from the Trade Bill to a possible Ford-Brezhnev summit in November. Kissinger and Ambassador Dobrynin joined in the meeting, as did United States Ambassador to the Soviet Union Walter J. Stoessel. After the meeting, Kissinger and Gromyko continued their discussions over lunch at the Soviet embassy. They went over the proposed letters to be exchanged between the administration and the Congress in which Soviet emigration policy was to be described.[27]

EXCEPTIONS FOR SECURITY

The question of Soviet citizens with access to sensitive secret information was considered. Kissinger told Jackson that he went over the question of emigrants exposed to security data five times with Gromyko, and Gromyko refused to set a precise number of years such an individual had to remain in the Soviet Union before receiving permission to emigrate. Perle had been tipped off that security exceptions constituted a potentially serious loophole detrimental to the intelligentsia whom the organized groups in this country and Jackson especially cared about. An anonymous, sympathetic American official had sent Jackson an unmarked envelope containing a copy of a confidential cable dispatched from the American Consulate in Leningrad to the State Department, which discussed a Soviet law setting a seven-year life on classified information. Jackson's inside information deflated Soviet and administration protests. Kissinger later admitted, "This is not an example of my super-clever weaseling."

Following up the Ford-Gromyko and Kissinger-Gromyko meetings, the foreign minister returned to the White House the next day for a brief thirty-minute noontime meeting. (Dobrynin and Kissinger again attended.) A high White House official said that there were no new subjects raised. The official indicated that an agreement was still in the offing on the Jackson amendment.

There were other indications that the Soviet leadership was going along with the substance of the three-letter exchange. Said the unidentified White House high official, "Agreement between the United States and Soviet leadership on this issue had been reached much earlier."[28] Jackson also personally heard after the meetings that the letters were acceptable.[29] Finally, in the week Gromyko was in the United States, an unidentified high-level Soviet official was reported complaining that "we've made our concessions; now where are our improved trade terms."[30]

THREE LETTERS BECOME TWO

At the same time that agreement was reached on waiving the Jackson amendment to the Trade Bill, the Senate passed on September 19 a series of amendments to the Export-Import Bank Bill that directly affected the trilateral negotiations. Jackson and Stevenson were the sponsors of the amendments that had been under consideration in the Congress since spring. In the context of the trilateral agreement, Jackson had agreed to granting at least temporarily trade concessions including credits to the Soviet Union. However, simultaneously, he was working hard to restrict credits to the Soviet Union. In effect, what he gave with one hand in the trilateral negotiations regarding the Jackson amendment to the Trade Bill, he seemed to take away with the other hand in the Export-Import Bank Bill.

One of the amendments passed by the Senate on September 19 prohibited granting further credits by the Export-Import Bank or any other agency of the government until the Trade Reform Act and the pending Jackson amendment were resolved.[31] On the surface, it seemed strange that a friend of the Export-Import Bank, Republican Senator Robert Packwood of Oregon, would have offered the amendment restricting bank operations. Behind the mystery, however, was the fact that Packwood was compelled to sponsor the amendment after Perle called a Packwood aide and threatened, "If he [Packwood] doesn't offer it, Jackson would."

Holding up the credits until the Jackson amendment was resolved was a perfectly understandable objective of Jackson. Less consistent with the spirit of the trilateral negotiations were other amendments that changed what the Soviets would get from a three-way agreement. These were the provisions of the original Stevenson-Jackson amendments to the bill originally introduced in June. They included: a ceiling of $300 million dollars on new credit commitments to the Soviet Union; a two-year limit on transactions with Communist countries; and a requirement that the president determine that transactions of over $40 million with Communist nations were in the nation's interests.[32]

It is not known if the Soviet government protested the Senate action on the Export-Import Bank. The previously quoted unidentified high Soviet official had expressed pique and impatience about not seeing American concessions in exchange for the Soviet concessions. That may or may not have referred to the Senate action. It is known, however, that on September 30 Kissinger's deputy Brent Scowcroft telephoned Jackson aide Dorothy Fosdick at home to inform her that Kissinger had just decided the third letter in the letter exchange would have to be dropped.

Given the sequence of events, one might speculate that the Soviets had decided to get tough after the Export-Import Bank restrictions passed the Senate and forced Kissinger to water down the degree to which he could express Soviet assurances that Ford was guaranteeing. However, in light of subsequent events it is more likely that Kissinger had his assistant call because after Kissinger and Gromyko had examined the two letters that Kissinger would write Jackson conveying Soviet assurances, it became absolutely clear that Soviet "assurances" were not so sure.

Another event also contributed to Kissinger's concern about how much he could state in letter form to Jackson. On September 26, Kissinger and Ford met with congressional leaders Hugh Scott, Hubert Humphrey, and Mike Mansfield. The purpose of the meeting was to discuss several anti-Turkey amendments pending in Congress. Near the end of the meeting, Ford mentioned the letters on emigration that were about to be released. Kissinger recalled what happened: "the difficulty arose at a meeting with the Congressional leadership in which we presented what had been discussed and pointed out what we could guarantee in the area in which we were not sure of what in fact would happen. And the unanimous opinion of the Congressional leadership was that if we could not be sure about certain aspects, then some of the formulations that had been used might lend themselves to misinterpretation later on."[33] Mansfield reportedly brought Kissinger up short when he asked if he really had a Soviet commitment to allow sixty thousand persons to emigrate. Kissinger said he did not. Mansfield explained that he believed Congress would interpret the third letter as a guarantee of such a commitment and if later it turned out that less than sixty thousand emigrated, the administration would be in trouble.

Mansfield also had difficulty accepting the unconventional letter arrangement. "I expressed my great concern that foreign policy was being made in that manner. . . . It is the responsibility of the executive branch to make agreements with foreign countries and any exchange of letters should be received by the President or Secretary of State, I was disturbed about this because of the precedent it created."[34] "If one Senator could do this," argued the majority leader, "why couldn't other Senators work out different agreements on other subjects?" Mansfield, a member of the Foreign Relations Committee, preferred the letters be exchanged with the Foreign Relations Committee and the House Foreign Affairs Committee rather than with Jackson.

The controversy over what assurances had actually been given had raged ever since Kissinger had returned from the Middle East in May. Some sources in June had downplayed the notion that Kissinger ever really said he had received assurances on numbers from the Soviet Union. Others had believed Kissinger either had assurances on numbers or at least said he did. Then the figure in question rose from forty-five to sixty thousand. Kissinger never did publicly clarify what the Soviet leaders had said they were willing to agree to. Thus, the general impression conveyed by Jackson had been allowed to persist that the Soviets were willing to give assurances on numbers of emigrants. The situation was so confused that even important members of the administration had assumed Kissinger had received Soviet assurances.

By early October it had become clear, however, that those so-called assurances were not so sure. Senate sources admitted to reporters who inquired on October 5 that Kissinger had never explicitly stated he had Soviet assurances on the number sixty thousand.[35] Specifically, Jackson had wanted to write in his letter to Kissinger that he understood that as "a minimum standard of initial compliance," the Soviet Union would permit sixty thousand emigrants a year. Kissinger was no longer willing to have Ford reply to Jackson in the third letter that "I can assure you that the Administration accepts them [Jackson's points including the sixty thousand figure] as appropriate guidelines."[36] At least, Kissinger was now telling the senators that they either had to take the situation as it was—with vague and ambiguous references about future Soviet behavior devoid of any written Soviet pledges—or leave it.

Jackson had no idea what had brought Kissinger to withdraw the third letter. All he knew was that he was furious. He suspected Kissinger of trying to trick him. Perle consulted NCSJ Chairman Lowell for his reaction. "It was a very bad day," Lowell recalled. "As a lawyer, I could see that without that third letter, the conditions in the second were not binding on anyone." Said a Senate source, "We were working on legislative language and suddenly there was a complete reneging on all that's been worked out. . . . This is the grossest violation of good faith in negotiations that I've ever heard of. It makes negotiating with the Russians look like handling a Sunday school class."[37] Another source publicly damned Kissinger's new offer to substitute the third letter he was withdrawing with an "emasculated" version that would say, "we will take note and consider" Jackson's second letter.[38]

Neither Kissinger nor Jackson wanted to discuss the matter, so strained was their personal relationship. Kissinger told associates in the White House that he wanted to avoid Jackson berating him or questioning his motives. Two days after Scowcroft called Fosdick, Kissinger sought a meeting. Perle's response was that Jackson would talk only if there were a prepared agenda that excluded backtracking on agreements that had already been reached.

At this point, the Jewish groups—in a rare gesture—independently intervened to get the negotiations going again. They wanted an agreement, pure and simple. They had no ulterior political motives or personal feelings at stake. The number of Soviet emigrants had dropped precipitously ever since the House of Representatives vote at the end of 1973. If the agreement unravelled completely—as it appeared to be doing—the Jews in the Soviet Union would bear the brunt of the fiasco. Jackson and Kissinger might blame each other. If that did not work, they both could blame the Soviet Union for negotiating in bad faith. Avoiding blame that could blight a public career might matter for Jackson and Kissinger. But it was inconsequential for the Jewish leaders. Their requirements were not as complicated as those of politician Jackson or diplomat Kissinger. What mattered for them was the Soviet Jews. Their job was to be single-minded—to get Soviet Jews who wanted to leave out of the Soviet Union.

This was "the hardest Jackson's office had ever been leaned on by the National Conference, which had for two years gone along faithfully with Jackson's tactical judgments."[39] Chairman Lowell let Jackson's office know that it would be inexcusable for Jackson to refuse to see Kissinger. Meanwhile Lowell contacted twenty-five top Jewish leaders and asked them to generate telegrams to President Ford—with copies to Kissinger—stating in the strongest language possible their outrage over the setback in the negotiations. With Jackson's encouragement, the leaders were also asked to indicate that Ford should know that he would be held personally responsible if the negotiations were not patched up.[40]

The three senators and Kissinger quickly arranged a meeting for October 8. On the eve of the meeting, Kissinger began to air—but not clarify—the ambiguity that had persisted throughout the trilateral negotiations. He explained what the areas of agreement were and were not. He stated he had assurances but did not say what they were:

> . . . the negotiations between the Senators and myself . . . arises from the fact that there are some assurances that have been given to me that I can defend and which I can transmit. There are some interpretations of these assurances which some of the Senators would like to make. And that is their privilege. And we understand that they would apply their interpretations as a test of Soviet good faith. What I cannot do is to guarantee things that have not been told to me. And so the question is whether we can work out something which makes clear that we take

the Senators' views very seriously, but which does not put us into a position of having to guarantee something beyond what has been discussed . . . we are here in an area of ambiguity, in which I have to say in fairness to the Senators concerned, they have always held the view there should be a fixed number. This is not something new caused by recent discussions, but it is something that they have always held. And I have always held the view that I could not guarantee something that has not been told to me.[41]

Kissinger told the press conference the day before his scheduled meeting with Jackson that "the question now is whether we can formulate a criterion that can be applied as a test without putting the Administration into the position of having misled them."[42] Instead of a new criterion, however, Javits found another way out of the impasse. Javits suggested dropping the third letter, which neither the president nor Kissinger was willing to write. Instead the operative paragraph from the third letter would be tacked on to the end of the first letter. Javits dictated the two new letters to Richard Perle and Morris Amitay. Javits, who was an attorney, explained that it expressed the same thing in two letters instead of the original three.

Javits, Jackson, and Ribicoff met with Kissinger for an hour on October 8. Kissinger told the gathering in Jackson's Capitol hideaway office that he wanted to avoid any accusations that he had broken a commitment. "Gromyko never promised more than forty-five thousand and he has since backed away from that," Kissinger said according to one report. So, said Kissinger, he personally could not commit himself to something to which the Soviets had not committed themselves.

Apparently the senators did not object. As stated earlier, Jewish activists in the Soviet Union and the United States opposed a quota anyway. The senators had virtually no other alternative but to accept the situation as it was or reject it completely. After a little more discussion, the senators handed Kissinger the two-letter arrangement inspired by Javits. Kissinger read it over several times, discussed it with his assistant Sonnenfeldt, and gave his assent subject to President Ford's approval. Kissinger said the administration would consider Jackson's letter merely as a threat of future congressional action if the Soviet Union did not behave according to "appropriate guidelines." It was not, Kissinger argued, legally binding. Jackson did not reject that interpretation, but he emphasized that Ford was still committing himself to removing MFN and credits after the agreed time if the conditions Jackson would write in his letter were not observed.[43]

Hours after the meeting, Kissinger flew to the Middle East. The following day, the three legislators were informed that the president had agreed to the two-letter device suggested by Javits. A reporter on the scene said the news was received by the legislators with "relief."[44] Although one of Jackson's staff aides characterized the arrangement as a "Kissinger defeat," as if he were keeping score between Kissinger and Jackson, the fact was that Jackson was willing to stop asking questions, clarifying the situation, or demanding more concessions to get an agreement once and for all. Jackson—the man who had made a political career of warning of Soviet perfidy and lately of criticizing Kissinger's diplomacy—was willing to accept the Kissinger package on Soviet emigration wrapped in ambiguity.

One remaining issue was left for Jackson to work out with President Ford: precisely how the repeal of the waiver of the Jackson amendment would work. This was the same legislative technicality that remained outstanding before the agreement had fallen apart September 30. Ford cared a great deal about the legislative language of the waiver and renewal of the waiver. Said one administration insider, "The President wasn't worried about these limitations—the assurances—on harassment and numbers, which Ford ever since coming into office, had taken it upon himself to guarantee. It was the procedure that put him on the spot—if the waiver lapsed."

A presidential bill signing ceremony October 11, which Jackson attended, presented the opportunity for Jackson and Ford to discuss the problem. Ford had insisted all along that the agreement last for two years after which the president could renew the tariff status for the Soviet Union, subject to a congressional veto if it was dissatisfied with the Soviet performance on emigration. Jackson had argued for a one-year provision or not more than eighteen months renewable only if Congress acted positively to renew the concessions. Jackson later told Congress that "in a personal discussion between the President of the United States and myself, the President gave his personal assurance—that if in this eighteen month period there is a course of action that is in violation of the agreement, he would act himself to cut off MFN and credits."[45] If the waiver lapsed a year or eighteen months after passage of the bill, it would put the debate over Soviet performance in the middle of election year, 1976, when Ford and Jackson would both be candidates.

On October 17, Kissinger met with the three senators. This time their Senate staffmen—Perle, Amitay, and Lakeland—were there as was Sonnenfeldt, who accompanied Kissinger. One of the staffmen attending recalled that Kissinger stated again that he couldn't assure a specific number of emigrants, but only that Gromyko had said that all the items spelled out in the letters added up to sixty thousand or more.

After the meeting of principals and staff, Perle and Amitay sat down with Alan Wolf, acting general counsel of the Special Trade Representative's office to do the final legislative drafting. During this late phase of legislative drafting, William Van Ness of Jackson's Interior Committee staff and Mark Sandstrom, a staff member of the Senate Finance Committee, were also involved. They wrote out the details for an intricate legislative device, which provided that for eighteen months the Soviet Union could enjoy trade concessions—including MFN and credits. After that, the president would have to request renewal of the agreement. Congress would have sixty days in which to renew the agreement by a vote of both houses of Congress. If Congress did not act, the renewal would become automatic unless one house vetoed it within ninety days. Concessions would then continue on an annual basis unless within sixty days after the president requested renewals the Congress vetoed the renewal request.

Jackson and Ford were both satisfied with the legislative arrangement. White House liaison Timmons called Perle to say that the president had agreed.[46] Jackson told the press the next day that "we reached an accord basically at about 8:15 P.M. and there was one item left which we worked out this morning with the President and the Secretary of State."[47] That "one item left" referred to a last-minute detail Kissinger raised when he read the draft late in the evening of October 17. He placed a phone call to Jackson at home, which woke up the senator. Kissinger argued that a ninety-day provision for renewal after the initial eighteen-month period was too long. Jackson agreed to change the ninety days to forty-five days.[48] Taking a jab at Kissinger, a trade official called Kissinger's changes "not material things"; They were merely "to show it was his [Kissinger's] deal."

Kissinger may have wanted to prove his point for the benefit of the individual actors immediately involved in the negotiations. Indeed, Jackson had agreed to less than sure "assurances" in exchange for relinquishing control over the fate of trade concessions for the Soviet Union and of the Trade Bill as a whole. Nevertheless, Jackson was more interested in having the public get the opposite impression that "the deal" was his—not Kissinger's and not the Soviet Union's.

DIPLOMACY BEFORE THE TV CAMERAS

Jackson, Javits, and Congressman Charles Vanik met with President Ford and Kissinger on October 18. In a forty-five-minute meeting in the Oval Office, Kissinger and Jackson signed the two letters culminating months of negotiations. Exactly two years to the day after the Soviet-American trade agreement was signed pledging American trade concessions to the Soviet Union, Kissinger and Jackson exchanged letters marking an accord meant to resolve the trade-emigration issue that had held up the original trade pact.

President Ford invited photographers into his office to take pictures of him with the legislators. His press secretary Ronald Nessen suggested that Jackson discuss the event with newsmen who had assembled in the White House briefing room. Perle and Amitay distributed mimeographed copies of the letter exchange, as Jackson conducted his second White House press conference of the year.

Jackson had exclusive control over the impression that the press received of the agreement. Neither the White House nor the State Department offered an official comment confirming, denying, or altering Jackson's statements. Kissinger held no press briefing on or off the record to elaborate, explain, or elucidate.

Javits, who was three weeks away from reelection in New York, attended the televised event, as did Charles Vanik, the House sponsor. Jackson made a point of explaining that Ribicoff "couldn't be here . . . due to a totally conflicting engagement." Ribicoff, who was no doubt busy campaigning for his reelection November 5, may have had additional reasons for not appearing. One of his staff members subsequently said that Ribicoff was concerned about the diplomatic consequences of a negative Soviet reaction to the fanfare of a White House announcement. "Ribicoff objected to Jackson-Javits effort to publicize the agreement. Ribicoff said he refused to come to town for it, and that Jackson was very foolish in getting on the podium in the White House."

Something other than a concern for the Soviet reaction may also have been operating. "In the end, Ribicoff's part in the campaign on the amendment was less open . . . ."[49] Ribicoff felt uncomfortable as a Jew taking such a conspicuous position on a "Jewish issue." He had been heard to say "I don't want to be the Jew boy who got the Jew deal." Toward the end of the campaign, he also began to realize the extent to which his staffman Morris Amitay had been far out in front of him.

Finally, Ribicoff was perhaps mindful of labor's negative reaction. Several weeks before, Ribicoff had persuaded the Finance Committee to wait and report out the Trade Bill to the full Senate after the election.[50] Possibly, Ribicoff had a similar concern in mind when he decided to take a low profile on the Jackson amendment and not appear at the White House on October 18.

Jackson controlled the October 18 events. Standing before the press, he boasted that "We have reached what I think is an historic understanding in the area of human rights." Jackson described his feat in unblushingly immodest terms. "I think it is a monumental accomplishment considering the fact that so many said it could never be accomplished. . . ." Jackson indicated that the Soviet government had capitulated. "Let me just say that what we started out with two years ago we have accomplished. I am not going to comment on what the Russians have done. I can only say that there has been a complete turn around here on the basic points that are contained in the two letters."

Jackson, the presidential candidate, was more interested in declaring victory for the benefit of his domestic audience and less concerned about the negative consequences that such publicity might have on the arrangement with the Soviet Union.[51] Such behavior served a domestic political purpose. But it could not have been designed to have worse diplomatic repercussions. Jackson had earlier indicated his understanding that it was essential not to embarrass the Soviet Union and to find a face-saving device for the Soviet leaders lest publicity about Soviet concessions push Soviet leaders to repudiate the agreement completely. But basking in the light of the TV cameras, Jackson exercised no self-restraint. He even made a point of singling out the controversial sixty thousand figure as a "benchmark" for measuring Soviet behavior and predicted that that number of emigrants would actually be exceeded. "I anticipate that it should go beyond sixty thousand based on the number of applications which we know exceed one hundred and thirty thousand."

The sixty thousand figure had already proven to be a particularly prickly problem. The removal of the third letter on October 8 clearly indicated that there were limits to what the Soviet leaders were willing to agree to. Jackson's letter stated "we understand that the actual number of emigrants would rise promptly from the 1973 level and would continue to rise to correspond to the number of applicants, and may therefore exceed sixty thousand per annum." Kissinger stated that "we have been assured" that certain practices will characterize Soviet emigration policy. Kissinger listed some of those assurances. He stated that he had not been assured, but rather it was his own "assumption that with the application of the criteria-for-practices and procedures set forth in that letter, the rate of emigration from the USSR would begin to rise promptly from the 1973 level and would continue to correspond to the number of applicants." Kissinger said that "the understandings in your [Jackson's] letter will be *among* the considerations to be applied by the President in exercising the authority" to waive the Jackson amendment.[52] Stating that Jackson's understandings would be "among the considerations" gave Kissinger and the Soviet Union a large loophole. It allowed for countervailing considerations that might justify the president's ignoring what Jackson had said in his letter about the per annum figure or about anything else. Jackson must have known and accepted that. However, he continued to claim that the agreement would mean sixty thousand or more would emigrate.

Jackson was optimistic about passage of the Trade Bill. At the August press conference, which seemed to anticipate his painful September 12 split with George Meany over Trade Bill strategy, he was not sure there would be time to pass the bill. On October 18, he predicted ". . . the Trade Bill should be signed into law sometime in December."

Jackson also answered questions about the Export-Import Bank Bill, which the Senate-House conference had not yet resolved. The Senate had rejected an October 8 House-Senate conference report that had gutted the Senate-passed Stevenson-Jackson ceiling of $300 million on loans to the Soviet Union by giving the president authority to raise the ceiling if he felt it was justified.[53] It was demanding another report that would make it impossible for the president to ignore the ceiling or the prohibition on credits to the Soviets for energy development without explicit congressional approval.[54] At the press conference, a reporter asked Jackson, "Is there any understanding as to how much the Russians will get in the next eighteen months?'' Jackson answered, ''We have had no understanding.''[55]

After the fanfare at the top level at the White House, the next level of actors—Perle, Amitay, Talisman, Lakeland, Silber, and Rogul—gathered for a celebration at the apartment of Israeli reporter Nahum Barnea and his wife, Tommi, a former employee at the embassy of Israel. The Israeli government also apparently felt it was safe to celebrate after maintaining a long public silence on the Jackson amendment. Prime Minister Rabin wrote to President Ford, ''Scoop,'' and Kissinger, marking the end of the process.[56]

Everyone still recognized, however, the need for, as Jackson put it, ''good faith in the implementation of the assurances contained in your [Kissinger's] letter of October 18 and the understanding conveyed by this letter.''[57] Stated NCSJ Chairman Lowell and Rabbi Israel Miller, president of the Conference of Presidents of Major American Jewish Organizations, ''. . . we will not forget that the real determination of the success of this agreement lies in the Kremlin. There can be only one measure of the effectiveness of today's announcement . . . and that is performance.''[58] ''We shall watch closely Soviet compliance with the terms of the understanding. . . .''[59]

THE SOVIETS WRITE A LETTER THAT KISSINGER ''FORGETS''

Even before the final exchange of letters at the White House on October 18, there were signs that the agreement was not firmly accepted by the Soviets. Jackson had boasted in September that the Soviets had come one hundred and eighty degrees. After that, there were indications that Jackson had spoken too soon. Then, after the highly publicized media event on October 18, there were even stronger indications that Jackson had also spoken too much.

On October 15, Brezhnev complained harshly that ''it is high time that there should be a clear understanding'' that ''utterly irrelevant and unacceptable'' conditions to trade with the Soviet Union should be avoided. Without naming it, he referred to the Jackson amendment as ''demands on questions totally unconnected with the area of trade and economics and lying completely within the domestic competence of states.''[60] Addressing an audience that included United States Secretary of Treasury William Simon, the party secretary declared that ''such attempts at interference in internal affairs do nothing but harm including the trade and economic relations between our two countries.''[61] Brezhnev probably knew that within days, the agreement between Kissinger and Jackson regarding Soviet emigration policy would be signed. His remarks may have been intended to serve as advance notification of Soviet unwillingness to be pinned down—prior notice that Kissinger's mediation between Jackson and the Soviet Union might be doomed to fail.[62]

The October 18 exchange of letters regarding emigration was intended to clear the way for fulfillment of the two-year-old promise of trade concessions. Instead, it further complicated the issue. On October 21, Nikolai Inozemtsev, vice-chairman of the Soviet State Planning Committee, told Western newsmen in a press conference that American trade laws were remnants of the "cold war." The fact that this Soviet official was attacking something that presumably would be altered by the October 18, 1974, Kissinger-Jackson reconciliation seemed to indicate that Soviet leaders were not themselves reconciled.

On the same day that Inozemtsev complained to newsmen in Moscow, Soviet officials stationed in the embassy in Washington also "bitched," in the words of a knowledgeable American lobbyist for East-West trade. "The Soviets," explained the lobbyist, who was in contact with the embassy, "are bothered by Jackson's benchmark." They "still feel in eighteen months it's something they'll be held to."

Apparently Soviet complaints compelled the administration to break the silence it had maintained since Jackson's White House press conference. On Monday, October 21, President Ford conferred with Secretary Kissinger aboard Air Force One. It was decided to issue a clarification about the sixty thousand figure, which Jackson had underscored. Ford instructed press secretary Ronald Nessen to issue a statement pointing out that Kissinger's letter contained no "specific number." Nessen stated, "all of the assurances we have received from the Soviet Union are" contained in that letter. "The Administration has agreed only that, as stated in the secretary's letter, they will be *among* considerations to be applied by the President" when he considers whether to renew the trade benefits after the eighteen-month trial period.[63]

Jackson unrelentingly responded:

The White House clarification serves to *underline* the fact that Secretary Kissinger's letter to me conveys the assurances of the Soviet Union. . . . With the Soviet assurances conveyed by Secretary Kissinger to me to end harassment and intimidation of those seeking to emigrate, and with the number of visas rising to correspond to the number of applicants, I believe that *more than sixty thousand* will emigrate each year. The sixty thousand figure . . . is . . . "a *minimum* standard of initial compliance," to be used, by the Congress and the President, in judging . . . the Soviets in the transition from their present restrictive policy to the future liberalized policy to which they are *committed* by the assurances in Secretary Kissinger's letter.[64]

Jackson was vindicating his claim of having a pledge for sixty thousand emigrants a year. Despite the warning signs from the Soviets that prompted American officials in the White House to clarify the situation, Jackson continued to insist publicly that the Soviets were committed by assurances they gave to Kissinger.

The next night, Kissinger left for three and one-half days of meetings with the Soviet leadership. The road leading to Moscow had been marked by the October 18 exchange of correspondence that was intended to settle the emigration issue once and for all, an October 19 lifting of a stop order on Soviet grain purchases, and an October 21 presidential clarification of the meaning of the exchange of letters with Jackson. But the secretary of state's trip to Moscow would still be his roughest ever.

The first meeting in Moscow on October 24 lasted from 11:00 a.m. to 2:00 p.m. Trade policy was discussed, but nothing more precise is known. Brezhnev and Kissinger and senior aides met again at 5:30 p.m. the same day; that meeting lasted three hours.[65] A final round of talks were held October 26 lasting seven and one-half hours and ending around midnight. The participants were bleary-eyed when they appeared at nine the next morning to leave from Moscow's Vnukovo airport.[66]

Later Kissinger explained that Brezhnev had been "livid" over Jackson's claims.[67] Reportedly Brezhnev "reacted violently to the manner" of Jackson's White House announcement. "The Soviets feel deeply wounded by the implication that they knuckled under to American demands affecting their internal affairs."[68] According to another report from Moscow, "there was . . . a profound display of grievance over the handling of the emigration-trade compromise. The Soviet leaders were upset that the compromise which it did not publicly admit to was handled so openly."[69] Kissinger told Brezhnev that he, too, had not expected the texts of the letters to be released.[70] But that did not calm Soviet anger.

The publicity generated by Jackson must have provided Brezhnev's domestic critics with useful ammunition with which to attack Brezhnev personally or at least to attack the policy of detente and trade with the West, or at the very least to attack the implication of that foreign policy for the internal treatment of dissidents, which had become a dominant issue in the West. Reports from Moscow on the eve of Kissinger's arrival indicated that "conservative doubters" were active.[71] United States government intelligence was also receiving "scattered reports that Brezhnev" was in "political trouble at home."

Kissinger had discussed the contents of his letter to Jackson with Soviet officials. He said they never complained about its contents. Rather it was the publicity that was upsetting.[72] Kissinger, however, never discussed the more detailed Jackson letter with the Soviets.[73] That may have been a shock.

Even so, Brezhnev might have been willing to acquiesce on the emigration issue if his domestic critics lacked public proof of it. Then, the problems created by releasing the letters were probably compounded by Jackson's publicly portraying the agreement as a Soviet concession. As a result, it made the arrangement difficult for Brezhnev to defend to the Politburo—the Soviet Union's top eleven men—who met while Kissinger was in Moscow.[74]

On the same day that Brezhnev had his emotional meeting with Kissinger, the *Economist Magazine* published an article summarizing the domestic pressures on Brezhnev and his government. Those pressures presumably led to the Soviet government's objections to the events of October.

> Mr. Brezhnev hates taking risks. . . . The Jackson deal may stir up an alarming amount of hope among the discontented inside Russia. It may destroy the remaining Soviet hopes of bringing any points of substance. It is bound to annoy the Arabs, who will accuse Russia of strengthening Israel by letting so many of its Jews go there. It will strengthen the position in American politics of Senator Jackson, a potential next president who has been branded in Moscow as a dangerous enemy. It will give Mr. Brezhnev's rivals among the Soviet hardliners a handle to use against him.[75]

The Soviets committed their protests to a formal note signed by Foreign Minister Andrei Gromyko and personally handed to Kissinger on October 26 while he was in Moscow. The strongly worded letter vehemently attacked both "the silence" (presumably of Kissinger) and the "attempts" (presumably of Jackson) "to ascribe to the elucidations . . . as some assurances and almost obligations on our part" regarding harassment or figures of emigrants.[76] The letter should be read in its entirety not only for its substance but also for the angry tone it conveys:

Dear Mr. Secretary of State,

> I believe it necessary to draw your attention to the question of the publication in the United States of materials of which the correspondence between you and Senator Jackson, create a distorted picture of our position as well as of what we told the American side on this matter.
>
> When clarifying the actual state of affairs in response to your request, we underlined that the question as such is entirely within the internal competence of our state. We warned at the time that in this matter we had acted and shall act in strict conformity with our present legislation on that score.
>
> But now silence is being kept about this very matter. At the same time, attempts are being made to ascribe to the elucidations that were furnished by us the nature of some assurances and almost obligations on our part regarding the procedure for the departure of Soviet citizens from the USSR. Some figures are even being quoted as to the supposed number of such citizens, and there is talk about an anticipated increase in that number as compared with previous years.

We resolutely decline such an interpretation. What we said, and you, Mr. Secretary of State, know this well, concerned only and exclusively the real situation concerning the given question. And when we did mention figures—to inform you of the real situation—the point was quite the opposite, namely about the present tendency toward a decrease in the number of persons wishing to leave the USSR and seek permanent residence in other countries.

We believe it important that in this entire matter, considering its principled significance, no ambiguities should remain as regards the position of the Soviet Union.

A. GROMYKO,
Minister of Foreign
Affairs of the USSR[77]

Gromyko had called for the end of "ambiguities"—the mortar that Kissinger had used to keep the shaky tripartite agreement together. Despite the Soviet attack on such "ambiguities," however, Kissinger chose to try to keep the arrangement together by perpetuating the ambiguity. Kissinger did not make the Soviet letter public, nor did he reveal its existence to anyone in Congress, not even Jackson. According to one of Kissinger's associates, Kissinger had discussed the letter with his top assistants when he received it. He decided to send it to Ford and also to the three most involved senators. One of his aides further explained that the letter "got lost in the shuffle" as Kissinger continued on a trip around the world after leaving Moscow. Kissinger returned to Washington on November 9 only to leave again in mid-November on another trip with Ford to the Summit at Vladivostok.[78] Kissinger's critics regarded the explanation that the letter got lost or that Kissinger forgot incredible.

Kissinger's "forgetting" may have been a convenient and conscious act. One of his associates later advanced this rationale for not sharing the contents of the letter with anyone outside his close staff circle: the letter was "ambiguously written to permit the Russians to go either way."[79] In other words, it may have been written and passed to the Americans for both nations to put in their diplomatic files marked "secret" as a kind of insurance or flank protection. It may have been intended for use only in an emergency by Gromyko, Dobrynin, Brezhnev, and others closely associated with detente and the emigration deal. It would surface only in the event that Brezhnev was under such heavy domestic attack that he would feel compelled to disavow the agreement. Kissinger may have hoped that with a little luck that day would never come. In the past Kissinger had expressed concern about domestic pressures on members of the Soviet élite associated with the policy of improving relations with the United States. In a private briefing to the Foreign Relations Committee in the spring of 1974, he had explained that

Nikita S. Khruschev eventually lost out to hard-liners in the Kremlin after he had tried to improve relations with the United States in the early sixties. Kissinger had argued that if Brezhnev tried and failed to do the same thing, it would be a long time before another Soviet leader would try again.[80] Not sharing the contents of the letter with Congress may have reflected Kissinger's sensitivity to the domestic pressures that may have prompted the protest letter in the first place. Kissinger might have figured that releasing the letter would have definitely precluded more time and breathing space for the Soviet leadership to temper its initial rage. He may have hoped that once the initial anger had subsided and Brezhnev had regained sufficient political strength vis-à-vis his critics, it would be time for the Senate vote on the Trade Bill and the Soviet Union would swallow its objections, ignore the Gromyko letter, and accept its much-delayed concessions without further ado.

There was basis for such hope. Although Brezhnev had been obviously upset by the publicity Jackson had given to the agreement and by Kissinger's silence when Jackson allegedly misconstrued the so-called Soviet "elucidations," Brezhnev never said he would actually rescind the agreement.[81] Kissinger pointed out at the time that Brezhnev had not disavowed the substance of the agreement but rather the humiliatingly noisy way in which it had been handled.[812]

FINAL SENATE CONSIDERATION

The Congress was in recess from several weeks before the election until November 18. Everyone—except perhaps Kissinger and the top Soviet leadership—thought the main issues of the Trade Bill had been resolved. The Senate Finance Committee—in particular committee staff—worked on the bill during the recess preparing the Trade Bill for the committee to approve and send to the Senate floor. The few critics of the Jackson-Kissinger compromise took their last opportunity to express their doubts before Senate passage.

The Executive Council of the AFL-CIO issued a stinging attack on the bill in general and the "Jackson-Kissinger agreement" in particular. This was the statement:

> The American public is being deceived. It is being led to believe that the sole obstacle to a new era in world trade has been resolved by the White House declaration . . . that the Soviet Union will soften its emigration policies. This is not true. . . . For the United States to expect that the Soviet Union will adhere to the Jackson-Kissinger agreement on emigration is to expect again the same scorn that has been heaped upon the United States in its earlier dealings with this nation. . . . The so-called "concession" by the Soviet Union, touted as relaxing bans on emigration of its citizens to Israel and other nations, is hollow indeed.

The Soviet Union has not confirmed the alleged change of policy. The agreement gives the Soviet Union most-favored-nation status before that nation demonstrates its willingness to allow the emigration of Soviet Jews—not after as stipulated in the Jackson Amendment. In effect, this would give the Russians an eighteen-month free ride. At the end of that period, we are told, the United States government would be satisfied of Russia's good faith if sixty thousand Soviet Jews and others had been allowed out. Even this benchmark figure has been brushed aside by the Soviet Union, and the President tells us there is no such agreement. There is no mechanism for checking Soviet claims of meeting emigration quotas. Soviet Jews applying for visas would continue to be harassed without any protection. And finally, the Soviet Union's record for breaching its word gives the world no guarantee that these promises allegedly made to Secretary Kissinger would be kept.[83]

Some members of the Finance Committee, particularly critic Harry Byrd, Jr. (Ind.-Va.), were as skeptical of the arrangement as the AFL-CIO was scornful. Byrd's criticism was fueled by distrust of detente with Communist Russia. In addition, said a Byrd aide, "The way Jackson and Kissinger handled this [agreement] raises problems. The letters really raised more questions than they answer. We don't know the language of the amendment [the waiver that was to accompany the letters], yet we are being asked to report the bill out." Other Finance Committee members shared Byrd's misgivings about the way the agreement was being handled. "There is a feeling Kissinger did not go out of his way to work with the committee. There is some unhappiness that Jackson circumvented the committee and did this on the floor where he got all the publicity."[84]

The committee had earlier resolved not to report the Trade Bill to the Senate floor until it had the opportunity to hear from Kissinger personally regarding the trilateral agreement. Byrd led an effort to have the secretary of state brief the committee during the week of November 12. Officially, Congress was in recess, but hearings were sometimes held during recess. Kissinger was scheduled to depart Sunday, November 16, with President Ford for a trip to Japan, Korea, and the Soviet Union. After that he was planning a trip to China for four days. He would therefore be out of the city when Congress returned November 18 from recess. To compound the problem, when Kissinger was scheduled to return to Washington, Congress would be recessing again for Thanksgiving, Thursday, November 28.

Therefore, Byrd asked Kissinger to appear during the one week of November 12 that both Kissinger and many of the Finance Committee members would be in town. Kissinger's office said that although Kissinger would be in town he was "unavailable." His refusal to appear delayed consideration of the Trade Bill until the first week in December when Congress and Kissinger would be in town at the same time.[85]

The Finance Committee met on November 18 to decide whether to report out the bill or wait until Kissinger could appear on December 2 at the earliest. The committee had not seen the legislative language that would necessarily be added to the bill permitting the president to waive Jackson's original restrictions. Ford, Kissinger, and the three senators had agreed to the waiver language, but the committee that was responsible for marking up the bill was still in the dark, save for leaks in the newspapers.

Byrd argued against reporting the bill to the full Senate until Kissinger appeared. Abraham Ribicoff—who had argued for a delay until after the election—now urged the committee not to bottle up the bill. Jackson joined Ribicoff's effort to end further delay, by telephoning Byrd to urge the Virginia Independent not to hold up the bill in the committee.

As a result, the committee decided to alter its original position. It ordered the bill reported November 20, while reserving judgment on the Soviet trade section of the bill. A committee spokesman said that the committee understood there would be no floor action until Kissinger appeared December 3. The question remains why Kissinger avoided testifying the week of November 12 and thus delayed final consideration of the Trade Bill, particularly in light of the fact that President Ford had welcomed Congress back on November 18 with a list of legislative goals including a special appeal for passage of the Trade Bill.[86] The forceful protest in the Gromyko letter of October 26 may have had something to do with it. Kissinger had withheld the letter from everyone in Congress, perhaps waiting for the criticism in the Soviet Union to subside. He may have been looking for sure signs that the Soviets would be willing to see the passage of the Trade Bill through and take their concessions despite their objections.

Signs that the letter exchange was in trouble persisted. Speaking to an American business audience on November 12. Soviet Ambassador Dobrynin asserted "bluntly" that increased United States trade with the Soviet Union was necessary if political detente was to be successful.[87] More or less the same view was echoed in Moscow days later by Deputy Minister of Trade Aleksei N. Manshulo, who was quoted in *Pravda* as saying, "It is useless to hope that détente in the full sense of this word is possible in conditions of trade discrimination. . . . Détente and discrimination are hardly compatible."[88]

Senator Walter F. Mondale was in Moscow the week of November 12 and spoke with Kosygin and Gromyko, who said the Soviets had no obligation to meet any standard of free emigration. Gromyko, who was particularly harsh, made remarks that seemed directly related to Jackson's public claims. He said the Soviet Union could not be held responsible for statements made in the United States. The Soviet Union alone could make and interpret its own emigration policy. At the time, Mondale did not know about the October 26 letter. Had he known, he might have recognized that

Gromyko's remarks in mid-November were reiterating the repudiation expressed in his October letter to Kissinger.

Mondale's report of his conversations was relayed from the American embassy in Moscow via carefully guarded diplomatic channels back to the State Department. Instructions on the Mondale cables alerted Kissinger's assistant Sonnenfeldt about the proper distribution of the material contained in the cables. It would not be unlikely that Kissinger learned in that way that the Soviet position remained unaltered since issuing its forceful protest of October 26.

Had Kissinger testified before the Finance Committee in mid-November when Byrd wanted, the secretary of state would have been expected to amplify on the assurances that were the basis for the compromise between the administration and Jackson. Detailing those assurances would have carried a risk of pushing the Soviet leadership to make public their protests, which were heretofore stated in a private, diplomatic note. Kissinger may have chosen to duck the issue in November to give Soviet tempers time to cool. It also gave Kissinger and Ford a chance to discuss the issue with the Soviet leadership at Vladivostok.

"Much has still to be done to really clear the way for the development of equitable trade and economic links between our countries." That was Brezhnev's testy greeting to President Gerald Ford whom he met for the first time at the Vladivostok Summit on November 23.[89] What else was said about the emigration issue at Vladivostok is rather unclear. Several months after the event, one of Kissinger's associates said that Gromyko's October 26 protest was reduced by remarks of Brezhnev at Vladivostok. According to one unidentified source, Brezhnev's speaking with Ford and Kissinger "reaffirmed that while they [the Soviets] did not like the [Kissinger-Jackson] letters, emigration would go forward, on the basis that they had explained earlier in the year."[90] Jackson, Ribicoff, Javits, and Vanik said they, too, were under the impression that "In the period since October 18 the assurances contained in Secretary Kissinger's letter have been reaffirmed on several occasions—by General Secretary Brezhnev in Vladivostok. . . . "[91]

Kissinger was given the opportunity on December 3—when he finally appeared before the Finance Committee—to clarify the entire situation, including what had transpired at Vladivostok. Faced with the necessity of amplifying on the assurances for the committee, Kissinger had to decide whether to heed Gromyko's warning to end the "silence" and "ambiguities." Kissinger had gotten as far as he had in the agreement as much by what he had not said as by what he had said. Clarifying the situation once and for all might destroy whatever chances existed for the agreement to stick. If he told the committee about Gromyko's letter, the senators would probably say there was no basis for any so-called agreement. They would have seen through the transparency of Kissinger's so-called assurances in the October 18 exchange of correspondence. The agreement would have evaporated in the light of public disclosure. If, on the other hand, Kissinger tried to reinforce the public's and Congress's impression that the Soviets were still in agreement on actual specifics and spelled that out, the Soviet government would have probably felt compelled to repudiate him publicly by making Gromyko's letter public knowledge. That, too, would have meant the end of any possible agreement.

Thus, Kissinger's performance before the Finance Committee December 3 displayed the quintessence of ambiguity. Rather than clarifying the situation, his statement was full of equivocation. He stated that "a satisfactory compromise was achieved on an unprecedented and extraordinarily sensitive set of issues," but warned,

> I must state flatly that if I were to assert here that a formal agreement on emigration from the USSR exists between our governments, that statement would immediately be repudiated by the Soviet government. . . . It was consistently made clear to us that Soviet explanations applied to the definition of criteria and did not represent a commitment as to numbers. If any number was used in regard to Soviet emigration, this would be wholly our responsibility; that is, the Soviet government could not be held accountable for or bound by any such figure.[92]

Neither Ribicoff, Jackson, Javits, the Soviets, nor anyone else—except perhaps George Meany and his close Senate ally Senator Vance Hartke and some political groups tougher than Jackson on the Soviet Union—objected to Kissinger's vague "assurances." Rather, Jackson interpreted Kissinger's December remarks to the Finance Committee as reconfirmation of prior Soviet assurances on emigration. He said that "Kissinger went beyond what had already been made public." This is part of what Jackson selected as significant in Kissinger's December remarks:

> I have had many conferences on this subject with Ambassador Dobrynin and conferences with Foreign Minister Gromyko. . . . In addition, when President Ford took office he had some conferences in which the statements which I have made here were reconfirmed by the same individuals. Finally, General Secretary Brezhnev has made analogous statements to President Nixon, to myself and recently to President Ford. This is the structure of the assurances that we have.

> SENATOR HARTKE: Are the assurances then made from Mr. Brezhnev, Mr. Gromyko and Mr. Dobrynin?

> SECRETARY KISSINGER: That is correct.[93]

If Jackson doubted Kissinger or the Soviets, he did not say so.

BATTLE OF THE LOBBIES

Thus, the stage was set for the full Senate debate of the Trade Bill to begin December 10. Jackson proceeded as planned by formally introducing the waiver, amendment number 2000, on December 9. Jackson's remarks to the Senate were unrevealing. He explained the strictly technical meaning of the waiver. Again, if he had doubts about the tripartite agreement, particularly after Kissinger's performance on December 3, he did not say so.[94]

The last legislative hurdle was to beat the clock as Congress raced to adjourn in time for Christmas. The leadership aimed to adjourn on December 20, leaving only ten days to resolve the Trade Bill and the Export-Import Bank Bill. The remaining issue was whether the Trade Bill with the Jackson-Kissinger compromise appended would pass in time or whether labor's unalterable opposition combined with the Senate's natural tendency to add amendments to a bill when it is being debated on the Senate floor would prevent Senate passage of the Trade Bill before adjournment. That question hinged on whether the Senate could evoke cloture cutting off debate and nongermane amendments that weighed down the bill and prevented the Senate's final consideration.

The race against the clock on the Trade Bill became a battle between the lobbies. NCSJ's Jerry Goodman commented on the shifting alliances, "At one point, we [the Jews] were sleeping with the labor movement. At another point, they [labor] got up and called themselves chaste."[95] Labor's tactic was to delay the bill to death, but as one Jackson staffer attested, "their lobbying was rotten." Jackson's role during this battle between his early allies—labor and the Jewish groups—was intriguing. Said Korey, "We were signalled by the White House. In this stage of the game, we were united with the White House in opposition to Meany." The White House conveyed to the Jewish activists in New York that Jackson was not doing enough to fend off labor's threat to the bill. The Jewish groups were asked to urge Jackson's office to involve itself more actively.[96] Jackson—along with Ribicoff and Javits—decided to sign the cloture petition, which was necessary to have a cloture vote scheduled.

The vote was scheduled for Friday, December 13. On Wednesday night—December 11—Richard Perle and Morris Amitay—who by then headed the American-Israel Public Affairs Committee—began placing telephone calls around the country to generate phone calls to the Senate offices to encourage an "aye" vote to invoke cloture. Perle struck gold when he called Abraham Bayer of the National Jewish Community Relations Advisory Council, which represents some eighty local groups and eight national Jewish organizations. Bayer at first said he could not help in the telephone campaign. He was preparing for a board meeting of forty Jewish community leaders the next day. Perle suggested that Bayer and his entire board drop their scheduled agenda and instead make calls back to the communities they represented to get the telephone calls pouring into the Senate offices to urge an "aye" vote.

At this point, Jewish groups, business groups, and the White House were all lobbying on the same side. President Ford lobbied personally as did his lobbying staff, GOP leaders Hugh Scott and Robert Griffin (R.-Mich.), acting Democratic leader Robert C. Byrd (D.-W.Va.), and self-appointed liberal whip Alan Cranston. Cranston found that liberals who would ordinarily heed labor's opposition instead supported cloture because they wanted to encourage detente with the Soviet Union and wanted the provisions on human rights to pass. Others stated their concern for the worsening world economic crisis and feared the adverse effects of not passing a Trade Bill to deal with the problem of international trade barriers.

Another important factor paving the way to a cloture vote was a deal struck by Trade Bill floor manager Russell Long and President Ford. Long reportedly agreed to bring the bill to a vote only after President Ford gave him a commitment not to oppose actively Senate passage of the cargo preference bill. The latter bill favored the maritime industry by requiring that 30 percent of all oil imported into the United States would eventually be transported in United States flag vessels. With the assurance that the president would see to it that a vote would be scheduled on cargo preference before Congress adjourned, Chairman Long threw his weight behind final consideration of the Trade Bill.[97]

The vote on cloture was taken on December 13, after only one day of debate on the bill. On the first try, by a healthy margin of seventy-one to nineteen (eleven more than the then required two-thirds of the members of the Senate present and voting), the Senate invoked debate-limiting cloture. The wide margin was a surprise to everyone—opponents and proponents alike. A not insignificant reason for the outcome was the fact that right before the roll on cloture was called, a "live" quorum call had been ordered requiring all senators to be present on the Senate floor. Before his captive audience, acting leader Robert Byrd announced that

If the Congress is unable to reach a final disposition of this bill one way or the other by the close of business next Friday [December 20, the date Congress was scheduled to adjourn], . . . we will have to continue in session beyond that date or we will be called back into session to act on this bill one way or another. So I would hope, in order to shorten the misery for all of us, that, Senators, if they can, vote for cloture, they will do it now rather than delay.[98]

After the cloture vote, four Jackson staffers—Perle, Fosdick, Silber, and Charles Horner—were given the privilege of remaining on the Senate floor for the rest of the debate. With his team in place and the way cleared for the legislative finale by virtue of the cloture vote, Jackson called up amendment number 200, the waiver provision that he, Javits, and Ribicoff had worked out with the Ford administration. His lengthy statement described the history of the amendment and the negotiations with the administration. He interpreted the meaning of the letters exchanged and explained the waiver section. This speech was intended to provide "legislative history" in the event that the legislation required future interpretation.[99]

DISREGARDING THE DOUBTERS

Jackson was sure of a legislative victory and he seemed assured that legislative victory would also spell diplomatic victory over the Soviet Union. His remarks about Kissinger, with whom he had clashed throughout the nine months of negotiations, were conciliatory. "I had my differences with Dr. Kissinger, but he stayed with it and in the end, we were able to reach the agreement, and that is the way negotiations are carried out."[100]

Jackson disregarded any signs that the agreement to which he had devoted so much energy might be built on shifting sands. Jackson chose not to interpret negatively the increase of harassment following the October 18 exchange of correspondence. In answer to Conservative James Buckley, he explained "I am not surprised—I am not at all surprised—by the harassment that continues before this arrangement is [put into] formal effect."[101] He gave no inkling that he thought the so-called Soviet assurances were not so sure.

> The assurances in Secretary Kissinger's letter are no less solemn, no less binding, and no less significant, because of the form in which they have been conveyed from Soviet representatives to President Ford and Secretary Kissinger and from President Ford and Secretary Kissinger to the Congress. The assurances conveyed in Secretary Kissinger's letter are broad and inclusive.[102]

A few senators criticized Jackson's arrangement with Kissinger and the Soviet Union. Vance Hartke, a close ally of labor, was skeptical of the Jackson-Ribicoff-Javits compromise. "I just daresay there is not a member of the Senate who understands exactly what this does. I am willing to say very simply that it does nothing. It is a propaganda vehicle. All it says, we hope and pray."[103]

Jackson also defended the agreement against right-wing critics. The Jewish Defense League considered the Jackson-Kissinger compromise a "sell-out." Right-wing criticism expressed in the Senate on December 13, however, arose from Jesse Helms (R.-N.C.) and Strom Thurmond (R.-S.C.), who introduced an amendment they claimed corrected some of the problems in the original Jackson amendment. They said their amendment—in contrast to the Jackson amendment—was concerned about other groups, not only Jews, and about other Communist countries, not only the Soviet Union. Their amendment dealt not so much with the right to emigrate as with the right to visit family living outside Communist borders and to return to homes in Communist lands.

Jackson fended off the challenge with the help of Javits and Ribicoff. Said Javits, "My colleagues and I would never have dreamed of confining this amendment, either in substance or in form to anything but all citizens of the Soviet Union. So it applies universally and without restraint or restriction of any kind or character."[104]

Whether Helms was distorting the picture or was simply confused by the rhetoric from the offices of the principal sponsors of the amendment that had dwelled almost exclusively on the question of Soviet Jews, Jackson and his colleagues had to deal with Helms's challenge. Jackson was solicitous in his remarks to Helms. "I am concerned that if the language of his [Helms's] amendment . . . is put in this bill, it might prejudice the agreement that we have already worked out [with the administration]. . . . Suppose we get together and discuss this matter after we vote on the pending amendment number 2000."[105]

The roll was called on amendment number 2000, the waiver. The final vote was eighty-eight to zero. Even Vance Hartke, Jesse Helms, and Strom Thurmond voted "aye." James Abourezk (D.-S.D.) nearly cast the single dissenting vote. The senator of Arab origin expressed to the Senate his resentment of what he perceived to be Jewish pressure. He told about being contacted by the B'nai B'rith in 1972 when he was serving in the House of Representatives. He questioned the early involvement in the Jackson amendment of AIPAC. Apparently Abourezk's first reaction was that if Jackson was sponsoring the amendment relating to Soviet Jewry, he should oppose it. Ironically, it took Richard Perle and Abraham Ribicoff huddling with the Arab senator on the Senate floor to convince Abourezk that the vote in question was on a waiver to the original Jackson amendment. Abourezk switched his vote and the waiver passed unanimously.[106]

Jackson still had to deal with the conservative challenge. There were private discussions off the Senate floor in the adjoining lobby. On behalf of Jackson, Ribicoff had sounded a public threat to fight Helms's amendment as originally introduced. "If the Senator from North Carolina would delete the word 'visit' I would be only too glad to recommend that we accept the Helms amendment. . . . In the event he fails to do so, the Senator from Washington [Jackson] will be constrained to move to table the Helms amendment. However, it would be my recommendation that if Senator Helms would delete just the word 'visit,' we could very easily accept the Helms amendment."[107] After further discussions in the Senate lobby, Helms agreed to the modifications demanded, and the Senate passed his amendment as modified. Later that day, in a move that caught Helms—as well as Jackson, Ribicoff, and Javits—by surprise, Senator Nelson moved to attach the Jackson waiver to the modified Helms amendment. Long, the floor manager, accepted the amendment.[108]

Jackson was not alone in wanting a final resolution to the problem. Aside from labor and a few conservative critics in the Senate, almost everyone—cosponsor and noncosponsor of the Jackson amendment, friends of Jackson and friends of the president—was anxious to resolve the twenty-seven-month fight. On December 13, the Senate finally voted on the Trade Bill, which now included both the original Jackson amendment and amendment number 2000, the waiver. Compared to the exciting battle over cloture and the unanimous passage of the waiver, the final vote on the Trade Bill as amended was anticlimactic. The vote was seventy-seven to four. Opposing were James Abourezk, Vance Hartke, James A. McLure, an outspoken anticommunist (R.-Idaho), who was apparently still unappeased by the adoption of the modified Helms-Thurmond amendment, and Lee Metcalf (D.-Mont.). After seven record votes and one quorum call—at 11:32 a.m., 11:49 a.m., 12:06 p.m., 12:16 p.m., 12:30 p.m., 3:48 p.m., 5:21 p.m., and 6:45 p.m.—the Trade Bill finally passed the Senate.[109] Ironically, the Trade Bill, which was inherently controversial, aside from the Jackson amendment, passed easily partly because debate had been diverted to the issue of the Jackson amendment.

Chairman of the Finance Committee Long announced the Senate representatives to the conference committee called for Wednesday, December 18, to resolve differences in the House and Senate versions of the Trade Bill. Only two days remained before Congress recessed for Christmas and adjourned the Ninety-third Congress.

THE EMPEROR HAD NO CLOTHES

As both the Trade Bill and the Export-Import Bank Bill conference committees were preparing to meet in Washington, the Central Committee of the Communist Party of the USSR—three hundred and sixty of the most powerful individuals in the Soviet Union—held its semiannual meeting in Moscow December 16. One cannot say what actually went on behind the Kremlin's closed doors. No doubt the gathering spanned the same political spectrum that existed in the eleven-man Polituro that had met before Gromyko handed his letter of protest to Kissinger on October 26 and that met again on December 18.[110] We know that on the afternoon of December 18, the Soviet government released the October 26 letter written by Gromyko to Kissinger that had remained secret for nearly two months. It was the first time since the Cuban missile crisis that the Soviet government had released diplomatic records.[111]

Accompanying the October 26 letter was a *Tass* statement that was widely distributed in the Soviet Union and the United States by the international wire services and by Soviet diplomats fanning out over Capitol Hill. The *Tass* statement discussed "bills" (in the plural referring, presumably, to the Trade Bill and the Export-Import Bank Bill), which had "been approved separately by the House of Representatives and the Senate, and after the finalizing of the texts in the House-Senate conference committee, they are subject to final endorsement by the two Houses." The statement said, "*Tass* is authorized to state that leading circles in the Soviet Union flatly reject as unacceptable any attempts, from who[m]ever they may come, to interfere in internal affairs that are entirely the concern of the Soviet state and no one else." The attempts mentioned were "provisions concerning, for instance, the departure of Soviet citizens for other countries, for making available economic information of a purely domestic nature to American institutions, etc."[112] The Soviet statement, however, stopped short of specifically rejecting American trade concessions if they were tied to Jackson's demands in the Trade Bill.

BREZHNEV AND HIS DOMESTIC CRITICS

Commentators, including Moscow-based diplomats, have explained the definitive Soviet protest as a product of a combination of domestic-based pressures. They believed Brezhnev was faced with the need to placate his conservative critics within the party by releasing the earlier letter to Kissinger to prove he was not giving too much away to Washington.[113] This period coincided with a period of political weakness for Brezhnev. Earlier it was speculated that Brezhnev may have felt himself on the political defensive and so decided to present Kissinger the letter of protest on October 26. After that, it seemed Brezhnev never recovered sufficient political strength to overcome domestic criticism against accommodating Jackson. For a period of six weeks in November and December, Brezhnev did not appear in public at all. He cancelled several meetings with foreign dignitaries including Senator Mondale. On December 29, he cancelled a much-heralded trip to Egypt, scheduled since November, indicating that his Egyptian policy may have also been under attack during this period.[114] Brezhnev was thought to be ill during this period, so any political weakness he was suffering was compounded by physical weakness.

To complicate matters, the Central Committee of the Communist Party was holding its semiannual meeting in Moscow, and Brezhnev could not ignore that event. He delivered a major speech. The Central Committee is generally a rubber-stamp for the Politburo, except during leadership crisis, when competing groups in the Politburo seek support from members of the Central Committee. December was such a period of crisis. During the meeting, there were signs of pressure on Brezhnev to withdraw the assurances on Jewish emigration and signs that the Kremlin might repudiate the original pact with the United States.

Those who may have challenged Brezhnev on the emigration issue included representatives of party and state bureaucracies who had opposed relaxation of internal controls of which unrestricted emigration was surely the most controversial. The advocates of internal control had been forced by the supporters of detente to accept compromises in their demands at various stages. After the November Vladivostok agreement, President Nikolai Podgorny expressed the rear-guard resistance to internal relaxation by asserting that it would be "intolerably short-sighted" not to take "full account" of foreign attempts to interfere in matters of "internal state policy." Added Podgorny, who in the past had opposed Brezhnev over detente and who had been associated with efforts to tighten the citizenship laws, "our internal affairs have never been and will never be a matter for political bargaining."[115] Leaving aside his critics, Brezhnev must have also personally resented the publicity surrounding the Jackson amendment agreement.[116] According to an account related from Moscow a month after this event,

. . . the word was being put out today that Brezhnev had personally decided the trade act should be rejected and presented that decision for ratification at the Communist Party plenum December 16.[117]

Both Brezhnev and Brezhnev's domestic critics had a number of reasons to be upset by the course of events in the United States that led to the stinging protest of December 18. The fallout from the Vladivostok agreement may have been part of the building pressure to issue the statement. On December 6, Jackson had circulated to the press a memorandum he had sent to his Senate colleagues calling for repudiation of the Vladivostok agreement on the grounds that the limitations were insufficient. Kissinger responded to that move saying that "If the pattern of the trade bill is repeated, then détente would be endangered."[118] Reportedly, it angered Brezhnev to think that American political figures might believe badgering successfully on the emigration issue suggested that the Soviets could be similarly forced to come to terms on nuclear arms accords.[119] Administration strategists were worried that Jackson's repudiation of the Vladivostok accord combined with the conditions he had already placed on MFN and credits would, in Kissinger's words, reach "a breaking point."[120]

Speculating on the reason for the December 18 Soviet blast, Kissinger also placed heavy emphasis on the negative impact of the credit restriction included in the Export-Import Bank Bill. "I believe," said Kissinger, "that the Soviet statements on Jewish emigration have been caused, in part, by Soviet disappointment with the credit restrictions. . . . The Soviet Union was much more interested in credits than it was in trade, because for the next four or five years, it will have very little in reciprocal trade."[121]

Finally, a middle-level Soviet embassy official who said he had been authoritatively briefed gave a *New York Times* reporter attending a Soviet embassy reception on December 19 an explanation of what led to the protest the day before, which emphasized the manner in which the so-called assurances were handled by both Jackson and the White House.

Moscow was furious with the exchange of letters on October 18. . . . In particular, the Soviet leaders were upset with Mr. Kissinger for having said that he had been assured that harassment would end.

If he had said "we expect" or "it is our understanding" that would have been better than "we have been assured," the diplomat said.

Moreover, the diplomat said, the fact that the letters were released by Mr. Jackson at the White House was irritating. He said the Soviet Union had expected that the details be made public in Congress, not in the White House. Of particular concern, the diplomat said, was the impression created by Mr. Jackson that the Soviet Union had agreed to permit sixty thousand Jews and others to leave in the first year of the accord.[122]

INTERPRETING THE SOVIET PROTESTS

It is hard enough years after the event to interpret the meaning of the protest. However, as the life of the Trade and Export-Import Bank bills were hanging in the balance in the final days of the Ninety-third Congress, Kissinger and Jackson had to react quickly. Jackson's office just happened to learn of the Soviet protest when a friend of staff member Tina Silber heard a radio broadcast and called the Jackson office with the news. Perle tried contacting the State Department for its interpretation of the events. He managed to reach Sonnenfeldt at the Sans Souci restaurant at lunch, but he was little help.

Meanwhile, Kissinger was lunching with Dobrynin. It is not known for sure what transpired over lunch. One report said Dobrynin "projected a scenario in which the October 1972 trade agreement would be placed in jeopardy."[123] Soviet embassy officials were also distributing the new statement over Capitol Hill. Some simply dropped off copies of the *Tass* protest without engaging in discussion of its import. Others spoke with members of Senate staffs and suggested that the Soviet protest spelled the end to the entire trade agreement of 1972. The Soviet Union, said one diplomat, could stop payments on lend-lease, which had been scheduled in the original 1972 agreement. Stopping payment meant pulling out of the 1972 pact.

The Soviet community in Washington, it appeared, was sending contradictory signals. A Jackson aide claimed that Soviet diplomats were informing congressmen not to worry about the protest because even though the Kremlin was upset by the publicity given to the compromise, it did not want to set back improvement in Soviet-American relations.[124] A "well-known Israeli lobbyist" said he got a phone call from a Soviet diplomat that day who said twice that the *Tass* statement "was nothing new" and that it should not worry him.[125] (The statement was not literally new, as it had been written on October 26, but the public release of the letter was new.)

Administration Interpretation. The official administration response was relaxed. The State Department was reported to be initially surprised by the

Tass statement. Later in the day of December 18—presumably after Kissinger's luncheon with Dobrynin—the following reassuring statement was issued: "The private communication from Foreign Minister Gromyko to the secretary of October 26, which was published by *Tass* today, does not in our view change the understandings referred to in the Secretary's letter to Senator Jackson of October 18." The announcement added that it "has always made clear" that there was no agreement on specific numbers of emigrants permitted to leave the Soviet Union.[126]

Jackson Interpretation. On Capitol Hill, the mood was also reported to be "surprisingly relaxed." "We should keep our cool," said Jackson. The senator who in the past had been known to show his temper over the way Kissinger had handled relations with the Soviet Union did not complain about not being informed earlier of the Gromyko letter. On Capitol Hill and in the State Department, the explicit omission in the *Tass* statement of an absolute rejection of the legislation was taken as evidence that the protests were merely "face-saving."[127] Jackson explained that the protests were intended for Soviet domestic consumption. He displayed a concern for the internal pressures on the Soviet leadership not displayed in the period after October 18, 1972. The only difficulty with his "face-saving" explanation is that there is some evidence Jackson may not have believed what he was saying.[128] Jackson was surprised by the Gromyko letter. He had no time to reflect on its significance and, given the short time left in the Ninety-third Congress, no choice but to refrain from objecting. His only refuge was to achieve a legislative victory, even if it were pyrrhic diplomatically. He downplayed the significance of the protests. In that sense, Jackson's reasoning was also a "face-saving" exercise.

One could interpret the October 26 letter as a flank-protecting exercise when it was written. But the release of the letter, on December 18, after all the previous indications of Soviet protests, could hardly be regarded as face-saving. Jackson was so close to the end of the battle. Final passage of the bill and the signature of the president would mark a dramatic legislative victory vis-à-vis the executive branch. Jackson could also construe final passage as proof that his hard-line approach of dealing with the Soviet Union worked. If Jackson admitted at that late date that the Soviet protests were not face-saving, but rather sure signs that something was wrong, it would have destroyed the chances for the legislation to pass. As for the diplomatic victory, if he said the Soviet Union was repudiating the agreement because his demands had been too stringent, he was, in effect, admitting that he had misjudged the reaction of the Soviet leadership. Downplaying the reaction assured legislative success and at least diminished the chances of being blamed for a diplomatic fiasco.

The Critics' Interpretation. The alignment of reactions to the Soviet protests were similar to the positions assumed during the Senate Trade Bill debate December 13. Those who had a stake in the original agreement belittled Soviet protests. Jackson, Javits, and Ribicoff on Capitol Hill and Henry Kissinger speaking for the administration insisted that the Soviet protests did not nullify the agreement. They were unwilling to recognize that the emperor had no clothes.

Only a very few individuals admitted that the emperor was in fact quite naked. During the December 13 Senate debate, Senators Hartke and Helms had criticized the agreement, even though they had voted for the waiver that was based on the assumption that an agreement existed. After the Soviet authorities released Gromyko's protest letter on December 18, George Meany of the AFL-CIO became the most outspoken insister that no agreement existed. That such an announcement might embarrass Jackson and Kissinger equally was of little consequence. According to an AFL-CIO spokesman, Meany had just told Jackson that "there is no inclination on Meany's part or on the AFL-CIO's part to make an early endorsement" of Jackson for president.[129]

Meany had a stake in heralding the inexistence of an agreement on emigration just as Jackson and Kissinger had a stake in insisting agreement still existed. Meany did not want an accord on Soviet trade concessions for both personal and professional reasons. Meany, a resolute anticommunist, opposed trading with the Soviet Union in principle. Meany also opposed an agreement because it removed the last roadblock in the way of final passage of the Trade Bill, which would "cause thousands of American workers to lose their jobs in order to increase the profits of American-based multinational corporations, whose greed is beyond belief and whose United States income tax breaks are fantastic."[130]

Meany attacked Jackson and Kissinger for their role in the so-called Soviet trade agreement. Meany said that Kissinger deceived the Congress and the American people for more than eight weeks. "Kissinger concealed the very agreement he was defending before the Committee." Meany also called Jackson "either a dupe of Kissinger or . . . he too misled the American people. . . . Jackson and others whooped the bill through under a Senate gag rule. . . . Senator Jackson continues the charade. He continues the fight for a measure that will rip off the American taxpayer, increase joblessness and benefit only the greedy, multinational corporations and the Soviet Union."[131]

TRADE BILL CONFERENCE

The December 18 Trade Bill conference met in the Capitol Building to decide once and for all the outcome of the Jackson amendment, particularly in light of the unexpected Soviet protest. The administration had issued an official statement reassuring the conferees that it was sticking by the October 18 exchange of correspondence. Trade officials William Eberle and Harold Malmgren also sat in on the conference to provide up-to-the-minute administration's reactions to the deliberations of the conference.

Malmgren also happened to be the bearer of Jackson's equally relaxed reaction to the December 18 events. He answered the telephone call that Richard Perle put in to Ribicoff, a conferee, to inform Ribicoff to "cool it," as that was what Jackson was doing. After the call, Ribicoff delivered a "three-minute discourse" to the conference. One of the House of Representative conferees remarked that "If the Russians don't like it, it must be good. Let's pass it." Long, who was chairman of the conference committee, said, "I don't pay attention to what the Russians say anyway."[132] So the conference decided to approve the Jackson amendment and its waiver as part of the Trade Bill.

EXPORT-IMPORT BANK CONFERENCE

Meanwhile, the Export-Import Bank Bill conference was also meeting on the afternoon of December 18. The *Tass* statement had complained about restrictions placed on lending. That may have referred to an earlier Export-Import conference on December 16, which decided to include a $300 million ceiling on loans to the Soviet Union. The December 18 conference maintained that provision with very little opposition by the administration. Jackson had kept close tabs on the months of legislative wrangling over the Export-Import Bank. In contrast, Kissinger focused almost exclusively on the negotiations with Jackson regarding the Trade Bill and ignored Export-Import Bank Bill developments even though they were so closely related.

Administration officials warned Kissinger that it was a mistake to ignore what was happening on the Export-Import Bank legislation because its outcome would inevitably affect the outcome of the three-cornered negotiations on trade and emigration. Said one official, "I'd bring it back to the White House and say we've got to settle both [Trade Bill and the Export-Import Bank Bill] at the same time. . . . At no point did we get anyone to agree . . . [that] it had to be handled at the same time." Another State Department source confirmed that "No one at the Kissinger level focused on what was happening on the credits." Reportedly, staff reports prepared by the State Department noted each of the three times that the Senate and House conferences met on the Export-Import Bank Bill.[133]

On December 3 Kissinger was given a chance to oppose the ceiling in public. Instead, he concentrated his attention almost exclusively on resolving the Jackson amendment in the Trade Bill. Senator Harry Byrd, Jr., the author of a credit ceiling that was compatible with the Stevenson-Jackson ceiling in the Export-Import Bank Bill and which enjoyed Jackson's support, asked Kissinger on December 3, "Do you oppose a ceiling on additional loans and guarantees to Russia?" Byrd pointed out in his question that the restriction was not actually in the Export-Import Bank Bill at that particular stage. However, Stevenson and Jackson had attempted to include it months before, and the final outcome of their efforts regarding that bill, which was still in conference, and the Trade Bill, which was still subject to amendments, was unresolved. Kissinger did not indicate concern that a credit ceiling would threaten Soviet-American relations nor did he convey a strong objection to the ceiling.[134]

The connection between the two pieces of legislation was becoming clearer but not to Kissinger, the one person who might have done something to avert it. Recalled an administration official, "I wrote a memo to Kissinger at least a week before the vote on Export-Import that we're going to get this limitation. Then it passed, and it [the ceiling] got put in the Trade Bill too. About four or five days afterward, he [Kissinger] said publicly that his people had not informed him about the ceiling. [But] he had a memo. . . . I remember sitting and talking with Henry and the President about this." Judging from remarks of a Kissinger associate denigrating Eberle and Export-Import Bank President William Casey, who were authorized to be liaisons between Congress and the executive branch on these issues, it appears that Kissinger must have discounted their warnings. Kissinger's associate claimed "Eberle was willing to throw the babies off the sled to get the Trade Bill going" and Casey "cared only about the Bank."

On December 13, the Senate passed the Byrd amendment to the Trade Bill, which added a ceiling of $300 million on all loans to the Soviet Union by any agency of the United States government, including the bank. On December 16, the Export-Import Bank Conference met and put the original Stevenson-Jackson ceiling (that had been weakened in an October conference) back into the bill. Ambassador Dobrynin had personally lodged an angry protest about the credit limitations and had focused Kissinger's attention on the problem.[135] However, Kissinger did little to try to get the December 18 Export-Import Bank Bill Conference to reverse the December 16 decision to include a ceiling. The conference decided to maintain the $300 million ceiling, which could be raised if both houses of Congress voted to do so by a concurrent resolution. As quoted earlier, Adlai Stevenson complained that "Kissinger himself, raised no strenuous objection" up until this point.[136]

Thus, the Export-Import Bank Bill Conference met, resolved its differences, and reported out the bill December 18. The House passed the report the same evening by 280 to 96 votes, and the Senate scheduled a vote for the next afternoon; the vote in the Senate was 71 to 24. Only after Congress had completed action on the bill did Kissinger order the State Department spokesman to denounce the credit limitation (which was incorrectly described as limiting loans to $75 million a year for four years) as "grossly discriminatory."[137]

The Trade Bill was in its second day of conference on December 19. The day before, the conferees had approved the Jackson amendment with the waiver previously worked out by Jackson and the administration. While State Department officials were less sanguine about the meaning of the Soviet protests than they had been the day before, the conferees nevertheless agreed on the conference report, which was quickly passed *pro forma* by both houses and sent to the president's desk for a signature or veto. Both houses adjourned December 20 leaving the president to deal with the problem of Soviet protests.

SOVIET PROTESTS CONTINUE

The Soviets never stopped protesting after the initial December 18 outcry. After the enactment of the two bills, protests appeared in *Izvestia, Pravda, Literaturnaia Gazeta,* and on radio.[138] Nevertheless, Kissinger seemed to hope the Soviet Union would not actually withdraw from the trade agreement. Said Kissinger in a December 23 interview, "I think the Soviets wanted to make clear ahead of time what their attitude was so later they could not be accused of having doublecrossed." Kissinger did not specify what he meant by "later." It might have meant in a matter of weeks—after final passage of the Trade Bill—or, it could have meant in eighteen months when the Congress would debate the issue of renewing MFN by reviewing Soviet behavior in the time elapsed.[139]

By December 28, any basis for hoping that the three-way pact had not been irrevocably destroyed began to disappear, when the highest official to comment on passage of the Jackson amendment, *Tass* Director General Leonid Zamyatin, hinted that the Soviet Union might retaliate economically. "In the present situation, the failure of one of the parties to honor its commitments cannot help but affect the commitments assumed by the other party under a series of commercial and financial agreements."[140] Zamyatin did not elaborate on what kind of retaliatory action the Soviets might take other than the previously stated threats to take Soviet business to other Western European nations. But his remarks about previous commitments may have referred to the October 1972 Trade Agreement and suggested that attaching new restrictions to that agreement provided an excuse for the Soviet Union not to comply with obligations, undertaken in 1972, to pay its lend-lease debt according to a mutually agreed-upon schedule.[141] Dobrynin had threatened Soviet noncompliance in his stormy meeting with Kissinger December 18, as did lower echelon Soviet embassy staff in conversations on Capitol Hill. But this was the first public hint that lend-lease might not be paid and thus that the October 1972 Trade Agreement would be nullified.

On January 3, the eve of Ford's signing the Trade Reform Act, the hint was made explicitly and conspicuously. Ambassador Anatoly Dobrynin told *Washington Post* correspondent Murray Marder that "the United States was told on December 18 that if the conditions for freer emigration of Soviet Jews known as the Jackson Amendment, are enacted into law and enforced, the Kremlin would consider the 1972 accord invalid, and each portion of it would be up for re-examination on a piece-by-piece basis." Although an unidentified State Department official said the Soviet Union had not described the 1972 agreement as "null and void," the official did admit that the Soviet Union had told the United States that "there are questions about the 1972 accord, and that they want to discuss the matter."[142]

While reporter Marder was picking up suggestions in Washington that the Soviet Union might pull out of the Trade Agreement, a similar message from the Soviet Foreign Ministry was suggested to Marder's *Washington Post* colleague in Moscow, Peter Osnos. A day after Marder spoke with Dobrynin, his source in the Washington community of Soviet diplomats, Osnos reported that "some Foreign Ministry officials are urging that the trade bill be renounced altogether."[143]

TO VETO OR NOT

The president had some tough choices to make. If he vetoed the Trade Bill to eliminate the provision on emigration and the credit ceiling, he would have to veto all the provisions authorizing negotiations to eliminate global trade barriers, which many inside the business world and out wanted. Vetoing would also eliminate the congressional grant of authority to extend MFN treatment to the Soviet Union, which was needed to fulfill the 1972 Trade Agreement. Ford had added up the Soviet protests issued on October 26, plus the December 18 warning that the Soviet Union might not stick by the Trade Agreement. But there still remained a slim chance that the Soviets would not pull out of the agreement completely. Kissinger was asked what he advised the president to do. He answered:

> . . . we were already at a very narrow margin. . . . Would I have recom-
> mended to the President that he not sign it? That's very hard to know.
> One has to remember that it was believed that the trade bill was in the
> essential interests of the United States and in the essential interests of a
> more open trading system among all of the industrialized countries. . . .
> therefore, to recommend the President to veto this because there were
> aspects of it in the granting of MFN to the Soviet Union would have
> been a very heavy responsibility. . . . I believed that, while it would be a
> close call, the agreement that was made with Senator Jackson would
> probably stick. And therefore I agree with those who say that it was en-
> tered into in good faith by all of the parties. So the issue never arose.[144]

On January 3, 1975, Ford signed the Trade Reform Act, Jackson amend-
ment and all. Its new designation became Public Law 93-618. In his brief speech at the bill-signing ceremony, Ford did not single out Henry Jackson by name, but he said, "I must express my reservations about the wisdom of legislative language that can only be seen as objectionable and discriminatory by other sovereign states."[145]

The decision to sign on the following day the Export-Import Bank Amendments (Public Law 93-646), which included the $300 million ceiling on loans to the Soviet Union was easier to make. Kissinger later explained the thinking behind that:

For the United States to veto legislation which made credits available to American business for trading with the whole world—because of an unsatisfactory limitation with respect to the Soviet Union at the end of a prolonged period of negotiations—was a decision which the President felt he could not take, and it is a decision with which I agreed. It came down to a fine judgment. It would not have changed the basic problem, anyway, because with the Export-Import legislation vetoed, the Soviet Union would have had no reason to put into effect the trade provisions in any event. So we were faced with a very difficult choice. In one case, they would get three hundred million; in the other case, they could get nothing.[146]

In either event—Export-Import Bank Bill, vetoed or not—Ford had already signed into law the Jackson amendment restriction of MFN and credits and the Byrd amendment loan ceiling in the Trade Reform Act.

SOVIET REPUDIATION

After Ford signed the Trade Bill, the administration still had leeway in the administrative application of the congressional restrictions. The president had the right to waive the express conditions of the Jackson amendment concerning emigration for a period of eighteen months. The president, however, was required to certify to Congress that waiving the restrictions would "substantially promote the objective freedom of emigration" and that he had received assurances from the Soviet Union that its emigration policies were leading to the objective of freedom of emigration.[147]

The administration would have had to interpret these requirements in such a way that the October 18 letter written by Kissinger concerning Soviet assurances on emigration were fulfilled. But the events of December 18 could have been as easily interpreted by the administration as having overtaken the assurances expressed in Kissinger's October 18 letter. Jewish community leaders spoke with Ford for seventy minutes on December 20 and urged Ford not to use his authority to extend Soviet MFN until he was convinced that, despite the December 18 letter and reported increase in harassment, "freer emigration will result."[148] Administration officials felt they had to resume discussions with Moscow to confirm Soviet assurances on emigration that the Soviet Union would not repudiate before Ford could certify to Congress Soviet compliance and then waive the restrictions against granting the trade concessions. Moreover, since the original 1972 Trade Agreement was written to extend concessions for three years and the Jackson amendment had cut that back to eighteen months, the administration had to open discussions with the Soviet Union to remove that technicality.

Kissinger explained how he went about complying with the new law in early January in talks with Dobrynin.

We informed the Soviet Union of the precise steps that would have to be taken under the Trade Act to implement the Trade Agreement [of 1972] and to put into effect the waiver provisions of the Jackson-Vanik Amendment . . . which made it impossible for us to apply the waiver without some Soviet action. . . . the Soviet Union informed us that they would not participate in these actions.[149]

On Friday, January 10, the Soviet government sent a letter, heretofore unpublished, which apparently indicated the Soviets' refusal to comply with the need to provide assurances on emigration or to make technical changes in the 1972 trade agreement. On Monday, January 13, Kissinger and Dobrynin concluded discussions regarding the handling of the January 10 letter. It was agreed that Kissinger would make a public statement that both governments had agreed to. It said that the Soviet government refused to accept the additional requirements to the 1972 Trade Agreement and would not "put into force the 1972 trade agreement." President Ford could not unilaterally write Congress that he had assurances when the Soviet government also stated that "such statements would be repudiated by the Soviet government."
Therefore Kissinger announced:

. . . that the 1972 Trade Agreement cannot be brought into force at this time and the President will therefore not take the steps required for this purpose by the Trade Act. The President does not plan at this time to exercise the waiver authority.

The $300 million ceiling in the Export-Import Bank Bill was, explained Kissinger, "really moot, because no new credits can be extended under the existing legislation."[150]

SUMMARY

Chapter 5 is the story of a delicately balanced, highly sensitive, and easily disturbable three-way negotiation that took place from August 1974 to January 1975. As the months passed in the legislative schedule of the Ninety-third Congress, second session, and the pressure of the November elections worked its effect, Jackson found that time was less and less on his side. Negotiating proved to be more difficult than legislating for presidential aspirant Henry Jackson. It demonstrated some of the institutional constraints on congressional involvement in foreign policy making. Compared to the difficulties of negotiating with two branches of government and a foreign country—including numerous actors with varying interests—getting the Jackson-Vanik amendment passed by the House of Representatives in 1973 had been simple.

The forum in which Jackson (aided by Ribicoff and occasionally prodded by Javits, both with their own domestic political considerations) negotiated was a difficult one. His personal relationships with his negotiating partners were not always the most congenial. Jackson once boasted, "Kissinger is afraid of me."[151] Moreover, no executive branch official wants Congress directly involved in bargaining with foreign nations. Kissinger was no exception, and his new patron Ford also had definite ideas about the prerogatives of the executive branch even though he was originally a creature of Congress.

In September, when the presidential deadlock was broken by Ford's appointment, Jackson had to decide once and for all whether to sign an agreement that was not iron-clad on Soviet Jewry or to hold out longer and possibly destroy the entire Trade Bill and lose his best chance for an emigration arrangement. George Meany would have preferred no accommodation and no bill. Practically at the last minute, Jackson demanded that the agreed number of emigrants be increased. One could have read that as an effort to drag out the negotiations further. Subsequent events indicated, however, that Jackson had decided to settle and was only trying to squeeze out one last concession. He got Javits and Ribicoff to agree to a higher number, and he thought he had gotten the administration and the Soviet Union to go along too. In any event, he proved how badly he wanted an agreement by finally parting ways with George Meany over legislative strategy on the Trade Bill and by accepting less than precise assurances conveyed by Kissinger from the Soviets. This was the domestic political price that Jackson had to pay for a diplomatic settlement. (Jackson may have incurred the wrath of Meany by compromising his amendment and later by voting cloture on debate on the Trade Bill thus paving the way for its final passage. But Jackson still fought for labor's viewpoint as it related to Export-Import Bank lending practices and as it related to export controls over technology and industrial techniques that United States firms tried to sell to the Soviet Union.)

Jackson—not unlike many politicians involved in the "art of compromise"—was anxious to achieve a legislative victory after years of battle and decided it best not to ask too many questions or press too hard for less ambiguous pledges lest he be left with nothing to show for his efforts. He disregarded the trouble signs from the Soviet Union and insisted on conveying to the American public that Soviet pledges existed where the remarks of Kissinger threw such claims in question. When Kissinger withdrew the third letter spelling out administration assurances, Jackson had little room to maneuver. Congress was recessing for the November election after which Jackson's influence over his Senate colleagues would decline. Adjournment of the Ninety-third Congress was a few months away, and all pending legislation would die in which case his leverage over the Soviet Union by means of his amendment to the bill would vanish. Earlier in September, he had advertised a victory and paid the price of compromise by angering the AFL-CIO and other interest groups.

Getting an agreement that all three parties could accept was not the end of Jackson's problems. Jackson still had the dilemma of any politician pursuing a diplomatic goal. In a matter not atypical of a politician, Jackson advertised his diplomatic successes, which angered his Soviet negotiating partner and jeopardized the success he was claiming. Publication of the October 18 exchange of correspondence was unavoidable. Congress would not have passed the necessary waiver merely on the basis of Kissinger's and Jackson's word.[152] The post-Vietnam and post-Watergate mentality encouraged congressional exercise of influence over foreign policy, including probing for answers to obvious questions about the agreement. However, that does not excuse Jackson from undiplomatically declaring a victory over the Soviets.

To assure the amendment's legislative life, particularly against right-wing detractors, Jackson also made certain claims that jeopardized its diplomatic life. In response to James Buckley's questioning hours before the final Senate vote about how to gauge Soviet compliance to Jackson's amendment on emigration, Jackson replied:

> I would give the Russians a little bit of latitude, but I would not wait very long. They have had a lot of lead time. They have known about this amendment for the last two years and they should be able to start at once. So I would expect then, the moment this becomes law, that the basic conditions that have been laid down in the exchange of letters, in the statute, in the colloquies made on the floor which are part of the legislative history, will apply and that the Soviets will carry them out once the law is passed.[153]

The menacing language Jackson employed could only have irritated the Soviet Union and increased the chances that the Soviets would change their minds about being a silent partner to any accord. Ironically, after Buckley heard Jackson's remarks, he announced that he was "going to take the liberty after leaving this chamber to contact the Voice of America and suggest that a synopsis of what we have said here be beamed to Russia."[154]

The same point applies to some of the provisions for the renewal of the waiver. As written and agreed to, the waiver in amendment number 2000 would expire eighteen months after the date of enactment of the Trade Bill.

Jackson explained in his colloquy with Buckley that "I would hope the bill would become law before the first of the year."[155] According to provisions for congressional review, in approximately June of the presidential election of the year 1976, a debate on Soviet compliance and renewal of the waiver would be held. The debate, that Jackson would surely dominate, would extend into the thick of the presidential campaign and eve of the presidential election—October 1976.[156]

These provisions made sense for Jackson, the politician. But it raised challenges to the Soviet Union that placed the agreement in diplomatic jeopardy. The original October 1972 Trade Agreement had pledged MFN for a period of three years. Jackson chiseled that down to eighteen months with an expiration coinciding with the most politicized period in American life—the final months of a presidential campaign. Finally Jackson's efforts to set a ceiling on loans to the Soviet Union may have also jeopardized his arrangement with the Soviets.[157]

Conclusion

6

I wonder whether we have not been trading in very short-term benefits for long-term benefits to the (Soviet Union). . . . Senator Jackson has been making capital out of this general fear for quite some time. . . . For whatever reason, in addition to patriotism, he does this, I will leave for others to judge. . . .

U.S. SENATOR CLIFFORD CASE (R.-N.J.)
JULY 22, 1974

Understanding American foreign policy requires an understanding of the domestic politics shaping its formulation. The Jackson amendment illustrates several major characteristics of American domestic political life that give our foreign policy its particularly American character. It underscores the fact that America is (1) a pluralistic democracy, (2) a land of immigrants, (3) an economic superpower, (4) a nation with a sense of moral responsibility for events occurring elsewhere, and (5) a country with a federal government featuring two separate but equal branches of government sharing foreign policy-making powers. These are "givens" in the American political environment that shape and inspire America's foreign policy. These givens are more important under certain conditions, as the Jackson amendment demonstrates.

The Jackson amendment was an American initiative that tried to harness economic might to gain a moral object in another nation. It unfolded over a relatively long period. There was ample opportunity for two presidents and every member of Congress to be involved. Congress asserted itself in a major foreign policy area against the will of the executive branch. It did so by attempting to extract political concessions from the Soviet Union in exchange for American economic concessions. A human rights objective—that everyone should have the right to emigrate—became both a rallying point and a convenient cause for a wide range of interest groups: ethnic, economic, and ideological.

In democratic America, the pluralistic pressures of American society find greatest expression when those policy-makers who are elected politicians take a stand on an issue. Considerations relating to policy-makers' chances of remaining in office affect what positions they will take. The key actors in this study were, with one exception, elected politicians: Jackson, Javits, Ribicoff, Nixon, and Ford.

The exception was Henry Kissinger, who was a diplomat with a specialized constituency: the Soviet government. The requirements of his office differed from those of elected officials, and these institutional differences were reason enough for the clashes that occurred over how to deal with the Soviet Union. The State Department—like many scholars and diplomats elsewhere—traditionally tries to depoliticize foreign policy-making. The Jackson amendment is a clear case of the kind of foreign policy issue that resists depoliticizing in America. Indeed, to the degree that Kissinger ignored the Congress and domestic forces, he undermined the conduct of his diplomacy with the Soviet Union.

One must examine foreign policy issues—in this case, the Jackson amendment—with an awareness that an issue may serve a dual function: to advance or sustain politicians' careers and to achieve foreign policy objectives. For example, why did so many congressmen sponsor the Jackson amendment? Why did a few influential senators decide to join Jackson even though they objected to the foreign policy it embraced and even though they were unable to make but cosmetic changes in Jackson's early 1972 drafts? Why did President Nixon choose not to oppose the amendment in the fall of election year 1972, while, after his reelection to a final term in office, he became the amendment's leading opponent? The point is that the politician's behavior is purposeful. The calculations of self-interest made by the subjects of this study changed in answer to the questions, "whose self-interest, in the light of which facts, and over what time periods."[1] A politician will say that he was motivated to support a particular issue like the Jackson amendment because it advanced a human rights objective overseas. He will claim that the position he held was in the national interest for various reasons. But he may appear to others to have responded or appealed to domestic interest groups, ethnic or otherwise. In fact, all these considerations may have existed. Everyone's motives are mixed.[2] They may be unfathomable to them or anyone else. But one thing is nearly certain. When, for example, a politician decided to sponsor (or in Nixon's case, not to oppose) the amendment, he was not ignoring the impact of this decision on his political future. Almost invariably—and there are rare exceptions—the highly visible postures assumed for a protracted time were good—or at least not harmful—for him politically.

THE PRESIDENTIAL POLITICS
OF HENRY JACKSON

In Senator Jackson's case, there were conceivably two dominant domestic political considerations and two dominant diplomatic objectives. Jackson was running for president of the United States. His two dominant concerns in the domestic arena corresponded to concerns of the Jews and George Meany of the AFL-CIO, who would be important in the presidential race that Jackson was facing in 1976. In Jackson's amendment, the Jews found a champion for Soviet Jewish emigration. Meany also found a possible means to block congressional passage of the Trade Reform Act as well as to express sympathy for Soviet Jewry and to retard the policy of detente with the Soviet Union, which featured among other things liberalization of Soviet-American trade.

Identifying Jackson's domestic political considerations helps to explain why Jackson fought so hard for his amendment. It also helps to explain why he eventually stopped fighting and began talking and compromising. Of course, it is impossible to probe Jackson's psyche and delve into his innermost motives to say finally that this or that motive was more important than another. It is safe to assume that at different stages in the history of the amendment, one objective was more important than the other. However, the vicissitudes in the negotiations suggest that factual changes in the position of Jackson's negotiating partners, Kissinger, Nixon, Ford, and the

Soviets; changing time considerations imposed by the congressional time-table, scheduling of the national elections, and Watergate deliberations; as well as oscillating political calculations in relationship to Jackson's allies among the Jewish interest groups and the AFL-CIO were all important considerations.

Assessing Jackson's amendment on domestic political grounds, it is clear that Jackson successfully built a loyal and useful political base through his outspoken efforts. Although the number of emigrants did decline after passage of the amendment, the general impression among Jews was that Jackson tried his best and that the decline was not his fault. Among the well-informed professional Jewish workers in Washington and New York, however, opinion was not so monolithic as it had been during the fight for the amendment. There was some feeling in retrospect that Jackson lacked good judgment at times during the campaign for his amendment. Nevertheless, the general feeling was that Jackson was a proven friend of the Jews. That yielded considerable financial assistance and electoral support for Jackson's presidential campaign. Having raised approximately two-thirds of his first million dollars from Jews, Jackson issued in early 1975 a major fund-raising letter intended to raise another $5 million in which he discussed his role as champion of the effort to link trade and Soviet concessions on emigration.[3] In the 1976 primaries, Jackson's Jewish support was considerable.

Assessing Jackson's domestic political success with Meany yields less clear-cut results. Meany's interest in retarding detente and trade were served. Meany also had his way on the Export-Import Bank Act (and Export Administration Act) thanks to Jackson's legislative hard work. However, Jackson angered Meany by compromising on the Jackson amendment, which paved the way for passage of the Trade Reform Act, which Meany opposed absolutely. He thought Jackson would not compromise, but he did. Meany accused Jackson of sacrificing labor on the Trade Bill "to get Jewish votes."[4] He was still calling him a "welsher" as much as a year after the breech.[5] But on February 16 of election year 1976, Meany "sounded friendlier" toward Jackson than he had for more than a year, and Jackson received significant AFL-CIO support in his campaign primaries.[6]

THE DIPLOMATIC RESULTS OF THE JACKSON AMENDMENT

In general, Jackson's amendment was good politics for Jackson and his congressional supporters. But was it good policy? In addition to short-run political gains, did he reap long-run (or even short-run) diplomatic dividends? Actually, Jackson's diplomatic objectives were two-fold. He wanted to retard detente and trade with the Soviet Union. At the same time his stated intention was to use trade as leverage to force Soviet authorities to permit free emigration of Jews. During most of the legislative history of the amendment, Jackson successfully pursued his dual domestic goals and dual diplomatic goals. However, just as the domestic goals were inevitably contradictory and he was forced to relinquish one of the goals—appealing to George Meany—when he compromised with Kissinger on Jewish emigration terms, so, too, did his dual foreign policy goals eventually clash. In the end, he managed to set back detente and trade liberalization, which the administration was trying to advance. But his particular effort to use trade as leverage on the Soviet Union to get more Jews out of the Soviet Union did not work.

The number of Jews who left the Soviet Union in 1975—a year after passage of the Jackson amendment—was approximately fourteen thousand. In 1976, Jews also left at the reduced annual rate of fourteen thousand. This was the lowest rate since 1971. (The 1977 figure was 16,737.) The declining trend began in early 1974 after passage of the Jackson amendment in the House of Representatives and after the October 1973 Yom Kippur War. Israel, after that war—and the resulting economic difficulties—was less attractive to Soviet Jews than it was after the June 1967 war. Soviet harassment—partly intended as a response to Jackson's involvement—was also a deterrent to applications. But the most dramatic incident depressing potential applications since January 1975 was the failure of the Jackson amendment to force the Soviet Union to soften its emigration policies. Jackson did not attain his stated diplomatic objective.

Jackson has charged, "It is the unwise policy of the President of the United States" (Ford) that resulted in lower emigration after passage of the Jackson amendment. "When I become President, they [the Soviet authorities] will know that they're dealing with someone that keeps his commitments and is very firm on certain issues of principle."[7] Jackson has attacked both Ford and Kissinger for watering down the effectiveness of his link between trade and emigration. "It was only after Henry Kissinger turned his back on the Amendment and pledged that the Ford Administration would try to destroy it that the Kremlin tightened up the screws again." He argued that withholding trade advantages would eventually cause the Soviet Union to buckle under to his demands. "We should stay firm, because three weeks later after passage of the amendment, Ford comes before the Congress and says: 'Let's repeal it. Change the law.' Well, if you're in the Russian government, what would you do? You'd just tighten the screws that much more. And that's not the way to bargain with them. I'm not going to change that one [the amendment]. Over my dead body they'll change it."[8]

But Jackson also contributed to the collapse of his own stated diplomatic objective by simultaneously pursuing other goals that ran counter to his emigration goal. His domestic goals impelled him to take actions that clashed with the linkage effort. Jackson's need to advertise his successes with the Soviet Union for the American press and public was apparently deeply resented in Moscow. The effort to link trade and emigration was also compromised by Jackson's other diplomatic goal: retardation of detente. He was hampering the removal of Soviet-American trade barriers at the same time that he was trying to use them as leverage. For example, he was heavily involved in setting a ceiling on Export-Import Bank loans, which he opposed on the grounds that they aided the Soviet Union. But by cutting back the loans, he was undercutting his leverage on the Soviet Union. His Export-Import Bank activity may have planted the seeds of destruction of the emigration agreement that he was part of. Conceivably, cutting back the loans was also interpreted by the Soviet Union as punishment since it thought the Nixon administration had already promised the loans in the United States-Soviet Trade Pact of 1972. In any case, withholding the loans undercut Jackson's bargaining position.

ATTEMPTING TO USE ECONOMIC CONCESSIONS FOR POLITICAL GAIN

Jackson's attempt to use leverage to extract political concessions from the Soviet Union is an illustration of an important tendency in American foreign policy. The United States, spanning a bountifully endowed continent, has often tried to apply its economic might to extract noneconomic concessions from other nations, in particular the Soviet Union. Commercial relations between the United States and the Soviet Union have never been a simple matter of dollars and cents.

This study has touched on several attempts in which the United States tied political conditions to trade with the Soviet Union. Detente was characterized by a conscious effort to coordinate economic and political relations with the Soviet Union. In Kissinger's words, ". . . our justification for increased trade with the Soviet Union has never been based primarily on economic grounds. . . . We see it as a tool to bring about or to reinforce a more moderate orientation of foreign policy and to provide incentives for responsible international behavior. . . ." Kissinger's approach was to induce—using carrots like MFN and Export-Import Bank loans. "I would judge that the foreign policy benefits of engaging in these (Export-Import Bank loans) justifies granting them. So I would do it not purely on commercial grounds but also on foreign policy grounds."[9]

Circumstantial evidence indicates that the Soviet Union's emigration policy was responding at least in part to the implicit incentive of receiving trade concessions from the United States. At the very least, Soviet sensitivity to courting Western public opinion may have played a role in the liberalization of emigration. During the period of nascent detente under the Nixon administration, a pattern existed in which American trade concessions accompanied Soviet emigration concessions. In mid-1971, the United States removed the requirement for general licenses for exporting to the Soviet Union; that coincided with the Twenty-fourth Congress of the Communist party where Brezhnev unveiled a strategy of political-military-economic bargaining with the West that has come to be known as detente. It also marked a notable increase in the number of emigrants permitted to leave. In the summer and fall of 1972, the United States sold tons of much-needed grain to the Soviet Union, signed the October 1972 trade pact, and Nixon found that it was in the United States' interest to give the Soviet Union Export-Import Bank loans. In the fall, the number of emigrants was heavy; there was a pledge that close to thirty-five thousand would be allowed to leave, and the education tax was temporarily suspended. In the spring of 1973, the first Export-Import Bank loans were extended to the Soviet Union, and the education tax on emigrants was removed. In March 1974 on the eve of Kissinger's trip to Moscow to discuss the senators' demands, $44.4 million worth of loans were released. Reports stemming from talks between the superpowers' foreign envoys said that the Soviets had agreed partially to some of the senators' demands. The timing in May 1974 of Nixon's intervention with the Export-Import Bank also seemed connected to a major breakthrough in the trilateral talks on emigration.

In the case of the Vietnam peace negotiation, the pattern was repeated in which the Nixon administration's advances with the Soviet Union accompanied advances in Soviet-American trade. In his first news conference as president of the United States, Richard Nixon told the world that he would try "to woo the Russians into a new and cooperative approach to a Vietnam compromise by dangling attractive bait before them—SALT, trade, and easing of tensions around Berlin, a European Security Conference." The Nixon administration carefully paced the liberalization of existing trade restrictions, first by granting more licenses for export to the Soviet Union and then by holding out the possibility of extending credits and most-favored-nation tariff treatment for use during negotiations on other subjects. Kissinger, however, has insisted that this linkage approach was more subtle than demanding strict *quid pro quos* for American trade concessions: "I am denying that we ever said to the Soviet leaders, 'If you do this for us in Vietnam, we will do that for you on trade.' You have to recognize that these are serious people, and we didn't come here to buy them."

Ironically, Kissinger and his colleagues were not aware of their greatest opportunity to use economic leverage for political purposes. Massive Soviet grain sales in this country were made in July and August of 1972 before

Kissinger was sufficiently aware to capitalize politcally on Soviet needs. However, even if the United States government did not force a conscious link at the time, the Soviets themselves were aware of their economic needs during the grain shortage year of 1972 and may have found it in their interest to cooperate with American efforts to get a Vietnam peace agreement.

The contrast between Kissinger's linkage on Vietnam and Jackson's on emigration is instructive. The demands Kissinger made on the Soviet Union were relatively marginal—cooperation with American efforts to negotiate a peace agreement with the Soviet's ally, North Vietnam. America's *quid pro quo* was kept so secret that Kissinger even denied ever trying to achieve Soviet cooperation for American trade. The major effort came at a time when the Soviet Union was committed to increasing trade in the West and had just suffered a disastrous harvest in 1972. As for American domestic constraints on using trade as a bargaining chip, America was in a position that is unlikely to be repeated soon in the future. The trade concessions America was offering had not built up a domestic constituency. At the time, trade—of grain or anything else—was beginning from practically zero. The grain sales caught almost everyone—including Kissinger—by surprise. In the beginning, it appealed to the farmers and to the general public at a time when the United States was in an unprecedentedly negative balance of trade. Only later, after the wheat had been sold and the trade concessions promised, were consumers and some farmers angered by distortions in the market place.

The Jackson attempt to link trade and emigration was anything but small and discreet. His desired change in Soviet behavior arguably touched the fundamental basis of the regime. It was big, political, and noisy. It dragged out over two and one-half years, thereby affecting the Soviet regime at times when it was not so needy of American trade concessions. By the fall of 1973, the multiplying prices of oil and gold—important Soviet commodities—gave the Soviet Union a $3 billion-a-year windfall. The harvest in the year the Soviet Union rejected Jackson's demands was the second best in history.[10] Jackson used trade overtly and as a weapon, a stick, not as a carrot. He withheld something the Soviet leaders thought America had already pledged in October 1972. Jackson's ability to wield that economic weapon was constrained by a growing constituency of industrial and agricultural businessmen who wanted to maintain what little trade had developed as a result of detente and to insure whatever future contracts might be made available by trading with the Soviet Union. As we have seen Jackson argue, his effort to apply economic pressure was counteracted by the administration, which was applying an incentive policy by continuing to give credits and promising to try to get MFN from the Congress in spite of Jackson.

The possibilities that Jackson would abandon his amendment and that the Nixon administration's pledge to grant credits and MFN would be fulfilled seemed to gain Soviet cooperation on the emigration question. In the spring of 1973, the Soviets quietly informed the administration that they were suspending the education tax, which was only months old and which had been suspended once before during the preelection period of 1972. The Soviets did not, however, agree to remove the tax from the books. The Soviet leadership seemed willing to cooperate in this small way in the spring of 1973, and again in the fall of 1974, when it came close to making an accommodation on more fundamental emigration policy, in hopes that Jackson would—in 1973—abandon his amendment and then—in 1974—compromise his amendment, and they would receive the trade benefits. Both times, the Soviet leaders seemed to have been operating as if in an incentive system—that is, if they cooperated, they would be rewarded.

Both times Jackson insisted that the concessions were insufficient. He demanded a fundamental change in Soviet emigration policy, including a specific benchmark of performance that sixty thousand Jews a year leave the Soviet Union. The Soviet leaders probably perceived this to be a serious challenge to their internal policies and potentially their very existence, as making concessions required relinquishing one means of intimidation by which the regime controls its domestic society.

The Soviet Union's apparent willingness to accommodate even Jackson's broader demands indicates that Jackson's linkage might have worked had he settled for small gains early and quietly. The question we cannot answer conclusively is whether domestic political considerations dictated by Meany's unequivocal opposition to a compromise with the administration and the Soviet Union, or Jackson's own desire to retard trade under any circumstances, or Jackson's view that he could extract more from the Soviet leaders determined his decision to reject these early Soviet offers. Clearly, Jackson would assert that it was the latter consideration. Even after the Jackson amendment had been rejected, Jackson's aide Richard Perle was still insisting that the Soviet Union was "feeling the pinch . . . so keep the trade pipeline closed until the cost becomes unbearably high" to Soviet authorities who would then let the Jews go.[11]

Past history suggests, however, that this expectation is overly optimistic. Trying to extract large political concessions from the Soviet Union by punitive means accompanied by a great deal of ostentatious publicity certainly has led to disappointment. Jackson and his staff have been undaunted and continue to operate on the premise that the Soviet Union needs economic help so badly that it will some day make concessions on Jackson's terms to get it. This does not seem to be a domestic political judgment, but it has, no doubt, won Jackson a particular following.

CONGRESSIONAL ASSERTIVENESS IN FOREIGN POLICY-MAKING

Jackson's efforts to reshape the trade-detente relationship the administration was developing with the Soviet Union illustrates another striking characteristic of American foreign policy-making, the separation of powers. When Senator Jackson introduced his amendment in October 1972, he warned, "It is important that the Russians understand they are dealing with not only the Administration but also with Congress."[12] Jackson was reminding the administration and the Soviets—what Senator Henry Cabot Lodge had shown President Wilson during the League of Nations fight—that Congress can have an important role in foreign policy-making.

The two and one-half year Jackson battle was a rare example of congressional assertiveness in foreign policy-making not witnessed in decades. Some elements of the Jackson amendment's legislative success may be idiosyncratic. One cannot ignore the fact that Congress in 1972 was entering a new phase of reassertiveness after a steady decline in influence dating from the period of Theodore Roosevelt and accelerating under the presidency of Franklin D. Roosevelt. Congress was reasserting itself after reaching the nadir of its foreign policy influence during the Vietnam war. At the same time the Democratically controlled Congress was asserting its power vis-à-vis the activist Republican President Richard M. Nixon. The same Congress that passed the Jackson amendment also enacted the Budget Act to counteract unprecedented levels of impoundment by the executive branch of congressionally appropriated funds. It was the same Congress that passed the War Powers Act in response to previous legislative impotence during the Vietnam War. The Watergate scandal, which rendered President Nixon so weak that his secretary of state admitted that Nixon hardly ruled in the last eighteen months in office, also accentuated the trend toward congressional reassertiveness and reinforced Jackson's claim that a congressional role in foreign policy-making was not only legitimate but necessary.

Leaving the idiosyncratic qualities of this period aside, it is worthwhile to analyze the Jackson amendment as an illustration of political skill in Congress. The Jackson amendment illustrates how a single politician directing a large and broad congressional coalition and interest-group alliance manages to influence United States foreign policy. It shows under what circumstances a congressman can effectively compete with the executive branch on foreign policy issues. Woodrow Wilson, an early student of Congress, recognized that Congress resembled a feudal governmental system in which barons compete for power with no one baron *primus inter pares*.[13] Jackson overcame this feudalism.

Jackson illustrated some of the qualities necessary for one congressman or senator to bring others into line. An important factor is *personality*.[14] Jackson was determined, dogged, and possessed a willingness to combat, disregard, and generally overcome his fellow legislators, committee chairman, Senate leadership, as well as the entire executive branch. Pugnacity and hard work achieved the legislative passage of the amendment. Jackson has described himself as having "a tiger in me—I don't let go."[15] Said Abraham Ribicoff, "I tip my hat to him for his consistent stubbornness. It is only because the Senator from Washington has been so persistent throughout these two years that we find the Jackson Amendment about to become part of the trade bill."[16] The other major senator in the alliance, Jacob Javits, remarked, "If running for President turns out to be a fantastic incentive to be Superman, then I think that's good for America, not bad. And he works like hell. God, he's working like hell."[17]

Jackson was aided by a reputation among his congressional colleagues as a *specialist* on Soviet affairs among a body of generalists. Because Congress must deal with so many issues, its membership has divided itself into committees more or less along functional lines. When it comes time for the Congress as a whole to consider a particular issue—for example, trade relations with the Soviet Union—the views of those members like Jackson specializing in the field have a disproportionate influence over the rest of the Senate and House membership. By virtue of his committee assignments, Jackson has devoted considerable personal and staff time to questions relating to the Soviet Union.

INFORMATION

Jackson's information—data and analyses necessary for a policy challenging the administration—was independent of the administration. This factor relates to the previously mentioned quality of Jackson as a specialist on Soviet affairs. Jackson's knowledge derived from information sources he had developed and that had accrued after twenty-four years in the Senate and twelve in the House of Representatives. Jackson's considerable seniority in Congress gave him control of a $3 million annual budget and assignment to many important committees where he employed some of his approximately one hundred staff members.[18] Jackson served on an estimated twenty-five subcommittees. He was chairman of the Special Investigations Subcommittee of Government Operations, which had special subpoena power, chairman of the Interior Committee, and chairman of several subcommittees of the Armed Services Committee. In addition, he served on the Joint Atomic Energy Committee. His *staff* included at least five full-time foreign policy experts—about five times more than most senators or congressmen. He drew strength from all of his staff. For example, Jackson's January 1975 statement reacting to Soviet rejection of his emigration demands was drafted by Richard Perle on the investigations subcommittee staff, issued by Jackson's personal office, and franked (mailed free) in an Interior Committee envelope.[19]

Augmenting his staff who were impressive qualitatively and quantitatively as information gatherers and information analyzers were outside consultants. *Academe* is an important information source. Jackson consulted university experts privately and through hearings. Executive branch agencies also provided information that was eventually used to challenge the administration's own position. Jackson was privy to legitimate as well as purloined information from the administration. He probably had the benefit of information and analyses of bureaucrats moonlighting from the executive branch when they disagreed with administration policy. For example, C.I.A. analyses on the Soviet Union's policy toward the Jews and on Soviet economic fortunes were helpful at several key moments in the history of the amendment. "We got our information. . . . I don't think any member of Congress with any seniority ever had a problem with information; most information is available," said Jackson staffer Perle. These remarks should be heeded by reformers of Congress who argue that lack of information deters Congress from asserting itself in United States foreign policy-making.

Interest groups also were useful conveyers of information. In the Jackson amendment case, these groups had transnational links within the Soviet Union, the country Jackson's policy was targeting. American Jewish groups had direct telephone, telegraph, and personal contact with Jews and other dissidents within the Soviet Union. They provided Jackson an independent source of information. Jackson, therefore, did not have to rely on traditional diplomatic channels of information to know about events within the Soviet Union—channels the executive branch controlled. During the three-way negotiations with the executive branch and the Soviet Union, this was an important factor permitting Jackson to formulate precise, finely tuned demands and to adjust them as he perceived necessary. By so doing, Jackson freed himself from Congress's traditional dependence on the administration for information on foreign affairs and equipped himself to shape his own competing policy and to challenge the administration on its own ground.

LEGISLATIVE SKILLS

Jackson followed a careful legislative strategy to maximize the chances that the issue of liberalization of emigration would become law. Jackson linked his amendment to an administration request for *authority* to grant the Soviet Union most-favored-nation treatment. Jackson's decision to link emigration to MFN capitalized on this constitutionally derived power of

Congress. By tradition, Congress has reinforced its power in the tariff-setting field by basing it on its authority to raise revenue. Foreign trade—in contrast to Congress's war powers, for example—is one of the foreign powers Congress has not let atrophy entirely, perhaps because it is directly important to domestic interests and involves so many federal bureaucracies.[20] Jackson appealed to Congress to play "its Constitutional role in establishing tariffs and regulating credits." "Congress," he said, "should not abdicate its responsibility to oversee the disposition of United States credits."[21]

Jackson also skillfully drafted his amendment to give him an effective bargaining position vis-à-vis the administration. Making MFN conditional on liberalization of emigration from the Soviet Union was an *"action-forcing device,"* a favored technique that has contributed to Jackson's legislative success. Since the president had to turn to Congress for authority to make foreign trade agreements relating to MFN, Jackson was dealing with the administration from a strong congressional position. If the administration wanted its authority, it was forced to act as the Jackson amendment prescribed.

He also capitalized on the fact that Congress is better equipped to *block* administration initiative than to initiate policy of its own.[23] Jackson blocked the administration's much desired trade pact until it accepted his free-emigration conditions. Eventually, Jackson held hostage both the Trade Reform Act and the Export-Import Bank Bill and thus thwarted the president's commitment to extend MFN and credits to the Soviet Union until the administration came to terms with him.

PACKAGING

Jackson also couched his amendment so it was not only legislatively linked to the administration, but so it also *appeared to follow logically* from administration policy. In other words, Jackson's amendment had an appearance of continuity and a claim of legitimacy borrowed from the administration. The administration had embraced an approach of "linkage" to carry out its detente policy with the Soviet Union. For example, the extension of trade concessions to the Soviet Union was linked to Soviet cooperation in other fields, such as in America's efforts to extricate its fighting forces from Vietnam. Jackson borrowed from Kissinger's handbook of success. He simply added another less modest and more politicized loop to Kissinger's chain of linking arrangements by insisting that the human rights issue of freedom to emigrate be linked to trade concessions. Jackson did not object to linkage. On the contrary, he embraced it in principle, while adapting it to other ends. The administration could not object to Jackson's approach since it was its own. It was reduced to debating the merits of the specific linkage that Jackson proposed.

Jackson portrayed his amendment in terms that *appealed* to the American public. Jackson was careful to line up support from both sides of the political aisle so he could claim it was nonpartisan. He appealed to universal principles of human rights. By evoking the right of free emigration, he appealed to principles popular to the American public that is made up of immigrants or scions of immigrants.

THE EXECUTIVE BRANCH AND CONGRESS

Jackson could not have engineered such congressional assertiveness in a vacuum. It took three years from the time Nixon came into office in 1969 to launch detente at the Moscow Summit in 1972. However, although the ground was well prepared for the bilateral relationship between the United States and Soviet Union's top leadership, the preparation of the domestic audience in the United States was faulty.

In 1972, Secretary of Commerce Peter Peterson issued a report on prospects for Soviet-American trade, which stated that Congress would be consulted regarding any changes in the then restrictive trade policy with the Soviet Union. As events unfolded in 1972, however, Congress was not consulted. The administration claimed it was being responsive to Congress during its negotiations with the Soviet Union by achieving an adequate lend-lease settlement, the only item the administration mentioned at the time as being a matter of congressional concern. During September and October of 1972, it disregarded the growing signs of public discontent and congressional demands that emigration be linked to trade terms. The October 18, 1972, trade pact was signed with no indication that such a linkage was made by the administration. Later, Kissinger even called the linkage *ex post facto.* "At no time were issues regarding Soviet domestic political practices raised. Indeed, not until after the 1972 agreements was the Soviet domestic order invoked as a reason for arresting or reversing the progress so painstakingly achieved."[24] The administration failed to consult Congress about its major policy initiatives as President Harry S. Truman had consulted with congressional leader Senator Arthur Vandenberg (R.-Mich.) during the post-World War II years. Once Congress had initiated its own policy in the form of the Jackson amendment and the administration had made itself aware of it, the executive branch's response was equally inadequate. The administration had a number of ways of responding to a congressional initiative: to ignore, confront, obstruct, and even cooperate.

In the earliest preelection 1972 period, Nixon did cooperate with Jackson on the assumption that such cooperation was a short-term, preelection expedient, since the Jackson amendment would die never to be reborn after the end of the Ninety-second Congress. Nixon's cooperation came at a strategic moment early in the Jackson amendment's history. It gave Jackson's effort important credibility and set it apart from other legislative efforts. It advanced the Jackson amendment just that much more as a future challenge to administration policy. From November 1972 to January 1973, after Nixon's reelection, the administration mostly ignored the amendment. Obstruction was tried in October 1973 during the Middle East War, as was confrontation during the House fight in December 1973. From March to October 1974, during the period of three-way negotiations, when it was perceived that all else had failed to avert passage of the Jackson amendment, the administration finally tried negotiating with Jackson as an equal.

In every phase, the executive branch proved to be unskillful in its dealing with Congress. As a result, it missed opportunities developing within the Congress that might have been used effectively to challenge Jackson. In September 1972, Javits' appeal for a substitute to the Jackson amendment was not heeded. Administration support for the Corman-Pettis proposal in September 1973 during Ways and Means Committee consideration was half-hearted. It embraced the idea of dropping Title IV completely—the authority for granting the controversial trade concessions and the Jackson amendment—from the Trade Bill so late in 1973 that the approach was by then untenable. In the Senate, it lent practically no support to those who might have wanted to find a compromise substitute to the Jackson amendment. It failed to recognize the opportunity to weaken support for Jackson in the Export-Import Bank legislation. Instead of turning the Export-Import Bank Bill to the administration's advantages, Kissinger, who disregarded the warnings of others in the administration, found his trade policy restricted even more by the Ex-Im Bill.

KISSINGER'S ROLE

The chief executive branch actors during the drama in the Senate were supposed to be Henry Kissinger and William Eberle, the president's Special Trade Representative. An executive decision was made giving Eberle—and not Peter Flanigan, who resigned June 25, 1974—total responsibility for the Trade Bill. However, Kissinger, a superior bureaucratic in-fighter, took control and kept a tight rein on the rest of the bureaucracy, Ambassador Eberle included. Kissinger told us "to keep our cotton-pickin' hands off," recalled a top Special Trade Representative official. Week after week, memoranda would be sent to Kissinger under Eberle's signature. Sometimes, there was no response; at other times, a message would come back from Kissinger's personal aide Lawrence Eagleberger that the secretary said again, "we don't want you involved."

Kissinger's Soviet expert Helmut Sonnenfeldt, elevated to counselor of the State Department, was known for "chewing out" members of the Special Trade Representative's office whenever they attempted to deal with

Jackson on the subject. After the Senate activity of 1974, A. Linwood Holton, State Department chief liaison with Congress from February 19, 1973, to December 1974, quit amidst much publicity that Holton felt "hamstrung by Kissinger's mania for secrecy, by the secretary's long absences from Washington and frequently by Holton's inability to gain access to Kissinger."[25]

Kissinger also isolated himself from those in Congress who might have helped to counter the Jackson amendment. The administration did nothing to help Javits in late 1972 before the amendment was initially introduced. Corman and Pettis were not given full backing by the administration when they tried to find a compromise to the Jackson amendment during deliberations in the Ways and Means Committee in 1973. Alan Cranston and Adlai Stevenson III were willing to help get around Jackson, but Kissinger did not seem interested. When Kissinger testified at the Finance Committee in 1974, he was unprepared and made avoidable mistakes. The Export-Import Bank legislation was an unnecessary and unfortunate surprise to him.

Kissinger's penchant for limiting the number of actors to maintain maximum flexibility was counterproductive. He aimed to avert congressional assertiveness in foreign policy. Then when finally forced to deal with Jackson, Kissinger limited involvement of others in Congress. As a result, Kissinger may have actually lost flexibility by passing up opportunities to neutralize Jackson's control over congressional will on the Soviet Jewry issue.

Contact with the Soviet government—via the Soviet embassy in Washington or any other means—was also strictly limited by Kissinger. Complained an anonymous top trade official:

> Dobrynin and Kissinger agreed between them that neither side was to carry on conversations and that there would be no channels of conversation except when they designate. . . . Trade discussions with Russia are not handled by trade people here in Washington. They are discussed totally in the context of political discussions. And when trade negotiators do talk, then others come along and tell the Russians to ignore the previous discussions because they don't count.

The liabilities of this exclusive two-man channel were incurred mostly by Dobrynin and the country he represented. By limiting his contacts, Dobrynin also limited his understanding of the situation, since Kissinger obviously misapprehended the mood of Congress. This was particularly damaging to Soviet interests in 1973 when the threat of Jackson's amendment was vastly underestimated. In 1974, it may have contributed to Soviet miscalculations based on ignorance of developments of other events in Congress. This observation also applies to the Soviet misreading of the Export-Import Bank Bill, which enormously complicated the 1974 negotiations on the Jackson amendment.[26]

INTEREST-GROUP INVOLVEMENT IN THE FORMATION OF FOREIGN POLICY

The involvement of interest groups in foreign policy-making in America is a major theme illustrated by this study, which also helps explain the amendment's legislative success. Hundreds of congressmen and three-quarters of the Senate sponsored the Jackson amendment because it attracted support from interests spanning America's political spectrum. Such extraordinary support for the amendment reflected its appeal to a wide array of interest groups—not just to the Jewish lobby. Indeed, for it to have been successful, such a controversial issue had to appeal to more than just one group.

The amendment, in fact, was a political *tour de force* for Jackson, running hard for president in 1976. His amendment—like a miniplatform—seemed to have something for practically everyone. Legislating reform of Soviet society attracted support from American Jewry and other ethnic and religious groups with brethren under Soviet rule. Generally liberal organizations like the Americans for Democratic Action and scores of otherwise liberal, artistic, professional, intellectual, and scientific groups that were concerned about dissident colleagues whose civil and human rights were being abused also embraced Jackson's notion that American pressure could change Soviet domestic practices. So did hard-line individuals like George Meany. Meany opposed trade with Communist Russia for ideological reasons. His unions also opposed extending government credits for Soviet-American transactions believing that this encouraged the transfer of United States plants and American technology to the Soviet Union, thus spurring Soviet competition against products made by American workers. Finally, Jackson was backed by traditionally conservative, anticommunist, patriotic groups inside and outside of the Pentagon, who opposed exporting American technology for fear it would be applied toward Soviet military projects or would generally benefit America's prime adversary.

JEWS AND FOREIGN POLICY INFLUENCE

Throughout the two-and-one-half-year battle over the Jackson amendment, Jackson was steering the Jewish groups, not vice versa. Interest groups may have shaped Jackson's policy as he anticipated the constituency for his position. However, lobby groups played a supporting role during the campaign for the amendment. For example, those Jews with primary power were Jewish staffers—whose power base was merely a desk in a senator's or representative's office—not professional workers for Jewish interest groups or Jewish campaign contributors. Groups of American Jews had been protesting Soviet practices for years and contacting senators and congressmen to join their cause, but the Jackson amendment as legislation was developed in Jackson's office and originally found little support from these groups. Jackson had to convince the more cautious Jewish leadership to follow his lead. Occasionally, he had to persuade, cajole, even threaten the leadership not to abandon the amendment in spite of opposition from the administration whose leverage over Israel was an important consideration.

The Jewish leaders' constituents were the members of their groups, to whom Jackson threatened to appeal over the leaders' heads if the leaders did not cooperate. Jackson also had allies among the Jewish professionals who—like bureaucrats in the government influencing their superiors—influence the policies their groups adopt by shaping the options the leadership and membership had to choose from. Workers for the National Conference on Soviet Jewry, for example, became advocates for Jackson's approach within the Jewish community. Reflected Philip Baum of the American Jewish Congress, "For two years we focused on a single tool to achieve our goal. Success for the amendment, we assumed, would be the beginning of success for our cause . . . we must seek additional initiatives and simply not rally around one piece of legislation."[27]

The Jewish groups relied on Jackson for legislative details and strategy. As a result, for example, the Jewish community was just as poorly informed about the significance of the Export-Import Bank legislation as were Kissinger and the Soviet Union. Assessed one professional when it was over, "everybody muffed it." Moreover, instead of being representatives for a group that purported to educate the Congress on Soviet Jewry, many of the Jewish professionals became lobbyists in Congress and guardians of the purity of a single piece of legislation, the Jackson amendment. Philip Baum concluded in retrospect, "that victory that we scored was a macho trip for the Jewish community, which is no substitute for statesmanship . . . the objective was to maximize the opportunity [for Jews] to leave, not to triumph."[28]

THE LIMITS AND STRENGTHS OF DOMESTIC POLITICS IN FOREIGN POLICY-MAKING

The characteristics of American political life that this study has identified make foreign policy-making in America inherently difficult. Attempts to enforce America's moral standards in the rest of the world—by using economic leverage or otherwise—tend to bring cries from other nations that America is inappropriately "meddling" in their internal affairs. Even when "leverage" exists—for example, when a sovereign nation is willing to accept our involvement, but does not want to be embarrassed by a public announcement of its accommodating American demands—American politicians are driven to claim credit publicly and the press feels the public has a right to know what its government is doing. Interest-group involvement in American foreign policy is a part of our pluralist democracy, but some interest groups have disproportionate influence and power. It is possible, therefore, that policy reflects not the will of the majority, but the will of highly leveraged, well-placed minorities.

Finally, negotiating with another nation is facilitated when the United States communicates clearly and continuity appears to exist so misunderstanding about American intentions will be minimized, whereas the Constitution dictates that foreign policy powers be shared equally between the Congress and the president. Instead of the government speaking with one voice, many voices are heard. Jackson has argued in the past that government should "speak with one voice." During the debate over his amendment, he claimed that "I don't inject myself into policy," but rather played a role to "tell Henry . . . stiffen Henry."[29] Jackson said he was Kissinger's bargaining chip in dealing with the Soviet leadership. He reinforced Kissinger. "Kissinger tells me how he tells the Russians I'm the problem. And he explains to them my strong stands, and he tells me what the Soviets say about me."[30] However, there is a thin line between strengthening and tying the administration's hands.

Having listed some limitations, one should also consider the advantages of a democratic foreign policy conducted by two branches of government and shaped by interest groups and politically ambitious policy-makers. Politicizing a foreign policy issue permits the opportunity for a larger group of actors with a broader, more representative range of views to deliberate on important issues. Although it runs the risk of spreading disagreements, it also carries the possibility of spreading agreement. It is a necessary condition for a broad public consensus to underpin a foreign policy.

Subjecting a policy to an open debate prevents surprises, as occurred in the development of a hostile public viewpoint toward the Vietnam war. At the outset of the war, Congress and the White House were both controlled by the same party and there was no politically ambitious policy-maker who detected any political bonus in criticizing America's early involvement in Vietnam. Criticism was reduced to a few outnumbered mavericks. Later, however, after much debate and dissent, the domestic support for American involvement proved to be insufficient to continue prosecution of the policy of American involvement.

Domestic political involvement allows for the systematic and legitimate handling of the increasing number of transnational issues that develop in a world of increasing technologically sophisticated communications and economic interdependency.

In the final analysis, the limitations inherent in our system are greatly determined by the ambitions of politicians who take it upon themselves to be foreign policy actors. The fact is that the underside of democracy is partisanship with all the negative connotations that are attached to that word. The paradox of American diplomacy in this instance is that while there is an impulse to improve human rights conditions overseas, there is also a domestic political impulse for elected officials to employ techniques that tend to undermine the effort. This is the thin line that both policy-makers and policy critics—diplomats and politicians—in the United States must walk in order to reap rewards abroad while satisfying the American public at home.

It is useless to pretend that politics stops at the water's edge. The roots of American political debate often originate beyond the water's edge. Additionally, our politics spill over our shores to affect our relations with other nations beyond the water's edge. But in the final analysis, what matters most is still what occurs within our borders: how we conduct our domestic political debate.

Afterword

Much of the present-day strain in the United States-Soviet relations is directly traceable to the period covered by this book. Indeed, trade relations—for which so many held out such great expectations during the early days of detente—have been frozen by the Jackson amendment, which is the law of the land to this day. Finding an accommodation on the trade-emigration linkage will, no doubt, be high on any American or Soviet agenda for rapprochement.

Whatever America's approach toward human rights policy vis-à-vis the Soviet Union should be in the future, it should not be benign neglect—as if our policy-makers could pursue this route for long against the basic impulses in American political life that drive an interventionist human rights policy and influence the choice of human rights objectives that American officials champion. Our concern has yielded results. But concern alone has not been enough; economic leverage has been an important component in whatever human rights advances in the Soviet Union that American policy has recently made possible.

Advancing human rights objectives is demonstrably far from risk free. Some fear that the ideological competition involved in a campaign for more freedom in the Soviet Union will revive the Cold War. And there is little doubt that today's cold warriors have used the human rights issues with mixed motives. But it can be argued that despite Soviet annoyance with America's human rights interference, there are certain Soviet military and economic needs which will restrain adverse Soviet reaction. In this vein, it is important that whatever human rights objectives are advanced, they should be linked (implicitly) to incentives—trade or otherwise. If not, American demands will appear to be merely rhetoric and not good faith efforts. Finally, an argument in favor of economic linkage for the purpose of advancing human rights can be borrowed from the commentator who pointed out:

> Unlike in the political sphere, advances in human rights are difficult to undo should the economic basis of the agreement disappear. While access to information may be cut off, what has already passed is in the hearts and minds of people, and cannot be expunged. Further, the process of *samizdat* would allow continued circulation of information even if the source were cut off. Likewise, the memories of easier emigration, or freer travel, are difficult to erase once allowed.[1]

Some would have the United States champion human rights issues other than emigration. That, however, would require reversing history which is based on realities of America's domestic political life. The fact is that would-be Jewish emigrants from the Soviet Union are allied to a well-organized and politically sophisticated community in this country who legitimately influence American policy-making. In addition, it can be argued that progress on this issue will encourage other efforts to advance other human rights objectives.

At the bottom of any policy considerations, however, should be the realization that the domestic scene in the Soviet Union shapes its policies just as it does in the United States. While the United States should continue to try to encourage liberalization in the Soviet Union, the basic impulse for improvement in human rights conditions in the Soviet Union will always be internal. Reform will have to evolve from within the Soviet Union. The best United States policy is one that capitalizes on that internal impulse from the so-called dissidents while also capitalizing on the desire of the Soviet leadership to keep a modicum of favor with its own people.

Appendixes

Measuring Soviet emigration policy is, unfortunately, limited by the statistics that are publicly available. Provided by the National Conference on Soviet Jewry, which compiles its data in cooperation with Israeli, Dutch, and American authorities, the figures tell only how many Jews get out of the Soviet Union. They do not reveal how many actually apply or how many who apply are rejected by Soviet authorities. (The Israeli figures for Soviet Jews requesting an invitation from a family in Israel as a necessary first step for a Soviet Jew to file an application is different from the actual number of applications.) Ideally, to measure Soviet policy, one would need to graph over time the proportion of applications to rejections.

The fluctuation in the numbers of emigrants should represent two major factors: (1) fluctuation in the number of applicants, and (2) fluctuation in Soviet government policy regarding the grant of permission for applicants to leave. These two factors are intimately interrelated. The more it appears to Soviet Jewry that Soviet authorities are permitting exit, the more applicants there are likely to be. Harassment and denials are important depressants in the number of applications filed. In addition, potential applicants also decide to apply formally based on their image of their future home. The attractiveness of life in Israel after the 1967 war was probably a positive factor in the number of applicants, in contrast to post-Yom Kippur War Israel.

APPENDIX 1

SOVIET JEWISH EMIGRATION
MEASURED BY ARRIVAL IN ISRAEL

	1967	1968	1969	1970	1971	1972	1973	1974	1975
January	—	—	—	—	108	3,004	2,500	2,365	899
February	—	—	—	—	71	1,796	2,751	1,581	890
March	—	—	—	—	636	1,977	2,174	1,726	525
April	—	—	—	—	1,578	2,845	2,821	1,579	708
May	—	—	—	—	1,049	2,804	2,171	1,222	477
June	—	—	—	—	1,138	3,070	1,929	1,230	648
July	—	—	—	—	661	2,163	2,240	1,293	448
August	—	—	—	—	524	2,061	2,660	1,318	627
September	—	—	—	—	995	2,128	3,065	1,092	624
October	—	—	—	—	1,328	2,840	4,200	1,384	673
November	—	—	—	—	1,835	3,760	3,814	1,214	872
December	—	—	—	—	3,000	3,120	3,039	864	904
TOTALS (Israel)	1,412	379	2,902	1,044	12,923	31,568	33,364	16,868	8,295

Arrivals—elsewhere (United States)	543	1,451	3,490	5,426
TOTALS (all countries)	32,122	34,805	20,358	13,721

Total to U.S.	1972-September 30, 1976	15,323
Emigration to U.S. and to Israel:	1972-September 1976	109,985

APPENDIX 2

1976 - 1978 EMIGRATION FIGURES

	1976		1977		1978	
	Vienna	Israel	Vienna	Israel	Vienna	Israel
January	969	428	1,245	582	1,761	865
February	1,218	646	1,063	443	1,812	842
March	1,391	671	1,030	569	2,038	914
April	1,115	529	1,204	522	1,938	756
May	1,120	637	1,193	789	1,958	993
June	1,173	645	1,268	529	1,983	767
July	823	422	1,305	643	1,899	814
August	815	471	1,474	686	2,275	862
September	1,030	579	1,622	758		
October	1,254	470	1,850	946		
November	1,542	772	1,543	936		
December	1,766	934	1,940	954		
TOTAL	14,216	7,204	16,737	8,357		

NOTES

INTRODUCTION: DOMESTIC POLITICS AND THE MAKING OF AMERICAN FOREIGN POLICY

1. Some scholars are more sensitive to the impact of the American domestic structure on the making of foreign policy. Three works that stand out are Ernest R. May, *The Making of the Monroe Doctrine* (Cambridge: Belknap Press of the Harvard Press, 1975); John Snetsinger, *Truman, the Jewish Vote and the Creation of Israel* (Stanford, Calif.: Hoover Institution Press, 1974); and Raymond H. Dawson, *The Decision to Aid Russia, 1941: Foreign Policy and Domestic Politics* (Chapel Hill: The University of North Carolina Press, 1959).

2. These examples are drawn from Gabriel Almond, *The American People and Foreign Policy* (New York: Praeger Publishers, 1968 edition), p. 183; Lawrence H. Fuchs, *The Political Behavior of American Jews* (Glencoe, Ill.: The Free Press, 1956), pp. 117-18; and Louis L. Gerson, *The Hyphenate in Recent American Politics and Diplomacy* (Lawrence: The University of Kansas Press, 1964), p. 102. Also see "Introduction," in Nathan Glazer and Daniel Moynihan, *Ethnicity* (Cambridge: Harvard University Press, 1975), pp. 23-24.

3. For a discussion on the 1912 abrogation of the United States-Russian Commercial Treaty, see Naomi W. Cohen, "The Abrogation of the Russo-American Treaty of 1832," *Jewish Social Studies* XXV, no. 1 (January 1963): 42. Other studies relating to Jews and United States diplomacy include Zosa Szaykowski, *Jews, Wars, and Communism*, vol. I, *The Attitude of American Jews to World War I, The Russian Revolutions of 1917, and Communism* (1914-1945) (New York: KTAV Publishing House, 1972); Cyrus Adler and Aaron M. Margalith, *With Firmness in the Right, American Diplomatic Action Affecting Jews* (New York: American Jewish Committee, 1946); Fuchs, *The Political Behavior of American Jews.*

4. Quoted in *Washington Post,* February 21, 1976, p. A3.

5. Carl J. Friedrich noted that action can be taken in anticipation of another's reaction. Friedrich, *Government and Politics* (New York: Harper Brothers, 1937). David Price described the "entrepreneurial" activities of legislators vis-à-vis interest groups. Price, *Who Makes the Laws?: Creativity and Power in Senate Committees* (Cambridge, Mass.: Schenkman Publishing Co., 1972), p. 322.

6. See Martha R. Cooper, "Implications of Electoral College Reform for American Jewry," *Analysis,* no. 55 (January 1976).

7. *New York Times,* April 17, 1976.

8. William Domhoff, *Fat Cats and Democrats* (Englewood Cliffs, N.J.: Prentice-Hall, 1972); George Thayer, *Who Shakes the Money Tree?* (New York: Simon and Shuster, 1973).

9. *Washington Star,* March 20, 1976. Another figure has two-thirds of Jackson's first million dollars provided by Jewish contributors. *The National Observer,* April 3, 1976. As of April 1976, Jackson had raised $4.5 million from private sources. *Washington Post,* April 23, 1976.

10. Herbert E. Alexander, *Political Financing* (Minneapolis, Minn.: Burgess Publishing Company, 1972), p. 194.

11. "George Meany: Fight over the Freeze," *Newsweek Magazine,* September 6, 1971.

12. *Transnational relations* is defined by Keohane and Nye as "contacts, coalitions, and interactions across state boundaries that are not controlled by the central foreign policy organs of government." These two scholars discuss "five major effects of transnational interactions and organizations." The fifth is most relevant to this discussion: "the emergence of autonomous ac-

tors with private foreign politics that may deliberately oppose or impinge on state policies." Robert O. Keohane and Joseph S. Nye, Jr., eds., *Transnational Relations and World Politics* (Cambridge, Mass.: Harvard University Press, 1972), pp. xi, xvii.

13. A classic example is Russell Warren Howe and Sarah Trott, "The Foreign Agent," *Washingtonian Magazine* 10, no. 3 (December 1974): 135-70. In contrast are several more sophisticated and scholarly studies: Donald Matthews, *U.S. Senators and Their World* (Chapel Hill: University of North Carolina Press, 1960); Andrew M. Scott and Margaret A. Hunt, *Congress and Lobbies: Image and Reality* (Chapel Hill: University of North Carolina Press, 1966); and Raymond A. Bauer, Ithiel de Sola Pool, and Anthony Dexter Lewis, *American Business and Public Policy: The Politics of Foreign Trade* (Chicago: Aldine-Atherton, 1972). They have pointed out how lobbyists can be used as service organizations and publicity bureaus for legislators. This study extends these works in this regard.

CHAPTER 1: THE SOVIET EMIGRATION MOVEMENT: THE U.S.S.R., ISRAEL, AND THE UNITED STATES

1. Quoted in Louis L. Gerson, *The Hyphenate in Recent American Politics and Diplomacy* (Lawrence: University of Kansas Press, 1964), p. 224.

2. Glazer and Moynihan, "Introduction," p. 23. Emphasis in original.

3. James Rosenau, "Foreign Policy as an Issue-Area," in *Domestic Sources of Foreign Policy,* ed. James Rosenau (New York: The Free Press, 1967), p. 31.

4. See Lionel Kochan, ed. *The Jews in Soviet Russia Since 1917* (London: Oxford University Press, 1972 edition). Also see Paula Stern, "The Water's Edge: The Jackson Amendment as a Case Study of the Role Domestic Politics Plays in the Creation of American Foreign Policy," Part I. Ph.D. Thesis, Fletcher School of Law and Diplomacy, April 1976.

5. Quoted in Susan Jacoby and Anthony Astrachan, "Who Gets Whom and What?" *Present Tense,* January 1974, p. 28.

6. Zev Katz, "After the Six-Day War," in *The Jews in Soviet Russia,* 2nd ed., ed. Lionel Kochan (London: Oxford University Press, 1972), p. 328.

7. Dimitri Simes, "Soviet Elite, Understanding the Solzhenitsyn Affair," *Dissent and Its Control in the USSR* (Washington, D.C.: Georgetown University Center for Strategic and International Studies, 1974), p. 17.

8. Leonard Schroeter, *The Last Exodus* (New York: Universe Books, 1973), p. 351.

9. Philippa Lewis, "The 'Jewish Question' in the Open: 1968-1971," in *The Jews in Soviet Russia,* ed. Lionel Kochan (London: The Oxford University Press, 1972 edition), p. 344.

10. Herman Edelsberg, "Showdown On Soviet Jewry," *National Jewish Monthly,* May 23, 1975, p. 6; Jeri Laber, Book Review, *New York Times,* May 25, 1975.

11. The following discussion relies heavily on, among other things, scattered references in Schroeter, *The Last Exodus.*

12. *American Jewish Yearbook,* 1971 (New York: American Jewish Committee, 1972), pp. 440-41.

13. Schroeter, *The Last Exodus,* p. 186.

14. Ibid., pp. 342-56.

15. Ibid., p. 334.

16. *American Jewish Yearbook,* 1965, vol. 66, p. 312.

17. Quoted from William W. Orbach, *Freethem Now* (1977), p. 125.

18. Earl Lefkovitz, "Pioneer in Soviet Jewry Movement Looks Back on Rocky Beginning," *The Cleveland Jewish News,* January 21, 1977.

19. Leonard Schapiro in "International Negotiations," Hearings before the Subcommittee on National Security and International Operations of the Committee on Government Operations, United States Senate, 91st Cong. 2d sess., part 2, April 16, 1970, p. 39.

20. *Congressional Record,* daily ed., December 13, 1974, p. S21420-1.

21. Schroeter, *The Last Exodus,* p. 334.

22. Orbach, *Free them Now,* p. 112.

23. Lester Milbrath categorized "hobby lobbyists" as individuals who "on their own initiative, spend their days on the Hill trying to influence legislators . . . however, since they represent themselves, they should not be considered lobbyists by our definition." Lester Milbrath, *The Washington Lobbyists* (Chicago: Rand McNally and Company, 1963), p. 11.

24. Orbach, *Free them Now,* p. 274.

25. Ibid., p. 276. Goodman recalled, "we had discussed export controls, the idea was in the wind," but he downplayed alleged opposition he may have had in June 1972 to linking trade and emigration.

26. Richard Nixon, "Khrushchev's Hidden Weakness," *Saturday Evening Post,* 1963, reprinted in Lloyd Gardner, ed., *The Great Nixon Turn-around* (New York: Viewpoints, 1973), pp. 63-64.

27. National Conference on Soviet Jewry News Bulletin, no. 35 (August 1, 1974): 2.

28. Testimony of Deputy Assistant Secretary for European Affairs Richard T. Davies, "Denial of Rights to Soviet Jews," Committee on Foreign Affairs, House of Representatives, Subcommittee on Europe, November 1, 1971, printed in Barbara Mihalchenko, "The Treatment of Jews in the Soviet Union: Developments During 1970-71," Congressional Research Service, Library of Congress, November 10, 1971. In 1971, as many as five hundred Soviet Jews were reported to be on the representation list of those the United States government was actively trying to help. Schroeter, *The Last Exodus,* p. 361.

29. "American Jews and Israel," *Times Magazine,* March 10, 1975, p. 27. December 1970, Soviet physicist Andrei Sakharov also wrote Nixon protesting the Leningrad trial. Schroeter, *The Last Exodus,* p. 175. Secretary of State William Rogers recalled that the Nixon administration's diplomatic response was not so quiet. "I sent a letter to Gromyko, and other things were done to bring pressure to bear and focus world opinion on the Russians. If we hadn't . . . forced the situation into the headlines, there would not have been a big fuss here. . . ." Quoted in Allen Drury, *Courage and Hesitation* (Garden City, N.Y.: Doubleday & Co., 1971), p. 286.

30. Testimony, Richard Davies, pp. CRS 45-60.

31. Averell Harriman, speech to East-West Trade Council, *Congressional Record,* November 2, 1972, p. E9047.

32. *American Jewish Yearbook, 1973,* p. 218.

33. William Safire, *Before the Fall* (New York: Doubleday, 1975), p. 575.

34. Ibid.

35. *American Jewish Yearbook, 1973,* p. 219.

36. Safire, *Before the Fall,* p. 451.

37. Schroeter, *The Last Exodus,* p. 337.

38. *New York Times,* August 20, 1972, p. 535.

39. *American Jewish Yearbook, 1973,* p. 219.

40. Glazer and Moynihan, "Introduction," p. 23.

CHAPTER 2: PRESIDENTIAL POLITICS AND DETENTE

1. Dear Colleague Letter, Henry Jackson et al., September 27, 1972.

2. Richard Perle showed a draft for legislation on trade to fellow participants of a Brookings Institution seminar on June 6, 1972,

3. Francis Miko, "Soviet-American Relations, 1969-1974: A Chronological Survey and Brief Analysis," Library of Congress, Congressional Research Service, JX 1428-Russia B74-113F, May 29, 1974.

4. Quoted in Daniel Yergin, " 'Scoop' Jackson Goes For Broke," *Atlantic Monthly*, July 1974, p. 86.

5. "Meet the Press," NBC Television Transcript, July 14, 1974, p. 3.

6. See William W. Prochnau and Richard W. Larsen, *A Certain Democrat* (Englewood Cliffs, N.J.: Prentice-Hall, 1972), p. 35.

7. For a definition of the *Jewish lobby,* see Hyman Bookbinder, "Ethnic Pressures and the Jewish Lobby—Myths and Facts," *Washington Letter, The American Jewish Committee,* September 1975.

8. For example, when the Jackson amendment was first formally introduced in Congress, the *New York Times* described it as "a direct result of the pressure" generated in the world Jewish community as a response to the education tax *(New York Times,* October 8, 1972).

9. See Bauer, Pool, and Dexter, *American Business,* pp. 477-79.

10. Rowland Evans and Robert Novak, "Israeli Support for the Jackson Amendment," *Washington Post,* March 19. 1973, p. A21.

11. Press Release, Jacob Javits, August 30, 1972. Democratic vice-presidential candidate in 1972, Sargent Shriver, has claimed he made the first speech suggesting that trade and emigration be linked. But most observers say that Javits was the first major public official to voice the idea.

12. See discussion of Perle's activities on other issues in Peter Ognibene, *Scoop* (New York: Stein and Day, 1976), pp. 225-27. Isolating what is the senator's role and what is the staff's in each stage of this history is impossible. It may be that the senator is giving a specific order to staff. It may be that the staff is operating with some personal discretion under general orders from the senator. It may be that a staffman literally interprets his boss's unstated desires and acts upon them much as the four knights did when King Henry II asked aloud in *Thomas a Becket:* "Who will rid me of this turbulent priest?" and thus was the archbishop of Canterbury killed. Or it may be pure staff initiative. However, in the final analysis, since the senator can fire his staff, the senator is ultimately responsible for the behavior of his staff.

13. Henry Jackson, *Congressional Record,* daily ed., December 13, 1974.

14. Abraham Ribicoff, Congressional Record, daily edition, December 13, 1974, p. S21416. On a general statement on Senate staff as "Political Actors in Their Own Right," see David Price, *Who Makes the Laws? Creativity and Power in Senate Committees* (Cambridge, Mass.: Schenkman Publishing Co., 1972), p. 329.

15. Lawrence Stern, "Washington Dateline: Two Henrys Descending," *Foreign Policy,* no. 18 (Spring 1975): 174.

16. Quoted in Stephen Isaacs, *Jews in American Politics* (New York: Doubleday, 1974), pp. 254-55.

17. Isaacs, *Jews,* pp. 255-58.

18. *Congressional Record,* daily ed., October 4, 1972, p. S16841.

19. Nahum Barnea, Title Unknown. Translated by Dalya Luttwack. *Davar Shavua*, July 26, 1974, pp. 5-7.

20. Goodman later downplayed Perle's claim that he opposed the Jackson amendment in its early stages.

21. There may have been a second inconclusive meeting in the bandage room. Franklin Silbey, "Senate Demands Quid Pro Quo on Soviet Jews, Trade," *The National Jewish Monthly*, November 1972, p. 10.

22. See Ognibene, *Scoop*, pp. 225-27. Stephen S. Rosenfeld, "If Everyone's Weak, Then Who's Strong?" *Present Tense* (Summer 1978), pp. 18-19.

23. Barnea, July 26, 1974; Silbey, "Senate Demands Quid Pro Quo," p. 10.

24. Carole Payne, "Abraham A. Ribicoff," Ralph Nader Congress Project 1972, Washington, D.C., pp. 15-16.

25. Stephen S. Rosenfeld, "The Politics of the Jackson Amendment: 'A Piece of Political Baggage with Many Different Handles,' " *Present Tense* (Summer 1974), p. 18. Emphasis added. The question of whether the Jackson amendment applied to Jews only is one of the fuzzier issues in this entire debate. Jackson, Javits, and Ribicoff stated later that the Jackson amendment was not intended to apply to Jews only.

26. *New York Times*, September 15, 1972, p. 1.

27. *New York Times*, September 14, 1972, p. 1.

28. Safire, *Before the Fall*, pp. 435-36. Also see Marvin Kalb and Bernard Kalb, *Kissinger* (New York: Little, Brown, 1974), pp. 346-47.

29. Hedrick Smith, *New York Times*, September 14, 1972, p. 1.

30. Tad Szulc, "Behind the Vietnam Cease-Fire Agreement: How Kissinger Did It," *Foreign Policy*, no. 15 (Summer 1974): 49.

31. *New York Times*, September 14, 1972.

32. *New York Times*, September 17, 1972. In 1974, Kissinger discussed this period. His version revealed the unimportance of domestic protests regarding emigration on his trade policy. "At no time were issues regarding Soviet domestic political practices raised. Indeed, not until after the 1972 agreements was the Soviet domestic order invoked as a reason for arresting or reversing the progress so painstakingly achieved.

This sudden ex-post-facto form of linkage raises serious questions." (Statement of Hon. Henry A. Kissinger, Secretary of State, Hearings, "Detente." Hearings before Committee on Foreign Relations, United States Senate, 93rd Cong., 2d sess., September 19, 1974, p. 252.)

33. *New York Times*, September 21, 1972, p. 13.

34. Richard Frank, "Trade Report," *National Journal*, November 15, 1972, p. 1806.

35. *New York Times*, December 28, 1975, pp. 1:7, 26:4.

36. Press Release, Henry Jackson, September 27, 1972.

37. Herbert Alexander, *Financing the 1972 Elections* (Lexington, Mass.: Lexington Books Company, 1976), p. 314.

38. Silbey, "Senate Demands Quid Pro Quo," p. 12; and Albright, p. 20.

39. Nahum Barnea, "The Balloon That Did Not Pop." Translated by Dalya Luttwack. *Davar Shavua*, August 9, 1974.

40. Silbey, "Senate Demands Quid Pro Quo," p. 10.

41. Ibid., p. 12.

42. Nahum Barnea, "The Jews Who Were a Disappointment." Translated by Dalya Luttwack. *Davar Shavua*, August 23, 1974.

43. See Donald R. Matthews and James A. Stimson on the importance of *cue taking* by

legislators who look to recognized and trusted colleagues in the Congress for cues on how to vote on matters not well known to an individual legislator. Cue taking applied to some degree in this case. Signers of a letter are the *cue givers.* Matthews and Stimson, *Yeas & Nays, Normal Decision Making in the United States House of Representatives* (New York: John Wiley & Sons, 1975).

44. According to Nahum Barnea's account, Perle and Amitay debated whether Magnuson, and not Jackson, should have been the primary sponsor.

45. Lawralyn Bellamy, "Senate Aides Rate Senator," Capitol Hill News Service, mid-November 1973.

46. As a practice, some senators—Sam Ervin (D.-S.C.), for example—did not cosponsor legislation.

47. *New York Times,* April 6, 1973, p. 14.

48. Hearings, "Russian Grain Transactions." Hearings before the Permanent Subcommittee on Investigations of Committee on Government Operations, United States Senate, 93rd Cong., 1st sess., July 20, 23, 24, 1974, p. 111.

49. Mark R. Levy and Michael Kramer, *The Ethnic Factor: How America's Minorities Decide Elections* (New York: Simon and Schuster, 1972), p. 119.

50. Orbach, *Freethem Now,* p. 279.

51. Ibid.

52. In another interview, Gunther recalled that Flanigan's office—not Commerce Secretary Peterson's office—returned his call saying that when the administration wants to take an initiative, it will do so on its own.

53. Press Release, Henry Jackson, "East-West Trade and Fundamental Human Rights," September 27, 1972.

54. For example, the impact of Rumania on the Jackson amendment was not changed in the legislative language. Gilmore recalled that Perle's "only concession was that legislative history" by means of a staged colloquy and formal statements in the *Congressional Record* would indicate that the amendment was not intended to harm Rumania's chances of getting most-favored-nation tariff treatment. In fact, the Jackson amendment hit Rumania and all "nonmarket countries."

55. Richard C. Bain and Judith H. Parris, *Convention Decisions and Voting Records,* 2nd ed. (Washington, D.C.: Brookings Institution, 1973), p. 329; also see Samuel Lubell, *The Future While It Happened* (New York: W.W. Norton and Company, 1973).

56. Safire, *Before the Fall,* p. 573.

57. *New York Times* says 17 percent (October 9, 1972). The *Ripon Society* said NBC reported 18 percent. The *Ripon Society* and Clifford W. Brown, Jr., *Jaws of Victory* (Boston: Little, Brown, 1973), p. 194.

58. *New York Times,* October 9, 1972.

59. Nixon had a high public regard for Jackson. In the beginning of his first administration, he offered Jackson the jobs of secretary of defense and secretary of state. The working relationship between Jackson's office and the White House was excellent, and until that period, there was a general agreement between Nixon and Jackson on national security questions. Prochnau and Larsen, *A Certain Democrat,* p. 243. Jackson's support of Nixon in Senate votes from 1969 to 1973 was higher than practically any other non-southern Democrat, according to the *Congressional Quarterly Almanac.* Americans for Democratic Action, Press Release, January 2, 1976. Some have actually argued that Jackson's Senate power derived from his unique relationship with Nixon. Ognibene, *Scoop,* p. 217.

60. Prochnau and Larsen, *A Certain Democrat,* pp. 70-173.

61. Ognibene, *Scoop,* p. 211.

62. Kurt Lauk, "The Jackson Amendment to SALT," unpublished manuscript, Stanford University, undated. Franz Schurmann, *The Logic of World Power: An Inquiry into the Origins. Currents, and Contradictions of World Politics* (New York: Pantheon Books, 1974), p. 542.

63. Robert Semple, Jr., *New York Times,* October 9, 1972; *Ripon Society* and Brown, *Jaws,* p. 194.

64. Evans and Novak, "Israeli Support for the Jackson Amendment," p. A8.

65. Ibid.

66. *New York Times,* October 3, 1972.

67. Richard S. Frank, "Trade Report/U.S. Sees Surplus, More Jobs in Early Years of Expanded Trade with Soviet Union," *National Journal,* November 25, 1972, pp. 1807-8.

68. *New York Times,* October 5, 1972, p. 1.

69. White House Press Conference, October 18, 1972.

70. *New York Times,* October 19, 1972.

71. Vladimir N. Pregelj, "Most-Favored-Nation Policy," Issue Brief No. IB 74139, Major Issues System date updated December 9, 1974, Congressional Research Service, Library of Congress. Also see Schroeter, *The Last Exodus,* p. 352.

72. *New York Times,* October 23, 1972.

73. *New York Times,* October 24, 1972, p. 3:5.

74. Szulc, "Behind the Vietnam Cease-Fire Agreement," pp. 54-55.

75. "What America Really Thinks of Nixon," *Newsweek,* August 28, 1972; George Gallup, "Nixon Popularity Hits 2-Year Peak on Soviet Trip," *Washington Post,* June 4, 1972; Louis Harris, "82 Percent Approve Summit Trip," *Washington Post,* June 27, 1972.

76. Safire, *Before the Fall,* p. 575.

77. *Rippon Society* and Brown, *Jaws,* p. 194.

78. Press Release, no. 294, Department of State, November 29, 1972. Emphasis added.

79. Edelsberg, "Showdown," p. 7. The White House's unwillingness to speak for the congressional concern reminds one of an observation by Tad Szule of a "favorite Kissinger ploy, espoused by Nixon of suggesting to 'difficult' clients that their real friends were in the White House. Nixon and Kissinger thought it gave them greater diplomatic leverage." Tad Szulc, *The Illusion of Peace* (New York: Viking Press, 1978), p. 98.

80. *New York Times,* December 2, 1972, p. 14:3.

81. Samuel O. Oglesby, "Soviet Emigration Policy: Exit Visas and Fees," Congressional Research Service, Library of Congress, April 11, 1973, pp. CRS 1, 7-8.

82. William Korey, "The Story of the Jackson Amendment 1973-1975," *Midstream,* March 1975, p. 10.

83. Steven Lazarus, "Trade Negotiations and Changing Attitudes," *United States Department of Commerce News,* January 16, 1973.

84. Henry Jackson, Interview, *U.S. News and World Report,* June 18, 1973.

85. Richard Nixon, *RN: Memoirs of Richard Nixon* (New York: Grosset & Dunlap, 1978), p. 876.

86. Stephen S. Rosenfeld, "The Politics of the Jackson Amendment," pp. 19-20.

CHAPTER 3: THE HOUSE OF REPRESENTATIVES

1. Vladimir N. Pregelj, "Most-Favored-Nation Principle: Definition, Brief History, and Use by the United States," Congressional Research Service, Library of Congress, October 26, 1972, update December 19, 1974, p. CRS-4.

2. Vanik had easily rounded up fifty-two cosponsors in his first hasty effort to introduce the House version of the Jackson amendment on October 10, 1972.

3. William Korey, "The Struggle over Jackson-Mills-Vanik," *American Jewish Yearbook, 1974-75* (New York: American Jewish Committee, 1976), p. 205.

4. *The Washington Lobby,* 2nd ed. (Washington, D.C.: *Congressional Quarterly,* September 1974), p. 118.

5. *Washington Post,* February 9, 1973.

6. Korey, "The Struggle," p. 205.

7. *New York Times,* February 7, 1973, p. 1.

8. Evans and Novak, "Israeli Support for the Jackson Amendment," p. A21.

9. Richard S. Frank, "Trade Report/Administration Between Domestic Overseas Interests in Drafting Trade Bill," *National Journal,* January 13, 1973, p. 53.

10. Frank, "Trade Report/Administration," p. 53.

11. John Herling, "George Meany and the AFL-CIO," *The New Republic* 73, no. 14 (October 4, 1975): 17.

12. Mark R. Levy and Michael S. Kramer, *The Ethnic Factor: How America's Minorities Decide Elections* (New York: Simon and Schuster, 1972), p. 151.

13. Joseph Albright, "The Pact of the Two Henrys," *New York Times Magazine,* January 5, 1975, p. 24.

14. U.S.-Soviet Trade Conference, Proceedings, National Association of Manufacturers, Washington, D.C.; also Korey, "The Story," p. 11.

15. Quoted in Oglesby, "Soviet Emigration Policy," p. CRS-8.

16. Korey, "The Struggle," pp. 203-34.

17. *New York Times,* March 13, 1973.

18. Korey, "The Story," p. 12.

19. Albright, "The Pact," p. 24.

20. *New York Times,* March 13, 1973, 53:5; Korey, "The Story," p. 12.

21. Korey, "The Struggle," p. 210.

22. Ibid., p. 211.

23. Marquis Childs, "A U.S.-Soviet Trade-Off on Tariffs?" *Washington Post,* March 13, 1973. In addition to the Colson and Shultz missions, Secretary of State William Rogers also discussed the emigration question with Foreign Minister Gromyko in Paris during this period.

24. Isaacs, *Jews,* p. 192.

25. Bookbinder, "Ethnic Pressures," pp. 7-8.

26. Evans and Novak, "Israeli Support for the Jackson Amendment," p. A21.

27. Edelsberg, "Showdown," p. 7.

28. Evans and Novak, "Israeli Support for the Jackson Amendment," p. A21.

29. *Congressional Record,* daily ed., March 15, 1973, pp. S4822-23.

30. Ibid., p. S4823.

31. Ibid., p. 4821.

32. William Korey reported that Jackson had planned to reintroduce his amendment after the administration had submitted its request for congressional authorization to fulfill the October 1972 trade pact, but Soviet activities pushed Jackson to act. Korey, "The Story," p. 12.

33. *New York Times,* March 27, 1973.

34. *New York Times,* March 21, 1973, p. 7:1; March 22, 1973, p. 3:1.

35. *Washington Post,* March 22, 1973.

36. *East-West Trade Council Newsletter* 1, no. 5 (March 28, 1973): 1.

37. Reprint, "Remarks by Senator Henry M. Jackson of the East-West Trade and Freedom of Emigration, National Press Club," of item placed in the *Congressional Record*, March 29, 1973.

38. *New York Times*, March 23, 1973, p. 5:1.

39. *New York Times*, March 30, 1973, p. 2:4.

40. Press Release, The White House, April 10, 1973, p. 8.

41. *Congressional Record*, April 10, 1973, Office of Senator Jackson, reprint of *Congressional Record*, April 10, 1973.

42. Sam Lipski, "Jackson Ahead in Battle to Free Soviet Jewry," *The Jerusalem Post Magazine*, April 27, 1973, p. 7.

43. Korey, "The Story," pp. 14-15.

44. Albright, "The Pact," p. 24.

45. Korey, "The Story," pp. 14-15.

46. *New York Times*, April 19, 1973, p. 12:4; press release, Henry M. Jackson, April 18, 1973.

47. Letter and enclosure, Andrew J. Biemiller, April 19, 1973.

48. Korey, "The Struggle," p. 214. While the White House was advertising the Soviet concessions to the select group of senators, Mills, and the American Jewish leadership, Brezhnev called an unexpected meeting with seven senators representing the Commerce Committee who were visiting in Moscow. Brezhnev assured the legislators that the tax had been suspended and the issue in effect was resolved. *International Herald Tribune*, April 25, 1973.

49. Korey, "The Struggle," p. 215.

50. V.O. Key refers to this form of pressure—"enlisting the support of a very few persons known to have great influence with an individual legislator"—as the "rifle" approach in contrast to the "shotgun" approach, which is a "general campaign in which all and sundry are asked to wire their congressmen." V.O. Key, *Politics, Parties, and Pressure Groups* (New York: Thomas Y. Crowell Co., 1952), p. 166. Others have discussed congressmen as pressure on lobbyists. Donald Matthews, *U.S. Senators and Their World* (Chapel Hill: University of North Carolina Press, 1960), p. 188; Lester W. Milbraith, "Interest Groups and Foreign Policy," in *Domestic Sources of Foreign Policy*, ed. James Rosenau (New York: The Free Press, 1967), pp. 250-51; Bauer, Pool, and Dexter, *American Business*, pp. 38, 441.

51. Isaacs, *Jews*, p. 256.

52. Barnea, "The Balloon."

53. Ibid.

54. William Korey, "Rescuing Russian Jewry: Two Episodes Compared," *Soviet Jewish Affairs* 5, no. 1 (1975): 8.

55. Lipski, "Jackson Ahead," p. 7; William Mehlman, "A Case of Bad Faith," *Times of Israel*, 1974?, p. 27.

56. Korey, "The Struggle," p. 215.

57. Albright, "The Pact," pp. 25-26.

58. Safire, *Before the Fall*, p. 575.

59. Barnea, "The Balloon."

60. Korey, "Rescuing Russian Jewry," p. 9.

61. Korey, "The Story," pp. 7-35.

62. Al Raphaeli, "Jews Said Persuaded by Nixon on Tax," *Jerusalem Post*, April 27, 1973.

63. *New York Times*, April 20, 1973, p. 1:3.

64. "Cabinet Meets on Issue of Soviet Jewry," *Jerusalem Post*, May 2, 1973, p. 2.

65. Edelsberg, "Showdown," p. 10; Matti Golan, *The Secret Conversations of Henry Kissinger: Step-by-Step Diplomacy in the Middle East* (New York: Quadrangle Press, 1976), p. 55.

66. *Jerusalem Post,* April 25, 1973.

67. *Jerusalem Post,* May 2, 1973, p. 2.

68. *Jerusalem Post,* May 2, 1973, p. 1.

69. *Jerusalem Post,* April 30, 1973.

70. *Jerusalem Post,* May 2, 1973.

71. *Jerusalem Post,* April 29, 1973.

72. Edelsberg, "Showdown," p. 10.

73. Korey, "Rescuing Russian Jewry," p. 9.

74. Quoted in Isaacs, *Jews,* p. 254; also Stephen Isaacs, "So Who Has the Power?" *Present Tense* 1, no. 4 (Summer 1974): 25.

75. Korey, "The Struggle," p. 216.

76. Albright, "The Pact," p. 26.

77. See "Trade Reform," Hearings before the House Ways and Means Committee, United States House of Representatives, 93rd Cong., 1st sess., part II, p. 3672.

78. *New York Times,* May 7, 1973, p. 1:3; August 14, 1973, p. 9:1.

79. Orbach, *Freethem Now,* p. 144.

80. Gabriel Almond distinguishes between "the *elected* or *political interest elite* and the *bureaucratic* staffs which have an importance in the field of interest group activity comparable to that of the governmental bureaucracy in official policy making. They too . . . enjoy powers in practice which are not formally recognized in the legal distribution of power." Almond, *The American People,* p. 140; V.O. Key, *Politics,* makes the same point, p. 155.

81. Harold B. Light, "Vanik Bill A Victory but Struggle Continues," *Exodus,* February-March 1974, p. 2.

82. Lipski, "Jackson Ahead," p. 7.

83. Korey, "Rescuing Russian Jewry," p. 10.

84. Albright, "The Pact," p. 26; Korey, "The Struggle," pp. 218-19.

85. Edelsberg, "Showdown," p. 10.

86. "Trade Reform," Hearings, p. 5671-72; Press Release, American Jewish Committee, May 20, 1973.

87. Korey, "The Struggle," p. 219.

88. *New York Times,* May 3, 1973, p. 3:4.

89. *New York Times,* June 2, p. 1:5; Korey, "The Struggle," said the list had eight hundred names, p. 219. This list was added to the State Department representation list, containing names of Soviet citizens refused an exit visa at least once. Kissinger took two lists to the Soviet Union. One was a list of conspicuous Jews denied the right to leave. The second was a list of people who had applied and had some connections with the United States because of either family in America or some claim to American citizenship.

90. *Washington Post,* May 10, 1973.

91. Barnea, "The Balloon." Donald Matthews, in *U.S. Senators,* and Lester Milbraith, in "Interest Groups," have discussed techniques by which indirect pressure on legislators from Washington organizations is communicated via constituents.

92. *New York Times,* June 2, 1973, p. 1:5.

93. *New York Times,* May 17, 1973, p. 12:5.

94. Korey, "The Struggle," p. 221.

95. Orbach, *Freethem Now,* p. 129.

96. "Statement on the Nixon-Brezhnev Meetings," *American Jewish Committee,* May 23, 1973.

97. *New York Times,* June 15, p. 1:4.

98. *Congressional Quarterly,* June 23, 1973, p. 1568; Szulc, *The Illusion of Peace,* p. 699. On April 23, he had tried out some of these same arguments on a delegation of seven senators from the Commerce Committee: Vance Hartke (D.-Ind.), Frank Moss (D.-Utah), Howard Baker, Jr. (R.-Tenn.), J. Glenn Beall, Jr. (R.-Md.), Robert Griffin (R.-Mich.), James Pearson (R.-Kans.) and Howard Cannon (D.-Nev.). *New York Times,* April 25, 1973, p. 3:4.

99. Mehlman, "Bad Faith," p. 28.

100. Orbach, *Free them Now,* p. 281.

101. Press Release, *American Jewish Committee,* June 25, 1973.

102. Szulc, *The Illusion of Peace,* p. 700; Korey, "The Struggle," p. 223. This probably reinforced those America-watchers in the Kremlin who believed that despite the apparent strength of the Jackson amendment, the capitalists would ultimately prevail and trade benefits would be granted without conditions.

103. *New York Times,* June 21, 1973, p. 17.

104. *New York Times,* July 3, 1973, p. 3:1.

105. *New York Times,* July 9, 1973, p. 14:4.

106. *New York Times,* July 21, 1973, p. 1:4.

107. "Detente," *Chronology,* p. 521.

108. *New York Times,* July 18, 1973, p. 6:6.

109. *New York Times,* August 22, 1973, p. 1:5.

110. *New York Times,* August 28, 1973, p. 34:5.

111. "A 51 to 12 percent majority supports 'giving Russian favored-nation status in trade as most Western nations now have with us' " and "a 72 to 14 percent majority supports 'expanding trade between the two countries' while an 84 to 4 percent majority favors agreement 'to get Russia to allow Jews to leave that country more easily.' " Louis Harris, "Majority See Summit as Breakthru," *Chicago Tribune,* June 23, 1973.

112. Carl Gershman, "The Soviet Dissidents and the American Left: Reviving the Democratic Faith," *The New Leader,* October 29, 1973, pp. 8-9.

113. "Detente," *Chronology,* p. 521.

114. Henry Jackson, "A Letter from Dr. Sakharov on Detente and Freedom of Emigration," *Congressional Record* 119, no. 134 (September 17, 1973), reprint. Jackson said the arrival of Sakharov's letter at that time was "ironic." Jackson's staffer Perle said that he had not had direct contact with Sakharov although he had spoken with Jews telephoning from the Soviet Union who were in contact with Sakharov.

115. *New York Times,* September 10, 1973, p. 1:5.

116. *Wall Street Journal,* September 11, 1973.

117. *Congressional Record,* September 17, 1973, reprint.

118. Korey, "The Struggle," p. 227.

119. Albright, "The Pact," p. 26.

120. Ibid.

121. Marilyn Berger, "Big Firms to Press Hill on Soviet Trade Benefit," *Washington Post,* September 16, 1973, pp. A1, A6:1.

122. Ibid.

123. Korey, "The Struggle," p. 227.

124. Ibid., p. 228.

125. In Moscow, *Newsweek* correspondent Jay Axelbank arranged for Lazarus to meet with a group of Moscow Jews including V.G. Levich, A.Y. Lerner, M.Y. Azbel, and A.Y. Voronel. This

group later accused Lazarus of trying to pressure them to stop their public campaign to emigrate. *(New York Times,* September 16, 1973, p. 1:5.) Henry Jackson elaborated on the "charge that he tried to advise them to lobby American citizens against my Amendment . . . this American official warned that the Soviet Government would 'wreak vengeance' on its Jewish citizens and that 'no one would be able to come to [their] aid' if the Jackson Amendment were to be approved by the Congress." Henry Jackson, speech, *Congressional Record,* daily ed., 119, no. 134 (September 17, 1973), reprint.

126. Korey, "The Struggle," p. 228.

127. *New York Times,* September 20, 1973, p. 11:1.

128. "Detente," *Chronology,* p. 522.

129. Korey, "The Struggle," p. 228.

130. Ibid., p. 229.

131. "Detente," *Chronology,* p. 522.

132. Hedrick Smith, *New York Times,* October 2, 1973.

133. Korey, "The Struggle," p. 230.

134. Edward R.F. Sheehan, "Step by Step in the Middle East," *Foreign Policy,* no. 22 (Spring 1976). See another version of the arms supply episode in Golan.

135. Barnea, "Jews," p. 15:1; Mehlman, "Bad Faith," p. 28.

136. Albright, "The Pact," p. 28. Orbach, *Freethem,* reported that Peter M. Flanigan also attended, p. 281.

137. Albright, "The Pact," p. 28.

138. Korey reported that Kissinger, not the Jewish leaders, was supposed to speak to Jackson and Vanik about the proposal, and if they agreed, the Jewish leaders would then respond to inquiries from legislators about the Jewish community position. Instead of consulting the sponsors, according to Korey's account, the Jewish leaders said they would go to their "constituency." (Korey, "The Struggle," p. 231.)

139. Statement of Peter Flanigan. Hearings, "Export-Import Bank of the United States," Subcommittee on International Finance, Committee on Banking, Housing and Urban Affairs, United States Senate, 93rd Cong., 1st sess., October 29, 1973, p. 55.

140. *Wall Street Journal,* October 31, 1973.

141. *New York Times,* October 31, 1973, p. 15:1.

142. *Washington Post,* November 2, 1973; *New York Times,* November 1973, p. 6:6:V; *Wall Street Journal,* November 2, 1973.

143. Matti Golan, *The Secret Conversations of Henry Kissinger: Step-by-Step Diplomacy in the Middle East* (New York: Quadrangle/The New York Times Book Co., 1976), pp. 172-73.

144. Albright, "The Pact," p. 26.

145. Barnea, "Jews."

146. Albright, "The Pact," p. 28; Korey, "The Struggle," p. 232; Mehlman, "Bad Faith," p. 29.

147. Korey, "The Struggle," p. 232.

148. Korey, "The Story," p. 25.

149. Mehlman, "Bad Faith," pp. 29-30.

150. Albright, "The Pact," p. 28.

151. Barnea, "Jews."

152. Albright, "The Pact," p. 28.

153. Ibid.; Mehlman, "Bad Faith," p. 260.

154. Albright, "The Pact," p. 28.

155. *New York Times,* November 8, 1973, p. 81:4.

156. *Wall Street Journal,* October 31, 1973.

157. *New York Times,* December 4, 1973, p. 1:2.

158. *New York Times,* December 7, 1973, December 15, 1973, p. 2:3.

159. *New York Times,* December 2, 1973, p. 13:1.

160. "Resolution on International Trade and Investment Adopted by AFL-CIO Convention, October 19, 1973," *Congressional Record,* November 8, 1973, p. H9778-79.

161. *International Herald Tribune,* April 25, 1973.

162. *The National Journal,* November 24, 1973.

163. Edelsberg, "Showdown," p. 10.

CHAPTER 4: THE SENATE, SOVIETS, AND NIXON NEGOTIATE

1. Quoted in Rosenfeld, "Politics," p. 33.

2. Albright, "The Pact," p. 29.

3. Ibid., p. 29.

4. Albright repeated that interpretation in his article and said that it was backed up by contemporaneous memos," Ibid., p. 29. A top official in the East-West Trade Bureau in the Commerce Department confirmed that even before September 1973, he and Perle and Morris Amitay had discussed elements of a compromise. A reporter who covered this dispute on a daily basis also recalled that even before the final House Ways and Means Committee vote, Perle said he could see where there was room for a compromise, but this reporter believed that Richard Perle was unduly revisionist in recalling that "all along Jackson was willing to compromise." Although the Jackson version may be accurate in portraying Jackson's long-range intent, some of the facts in the story have been contradicted by one actor, who was supposed to be the catalyst for Jackson's overture to Kissinger: William Eberle. Eberle has stated specifically, "My contacts with Jackson or his staff were all indirect at least through May."

5. Henry Jackson, *Congressional Record,* December 13, 1974, reprint.

6. Charles Bartlett, "Jackson Breakthrough," *Washington Star,* February 11, 1974, p. A13.

7. Quoted in *Washington Star-News,* March 8, 1974.

8. *The Times,* London, June 12, 1974.

9. Hearings, "The Trade Reform Act," Senate Finance Committee, Unted States Senate, 93rd Cong., 2nd sess., March 7, 1974, pp. 478-79.

10. Ibid., p. 464.

11. Ibid., p. 479.

12. Henry Jackson, *Congressional Record,* December 13, 1974, p. 2, reprint.

13. Marilyn Berger, "Soviet Emigration Assurances, Trade Bill Linked," *Washington Post,* March 19, 1974, p. A12.

14. *Boston Globe,* March 24, 1974, p. A-3.

15. *New York Times,* March 25, 1974, p. 1.

16. *New York Times,* March 21, 1974, p. 18.

17. *New York Times,* March 29, 1974, p. 1.

18. *New York Times,* March 30, 1974, p. 1.

19. *New York Times,* April 10, 1974, p. 51.

20. Albright, "The Pact," p. 29.

21. Hearings, "Detente," October 8, 1974.

22. *New York Times,* March 30, 1974.

23. *Washington Post,* April 27, 1974.

24. Henry Kissinger, Hearings, "Emigration Amendment," Finance Committee, United States Senate, 93rd Cong., 2nd sess., December 3, 1974.

25. *Washington Post,* April 26, 1974.

26. Kissinger, Hearings, "Emigration Amendment"; *Washington Post,* April 26, 1974.

27. Albright, "The Pact," p. 29.

28. "Some had felt the President might wait to announce final approval of the loan until his expected visit to Moscow next month." Others have suggested that the loan decision resulted from Soviet official warning that the Soviet Union might go elsewhere if it failed to receive the loan and from American businessmen, "frantic" that contracts might be lost lest the loan be granted, who lobbied successfully for the decision. *Washington Post,* May 22, 1974, p. A1.

29. *Statement of Russell Long,* May 23, 1974.

30. *Washington Post,* May 25, 1974.

31. Richard S. Frank, "Trade Report Credits to Soviet Threatened by Eximbank Bill Amendments," *National Journal,* May 11, 1974, p. 684.

32. Andrew Biemiller, Hearings, "The Role of the Export-Import Bank and Export Controls in United States International Economic Policy," Hearings Subcommittee on International Finance of the Committee on Banking, Housing and Urban Affairs, United States Senate, 93rd Cong., 2d sess., S. 1890, p. 242.

33. William Korey, Leadership Convocation, Synagogue Council of America, September 10, 1975.

34. "National Conference of [sic] Soviet Jewry," Additional Statements and Data, Hearings Senate Banking Committee, pp. 562-70.

35. The National Conference on Soviet Jewry protested against specific loans to the Soviet Union, which, they argued, contradicted the policy of exerting economic pressure on the Soviets for the purpose of forcing liberalization of emigration. "The Need for Passage of the Jackson Amendment," excerpts from remarks made by Stanley H. Lowell, chairman, National Conference on Soviet Jewry, at the NCSJ Board Meeting, Washington, D.C., June 3, 1974.

36. Press Release, Adlai Stevenson, January 21, 1975.

37. *Congressional Record,* daily ed., June 17, 1974, pp. S10681-687.

38. *Washington Post,* June 19, 1974.

39. Albright, "The Pact," p. 30.

40. Rosenfeld, "Politics," p. 33.

41. "The Role of National Jewish Leadership in Jackson-Mills-Vanik," January 7, 1974, pp. 26, 33, 36.

42. "Trade Reform Act." March 7, 1974, p. 477.

43. "Trade Reform Act," April 10, 1974, part 5, pp. 2240-41, 2245.

44. Tom Braden, "Senator Kennedy: Seeking Options for Detente," *Washington Post,* April 20, 1974.

45. Cranston's count in April showed that thirty-eight of the original cosponsors were ready to get off the Jackson amendment if a compromise would be offered. That figure indicated a majority of the committee and the Senate would be prepared to pass a substitute. The count vaguely coincided with an administration head count indicating that Jackson had a sure sixty-two—not all seventy-eight cosponsors—for an up and down vote on the Jackson amendment.

46. For example, see Speech, Senator George Aiken (R.-Vt.), *Congressional Record,* May 21, 1974, pp. 8668-69.

47. Paul F. Levy, "More Jews Expected to Leave Russia," *Wisconsin Jewish Chronicle,* June 28, 1974, pp. 1, 18.

48. Statement by Stanley H. Lowell, June 5, 1975, circulated to United States senators and congressmen by the National Conference on Soviet Jewry on June 11, 1974.

49. "Congress Criticized by Nixon," *Wisconsin Jewish Chronicle,* June 14, 1974, pp. 3, 13.

50. These remarks also may have been intended for Soviet officials listening and waiting for Nixon to arrive for his last summit in Moscow. *Washington Post,* June 8, 1974.

51. *New York Times,* June 7, 1974, pp. 1:3, 10:4.

52. *Washington Post,* June 6, 1974, pp. A1, A11, col. 1.

53. *New York Times,* June 21, 1974, pp. 8, 3:1.

54. *New York Times,* June 21, 1974.

55. *New York Times,* June 22, 1974, pp. 1:3, 2:3.

56. Albright, "The Pact," p. 28.

57. Ibid., p. 30; Marvin Schick, Letter to the Editor, the *Jewish Press,* August 16, 1974.

58. Levy and Kramer, *Ethnic Factor,* pp. 120-21.

59. *Near East Report* XVII, no. 26 (June 26, 1974): 152.

60. Ibid.

61. *Washington Post,* June 24, 1974, pp. A1, A20; *Washington Post,* June 12, 1974.

62. *New York Times,* June 18, 1974, p. 3.

63. *New York Times,* June 28, 1974.

64. *New York Times,* June 30, 1974, pp. L:8, 20:3.

65. *New York Times,* July 19, 1974, p. 3:1; *East-West Trade Council Newsletter* 11, no. 11 (July 22, 1974): 1; *Wisconsin Jewish Chronicle,* August 1, 1974, pp. 1, 19.

66. *New York Times,* June 5, 1974.

67. Rowland Evans and Robert Novak, "The Detente Lobby and the Jackson Amendment," *Washington Post,* July 17, 1974.

68. Nahum Barnea, first of series, *Davar Shavua,* July 26, 1974.

69. Schick, Letter to the Editor, August 16, 1974.

70. Albright, "The Pact," p. 30.

71. George Gallup, "Approval of Nixon Levels Off to 29% at Year End," *Washington Post,* January 6, 1974.

72. *New York Times,* June 23, 1974, section 4. Although the parliamentarians' trip occurred in the spring, the plans for the trip were probably set in motion months earlier. Norman Cousins, the American journalist, noted from his own perspective marked change in Soviet understanding of American domestic political realities. Norman Cousins, "From Hanover to Tbilsi," *Saturday Review World,* June 15, 1974, p. 5.

73. Not until spring 1974 did the Soviet Union give Watergate serious thought. Hedrick Smith, *The Russians* (New York: Quadrangle/The New York Times Book Company, 1976), pp. 242-43.

74. Jackson was not the only one who downplayed Soviet economic recovery. One of his aides argued at the time that "trade is as important for the Soviet Union as it was two years ago; they have five year programs built upon certain expectations." An aide of Senator Ribicoff who worked intimately with the Jackson office also said, "I continue to believe trade is very, very important to the Soviet Union" and specifically took issue with Soviet trade expert Marshall Goldman's testimony before the Senate Banking Committee about increased Soviet hard currency earnings. Hearings, "Export-Import Bank," April 25, 1974, pp. 325-41.

Counterbalancing the Goldman analysis and reinforcing Jackson's perception of economic vulnerability was the opinion of another source of economic expertise outside the orbit of Henry

Jackson: the Central Intelligence Agency. The CIA concluded in a study reported in August 1974 that "Moscow now considers trade with the developed world as essential to close the technological gap." *Wall Street Journal*, August 16, 1974, p. 2.

75. "Of Course the Kremlin Will Not Go Quietly," *Los Angeles Times*, October 1, 1978.

76. In early February Peter Flanigan repeated the veto threat. He told Senator Javits that the president would still veto the Trade Bill with the Jackson-Vanik language.

77. Hearings, Trade Reform Act, part 2, p. 457.

78. Ibid., p. 463.

79. *The Washington Star Newspaper*, October 16, 1975. Also see Henry Brandon, "Ford Can Listen, Kissinger's Talking," *New York Times*, August 25, 1975.

80. United States Senator Walter F. Mondale wrote that "the (Nixon) Administration viewed the trade bill primarily as a vehicle to advance its detente objectives." Walter F. Mondale, "Beyond Detente: Toward International Economic Security," *Foreign Affairs* 53, no. 1 (October 1974): 15. Mondale occasionally consulted William Pearce, a former top official in the Office of the Special Trade Representative. Mondale, at the time the article was written, also employed David Aaron, a former national security staffer for Henry Kissinger.

CHAPTER 5: PRESIDENT FORD

1. Jacob Javits, *Congressional Record*, daily ed., December 13, 1974, p. S21416.

2. "President Gerald R. Ford," *Near East Report* XVIII, no. 3 (August 14, 1974): 177-80.

3. *New York Times*, August 14, 1974.

4. J.F. ter Horst, "Trade Bill Compromise," *Washington Star-News*, October 23, 1974.

5. Ibid.

6. Press Release, The White House, Press Conference on Senator Abraham A. Ribicoff, Senator Henry M. Jackson, and Senator Jacob K. Javits, August 15, 1975. Later Ribicoff and Javits seconded this view. *Congressional Record*, daily ed., December 13, 1974, p. S21416.

7. Henry Brandon, "Ford Can Listen."

8. Albright, "The Pact," p. 30.

9. Quoted in *Washington Post*, August 16, 1974, pp. A1, A2:1.

10. Press Conference, August 15, 1974. Emphasis added.

11. *Washington Post*, August 23, 1974.

12. It is not clear whether this referred to Jackson and staffers Perle and Amitay or Jackson and Ribicoff and Javits.

13. Albright, "The Pact," p. 30.

14. Jacob Javits, *Congressional Record*, daily ed., December 13, 1974, p. S21427. Emphasis added.

15. *Wall Street Journal*, September 9, 1974.

16. Memorandum of Conversation. "Jewish Activists and United States Senators," Rossiya Hotel, Moscow, June 29, 1975, p. 3.

17. *Washington Post*, September 7, 1974.

18. John Herling, "Change and Conflict in the AFL-CIO," *Dissent*, Fall 1974, p. 481.

19. Victor Riesel, "Scoop's China Visit Helps Ted," *Human Rights*, August 3, 1974, p. 697.

20. He commented on the Export-Import Bank. "This isn't trade. This is an economic aid program. This is a welfare program for the benefit of the Soviet leaders." Hearings, "Detente," pp. 381, 383, 410.

21. R. W. Apple, Jr., "Puritan for President," *The New York Times Magazine* (November 23, 1975):58; Albright, "The Pact," p. 34.

22. Albright, "The Pact," p. 34.

23. John Herling, "George Meany and the AFL-CIO," *The New Republic* 173, no. 14 (October 4, 1975): 17.

24. See earlier reference to article in *Washington Post,* September 6, 1974, for example.

25. *Washington Post,* September 19, 1974, p. A18.

26. *Washington Post,* September 21, 1974, pp. A1, A6:6.

27. Albright, "The Pact," p. 30.

28. *New York Times,* September 22, 1974; *Washington Post,* September 22, 1974. Kissinger and Gromyko were scheduled to meet one more time in New York over dinner Tuesday, September 24, 1974, *Washington Post,* September 21, 1974.

29. Albright, "The Pact," p. 30.

30. American Enterprise Institute, News summaries, October 5, 6, 7, 1974.

31. *Congressional Record,* daily ed., September 19, 1974, p. S17183.

32. "Limits on Export-Import," *Near East Report* XVIII, no. 39 (September 25, 1974): 203; "Senate Export-Import Action Makes House Bill Look Great," *East-West Trade Council Newsletter* II, no. 15 (September 30, 1974): 3-4.

33. The Secretary of State Press Conference, October 7, 1974, p. 4.

34. Albright, "The Pact," p. 31.

35. *New York Times,* October 6, 1974.

36. Ibid: Albright, "The Pact," p. 30.

37. *Exodus* 5, no. 9 (September-October 1974): 1.

38. *New York Times,* October 6, 1974, pp. 1:7, 8:1.

39. Albright, "The Pact," p. 31.

40. Ibid.

41. Secretary of State Press Conference, October 7, 1974, pp. 4-5.

42. Ibid.

43. *New York Times,* October 9, 1974.

44. Albright, "The Pact," p. 34.

45. *Congressional Record,* daily ed., December 13, 1974, p. S21421.

46. Albright, "The Pact," p. 34.

47. The White House Press Conference of Henry M. Jackson, Jacob Javits, and Charles A. Vanik, White House Briefing Room, October 18, 1974, 10:46-11:14 a.m.

48. Albright, "The Pact," p. 34.

49. Barnea, "The Balloon."

50. A. Ribicoff's staffman denied that Ribicoff had argued for the delay with labor's reaction in mind.

51. This is an example of what Mayhew calls "advertising" and "credit claiming" behavior of congressmen. It applies to all elected or would-be elected politicians. David R. Mayhew, *Congress: The Electoral Connection* (New Haven: Yale University Press, 1974), p. 76.

52. Emphasis added.

53. Export-Import Bank Act Amendment, Conference Report, no. 93-1439, October 8, 1974.

54. National Conference on Soviet Jewry News Bulletin, no. 40, October 18, 1974, p. 2.

55. Press Conference, The White House, Henry Jackson, Jacob Javits, Charles Vanik, October 18, 1974.

56. *Wisconsin Jewish Chronicle,* October 31, 1974.

57. Letter, Henry M. Jackson to Secretary of State Kissinger, October 18, 1974.

58. Quoted in *Washington Post*, October 19, 1974.

59. *Near East Report* XVIII, no. 43 (October 23, 1974): 719.

60. *Quoted in Washington Post*, October 22, 1974.

61. *New York Times*, October 16, 1974.

62. It may also have been an unguarded outburst of anger reflecting Soviet impatience with the mounting interference that Simon's government was inserting in the trade relationship between the two superpowers. The October 18, 1972, Trade Agreement was still not in force. Even if all went well regarding the trilateral emigration agreement, the concessions would not be assured until final passage of the Trade Bill in December 1974, at the earliest. The Export-Import Bank legislation was complicating the trade picture, too. On October 5, a new development agitated Soviet-American trade relations. An executive decision in the White House was made to block all trade in grains with the Soviet Union. Ostensibly, the stop order was designed to prevent a recurrence of disruptions in the United States marketplace that had occurred after the massive Soviet purchases of grain in the summer of 1972. Eventually the two countries agreed on pacing Soviet purchases to prevent disruptions of the American economy. The announcement of the new agreement was made on October 19, 1974. The timing of the announcement—one day after the trade-emigration letters were exchanged—is intriguing. One might hypothesize that even if economic considerations had forced the original temporary stop order, diplomatic considerations might have affected the timing of the announcement that the stop order had been removed. Both the removal of the stop order and the final letter exchange—which ostensibly cleared up two major sources of Soviet agitation—preceded Kissinger's embarkation for Moscow to arrange a minisummit and discussions on strategic arms limitations for the new president and Party Chief Brezhnev. *New York Times*, October 20, 1974, pp. 1:1, 61:3.

63. Release, "Statement by the Press Secretary on the Agreement Concerning Soviet Emigration and the Trade Bill," The White House Press Secretary (Tucson, Arizona), October 21, 1974. Emphasis added.

64. Press Release, Senator Henry M. Jackson, "On Agreement on Trade and Emigration," October 21, 1974. Emphasis added.

65. *Washington Post*, October 25, 1974.

66. *Washington Post*, October 28, 1974, pp. A1, A4:1.

67. "Last Tangle in Moscow," *Newsweek*, December 30, 1974, p. 27.

68. *New York Times*, October 28, 1974.

69. *Washington Post*, October 28, 1974.

70. *New York Times*, November 20, 1974. If so, that was a rather lame excuse since Ford had been quoted suggesting a "definitive leak" (which was a Kissinger idea) to deal with the letters.

71. This was given as a possible reason for Brezhnev to seek an early meeting with Ford. One of the purposes of Kissinger's trip to Moscow was to arrange such a meeting. *New York Times*, October 22, 1974, pp. 1:6, 5:1.

72. *New York Times*, January 16, 1975, pp. 1:8, 18:3.

73. Frank Starr, "Was Jackson Taken?" *Wisconsin Jewish Chronicle*, November 14, 1974, p. 7.

74. *Washington Post*, January 24, 1975, pp. A2, A21.

75. "Buying People's Freedom," *The Economist Magazine*, October 26, 1974, reprinted in Hearings, "Emigration Amendment," p. 110.

76. Released by the Embassy of the Union of Socialist Soviet Republics, Washington, D.C., December 18, 1974.

77. Ibid.

78. *Washington Post,* February 17, 1975.

79. Ibid.

80. *New York Times,* April 21, 1974, pp. 1:7, 16:1.

81. *New York Times,* October 28, 1974.

82. *Washington Post,* February 17, 1975, pp. A1, A7.

83. Mimeograph, "Statement by the AFL-CIO Executive Council on Pending Trade Legislation," November 7, 1974, Washington, D.C., pp. 1, 4, 5.

84. *Washington Post,* November 19, 1974, p. A10.

85. *Journal of Commerce,* November 12, 1974, p. 1.

86. *Washington Post,* November 19, 1974.

87. *New York Times,* November 13, 1974.

88. *New York Times,* November 20, 1974, p. 5.

89. Quoted in *New York Times,* November 25, 1974.

90. Quoted in *Washington Post,* February 17, 1975.

91. Joint Statement by Senators Jackson, Ribicoff, and Javits, and Congressman Vanik on East-West Trade and Freedom of Emigration, January 15, 1975, p. 1; Albright, "The Pact," p. 16.

92. Hearings, "Emigration Amendment," December 3, 1974.

93. Henry Jackson, "East-West Trade and Freedom of Emigration," *Congressional Record,* January 30, 1975, p. 203, reprint.

94. *Congressional Record,* daily ed., December 9, 1974, p. S20859.

95. Jerry Goodman, Statement, Synagogue Council of America, Leadership Convocation, September 10, 1975.

96. Korey, Statement, September 10, 1975.

97. *Washington Post,* December 14, 1974, pp. A1, A4:1. There was also a successful effort to prevent James Buckley from introducing an amendment to deregulate natural gas, which would have attracted counteramendments and precipitated a long debate that would have killed the bill.

98. Robert Byrd, *Congressional Record,* daily ed., December 13, 1974.

99. Henry Jackson, *Congressional Record,* December 13, 1974, pp. S21407-15.

100. Ibid., p. S21416.

101. Ibid., p. S21420.

102. Ibid., p. S21409.

103. Hartke, *Congressional Record,* December 13, 1974, p. S21383.

104. Javits, *Congressional Record,* December 13, 1974, p. S21417. Jackson reinforced Javits, p. S21418.

105. Jackson, *Congressional Record,* December 13, 1974, p. S21418.

106. Abourezk, *Congressional Record,* December 13, 1974, p. S21425.

107. Ribicoff, *Congressional Record,* December 13, 1974, p. S21412.

108. Nelson, *Congressional Record,* December 13, 1974, p. S21448.

109. James Buckley, *If Men Were Angels* (New York: G.P. Putnam's Sons, 1975), p. 125.

110. William Safire, "The Rabbit Punch," *New York Times,* February 3, 1975, p. 25.

111. "Last Tangle in Moscow," *Time Magazine,* December 30, 1974, p. 28.

112. Soviet Embassy Press Release, *"Tass* Statement," December 18, 1974.

113. Victor Zorza, "Brezhnev's Political Health," *Washington Post,* January 9, 1975, p. A23.

114. See Paula Stern, "Egypt and Soviet Policy," *Washington Post,* January 13, 1975. There

may be some connection between the repudiation of the emigration accord and desire on the part of the Soviet Union to appeal to its Arab friends. *New York Times,* January 16, 1975.

115. Korey, "The Story," pp. 31-32. For further speculation along these lines see Victor Zorza, "Brezhnev and the Emigration Issue," *Washington Post,* December 27, 1974, p. A17. For earlier reference to Podgorny's activities, see p. 214.

116. Victor Zorza. "The Kremlin's 'Collective Leadership,' " *Washington Post,* January 30, 1975, p. A21.

117. *Washington Post,* January 16, 1975, p. A30; Marshall I. Goldman, *Detente and Dollars: Doing Business with the Soviets* (New York: Basic Books, Inc., 1975), p. 69.

118. Press Conference, Secretary of State, December 7, 1974, p. 8. Kissinger discussed the connection between the Vladivostok and emigration agreements again on January 14. Press Conference, Secretary of State, "Soviets Reject Trade Agreement, January 14, 1975," *Washington Post,* February 17, 1975.

119. *Washington Post,* January 16, 1975. Soviet official of the U.S.A. Institute, Yuri Shvedkov, said, "The feeling was he [Jackson] would ask for more and more reports and if we give it, he'll ask for more. . . ."

120. *Washington Post,* December 29, 1974, pp. A1, A17:1.

121. *Business Week* Interview, given December 23, 1974, reviewed by Department of State, December 25, reprinted in *Washington Post,* January 3, 1975, p. A17.

122. *New York Times,* December 21, 1974.

123. Korey, "The Story," p. 30.

124. *New York Times,* December 21, 1974.

125. *New York Times,* December 20, 1974.

126. *New York Times,* December 19, 1974, pp. 1:7, 18:5.

127. Javits and Ribicoff's remarks essentially echoed Jackson. *Washington Post,* December 19, 1974; *Washington Post,* February 17, 1975.

128. John Luneau cites an interview with Professor Uri Ra'anan, advisor to Senator Jackson, as evidence that Jackson's public and private assessments of the protests differed. Luneau, "Congressional Trade Restrictions and US/Soviet Diplomacy from 1972-1975: A Case Study of Detente," unpublished manuscript, The Fletcher School of Law and Diplomacy, May 9, 1975.

129. *Washington Post,* December 21, 1974.

130. Ibid.

131. "News from the AFL-CIO" Press Release, "The Politics of Deceit," signed by George Meany, December 20, 1974.

132. *New York Times,* December 19, 1974.

133. *Washington Post,* February 17, 1974, pp. A1, A7.

134. Hearings, "Emigration Amendment," December 3, 1974, p. 59.

135. *New York Times,* December 20, 1974.

136. Press Release, Senator Adlai E. Stevenson, "$300 Million in New Credits for Soviet Union Isn't 'Peanuts,' " January 21, 1975.

137. An unnamed State Department official was reported to say "Three hundred million is peanuts in Soviet terms." The official, later identified as Kissinger, gave an exaggerated interpretation of the ceiling and called it "an insult . . . an absurdity." William Safire, "The Rabbit Punch," *New York Times,* February 3, 1975, p. 25; *New York Times,* December 20, 1974; *Washington Post,* December 20, 1974, pp. A1, A6:1. The fact is that loans were limited to $300 million, but provision was made for increasing the ceiling if both houses deemed it advisable.

The $300 million figure was originally suggested to Congress by Export-Import Bank officials since it represented the amount of loans for which American companies had already applied to do business in the Soviet Union.

138. *New York Times,* December 22, 1974; *New York Times,* December 23, 1974, p. 14.

139. *Business Week* interview.

140. *New York Times,* December 29, 1974, pp. 1:1, 5. His article appeared in *Sovetkaiia Rossia,* a daily of the province of the Russian Republic. It may have been intended for a domestic audience, but it did not escape notice in America.

141. The Soviet Union had agreed to pay three installments totaling $48 million on October 18, 1972, July 1, 1973, and July 1, 1975. After that, the balance of the $700 million obligation was to be paid in annual installments after Soviet receipt of MFN. In fact, the Soviets did pay its July 1, 1975, installment, in spite of their protests.

142. *Washington Post,* January 4, 1975, pp. A1, A7:1.

143. *Washington Post,* January 5, 1975, pp. A1, A19:1.

144. Press Conference, Secretary of State, January 28, 1975, p. 4.

145. *Washington Post,* January 4, 1975, pp. A1, A12:1.

146. Press Conference, January 14, 1975.

147. Trade Act of 1974, Summary of the Provisions of H.R. 10710, "Prepared for Committee on Finance and Committee for Ways and Means," December 30, 1974, p. 18.

148. The group suggested that Soviet compliance with the standards spelled out in the Jackson amendment be reviewed "after four to six months." *New York Times,* December 21, 1974. The January 3, 1975, news bulletin of the National Conference on Soviet Jewry repeated the official position of the Jewish community on the subject.

149. Press Conference, Secretary of State, "Soviets Reject Trade Agreement," January 14, 1975.

150. Ibid.

151. Stanley Karnow, "Jackson's Bid," *New Republic,* May 25, 1974, p. 19.

152. For Jackson's personal defense, see Henry Jackson, "East-West Trade and Freedom of Emigration," *Congressional Record,* January 30, 1975, p. 3, reprint.

153. Jackson, *Congressional Record,* December 13, 1974, p. S21421.

154. Buckley, *Congressional Record,* December 13, 1974, p. S21421.

155. Jackson, *Congressional Record,* December 13, 1974, p. S21421.

156. Ibid., pp. S21410-11.

157. William Korey construed the Export-Import Bank legislation as "completely unrelated to the Jackson Amendment." Korey, "The Struggle," p. 165.

CHAPTER 6: CONCLUSION

1. Bauer, Pool, and Dexter, *American Business,* p. 473.

2. Motives of "political types" is a question for another study. Harold D. Lasswell sees personality as the root. "Political types," he has written, are power-seekers with "private motives displaced on public objects rationalized in terms of public interest." Harold D. Lasswell, *Power and Personality* (New York: Viking, 1948), p. 38. V.O. Key's focus, in contrast, is group oriented. "At bottom, group interests are the animating forces in the political process." Key, *Politics,* p. 23.

3. *New York Times,* February 7, 1975, pp. 1:7, 10:4.

4. Rowland Evans and Robert Novak, "Meany and Scoop, Once Again," *Washington Post,* February 23, 1976.

5. Apple, "Puritan for President," p. 58.

6. Damon Stetson, "Meany Sees Ford Lacking in Compassion for Jobless," *New York Times,* February 17, 1976, p. 16.

7. Lawrence R. Tarnoff, "Jackson Seeks Change of Heart," *The Wisconsin Jewish Chronicle,* April 1, 1976.

8. Quoted in "Candidates' Views on Jewish Issues," *The Wisconsin Jewish Chronicle,* April 1, 1976, p. 5.

9. Hearings, "Emigration Amendment," December 3, 1974, pp. 66-67, 96-97. For a general discussion see "The Government's Role in East-West Trade—Problems and Issues," Summary Statement of Report to the Congress, Comptroller General of the United States, February 4, 1976. For remarks similar to Kissinger's, see testimony of Helmut Sonnenfeldt in Hearings, "Export-Import Bank of the United States," S. 1890, pp. 493-95. In this context, there were rumors that Kissinger's office had pressured the bank to relax its normal lending criteria. Goldman I. Marshall, *Detente and Dollars: Doing Business with the Soviets* (New York: Basic Books, 1975), p. 146.

10. *New York Times,* January 11, 1975; Franklyn D. Holzman and Robert Levgold. "The Economics and Politics of East-West Relations," in C. Fred Bergsten and Lawrence B. Krause, *World Politics and International Economics* (Washington, D.C.: The Brookings Institution, 1975), p. 168.

11. Richard Perle, statement before a rally sponsored by the Union of Councils for Soviet Jewry, Washington, D.C., June 17, 1975.

12. *New York Times,* October 5, 1972.

13. Woodrow Wilson, *Congressional Government: A Study in American Politics* (Boston: Houghton Mifflin Co., 1885), chapter 9.

14. Stephen K. Bailey and Howard D. Samuel underlined the "importance of individual will and inventiveness as energizing social forces" applicable to the Congress, and indeed any form of human endeavor. Stephen K. Bailey and Howard D. Samuel, *Congress At Work* (New York: Henry Holt and Company, 1956), pp. 194-95. David Price, *Who Makes the Laws?* also considers the general question of "personal traits and skills" as "prime determinants of legislative effectiveness," p. 317.

15. *Time Magazine,* April 12, 1976.

16. Ribicoff, *Congressional Record.* December 13, 1974, p. S21416.

17. *Washington Post,* February 18, 1975.

18. NBC News, Catherine Machin reporting, 6:30 p.m., February 6, 1975.

19. *Washington Post,* February 18, 1975.

20. Milbraith, "Interest Groups and Foreign Policy," p. 236.

21. Press Release, Henry Jackson, January 26, 1975.

22. Apple, "Puritan for President," p. 57.

23. Key, *Politics,* pp. 167-68.

24. Statement of Honorable Henry A. Kissinger, Secretary of State, Hearings, "Detente," September 19, 1974, p. 252.

25. *Washington Post,* December 28, 1974, p. A2.

26. Dobrynin was not alone in thinking the Jackson amendment might be much ado about nothing. The Soviet embassy official assigned occasionally to visit Perle and Amitay said as late

as August 2, 1974, that he believed various branches of government in the United States seem to fight but actually coordinated their views. In his view, decisions in America are ultimately based on what is more profitable for the capitalists.

27. Philip Baum, "Remarks to Synagogue Council of America," September 10, 1975.

28. Ibid.

29. Quoted in *Washington Post,* March 29, 1974.

30. Quoted in *New York Times,* June 1, 1974.

AFTERWORD

1. Douglas G. Scrivner, "The Conference on Security and Cooperation in Europe: Implications for Soviet-American Detente," *Denver Journal of International Law and Policy* 6, no. 1 (Spring 1976), p. 158.

Bibliography

This bibliography indicates some of the more important printed material the author consulted in preparing this study. The primary sources in this list include government publications of the executive branch and the Congress, newspaper accounts, transcripts of news events, and literature prepared by some of the major interest groups involved.

What is not in this list, that is, what is not printed material, is perhaps more important than what is included here. Interviews and notes of conversations recorded as the events were occurring were most valuable. Because many of the individuals involved may not have revealed their thinking to the author had they known it would be committed to paper, this study does not reveal these sources. Of course, many of these same sources did know of the author's intentions to write a study of the Jackson amendment. Many of these same sources were formally interviewed after the events. The author was in repeated contact with scores of offices in the Senate and House of Representatives, including those of the major actors: Jackson, Ribicoff, Javits, and Vanik. In addition, executive branch offices in the White House and the agencies—State Department, Commerce Department, and Central Intelligence Agency—were contacted. Other executive bureaucracies represented in the author's contacts include the National Security Council, the Special Trade Representative's Office, and the Council on International Economic Policy.

Interviews and conversations with professional workers for Jewish and other ethnic groups, business, farm, and labor interests were also helpful. In addition, officials of the Soviet Union and Israel contributed helpful data.

Having stated what information was available—both that listed and that not listed—it is important to note what was not available to the author at all. The internal, official State Department record is not officially available. Nor are there transcripts of Soviet governmental deliberations. Jackson's office also withheld potentially useful memoranda and records of meetings.

U.S. GOVERNMENT PUBLICATIONS

EXECUTIVE BRANCH

Central Intelligence Agency. "Recent Developments in Soviet Hard Currency Trade." January 1976.

Department of Commerce. "U.S.-Soviet Commercial Relationships in a New Era." By Peter G. Peterson, Secretary of Commerce. August 1972; "The United States Role in East-West Trade: Problems & Prospects." By Rogers Morton, Secretary of Commerce. August 1975; Department of Commerce News. "Trade Negotiations and Changing Attitudes." By Steven Lazarus. January 16, 1973.

Department of State. "American Foreign Policy, Current Documents." 1963-1964.

Public Papers of the Presidents, 1969, 1970, 1971, 1972. United States Government Printing Office.

Weekly Compilation of Presidential Documents. Vol. 5, Nos. 1-26, 1969.

CONGRESS

"Background Materials Relating to the United States-Soviet Union Commercial Agreements." Committee on Finance. United States Senate. 93rd Congress, 2nd Session. Committee Print, U.S. Government Printing Office, 1974, 29-849.

"Briefing on East-West Trade." Hearing before the Subcommittee on International Trade Investment and Monetary Policy of Committee on Banking, Currency, and House, House of Representatives. 94th Congress, 1st Session. March 19, 1975.

"Century Old Tradition of American Initiatives on Behalf of Oppressed Minorities, The." By William Korey. Appendix B to Testimony of Stanley Lowell, National Conference on Soviet Jewry, to Senate Finance Committee on The Trade Reform Act of 1973. Hearings, Part 5. 93rd Congress, 2nd Session.

"Detente: An Evaluation." Committee Print, Subcommittee on Arms Control of the Committee on Armed Services. United States Senate. U.S. Government Printing Office, 1974, 34-347.

"Detente." Hearings before the Committee on Foreign Relations, United States Senate. 93rd Congress, 2nd Session. August 15, 20, 21; September 10, 12, 18, 19, 25; October 1, 8, 1974. U.S. Government Printing Office, 1975.

"Detente." Hearings before the Subcommittee on Europe, Committee Foreign Affairs. House of Representatives. 93rd Congress, 2nd Session. May 8, 15, 22; June 9, 12, 26; July 17, 25, and 31, 1974. U.S. Government Printing Office, 1974.

"East-West Trade and Investment Policy Issues: Past and Future." By Franklyn Holzman. Soviet Economic Prospects for the Seventies. Joint Economic Committee. Congress of the U.S. 93rd Congress, 1st Session. June 27, 1973.

"Foreign Assistance Authorization" (Testimony and Cross-Examination of Henry Kissinger). Hearings before the Committee on Foreign Relations. U.S. Senate. 93rd Congress, 2nd Session. June 7, 21, 26; July 24, 25, 1974.

"Foreign Economic Policy for the 1970's. Part 6—East-West Economic Relations." Hearings before the Subcommittee on Foreign Economic Policy of the Joint Economic Committee. Congress of the U.S. 91st Congress, 2nd Session. December 7, 8, 9, 1970. U.S. Government Printing Office, 1971.

"International Negotiation." Hearings, Subcommittee on National Security and International Operations. Committee on Government Operations. United States Senate. 91st Congress, 1st Session. Part 1—with Robert Conquest. U.S. Government Printing Office, December 15, 1969, 38-736.

"International Negotiations." Hearing—Subcommittee on National Security and International Operations of Committee on Government Operations. United States Senate. 91st and 92nd Congress, 2nd Session. Part 2.

"Kissinger's Role in Wiretapping, Dr." Hearings before the Committee on Foreign Relations. United States Senate. 93rd Congress, 2nd Session. Executive hearings held on July 10, 15, 16, 23, 30, 1974, and made public September 29, 1974. Executive hearings held on September 10 and 17, 1973, and made public October 4, 1973; further declassified and made public September 29, 1974.

"Negotiation and Statecraft." Hearings, Permanent Subcommittee on Investigations, Committee on Government Operations. United States Senate. Part 2—with Leopold Labedz. 93rd Congress. July 12, 1973. U.S Government Printing Office, 1973, 5270-01925.

"Nomination of Henry A. Kissinger." Hearings before the Committee on Foreign Relations. United States Senate. 93rd Congress, 1st Session. Part II, September 7, 10, 11, 14, 1973. Part II: Executive hearings held on September 10 and 17, 1973, and made public October 4, 1973.

"Nominations of Helmut Sonnenfeldt, Donald C. Alexander, and Edward C. Schmultz." Hearings before Committee on Finance. United States Senate. 93rd Congress, 1st Session. May 15, 1973, and October 1 and 2, 1973.

"Role of the Export-Import Bank and Export Controls in U.S. International Economic Policy, The." Hearings before the Subcommittee on International Finance of the Committee on Banking, Housing and Urban Affairs. United States Senate. 93rd Congress, 2nd Session. April 2, 5, 10, 23, 25 and 26; May 2, 1974.

"Russian Grain Transactions." Hearings before the Permanent Subcommittee on Investigations of Committee on Government Operations. United States Senate. 93rd Congress, 1st Session. Part I, July 20, 23, 24. Part II, October 9, 1973.

"Russian Grain Transactions." Report of the Committee on Government Operations. United States Senate. Made by Its Permanent Subcommittee on Investigations. July 29, 1974. 93rd Congress, 2nd Session. Report No. 93-1033.

"Soviet-American Relations, 1969-74: A Chronological Summary and Brief Analysis in 'Detente.'" Hearings before the Subcommittee on Europe. Committee on Foreign Affairs. House of Representatives. 93rd Congress, 2nd Session. May 18, 19, 22; June 10, 12, 26; July 17, 25, 31, 1974.

"Soviet Bloc Trade Hopes: Reactions to the Trade Act of 1974." Report of a Study Mission to the Soviet Union and Four Eastern European Nations. 94th Congress, 1st Session. June 28, 1975. Committee on International Relations, U.S. Government Printing Office, 1975, 53-957.

"Summary Statement of Report to the Congress, the Government's Role in East-West Trade—Problems and Issues." Comptroller General of the United States, February 4, 1976.

"Trade Act of 1974, Summary of the Provisions of H.R. 10710." Prepared by Staffs of Senate Finance and House Ways and Means Committees. Printed by Committee on Finance. U.S. Government Printing Office, December 30, 1974.

"Trade Reform Act of 1973, The." Hearings before the House Ways and Means Committee. 93rd Congress, 1st Session.

"Trade Reform Act of 1973, The." Hearings before the Senate Finance Committee. 93rd Congress, 2nd Session.

"United States East European Trade: Considerations Involved in Granting Most-Favored-Nation Treatment to the Countries of Eastern Europe." By Anton F. Malish, Jr. United States Tariff Commission. Staff Research Studies No. 4, 1972.

"U.S.-Soviet Commercial Relations." By Edward T. Wilson; David K. Katz; Suzanne F. Porter; Bonnie M. Pounds; and Gilbert M. Rodgers. Soviet Economic Prospects for the Seventies. A Compendium of Papers, submitted to the Joint Economic Committee. Congress of the United States. June 27, 1973.

"U.S.-Soviet Commercial Relations: The Interplay of Economic, Technology Transfer, and Diplomacy." By John P. Hardt (senior specialist in Soviet economics) and George D.

Holliday (research analyst in economics)—Economics Division, Congressional Research Service, Library of Congress. Prepared for the Subcommittee on National Security Policy and Scientific Developments of the Committee on Foreign Affairs. U.S. House of Representatives, June 10, 1973. U.S. Government Printing Office, 1973.

THE LIBRARY OF CONGRESS, CONGRESSIONAL RESEARCH SERVICE

"Congressional Oversight: A Select Bibliography." By Walter J. Oleszek. October 28, 1968.

"East-West Commercial Relations: Issue Brief Number IB 74110." By John P. Hardt. July 1, 1975.

"Foreign Policy Resolution by the Congress: An Analysis Based on Selected Cases Since 1950; with Synopses and Notes on Historical Background." By Ernest S. Lent. May 25, 1966.

"History of the Export-Import Bank of the United States." By George D. Holliday. August 29, 1974.

"The Role of Foreign Policy Making—A Selected Bibliography." By Marjorie Ann Browne. December 3, 1971.

"Soviet American Relations, 1969-1974: A Chronological Summary and Brief Analysis." By Francis T. Miko. JX 1428-Russia B 74-113F. May 29, 1974.

"Soviet Emigration Policy: Exit Visas and Fees." By Samuel C. Oglesby. April 11, 1973.

"The Soviet Exit Fee: A Summary of Pro-Con Discussion." By Samuel Oglesby. March 1973.

"The Treatment of Jews in the Soviet Union: Developments During 1970-71." By Barbara Michalchenko. E 190. For U.S.S.R. 71-229F. November 10, 1971.

NEWSPAPERS

American Enterprise Institute. *Press Summaries.* 1972-74.
Christian Science Monitor. 1972-73.
Jerusalem Post. April 19, 1973-May 4, 1973.
The New York Times. 1972-April 1976.
The Washington Post. 1972-April 1976.
The Washington Star-News. 1972-April 1976.

OTHER PERIODICALS

American Jewish Committee. *Washington Letter.* 1974-75.
The Congressional Record. Daily edition. 1972-74.
East-West Trade Council. 1973-74.
Exodus. An Organ of the Union of Councils for Soviet Jewry. Published by Soviet Jewry Action Group, San Francisco. 1973-74.
Human Events. 1974.
National Conference on Soviet Jewry. *News Bulletin.* 1973-74.
The National Journal. 1972-74.
Near East Report. American-Israel Public Affairs Committee. 1972-74.

TRANSCRIPTS (Radio-Television, Press Conferences)

Henry Jackson, Press Releases. 1972-1975.
"Meet the Press," National Broadcasting Corporation. July 14, 1974.
Press Conference, The White House. October 18, 1972.
Press Conference, The White House. Peter M. Flanigan, March 22, 1973.
Press Conference, The White House. April 10, 1973.
Press Conference, The White House. August 18, 1974.
Press Conference, The White House. October 18, 1974.
"Sixty Minutes," Columbia Broadcasting Corporation. Vol. VI, No. 1. January 6, 1974.

BOOKS

Adler, Cyrus, and Margalith, Aaron M. *With Firmness in the Right: American Diplomatic Action Affecting Jews 1840-1945.* New York: The American Jewish Committee, 1946.

Adler-Karlsson, Gunnar. *Western Economic Warfare: 1947-1967, A Case Study in Foreign-Economic Policy.* Stockholm: Almquist & Wiksell, 1968.

Alexander, Herbert E. *Financing the 1968 Election.* Lexington, Massachusetts: Heath-Lexington Books, D.C. Heath & Co., 1971.

———. *Political Financing.* Minneapolis, Minnesota: Burgess Publishing Co., 1972.

——— (with Eugenia Grohman). *Financing the 1972 Election.* Lexington Massachusetts: ington Books Co., 1976.

Almond, Gabriel A. *The American People and Foreign Policy.* 2nd ed. 8th printing. New York: Frederick A. Praeger, 1968.

American Jewish Yearbook 1971. New York: American Jewish Committee, 1972.

Bailey, Stephen Kemp. *Congress Makes a Law.* New York: Vintage Books, 1950.

———. *Congress Makes a Law: The Story Behind the Employment Act of 1946.* New York: Columbia University Press, 1950.

———. *Congress At Work.* New York: Holt, 1956.

Bailey, Thomas A. *America Faces Russia: Russian-American Relations from Early Times to Our Day.* Ithaca, New York: Cornell University Press, 1950.

Bain, Richard C., and Parris, Judith H. *Convention Decisions and Voting Records.* 2nd ed. Washington, D.C.: The Brookings Institution, 1973.

Barone, Michael; Ujifusa, Grant; and Matthews, Douglas. *The Almanac of American Politics: The Senators, The Representatives—Their Records, States and Districts, 1972.* Boston: Gambit, 1972.

Barron, John. *KGB: The Secret Work of Soviet Secret Agents.* New York: Readers Digest Press, 1974.

Bauer, Raymond A.; de Sola Pool, Ithiel; and Dexter, Lewis Anthony. *American Business and Public Policy—The Politics of Foreign Trade.* Chicago: Aldine Atherton, 1972.

Binder, Leonard. *The Middle East Crisis: Background and Issues.* Chicago: University of Chicago Center for Policy Study, 1969.

Bliss, Howard, and Johnson, M. Glen, eds. *Consensus at the Crossroads: Dialogues in American Foreign Policy.* New York: Dodd, Mead & Co., 1972.

Bonavia, David. *Fat Sasha and the Urban Guerrilla.* New York: Atheneum, 1973.

Brandon, Henry. *The Retreat of American Power.* Garden City, New York: Doubleday & Co., 1973.

Browder, Robert Paul. *The Origins of Soviet-American Diplomacy.* New Jersey: Princeton University Press, 1953.

Brown, Alan A., and Neuberger, Egon, eds. *International Trade and Central Planning (An Analysis of Economic Interaction).* Berkeley and Los Angeles: University of California Press, 1968.

Brzezinski, Zbigniew. *Alternative to Partition.* New York: Council on Foreign Relations and McGraw Hill Book Co., 1965.

———, and Huntington, S.K. *Political Power: USA-USSR.* New York: Viking Press, 1964.

Buckley, James L. *If Men Were Angels.* New York: G. P. Putnam's Sons, 1975.

Business International S.A. *Doing Business With the U.S.S.R.* Geneva, Switzerland, 1971.

Chesler, Evan R. *The Russian Jewry Reader.* New York: Behrman House, in cooperation with Anti-Defamation League of B'nai B'rith, 1974.

Clapp, Charles L. *The Congressman: His Work as He Sees It.* Garden City, New York: Anchor Books, Doubleday & Co., 1964.

Cohen, Richard. *Let My People Go!* New York: Popular Library, 1971.

Dahl, Robert A. *Congress and Foreign Policy.* New York: Harcourt, Brace and Co., 1950.

———. *Democracy in the United States: Promise and Performance.* 2nd ed. Chicago: Rand McNally and Co., 1972.

Dawson, Raymond H. *The Decision to Aid Russia, 1941: Foreign Policy and Domestic Politics.* Chapel Hill: The University of North Carolina Press, 1959.

Destler, I.M. *Presidents, Bureaucrats and Foreign Policy: The Politics of Organizational Reform.* New Jersey: Princeton University Press, 1974.

Domhoff, G. William. *Fat Cats and Democrats: The Role of the Big Rich in the Party of the Common Man.* Englewood Cliffs, New Jersey: Prentice-Hall, 1972.

Drury, Allen. *Courage and Hesitation.* Garden City, New York: Doubleday & Co., 1971.

Dunn, Delmer D. *Financing Presidential Campaigns.* Washington, D.C.: The Brookings Institution, 1972.

Durasoff, Steve. *Pentecost Behind the Iron Curtain.* Plainfield, New Jersey: Logos International, 1972.

Flanigan, William H. *Political Behavior of the American Electorate.* Boston: Allyn and Bacon, 1968.

Fox, Douglas M. *The Politics of U.S. Foreign Policy Making: A Reader.* Pacific Palisades, California: Goodyear Publishing Co., 1971.

Froman, Lewis A., Jr. *Congressmen and Their Constituents.* Chicago: Rand McNally and Co., 1963.

Frye, Alton. *A Responsible Congress: The Politics of National Security.* New York: McGraw-Hill Book Co., 1975.

Fuchs, Lawrence H. *The Political Behavior of American Jews.* Glencoe, Illinois: The Free Press, 1965.

Gardner, Lloyd C. *The Great Nixon Turnaround: America's New Foreign Policy in the Post Liberal Era.* New York: New Viewpoints, 1973.

Gati, Charles, ed. *Caging the Bear: Containment and The Cold War.* New York: The Bobbs-Merrill Co., 1974.

George, Alexander L.; Hall, David K.; and Simons, William E. *The Limits of Coercive Diplomacy: Laos, Cuba, Vietnam.* Boston: Little, Brown and Co., 1971.

Gerson, Louis L. *The Hyphenate in Recent American Politics and Diplomacy.* Lawrence: The University of Kansas Press, 1964.

Glazer, Nathan, and Moynihan, Daniel P. *Ethnicity: Theory and Experience.* Cambridge, Massachusetts: Harvard University Press, 1975.

Golan, Matti. *The Secret Conversations of Henry Kissinger: Step-by-Step Diplomacy in the Middle East.* New York: Quadrangle/The New York Times Book Co., 1976.

Goldman, Marshall I. *Detente and Dollars: Doing Business with the Soviets.* New York: Basic Books, 1975.

Gordon, Charles, and Rosenfield, Harry N. *Immigration Law and Procedure.* Rev. ed. New York: Matthew Bender, 1972.

Green, Mark; Fallows, James M.; and Zwick, David R. *Who Runs Congress?* New York: Bantam/Grossman Books, 1972.

Griffith, Ernest S. *Congress: Its Contemporary Role.* New York: New York University Press, 1951.

Halperin, Morton H. *Bureaucratic Politics and Foreign Policy.* Washington, D.C.: The Brookings Institution, 1974.

Hamilton, Martha M. *The Great American Grain Robbery and Other Stories.* Washington, D.C.: Agribusiness Accountability Project, 1972.

Handlin, Oscar. *Immigration as a Factor in American History.* Englewood Cliffs, New Jersey: Prentice-Hall, 1959.

Hardt, John P. *Tariff, Legal and Credit Constraints on East-West Commercial Relations.* Ottawa, Canada: Carleton University Institute of Soviet and East European Studies, East-West Commercial Relations Series, Special Study, May 1975.

Haviland, Field H., Jr. *The Formulation and Administration of United States Foreign Policy* (A Report for the Committee on Foreign Relations of the United States Senate). Washington, D.C.: The Brookings Institution, 1960.

Herring, George C., Jr. *Aid to Russia 1941-1946: Strategy, Diplomacy, The Origins of the Cold War.* New York: Columbia University Press, 1973.

Hoffman, Erik P., and Fleron, Frederic J., Jr. *The Conduct of Soviet Foreign Policy.* Chicago: Aldine Atherton, 1971.

Hoffman, Stanley. *Gulliver's Troubles, or the Setting of American Foreign Policy.* New York: McGraw-Hill Book Co., 1968.

Isaacs, Stephen D. *Jews and American Politics.* Garden City, New York: Doubleday & Co., 1974.

Jackson, Senator Henry M., ed. *The Secretary of State and the Ambassador: Jackson Subcommittee Papers on the Conduct of American Foreign Policy.* New York: Praeger Publishers, 1964.

Jewell, Malcolm E. *Senatorial Politics and Foreign Policy.* Lexington, Kentucky: University of Kentucky Press, 1962.

Kalb, Marvin, and Kalb, Bernard. *Kissinger.* Boston: Little, Brown and Co., 1974.

Kennan, George F. *American Diplomacy 1900-1950.* Chicago, Illinois: The University of Chicago Press, 1951.

―――. *Russia Leaves the War: Soviet American Relations 1917-1920.* Princeton, New Jersey: Princeton University Press, 1956.

Kennedy, John Fitzgerald. *A Nation of Immigrants.* New York: Anti-Defamation League of B'nai B'rith, 1963.

Keohane, Robert O., and Nye, Joseph S., Jr., eds. *Transnational Relations and World Politics.* Cambridge, Massachusetts: Harvard University Press, 1972.

Key, V.O., Jr., *Politics, Parties and Pressure Groups.* 3rd ed. New York: Thomas Y. Crowell, 1952.

Knorr, Klaus. *Power and Wealth: The Political Economy of International Power.* New York: Basic Books, 1973.

Kochan, Lionel. *The Jews in Soviet Russia Since 1917.* London: Oxford University Press, 1970 ed. and 1972 ed.

Korey, William. *The Soviet Cage: Anti-Semitism in Russia.* New York: The Viking Press, 1973.

LaFeber, Walter. *America, Russia, and the Cold War 1945-1966.* New York: John Wiley and Sons, 1967.

Lasswell, Harold Dwight. *Power and Personality.* New York: The Viking Press, 1962.

Lesh, Donald R. *A Nation Observed.* Washington, D.C.: Potomac Associates, 1974.

Levitan, Tina. *Jews in American Life.* New York: Hebrew Publishing Co., 1969.

Levy, Mark R., and Kramer, Michael S. *The Ethnic Factor: How America's Minorities Decide Elections.* New York: Simon and Schuster, 1972.

Lubell, Samuel. *The Future While It Happened.* New York: W.W. Norton and Co., 1973.

McKitterick, Nathaniel. *East-West Trade: The Background of U.S. Policy.* New York: 20th Century Fund, March 1966.

McMillan, Carl H., ed. *Changing Perspectives in East-West Trade.* Lexington, Massachusetts: Lexington Books, 1974.

Marer, Paul. *Soviet and East European Foreign Trade 1946-1969: Statistical Compendium and Guide.* Bloomington, Indiana: Indiana University Press, 1972.

Matthews, Donald R. *U.S. Senators and Their World.* Chapel Hill: University of North Carolina Press, 1960.

———, and Stimson, James A. *Yeas and Nays: Normal Decision-Making in the U.S. House of Representatives.* New York: John Wiley and Sons, 1975.

May, Ernest R. *American Imperialism: A Speculative Essay.* New York: Atheneum, 1968.

———. *The Making of the Monroe Doctrine.* Cambridge, Massachusetts: The Belknap Press of Harvard University Press, 1975.

Mayhew, David R. *Congress: The Electoral Connection.* New Haven: Yale University Press, 1974.

Milbrath, Lester W. *The Washington Lobbyist.* Chicago: Rand McNally and Co., 1963.

Moe, Ronald C., ed. *Congress and the President: Allies and Adversaries.* Pacific Palisades, California: Goodyear Publishing Co., 1971.

Nagorski, Zygmunt, Jr. *The Psychology of East-West Trade: Illusions and Opportunities.* New York: Mason and Lipscomb Publishers, 1974.

Neal, Fred Warner, and Harvey, Mary Kersey. *The Nixon-Kissinger Foreign Policy: Opportunities and Contradictions.* Vol. 1, Pacem in Terris III. Santa Barbara, California: Fund for the Republic, 1974.

———. *The Requirements of Democratic Foreign Policy.* Vol. IV, Pacem in Terris III. Santa Barbara, California: Fund for the Republic, 1974.

Newhouse, John. *Cold Dawn: The Story of SALT.* New York: Holt, Rinehart and Winston, 1973.

Nichols, David. *Financing Elections, The Politics of an American Ruling Class.* New York: New Viewpoints, A Division of Franklin Watts, 1974.

Novak, Michael. *The Rise of the Unmeltable Ethnics: Politics and Culture in the Seventies.* New York: The Macmillan Co., 1972.

Owen, Henry, ed. *The Next Phase in Foreign Policy*. Washington, D.C.: The Brookings Institution, 1973.

Paterson, Thomas G. *Soviet-American Confrontation: Post War Reconstruction and the Origins of the Cold War*. Baltimore: The John Hopkins University Press, 1973.

Patolichev, Nikolai. *USSR Foreign Trade: Past, Present and Future*. Moscow: Novosti Press Agency Publishing House, 1967.

———. *USSR Foreign Trade: Yesterday, Today, Tomorrow*. Moscow: Novosti Press Agency Publishing House, no date.

Pisar, Samuel. *Coexistence and Commerce—Guidelines for Transactions Between East and West*. New York: McGraw-Hill Book Co., 1970.

Price, David E. *Who Makes the Laws? Creativity and Power in Senate Committees*. Cambridge, Massachusetts: Schenkman Publishing Co., distributed by General Learning Press, 1972.

Prochnau, William W., and Larsen, Richard W. *A Certain Democrat: Senator Henry M. Jackson*. Englewood Cliffs, New Jersey: Prentice-Hall, 1972.

Redman, Eric. *The Dance of Legislation*. New York: Simon and Schuster, 1973.

Ripon Society, The, and Brown, Clifford W., Jr. *Jaws of Victory: The Game-Plan Politics of 1972; The Crisis of the Republican Party, and the Future of the Constitution*. Boston: Little, Brown and Co., 1973.

Robinson, James A. *Congress and Foreign Policy-Making—A Study in Legislative Influence and Initiative*. Homewood, Illinois: The Dorsey Press, 1967.

Rogoff, Harry Hillel. *An East Side Epic: The Life and Work of Meyer London*. New York: The Vanguard Press, 1930.

Rosenau, James N., ed. *Democratic Sources of Foreign Policy*. New York: The Free Press, 1967.

Safire, William. *Before The Fall*. Garden City, New York: Doubleday & Co., 1975.

Scammon, Richard M., and Wattenberg, Ben J. *The Real Majority*. New York: Coward-McCann, 1970.

Schell, Jonathan. *The Time of Illusion*. New York: Alfred A. Knopf, 1976.

Schlesinger, Arthur M., Jr. *The Imperial Presidency*. Boston: Houghton Mifflin Co., 1973.

Schroeter, Leonard. *The Last Exodus*. New York: Universe Books, 1974.

Schurmann, Franz. *The Logic of World Power—An Inquiry into the Origins, Currents and Contradictions of World Politics*. New York: Pantheon Books, A Division of Random House, 1974.

Schwartz, Morton. *The Foreign Policy of the USSR: Domestic Factors*. Encino and Belmont, California: Dickerson Publishing Co., 1975.

Scott, Andrew M., and Dawson, Raymond H. *Readings in the Making of American Foreign Policy*. New York: The Macmillan Co., 1965.

Scott, Andrew M., and Hunt, Margaret A. *Congress and Lobbies—Image and Reality*. Chapel Hill: The University of North Carolina Press, 1966.

Shub, Anatole. *The New Russian Tragedy*. New York: W.W. Norton and Co., 1969.

Skillings, H. Gordon, and Griffiths, Franklyn. *Interest Groups in Soviet Politics*. Princeton New Jersey: Princeton University Press, 1971.

Smith, Hedrick. *The Russians*. New York: Quadrangle/The New York Times Book Co., 1976.

Snepp, Frank. *Decent Interval*. New York: Random House, 1977.

Snetsinger, John. *Truman, the Jewish Vote, and the Creation of Israel.* Stanford, California: Hoover Institution Press, Stanford University, 1974.

Szajkowski, Zosa. *Jews, Wars, and Communism, Vol. I. The Attitude of American Jews to World War I, the Russian Revolutions of 1917, and Communism (1914-1945).* New York: KTAV Publishing House, 1972.

Thayer, George. *Who Shakes the Money Tree? American Campaign Practices from 1789 to the Present.* New York: Simon and Schuster, 1973.

Trager, James. *Amber Waves of Grain.* New York: Arthur Fields Books, 1973.

Treadgold, Donald W. *Twentieth Century Russia.* 4th ed. Chicago: Rand McNally and Co., 1962.

Truman, David B. *The Congress and America's Future.* 2nd ed. Englewood Cliffs, New Jersey: Prentice-Hall, 1973.

Ulam, Adam B. *The Rivals: America and Russia Since World War II.* New York: The Viking Press, 1971.

Weaver, Warren, Jr. *Both Your Houses: The Truth About Congress.* New York: Praeger Publishers, 1973.

Wilcox, Francis O. *Congress, the Executive and Foreign Policy.* New York: Council on Foreign Relations-Harper and Row, 1971.

Wilczynski, J. *The Economics and Politics of East-West Trade (A Study of Trade Between Developed Market Economics and Centrally Planned Economics in a Changing World).* London: Macmillan, 1969.

Wiles, P. J. *Communist International Economics.* New York: Frederick A. Praeger, 1969.

Williams, William Appleton. *American-Russian Relations 1781-1947.* New York: Rinehart, 1952.

Wilson, Woodrow. *Congressional Government: A Study in American Politics.* Boston: Houghton Mifflin Co., 1885.

Wolf, Thomas A. *U.S. East-West Trade Policy: Economic Warfare Versus Economic Welfare.* Lexington, Massachusetts: Lexington Books, D.C. Heath & Co., 1973.

MONOGRAPHS

Brill, Steven. "Senator Henry M. Jackson: Liberal?" Distributed by Americans for Democratic Action. August 14, 1975.

Coalition for a Democratic Majority, A Statement by the Foreign Policy Task Force of the. "The Quest for Detente." July 31, 1974.

"Dissent and Its Control in the USSR." Seminar: The Center for Strategic and International Studies, Georgetown University. January 21, 1974.

"Ethnic Lobbying: An American Tradition, A Background Memorandum." The American Jewish Committee, Institute of Human Relations. New York, New York, November 1975.

Katz, Zev. "Jewish Emigration—A Profitable Enterprise for the Soviet State." Center for International Studies. Massachusetts Institute of Technology.

Kohler, Foy D.; Goure, Leon; and Harvey, Moses. "The Soviet Union and the October, 1973 Middle East War: The Implications for Detente." Monograph in International Affairs: Center for Advanced International Studies, University of Miami, 1974.

"Jackson Record, The Truth About the: A Staff Study for the Jackson for President Committee." December 1975.

MacKown, Craig, and Bortz, Arnold. "Jacob K. Javits." Ralph Nader Congress Project. August 1972.

Merrill, Stephen A. "Wilbur D. Mills." Ralph Nader Congress Project. August 1972.

"Shull to Senator Henry Jackson, Letter from Leon." Press Release, Americans for Democratic Action. January 2, 1976.

Skoczylas, Elehie. *The Realities of Soviet Anti-Semitism.* Philadelphia, Pennsylvania: Foreign Policy Research Institute, January 1965.

"Soviet Internal and External Policies: Their Influence on U.S. Foreign Relations." Center for Strategic and International Studies Report, Georgetown University, July 16, 1974.

"Soviet Union and the Western Crisis, The—1975." Center for Strategic and International Studies, Georgetown University, February 14, 1975.

Sussman, Robert. "Henry M. Jackson." Ralph Nader Congress Project. August 1972.

"Understanding the Solzhenitsyn Affair—Dissent and Its Control in the USSR." Report, Georgetown University Center for Strategic and International Studies, February 1974.

ARTICLES

Abrams, Elliott, and Abrams, Franklin. "Immigration Policy—Who Gets In and Why?" *The Public Interest,* Vol. 38 (Winter 1975): pp. 3-29.

Agursley, Mikhail. "Selling Anti-Semitism in Moscow." Translated by Peter Reddaway. *New York Review of Books* (November 16, 1972).

Albright, Joseph. "The Pact of Two Henrys." *New York Times Magazine* (January 5, 1975): pp. 16-34.

———. "Some Deal: The Full Story of How America Got Burned and the Russians Got Bread." *New York Times Magazine* (November 25, 1973): pp. 36-37, 84-102.

Allison, Graham. "Conceptual Models and the Cuban Missile Crisis." *American Political Science Review,* Vol. LXIII, No. 3 (September 1969): pp. 689-718.

Allison, Graham T., and Halperin, Morton H. "Bureaucratic Politics: A Paradigm and Some Policy Implications." *World Politics (Supplement) Theory and Policy in International Relations,* Vol. XXIV (Spring 1972): pp. 40-79.

Allison, Graham; May, Ernest; and Yarmolinsky, Adam. "Limits to Intervention." *Foreign Affairs* (January 1970): pp. 245-61.

"American Jews and Israel." *Time Magazine* (March 10, 1975): pp. 14-27.

"American Review of East-West Trade, The." Vol. 1, No. 5 (May 1968).

Apple, R.W., Jr. "Puritan for President." *The New York Times Magazine* (November 23, 1975): pp. 27, 48-61.

Aspin, Les. "Why Doesn't Congress Do Something?" *Foreign Policy,* No. 15 (Summer 1974): pp. 70-82.

Baldwin, Hanson W. "Red Flag Over the Seven Seas." *The Atlantic Monthly,* Vol. 214, No. 3 (September 1964): pp. 37-43.

Barnea, Nahum. "The Balloon That Did Not Pop." Translated by Dalya Luttwack. *Davar Shavua* (Israel: August 9, 1974): Part II.

———. "Jackson, the Minister of the Jews." Translated by Dalya Luttwack. *Davar Shavua* (Israel: October 25, 1974): Part IV.

———. "The Jews Who Were a Disappointment." Translated by Dalya Luttwack. *Davar Shavua* (Israel: August 23, 1974): Part III.

———. Title Unknown. Translated by Dalya Luttwack. *Davar Shavua* (Israel: July 26, 1974): pp. 5-7, Part I.

Bartlett, Charles. "Jackson Breakthrough?" *Washington Star* (February 11, 1974): p. A13.

Berger, Marilyn. "Soviet Emigration Assurance, Trade Bill Linked." *The Washington Post* (March 19, 1974): p. A-12.

Berman, Harold J., and Garson, John R. "Possible Effects of the Proposed East-West Trade Relations Act Upon U.S. Import, Export, and Credit Controls." *Vanderbilt Law Review,* Vol. 20, No. 2 (March 1967): pp. 270-302.

———. "United States Export Controls—Past, Present, and Future." *Columbia Law Review,* Vol. 67, No. 5 (May 1967): pp. 791-891.

Bernstein, Marver H. "U. S.-Israel Relations: One Year After the October War." *Analysis,* No. 48 (November 15, 1974).

Berry, Mary Clay. "A Reform in Search of a Definition: Who Is a Lobbyist Anyway?" The Alicia Patterson Foundation (March 10, 1976).

Bociurkiu, Bohdan R. "The Shaping of Soviet Religious Policy." *Problems of Communism* (May-June 1973): pp. 37-51.

Bookbinder, Hyman. "Ethnic Pressures and the Jewish Lobby—Myths and Facts." *Washington Letter, The American Jewish Committee* (September 1975).

Braden, Tom. "Senator Kennedy: Seeking Options for Detente." *Washington Post* (April 20, 1974).

Brainard, Lawrence. "Credit's Role in U.S.-Soviet Trade." *International Finance* (July 14, 1975): pp. 7-8.

Brumberg, Abraham. "Dissent in Russia." *Foreign Affairs,* Vol. 52, No. 4 (July 1974): pp. 781-98.

Brzezinski, Zbigniew. "The Balance of Power Delusion." *Foreign Policy,* No. 4 (Summer 1972): pp. 54-59.

———. "The Economics of Detente: A U.S. Portfolio in the U.S.S.R.?" *The New Leader* (August 5, 1974): pp. 5-7.

———. "How the Cold War Was Played." *Foreign Affairs,* Vol. 51, No. 1 (October 1972): pp. 81-209.

Cameron, Juan. "Scoop Jackson Comes Down With Presidential Fever." *Fortune Magazine* (June 1974): pp. 123-27, 233, 235.

Cattel, David T. "Soviet Foreign Policy." *Current History,* Vol. 49, No. 290 (October 1965): pp. 208-13.

Cohen, Naomi W. "The Abrogation of the Russo-American Treaty of 1832." *Jewish Social Studies,* Vol. XXV, No. 1 (January 1963): pp. 3-41.

"Congress & Foreign Policy." *The Annals of the American Academy of Political and Social Science.* Vol. 289 (Philadelphia: September 1953).

Conquest, Robert. "A New Russia? A New World?" *Foreign Affairs,* Vol. 53, No. 3 (April 1975): pp. 482-97.

Cooper, Martha R. "Implications of Electoral College Reform for American Jewry." *Analysis,* No. 55 (January 1976).

Cousins, Norman. "From Hanover to Tbilsi." *Saturday Review World* (June 15, 1974): pp. 4-8.

———. "A Report on Jews in the USSR." *Saturday Review World* (June 1, 1974): p. 4.

Draper, Theodore. "Detente." *Commentary,* Vol. 57, No. 6 (June 1974): pp. 25-47.

————. "Appeasement and Detente." *Commentary Magazine* (February 1976): pp. 27-38.

Eberle, William D. "World Trade: America's Strategy." *The Atlantic Community Quarterly,* Vol. II, No. 3, pp. 339-47.

Edelsberg, Herman. "Showdown on Soviet Jewry." *The National Jewish Monthly* (May 1973): pp. 6-10.

"Editorial: U.S.-East European Trade Prospects Brightened by Paris Peace Talks." *The American Review of East-West Trade,* Vol. 1, No. 5 (May 1968): pp. 5-6, 71.

"Editor's Notes." *USSR* (March 1964): p. 60.

Effron, Mark, and Sandler, Andrea. "Peixotto's Mission, Why Freud Joined Up, and How We Went to War." *The National Jewish Monthly,* Vol. 89, No. 11 (July-August 1975): pp. 20-40.

Ettinger, S. "The National Awakening of Russian Jews." Translated by David Aberbach. *The Jewish Quarterly* (London: Winter 1973): pp. 9-14.

Evans, Rowland, and Novak, Robert. "Israeli Support for the Jackson Amendment." *The Washington Post* (March 19, 1973): p. A21.

Fein, Leonard. "The Domestic Element: American Jewry and U.S.-Israel Relations." *Analysis,* No. 49 (December 1, 1974).

Frank, Richard S. "Trade Report/Credits to Soviets Threatened by Exim Bank Bill Amendments." *The National Journal* (May 11, 1974): pp. 692-99.

————. "Trade Report/Pact with Soviets Offers Economic Political Gains Once U.S. Solves Policy Questions." 1st in 2-part series. *National Journal* (November 18, 1972): pp. 1763-72.

————. "Trade Report/ U.S. Sees Surplus, More Jobs in Early Years of Expanded Trade with Soviet Union." 2nd of 2-part series. *National Journal* (November 25, 1972): pp. 1799-1808.

Friedberg, Maurice. "The State of Soviet Jewry." *Commentary* (January 1965): pp. 38-43.

Friedgut, Ted. "Jewish Nationalism and the Soviet System." *Problems of Communism,* Vol. XXIII, No. 1 (January-February 1974): pp. 85-88.

Frye, Alton. "Congress: The Virtues of Its Vices." *Foreign Policy,* No. 3 (Summer 1971): pp. 108-28.

Garvey, Bruce. "Kissinger Calls Nixon 'Unpleasant.' " *The Washington Post* (October 16, 1975): p. 1, Column 7.

Gati, Charles. "The Forgotten Region." *Foreign Policy,* No. 19 (Summer 1975): pp. 135-45.

Gershman, Carl. "The Soviet Dissidents and the American Left Reviving the Democratic Faith." *The New Leader* (October 19, 1973): pp. 8-9.

Glazer, Nathan, and Moynihan, Daniel P. "Why Ethnicity?" *Commentary,* Vol. 58, No. 4 (October 1974): pp. 33-39.

Herling, John. "George Meany and the AFL-CIO." *The New Republic,* Vol. 173, No. 14 (October 4, 1975): pp. 13-19.

Hilsman, Roger. "Congressional-Executive Relations and the Foreign Policy Consensus." *American Political Science Review,* Vol. LII, No. 3 (September 1958): pp. 725-44.

Hodnett, Greg. "Succession Contingencies in the Soviet Union." *Problems of Communism,* Vol. XXIV, No. 2 (March-April 1975): pp. 1-21.

Holbrooke, Richard. "Washington Dateline: The New Battlelines." *Foreign Policy,* No. 13 (Winter 1973-74).

Holzman, Franklyn D., and Legvold, Robert. "The Economics and Politics of East-West Relations." In C. Fred Bergsten and Lawrence Krause, *World Politics and International Economics* (Washington, D.C.: The Brookings Institution, 1975), pp. 275-322.

"How Henry Did It in Viet Nam." *Time Magazine* (June 10, 1974): pp. 41-42.

Howe, Russell Warren, and Trott, Sarah. "The Foreign Agent." *Washingtonian Magazine*, Vol. 10, No. 3 (December 1974): pp. 135-70.

Isaacs, Stephen D. "So Who Has the Power? (How Dare You Push in Foreign Policy)." *Present Tense*, No. 4 (Summer 1974).

"Israeli Lobby: Instant Votes When Needed, The." *Congressional Quarterly* (October 27, 1973): pp. 2858-59.

Jacoby, Susan, and Astrachan, Anthony. "Soviet Dissent: An Ebb Tide." *World* (June 19, 1973): pp. 13-19.

———. "Who Gets Whom and What." *Present Tense* (January 1974): pp. 21-28.

Javits, Jacob. "Concern for Oppressed Jewry: An American Tradition." *The Jewish Veteran* (July-August 1973): pp. 21, 24-25.

Johnson, George E. "Which Promised Land? The Realities of American Absorption of Soviet Jews." *Analysis*, No. 47, Special Issue (November 1, 1974).

Karnow, Stanley. "Jackson's Bid." *The New Republic* (May 25, 1974): pp. 17-21.

Kaser, Michael. "Soviet Trade Turns to Europe." *Foreign Policy*, No. 9 (Summer 1975): pp. 123-34.

Kissinger, Henry A. "Domestic Structure and Foreign Policy." *Daedalus*, Vol. 95 (1966): pp. 503-29.

Kleiman, Robert. "Durability of Detente, The." *The Alicia Patterson Foundation Newsletter* (New York: September 17, 1973).

———. "Interdependence, Autarchy, Ideology." *The Alicia Patterson Foundation Newsletter* (September 19, 1973).

Korey, William. "August 12: The Anniversary of a 'Secret' Soviet Crime." *New York Times* (August 12, 1972).

———. "Rescuing Russian Jewry: Two Episodes Compared." *Soviet Jewish Affairs*, Vol. 5, No. 1 (1975): pp 3-19.

———. "Story of the Jackson Amendment, 1973-1975, The." *Midstream*, Vol. XXI, No. 3 (March 1975): pp. 7-35.

———. "Struggle over the Jackson Amendment, The." *American Jewish Yearbook* (New York: American Jewish Committee, 1976): pp. 160-70.

———. "Struggle over the Jackson-Mills-Vanik Amendment, The." *American Jewish Yearbook* (New York: American Jewish Committee, 1974-75): pp. 203-34.

Leonard, Wolfgang. "The Domestic Politics of the New Soviet Foreign Policy." *Foreign Affairs* (October 1973): pp. 59-74.

Levenberg, S. "Tragedy of a Movement." *World Jewry*, Vol. XVI, No. 1 (1973): pp. 19-21.

Lefkovitz, Earl. "Pioneer in Soviet Jewry Movement Looks Back on Rocky Beginnings." *The Cleveland Jewish News* (January 21, 1977).

———. "Soviet Jewry Movement Facing Difficult Period." *The Cleveland Jewish News* (January 28, 1977).

Lipski, Sam. "Jackson Ahead in Battle to Free Soviet Jewry." *The Jerusalem Post Magazine* (April 27, 1973): p. 7.

Lowendron, Barry F. "National Sovereignty vs. Human Rights." *SAIS Review*, Vol. 19, No. 2 (1975): pp. 3-7.

Mansfield, Harvey C., Sr. "Congress Against the President." *Proceedings of the Academy of Political Science,* Vol. 32, No. 1 (New York: 1975).

Meany, George. "Let the Debate Begin!" *AFL-CIO, Free Trade Union News,* Vol. 29, No. 8 (September 1974): pp. 5-9.

Mehlman, William. "A Case of Bad Faith." *Times* of Israel (No date [1974?]): pp. 26-31.

Metzger, Stanley D. "Most-Favored-Nation Treatment of Imports to the U.S. from the U.S.S.R." *The International Trade Law Journal,* Vol. 1, No. 1 (Spring 1975): pp. 79-86.

Meyer, Herbert E. "Why the Russians Are Shopping in the U.S." *Fortune* (February 1973): pp. 66-71, 146, 148.

"Miracle Worker Does It Again, The." *Time Magazine* (June 10, 1974): pp. 34-40.

Mondale, Walter F. "Beyond Detente: Toward International Economic Security." *Foreign Affairs,* Vol. 53, No. 1 (October 1974): pp. 1-24.

Moynihan, Daniel P. "Was Woodrow Wilson Right?" *Commentary,* Vol. 57, No 5 (May 1974): pp. 25-31.

Odom, William F. "Who Controls Whom in Moscow." *Foreign Policy,* No. 19 (Summer 1975): pp. 109-22.

Rakowska-Harmstone, Theresa. "Ethnic Politics in the USSR." *Problems of Communism* (May-June 1974): pp. 1-22.

Reeves, Richard. "The Inevitability of Scoop Jackson." *New York* (December 17, 1973): pp. 51-54, 59-62.

Riesel, Victor. "Scoop's China Visit Helps Ted." *Human Events* (August 3, 1974).

Roberts, Chalmers. "Foreign Policy Under a Paralyzed Presidency." *Foreign Affairs,* Vol. 52, No. 4 (July 1974): pp. 675-89.

Rosecrance, Richard. "Detente or Entente?" *Foreign Affairs,* Vol. 53, No. 3 (April 1975): pp. 464-81.

Rosenfeld, Stephen S. "The Politics of the Jackson Amendment (A Piece of Political Baggage With Many Different Handles)." *Present Tense,* Vol. 1, No. 4 (Summer 1974): pp. 17-23.

———. "If Everyone's Weak, Then Who's Strong?" *Present Tense* (Summer 1978), pp. 18-19.

Rubin, Vitaly. "Moscow Testimony: Is There Any Hope for Those Who Choose to Stay?" *Present Tense,* Vol. 2, No. 3 (Spring 1975): pp. 55-59.

Safire, William. "Puppet as Prince." *Harper's Magazine,* Vol. 250, No. 1498 (March 1975): pp. 12-17.

"Scent of Honey, The—A Survey of East-West Trade." *The Economist,* Vol. 245 (June 1973): pp. 1-49.

Schick, Marvin. "Letter to Editor." *The Jewish Press* (New York, August 16, 1974).

Schlesinger, Arthur, Jr. "Congress and the Making of American Foreign Policy." *Foreign Affairs,* Vol. 51, No. 1 (October 1972): pp. 78-113.

Sheehan, Edward R.F. "Step by Step in the Middle East." *Foreign Policy,* No. 22 (Spring 1976): pp. 3-70.

Shulman, Marshall D. "Toward a Western Philosophy of Coexistence." *Foreign Affairs* (October 1972): pp. 35-58.

Silbey, Frank. "Senate Demands *Quid Pro Quo* on Soviet Jews, Trade." *The National Jewish Monthly* (November 1972): pp. 10-11.

Smith, Hedrick. "Russians Mean Business, The." *The Atlantic.* Vol. 234, No. 6, pp. 41-48.

Spiegel, Steven. "The Fate of the Patron: American Trials in the Arab-Israeli Dispute." *Public Policy,* Vol. XXI, No. 2 (Spring 1973): pp. 73-202.

Stern, Lawrence. "Washington Dateline: Two Henrys Descending." *Foreign Policy,* No. 18 (Spring 1975): pp. 168-81.

Stern, Paula. "Egypt and Soviet Policy." *The Washington Post* (January 13, 1975).

———. "Russians and Americans: Talking About SALT." *The Sunday Washington Star and Daily News* (July 1, 1973): p. D-2.

———. "Too High A Price." *The Progressive* (October 1973): pp. 54, 58.

Szulc, Tad. "Behind the Vietnam Cease-Fire Agreement: How Kissinger Did It." *Foreign Policy,* No. 15 (Summer 1974): pp. 21-69.

Tanter, Raymond, and Ullman, Richard. "Introduction." *World Politics, A Quarterly Journal of International Relations Supplement—Theory and Policy in International Relations.* Edited by Raymond Tanter and Richard H. Ullman, Vol. XXIV (Spring 1972): pp. 3-6.

"Undercover." Published by Soviet Jewry Committee of Jewish Community Council of Greater Washington, No. 27 (December 11, 1972); No. 29 (February 2, 1973).

Walker-Leigh, Vanya. "Trade Bill May Be Approved by the Autumn." *The Times* (London: June 12, 1974).

"The Washington Lobby." *Congressional Quarterly* (September 1974).

Wick, Adele E. "Perspectives of East-West Trade: A Definition of Detente." *Tower International,* Newsletter No. 14 (October 1973).

Wieck, Paul R. "Henry Jackson's Way with Money." *The New Republic* (February 15, 1975).

Will, George F. "Only Business?" *New York Times Magazine* (December 23, 1973): pp. 10-36.

Wills, Gary. "Cato's Gang." *The New York Review of Books,* Vol. XXIII, No. 3 (March 4, 1976): pp. 21-23.

Windsor, Philip. "America's Moral Confusion." *Foreign Policy,* No. 13 (Winter 1973-74): pp. 139-53.

Wright, Robert B. "East-West Trade— The Position of the State Department." *The American Review of East-West Trade,* Vol. No. 5 (May 1968): pp. 21-26.

Yergin, Daniel. "Great Expectations: Trade with Russia." *The Yale Review,* Vol. LXV, No. 2 (December 1975): pp. 175-93.

———. " 'Scoop' Jackson Goes for Broke." *Atlantic Monthly* (July 1974): pp. 76-86.

Zwick, Paul R. "Henry Jackson's Way with Money." *The New Republic,* Vol. 172, No. 7, Issue 3136 (February 15, 1975): pp. 14-15.

UNPUBLISHED MANUSCRIPTS

Johnson, Victor C. "Congress and Foreign Policy: The House Foreign Affairs and Senate Foreign Relations Committees." Ph.D. Thesis, University of Wisconsin, Madison, Wisconsin, 1975.

Lauk, Kurt J. "The Jackson Amendment to SALT I." Unpublished Manuscript, Stanford University. No date.

Luneau, John P. "Congressional Trade Restrictions and U.S./Soviet Diplomacy from 1972-1975: A Case Study of the Learning/Teaching Process Between the Two Superpowers in the Initial Stages of 'Detente.'" Unpublished Manuscript, The Fletcher School of Law and Diplomacy, May 9, 1975.

Orbach, William W. "Freethem Now: The American Movement to Aid the Jews Within the Soviet Union," 1977.

Pfiffner, James Price. "Presidential Impoundment of Funds and Congressional Control of the Budget." Ph.D. Thesis, University of Wisconsin, 1975.

"The Role of National Jewish Leadership in Jackson-Mills-Vanik," January 7, 1974.

Index

ABOUT THE AUTHOR
Paula Stern, Commissioner of the United States International Trade Commission, was an International Affairs Fellow at the Council on Foreign Relations in 1978. A former legislative assistant and policy analyst, her articles have appeared in the *Atlantic Monthly*, the *New Republic*, the *New York Times*, and the *Washington Post*.